E
169.1
.A472155
2006

# American Icons

# AMERICAN ICONS

## An Encyclopedia of the People, Places, and Things that Have Shaped Our Culture

### VOLUME TWO

Edited by Dennis R. Hall
and Susan Grove Hall

**GREENWOOD PRESS**
Westport, Connecticut • London

Library of Congress Cataloging-in-Publication Data

American icons: an encyclopedia of the people, places, and things that have shaped our culture/edited by Dennis R. Hall and Susan Grove Hall.
  p. cm.
  Includes bibliographical references and index.
  ISBN 0–275–98421–4 (set : alk. paper)—ISBN 0–275–98429–X (vol. 1 : alk. paper)—ISBN 0–275–98430–3 (vol. 2 : alk. paper)—ISBN 0–275–98431–1 (vol. 3 : alk. paper)
  1. United States—Civilization—Encyclopedias. 2. Popular culture—United States—Encyclopedias. 3. Americana—Encyclopedias. I. Hall, Dennis, 1942– II. Hall, Susan G., 1941–
  E169.1 .A472155 2006
  306.0973'03—dc22       2006006170

British Library Cataloguing in Publication Data is available.

Copyright © 2006 by Dennis R. Hall and Susan Grove Hall

All rights reserved. No portion of this book may be reproduced, by any process or technique, without the express written consent of the publisher.

Library of Congress Catalog Card Number: 2006006170
ISBN: 0–275–98421–4 (set)
    0–275–98429–X (vol. 1)
    0–275–98430–3 (vol. 2)
    0–275–98431–1 (vol. 3)

First published in 2006

Greenwood Press, 88 Post Road West, Westport, CT 06881
An imprint of Greenwood Publishing Group, Inc.
www.greenwood.com

Printed in the United States of America

The paper used in this book complies with the Permanent Paper Standard issued by the National Information Standards Organization (Z39.48–1984).

10 9 8 7 6 5 4 3 2

# Contents

Guide to Related Topics     xi
Preface     xvii
Acknowledgments     xxi

**VOLUME ONE**

| | |
|---|---|
| Alamo, *Richard R. Flores* | 1 |
| Muhammad Ali, *J. Peter Williams* | 9 |
| Amish, *David L. Weaver-Zercher* | 15 |
| Antiperspirant, *Jimmy Dean Smith* | 22 |
| Art Fair, *Mary Carothers and Sharon Scott* | 28 |
| Fred Astaire, *Michael Dunne* | 35 |
| Lucille Ball, *Rhonda Wilcox* | 40 |
| Banjo, *Jack Ashworth* | 45 |
| Barbie, *Dawn Heinecken* | 51 |
| Bear, *Richard Sanzenbacher* | 58 |
| Beats, *Jason R. Kirby* | 65 |
| Betty Crocker, *Pauline Adema* | 73 |
| Bomb, *Margot A. Henriksen* | 82 |
| Daniel Boone, *Richard Taylor* | 90 |
| Boy Scout Knife, *R. H. Miller* | 101 |

| | |
|---|---:|
| Capitol, *Karelisa V. Hartigan* | 107 |
| Johnny Carson, *David Lavery* | 114 |
| Johnny Cash, *Don Cusic* | 120 |
| Cell Phone, *John P. Ferré* | 128 |
| Ray Charles, *Reginald Martin* | 134 |
| Julia Child, *Sara Lewis Dunne* | 139 |
| Computer Chip, *Michael Bertz* | 145 |
| Coney Island, *Judith A. Adams-Volpe* | 151 |
| Couch, *Dennis Hall* | 159 |
| Courtroom Trial, *David Ray Papke* | 166 |
| Joan Crawford, *Claude J. Smith* | 173 |
| Crayola Crayon, *Elizabeth Armstrong Hall* | 180 |
| George Armstrong Custer, *Michael C. C. Adams* | 186 |
| James Dean, *Geoffrey Weiss* | 192 |
| Dinosaur, *Mark A. Wilson* | 198 |
| Dollar Bill, *Heinz Tschachler* | 205 |
| Bob Dylan, *Edward P. Comentale* | 213 |
| Albert Einstein, *Anthony O'Keeffe* | 220 |
| Emergency Room, *Robert Wolosin* | 226 |
| Flea Market, *Michael Prokopow* | 233 |
| Ford Mustang, *Susan Grove Hall* | 242 |
| Gettysburg, *Randal Allred* | 249 |
| GI, *Michael Smith* | 258 |
| Golden Gate Bridge, *Kenneth M. Sanderson and Laura Kennedy* | 266 |
| Billy Graham, *David Fillingim* | 271 |
| Grateful Dead, *Nicholas Meriwether* | 277 |

## VOLUME TWO

| | |
|---|---:|
| Guardian Angel, *Scott Vander Ploeg* | 285 |
| Gun, *Michael C. C. Adams* | 292 |

## CONTENTS

| | |
|---|---|
| Halloween Costume, *Sylvia Grider* | 298 |
| Hard-Boiled Detective, *Brendan Riley* | 304 |
| Harley-Davidson Motorcycle, *Wendy Moon* | 310 |
| Ernest Hemingway, *R. H. Miller* | 316 |
| Jimi Hendrix, *Joy Haenlein* | 322 |
| Audrey Hepburn, *Lucy Rollin* | 329 |
| Hershey Bar, *Dennis Hall* | 336 |
| Hollywood, *Thomas B. Byers* | 343 |
| Horse, *Barrett Shaw* | 349 |
| Indian Scout, *Tom Holm* | 356 |
| Martin Luther King, Jr., *Ricky L. Jones* | 363 |
| Evel Knievel, *Randy D. McBee* | 369 |
| Kodak Camera, *Richard N. Masteller* | 375 |
| Las Vegas, *Lawrence E. Mintz* | 382 |
| Rush Limbaugh, *Thomas A. Greenfield* | 388 |
| Charles A. Lindbergh, *Roger B. Rollin* | 396 |
| List, *Dennis Hall* | 404 |
| Log Cabin, *William J. Badley with Linda Badley* | 412 |
| Lorraine Motel, *Thomas S. Bremer* | 419 |
| Jessica Lynch, *Anna Froula* | 425 |
| Loretta Lynn, *Don Cusic* | 431 |
| *MAD* Magazine, *Charles Hatfield* | 438 |
| Madonna, *Diane Pecknold* | 445 |
| McDonald's, *Betsy Beaulieu* | 452 |
| Mexican-American Border, *Susana Perea-Fox and Iván Figueroa* | 458 |
| Miami, *Gary Harmon* | 465 |
| Mickey Mouse, *M. Thomas Inge* | 473 |
| Miss Manners, *Dennis Hall* | 481 |
| Marilyn Monroe, *Ann C. Hall* | 486 |

| | |
|---|---|
| Mount Rushmore, *Susan Grove Hall with Dennis Hall* | 493 |
| Muppets, *Robert Barshay* | 501 |
| NASCAR's Bristol Motor Speedway, *Barbara S. Hugenberg and Lawrence W. Hugenberg* | 509 |
| Niagara Falls, *Patrick McGreevy* | 516 |
| Jack Nicholson, *Thomas A. Van* | 522 |
| Olmsted Park, *Thomas J. Mickey* | 530 |
| One-Room Schoolhouse, *Ray B. Browne* | 536 |
| Oscar, *Robert Holtzclaw* | 542 |
| Patchwork Quilt, *Judith Hatchett* | 549 |
| Walter Payton, *Clyde V. Williams* | 558 |
| Polyester, *Patricia A. Cunningham* | 565 |
| Poster Child, *Mary Johnson* | 572 |
| Elvis Presley, *George Plasketes* | 578 |

## VOLUME THREE

| | |
|---|---|
| Railroad, *Arthur H. Miller* | 585 |
| Robot, *Ira Wells* | 592 |
| Eleanor Roosevelt, *Maurine H. Beasley* | 597 |
| Rosie the Riveter, *Kathleen L. Endres* | 601 |
| Route 66, *Thomas A. Greenfield* | 607 |
| Babe Ruth, *J. Peter Williams* | 614 |
| Scrapbook, *Patricia Prandini Buckler* | 621 |
| Tupac Shakur, *Mickey Hess* | 628 |
| Spaceship, *Angela Hague* | 634 |
| Sports Bar, *William R. Klink* | 641 |
| Stadium, *Sylvester Frazier, Jr.* | 648 |
| Stonewall, *Thomas Piontek* | 655 |
| Suburbia, *Philip C. Dolce* | 662 |
| Superman, *P. Andrew Miller* | 669 |

## CONTENTS

| | |
|---|---|
| Tara, *Diane Calhoun-French* | 676 |
| Tattoo, *Karen Aubrey* | 683 |
| Henry David Thoreau, *Daniel S. Kerr* | 690 |
| Tractor, *Robert T. Rhode* | 698 |
| Tupperware, *Judith Hatchett* | 705 |
| Underground Railroad, *J. Blaine Hudson* | 713 |
| Viagra, *Bennett Kravitz* | 720 |
| Video Game, *Ken S. McAllister and Judd Ethan Ruggill* | 727 |
| Vietnam Veterans Memorial, *Linda Marie Small* | 733 |
| Wal-Mart, *Richard Daniels* | 739 |
| John Wayne, *David Magill* | 746 |
| Whistler's Mother, *Elaine A. King* | 752 |
| Oprah Winfrey, *R. Mark Hall* | 760 |
| Witch, *Linda Badley* | 767 |
| Tiger Woods, *Michael K. Schoenecke* | 776 |
| Wright Brothers, *Roger B. Rollin* | 783 |
| Zipper, *Robert Friedel* | 790 |
| Selected Bibliography | 797 |
| Index | 801 |
| About the Contributors | 849 |

# Guide to Related Topics

**Art and Architecture**
Art Fair
Capitol
Coney Island
Crayola Crayon
Dollar Bill
Golden Gate Bridge
*MAD* Magazine
Mickey Mouse
Mount Rushmore
Olmsted Park
Patchwork Quilt
Whistler's Mother

**Commerce, Consumers, and Marketing**
Art Fair
Barbie
Betty Crocker
Coney Island
Crayola Crayon
Dollar Bill
Flea Market
Ford Mustang
Halloween Costume
Hershey Bar
Kodak Camera
Las Vegas
Log Cabin
McDonald's
Polyester
Poster Child
Elvis Presley
Scrapbook
Tupperware
Wal-Mart

**Community or Civic Identity**
Amish
Courtroom Trial
Dollar Bill
Albert Einstein
Golden Gate Bridge
Billy Graham
Gun
Harley-Davidson Motorcycle
Hollywood
Martin Luther King, Jr.
Rush Limbaugh
List
Log Cabin
Mexican-American Border
Miami
Mickey Mouse
Mount Rushmore
Olmsted Park
One-Room Schoolhouse
Patchwork Quilt
Stonewall
Suburbia

## Femininity

Lucille Ball
Barbie
Joan Crawford
Hard-Boiled Detective
Audrey Hepburn
Horse
Jessica Lynch
Loretta Lynn
Madonna
Marilyn Monroe
Patchwork Quilt
Eleanor Roosevelt
Rosie the Riveter
Tupperware
Oprah Winfrey
Witch

## Film

Alamo
Fred Astaire
Joan Crawford
James Dean
Hard-Boiled Detective
Harley-Davidson Motorcycle
Audrey Hepburn
Hollywood
Kodak Camera
Mickey Mouse
Marilyn Monroe
Mount Rushmore
Jack Nicholson
Oscar
Tara
John Wayne

## Foodways

Betty Crocker
Julia Child
Coney Island
Hershey Bar
McDonald's

## Generational Change and Counterculture

Muhammad Ali
Beats
Crayola Crayon
James Dean
Dinosaur
Bob Dylan
Ford Mustang
Grateful Dead
Harley-Davidson Motorcycle
Evel Knievel
*MAD* Magazine
Muppets
Rosie the Riveter
Stonewall
Tattoo

## Hero

Muhammad Ali
Daniel Boone
George Armstrong Custer
GI
Hard-Boiled Detective
Ernest Hemingway
Charles A. Lindbergh
Elvis Presley
Babe Ruth
Superman
John Wayne

## Home and Family

Betty Crocker
Couch
Flea Market
Log Cabin
Muppets
Patchwork Quilt
Rosie the Riveter
Scrapbook
Suburbia
Tara
Tupperware

# GUIDE TO RELATED TOPICS

Wal-Mart
Whistler's Mother

**Law**
Courtroom Trial
Gun

**Leisure, Travel, and Pilgrimage**
Coney Island
James Dean
Flea Market
Gettysburg
Halloween Costume
Kodak Camera
Las Vegas
Lorraine Motel
Mount Rushmore
NASCAR's Bristol Motor Speedway
Niagara Falls
Elvis Presley
Railroad
Route 66
Stadium
Video Game
Vietnam Veterans Memorial

**Literature**
Beats
Ernest Hemingway
*MAD* Magazine
Tara
Henry David Thoreau
Zipper

**Masculinity**
Bear
Boy Scout Knife
Ernest Hemingway
Jack Nicholson
Robot
Sports Bar
Viagra
John Wayne

**Medicine**
Emergency Room
Viagra

**Music**
Banjo
Beats
Johnny Cash
Ray Charles
Bob Dylan
Grateful Dead
Jimi Hendrix
Loretta Lynn
Madonna
Elvis Presley
Tupac Shakur

**Myth**
Alamo
Amish
Daniel Boone
Boy Scout Knife
James Dean
Gettysburg
Hollywood
Indian Scout
Jessica Lynch
Route 66
Tupac Shakur
Spaceship
Tara
Henry David Thoreau
Underground Railroad
Oprah Winfrey
Witch

**Nature**
Bear
Daniel Boone
Dinosaur
Horse
Indian Scout
Niagara Falls

### Race and Ethnicity
Alamo
Muhammad Ali
Banjo
Beats
Johnny Cash
Ray Charles
George Armstrong Custer
Jimi Hendrix
Indian Scout
Martin Luther King, Jr.
Evel Knievel
Lorraine Motel
Jessica Lynch
Mexican-American Border
Walter Payton
Tupac Shakur
Tattoo
Underground Railroad
Oprah Winfrey
Tiger Woods

### Radio and Television
Lucille Ball
Johnny Carson
Julia Child
Emergency Room
Rush Limbaugh
Muppets
Oscar
Superman
Oprah Winfrey

### Religion and Spirituality
Amish
Emergency Room
Billy Graham
Grateful Dead
Guardian Angel
Audrey Hepburn
Martin Luther King, Jr.

Olmsted Park
Henry David Thoreau

Poster Child
Witch

### Science and Technology
Bomb
Cell Phone
Computer Chip
George Armstrong Custer
Dinosaur
Albert Einstein
Emergency Room
Gun
Charles A. Lindbergh
Niagara Falls
Polyester
Railroad
Robot
Spaceship
Tractor
Video Game
Wright Brothers
Zipper

### Social Class, Sophistication, and Style
Antiperspirant
Fred Astaire
Couch
Joan Crawford
Audrey Hepburn
Hollywood
Miss Manners
Polyester
Tattoo

### Sports
Muhammad Ali
Ford Mustang
Horse
Evel Knievel
NASCAR's Bristol Motor Speedway
Walter Payton
Babe Ruth

# GUIDE TO RELATED TOPICS

Sports Bar
Stadium
Tiger Woods

**War**

Bomb
George Armstrong Custer
Gettysburg
GI
Gun
Indian Scout
Jessica Lynch
Rosie the Riveter
Vietnam Veterans Memorial

# Preface

We can best introduce you to these entries by giving you the same description we sent to their writers, when asking them to contribute to the collection. We invited them to interpret a cultural "icon" in an essay for a wide readership, from casual readers in public libraries, to investigating students, to scholars researching patterns in American culture and popular culture. We asked for the essay to make cultural scholarship accessible to the general reader, and also to add to critical understanding of the subject and of its "iconic" character.

The term "icon"—as we pointed out to the writers—is now used everywhere. It has mushroomed in popular usage, coinciding with the growth of interest in popular culture and of popular culture studies. What does it mean when we say some person, place, or thing is an icon? We have speculated about features of people, places, and things commonly characterized as iconic. We have also tested lists of "icons" with various age groups, looking for patterns of recognition, understanding, agreement, and disagreement. We have surveyed scholarly research, studied the programs of recent conferences on popular culture and other fields, and attended many presentations, attempting to identify the popular phenomena which are now commanding attention, and to locate the best understandings of this attention. In the process of these discussions and research, we realized that "icons" generate strong reactions.

We gave writers our hypothesis about features that we came to associate with an icon. These qualities include the following:

—An icon generates strong responses; people identify with it, or against it; and the differences often reflect generational distinctions. Marilyn Monroe, for instance, carries meanings distinctly different for people who are in their teens and twenties than for people in their sixties and older.

—An icon stands for a group of related things and values. John Wayne, for example, images the cowboy and traditional masculinity, among many other associations, including conservative politics.

—An icon has roots in historical sources, as various as folk culture, science, and commerce; it may supersede a prior icon; it reflects events or forces of its time. The log cabin has endured as an influential American icon, with meanings and associations evolving from our colonial past through the present.

—An icon can be reshaped within its own image, or extended in updated images by its adaptations or imitators. The railroads and trains, for instance, have shifted from carrying associations of high technology and the modern, to conveying ideas of nostalgia and a retreat from high technology.

—An icon moves or communicates widely, often showing the breakdown of former distinctions between popular culture and art or historic American culture. Icons like "Whistler's Mother" and the patchwork quilt are both revered as high art and widely accepted as popular art.

—An icon can be employed in a variety of ways, and used in visual art, music, film, and other media. For example, references in text or graphics to Ernest Hemingway or to Mount Rushmore or to the gun add meanings to every artistic text in which they appear.

—An icon is usually successful in commerce. Every advertising campaign, every corporation, hopes to become the next Mickey Mouse, the next Las Vegas, the next Golden Arches.

In our invitations to the writers, then, we suggested that the essays should reveal an icon's origins and changes, its influences, and the meaning of its enduring appeal—and repulsive reactions. When the articles began to arrive, though, we found we had underestimated either the subjects or the authors, or both; the essays were fascinating for many reasons we had not anticipated. We have been surprised by the insights they offer, and pleased to learn much that we had not envisioned having importance, complexity, or charm. And as their numbers mounted to over a hundred, we continued to be surprised by what we learned, and increasingly curious, as the entries touched on related topics from differing viewpoints, and added to the attractive qualities of icons—and to their dubious qualities as well.

These items we call icons hold a depth of significance we had not foreseen; it's fortunate we did not attempt or request any definition of an icon, or of its appeal, because neither would have held true. We sought, instead, the range of meanings an icon holds for people. As we see it still, this range of meanings, plus people's disagreements about an icon's meanings and value, reflect the cultural resonance it holds, and provide the best indication of its character. In other words, a contest of possible meanings and values makes up the drawing power of an icon, and makes it dynamic, rather than static, evolving, rather than securely definable.

There are more icons than any three volumes could address. In making a selection, we have aimed at a representation of various kinds of icons, so that the entries treat principles and modes of differing types. Our arrangement of the icons into alphabetical order illustrates our idea of the equal, or random, relationship among icons, and the curious fact that out-of-the-way places,

# PREFACE

and small items we take for granted, influence popular thinking as importantly as the hero or celebrity who is touted by media. The entries themselves illustrate a variety of approaches for understanding icons. Indeed, our basic purpose is to furnish useful demonstrations of how to "read" cultural artifacts, to make readers alert to such significant things around us, and to enable readers to interpret them.

Thus these writings should generate thought, not necessarily agreement. They are entries with lively variations in style and method, and often the writer rhetorically "animates" the subject. They present distinct viewpoints, but in ways that are thought-provoking and inviting of response. Icons may well be controversial in their very basis; these entries, separately, and much more in their convergences, should stir question and even dispute.

The entries provide a fund of themes and perspectives for study and scholarship. Among them are intriguing suggestions of possible patterns and modes among icons of differing types, related to such important concepts as identity, generational differences, and myths. Linking many of the essays are intersections of meaning, and webs of associations. To those who are or will be engaged in the study of icons, this collection will bring a wealth of resources, and make them accessible as subjects in the index.

# Acknowledgments

We first thank the many people who shared their thoughts and opinions about icons with us as we developed our plans for this collection. These discussions—including the arguments—increased our understanding, stirred our curiosity, and encouraged our efforts to gather together the best voices for a worthwhile forum on the large but mysterious presence in our midst of those people, places, and things we call iconic.

We thank our writers for the help, encouragements, and pleasures they have given us. Some of the contributors we have known through many years of hearing their presentations at popular culture and literary conferences, and sharing critical discussions with them. Others we found as we searched for current writing, scholarship, and teaching on iconic subjects, or in the disciplines which study them; through subsequent conversations with them, we've enjoyed getting to know some very lively and original thinkers. We're appreciative that popular culture scholars ranging from the long-established to new contributors joined efforts with us, so the collection represents the flourishing vitality of popular culture studies. Our energy for this project has not flagged, because we kept hearing, from old associates and new, that they themselves looked forward to the finished volumes with great interest.

We are grateful to Eric Levy for asking us to consider editing a collection of essays on icons, whose suggestion started our thinking and investigation. Eric was then at Greenwood Press, where he was editor of *The Greenwood Guide to American Popular Culture*, essays on research and bibliography co-edited by M. Thomas Inge and Dennis Hall. Eric has moved to the Wesleyan University Press. Since then we have enjoyed having the attentive help of Lisa Pierce with the many questions and issues involved in bringing this collection to publication.

To the University of Louisville English Department and its chair, Susan M. Griffin, we are very grateful for the moral and material support they have given our efforts.

The University of Louisville Ekstrom Library and its librarians have provided help at every stage of our research on icons and preparation of this collection.

The Louisville Free Public Library has furnished many resources necessary for surveying and selecting popular icons, for finding books and articles with perspectives on them, and for fact-checking all kinds of matters from quotations to bibliographies. Their interlibrary loan and information services librarians have given us especially timely, needed help. Ruth Ellen Flint, information specialist at the Highlands–Shelby Park Branch, deserves our special thanks, because we took to her our problems of the most esoteric matters of fact, and she has never yet failed to devise a stratagem for finding the obscure detail which so often has seemed the key to correctness.

# Guardian Angel

## Scott Vander Ploeg

The most resilient manifestation of the guardian angel in American popular culture appears in the 1947 Frank Capra classic Christmas movie, *It's a Wonderful Life*, starring Jimmy Stewart as George Bailey, perhaps his most endearing role. As George is contemplating suicide by jumping from the town bridge he is confronted by his guardian angel, Clarence Oddbody, who explains that he has been assigned by the higher authority of the archangels, and consequently by God, to save George. George assumes that Clarence is a deluded old man. But if Clarence can convince George to turn back from self destruction, he will earn his wings, graduating to first-class angel status. Clarence convinces George that his life is indeed worth living by showing him what an awful place Bedford Falls would have been if George had never been born.

Replayed on television incessantly during the holiday season, this movie capitalizes upon Biblical precedents and secular usages and so contributes to keeping the guardian angel strongly entrenched in the contemporary world view. The details of the guardian angel story in *It's a Wonderful Life* are only slightly different, for cinematic purposes, from the traditional associations of guardian angel. Clarence has a personal interest in George—getting his wings, as well as protecting him, suggesting a promotion among the hierarchy that is not consistent with tradition. The movie introduces and popularizes the notion that when a bell rings, it signifies that an angel has earned its wings. Now, it is common parlance to refer to getting or earning one's wings, and the imagined occasion is often heralded by the ringing of a bell. The movie is so broadly known that an episode of *The Fresh Prince of Bel-Air* (1990–1996) included a cameo appearance by Tom Jones as a guardian angel offering to rescue Will Smith's TV cousin, Carlton Banks, in a plot similar to that of Capra's movie.

The wider cultural manifestations of the guardian angel are legion, and range from high culture operatic works to pop culture movies and television shows. The concept of an angel is pervasive to Western civilization, so much so that Mortimer Adler and Robert Hutchins include it as the first entry in

Henry Travers and James Stewart in Frank Capra's holiday classic *It's a Wonderful Life*, 1946. RKO/The Kobol Collection.

*The Great Ideas: A Syntopicon of Great Books of the Western World*. Milton's depiction of angel multitudes and their individual involvement in the story of Adam and Eve in *Paradise Lost* is part of an ongoing project in our culture that seeks to establish personal connection between deity and individual. Guardian angels figure prominently in the "holy cards" distributed to Catholic grade school children as rewards for work well done. Far apart in time and purpose, in the early 1990s a fad of guardian angel materials bloomed from book publications seeking to provide explanation and instruction in how the individual can better contact and utilize his or her angels. Such materials as tarot-styled angel cards (*The Angel Oracle*) and, packaged with a booklet, a stuffed angel-effigy doll, accompanied by golden purse and "blessing cards" (Crain), emphasize the connection between spiritual agency and the common consumer. Until the 1990s, William D. Webber points out, only eight books on angels were available in print, and five of those were "denominational books" specific to particular doctrines and practices. By the end of the decade, however, some 300 books about angels had been published. The literary critic Harold Bloom identified angelology, along with interest in dreams and the "near-death experience," as a main cultural concern emerging with the approach of the millennium; for Bloom the aim of this quest was an image of the spiritually essential "primordial person," who would be the "guardian angel, or heavenly twin" (2, 10).

Hollywood long ago found that audiences embraced angels, as the use of "angel" in the title of so many movies suggests, perhaps most notably *Angels with Dirty Faces* (1938), but the guardian angel often took the guise of a friendly ghost as in the *Topper* movies (1937, 1938, 1941, 1979). The guardian angel proper figures more conspicuously in *Angel on My Shoulder* (1946, 1980), *The Bishop's Wife* (1947), *Angels in the Outfield* (1951, 1994), *The Angel Who Pawned Her Harp* (1954), and *The Angel Levine* (1970), among many others. And there has been something of a revival of motion pictures relying heavily on the saving grace of a guardian angel, including the remake of *Angels in the Outfield* (1994), *Michael* (1996), *City of Angels* (1998), *The Preacher's Wife* (1996), and, with an ironic presentation, *Dogma* (1999). Furthermore, the essential concept of aid from the spiritual realm can be found in many movies of that period that do not rely on traditional guardian angel entities, such as *Ghost* (1990) and *Field of Dreams* (1989).

Television and the mass media are also now well populated with guardian angels. Michael Landon created a guardian angel role in *Highway to Heaven* (1984–1989), and Della Reese stared in the television series *Touched by an Angel* (1994–2003). Amid these happy-ending TV series, Sophy Burnham published her bestselling *A Book of Angels: Reflections on Angels Past and Present and True Stories of How They Touch Our Lives* in 1990, followed by its readers' responses in *Angel Letters* (1991), and Eileen Elias Freeman brought out *Touched by Angels: True Cases of Close Encounters of the Celestial Kind* in 1993. Though negligibly different in detail, the stories these publications tell are of angelic interventions and the turning of individuals from godless lives heading for destruction to positive and generous behavior full of gladness, gratitude, and godliness. Stories of good deeds are often interpreted as particular manifestations of angelic forces. These books launched a raft of angel goods into the popular culture, such that miniature guardian angel pins became common adornments, guardian angel paintings and posters and tattoos were suddenly desired commodities. At crane-style arcade games in Wal-Marts across America, for fifty cents you could win a guardian angel pin for your favorite occupation, including one for truck drivers. Other motorists sported bumper stickers claiming that their "guardian angels were riding with them." The guardian angel became ubiquitous.

Moreover, the guardian angel story became a common device for explaining happy coincidences, surprising or unexpected recoveries, ghostly presences that "save" individuals, and any gesture of compassion or sacrifice for the good of others. The story had a precedent in American literature. The "Good Samaritan" as guardian angel had been fully developed a century earlier, in Oliver Wendell Holmes's sentimental novel *The Guardian Angel* (1875). In its story, Master Byles Gridley, a fusty old philosopher, intervenes to protect a young girl, appropriately named Myrtle Hazard, from the perils of the male-dominated society in which she grows up. Although his good deeds have no hint of supernatural or divine agency behind them, Gridley is named as her guardian angel in the book's last sentence. Many of the late twentieth-century angel-themed books, such as Freeman's *Angelic Healing* and the authorless *When God Sends an Angel*, consist of compilations of stories of lucky outcomes and miraculous occurrences that are attributed to angelic intervention. Often the miracles are instances of good deeds performed by strangers. Both Sophy Burnham's and Eileen Freeman's experiences include numerous incidents in which they were warned by a voice or image and then averted injury to self or another; Burnham reflects on explanations such as telepathy or intuition but finds them insufficient in contrast to religious perspectives on prayer, angels, and, most of all, individual conviction (*A Book of Angels* 51–

61). Clearly the mass of believers who avidly watch the television shows and movies and seek these books agree with their concept of supernatural agency involved in daily survival, because it is basic to the plots, and, in the books, the introductory part of the memoir which must establish credibility (Burnham, *A Book of Angels* 6–17; Freeman, *Touched by Angels* 1–19).

The imagery of guardian angels often involves depiction of a ghostly presence, typically floating or flying and sporting large wings attached from the back and shoulders, the whole shown as translucent or diaphanous. In many paintings, lithographs, and poster depictions from the Victorian era, the angel is following a child or young children as they contend with metaphors of a dangerous world. In several such paintings, the children are alone, except for the angels behind and above them, the children's youth seeming at odds with their solitary status. The children are crossing bridges over streams, or playing near a cliff edge, suggesting the danger of falling, or they are toddling through a forest and in danger of remaining lost. Protection is the prime function of such angelic presences, though in most cases the angel's action is muted or passive.

The strong appeal of guardian angels often reveals an equally strong sense of a pervasive threat lurking in the world, as true for adults as for children. A divine protector is needed because it is believed that the individual cannot withstand the dangers that beset us. This threat perhaps explains why some of the guardian angel stories take the form of crime or detective movies and fiction. John Wall's *Guardian Angel in the Underworld*, for example, is a tale of good guys stopping gangsters, largely through the work of a woman who seeks to right the wrongs done to her own family. While guardian angels are not often represented as engaged in physical acts of protection, the avenging

A 1910 vintage greeting card showing a guardian angel watching over a sleeping child. Courtesy of Shutterstock.

or killer angels of ancient tradition lurk in the background; the possibility of a guardian angel's physical, even violent, intervention is commonly assumed and is a source of comfort. It is worth noting that the vigilante group in New York city who organized to fight street crime called themselves "The Guardian Angels." They saw their activity of enforcing law in the absence of official control as a kind of protection. Batman likewise functions as a type of guardian angel, relying on his utility belt and muscle instead of supernatural agency.

In Burnham's *Book of Angels*, she recognizes a psychological connection between the habit of young children to develop imaginary friends and the belief in angels who guard us. She explains that young children who reveal the presence of such imaginary friends are actually more in tune with their awareness than adults, and thus are reporting the real existence of guardian angels (41–45). Her explanation does not admit, or even seem capable of accepting the possibility, that the guardian angels of her adult world resemble the child's imaginary friends; but it bespeaks a sense of guardian angel belief deriving out of individual need for companionship. For many, the fact of being alone is a bane, a dismal situation that the guardian angel defeats by mere presence. Wordsworth's poetry answers the dread of loneliness by affirming the child's beliefs in spiritual beings; religion addresses it in creating heavens including angels; in common, art and religion value imagination. For Burnham, poets including Dante, Wordsworth, Blake, and Rilke; artists such as Dürer, Doré, Blake, and Gustave Moreau; and religions from Judaism, Medieval Christianity, Islam, to Swedenborgianism all convey images of angels and therefore, in her perspective, confirm her belief in angels (161–92). She mentions only agreements among these, not differences.

The good and bad angels that are popularly thought to sit on our shoulders and advise us alternately between good and evil are vestiges of medieval drama that can be found in literary treatments ranging from Christopher Marlowe's *Dr. Faustus* to Walt Disney's Donald Duck. Latent in the public consciousness related to recent angel phenomena may be ancient concepts that each individual is allocated a guardian angel to watch over and protect the individual. Evidence of belief in angel guardians dates back to Sumerian civilization circa 3,000 B.C.E. and Egyptian Ishtar cults of the 1,800 B.C.E. range. The concept of personal guardian angels, presented by Aquinas and Augustine and debated in other Catholic patristic sources, has found comfortable placement among modern Protestant evangelicals, beginning with Billy Graham. When Graham first became interested in preaching about angels, however, he found very little about them in his library, and nothing written in the twentieth century. He noted the numerous shelves of books devoted to the devil, along with the occult and demons, and, reflecting that the Bible gives more importance to angels as divine ministers and human guardians than to the diabolical fallen angels, he began the study leading to his 1975 publication, *Angels: God's Secret Agents* (ix–x). Graham's book is a diverse treatment of angel stories expanded from Biblical references.

Although the idea of specific guardian angels assigned to each individual may be consistent with Protestantism's emphasis on personal relations with the deity, it is not Biblical, and not part of Graham's view. Graham relates Biblical passages to twentieth-century accounts of activities of angels, such as the rescue of a missionary and his wife from a murderous tribe, and, during World War II, Captain Eddie Rickenbacker's account of the gift of a gull which saved him and six fellow airmen from starvation after they were shot down in the Pacific Ocean (3–4).

Graham extended the personal ministry of angels, in his book and preaching, by integrating his witness of world events in his experience as an advisor to presidential administrations with the Bible's testimony about supernatural conflict; the warfare in the world, in this perspective, stems from attacks of demonic forces on God and the holy angels (75–76). Graham also implied the danger of being unaware of the spiritual hosts of good and evil in contending that "We live in a perpetual battlefield—The great War of the Ages continues to rage," so that a denial of angels and devils amounts to ignorance of the real conflict (65–67). More to the point of individual understanding and decision-making, and to the elevation angels have received in the 1990s, however, Graham emphasized the ultimate personal relationship with angels: "Today we have the choice of whether or not to receive the ministry of angels" crucial in our own futures, involving our death, judgment, and eternity (139). Again, present-day stories, of dying people, illustrate Biblical references to angels' actions in greeting, escorting, and singing to people (152–55).

More recent accounts of angelic intervention follow Graham's ideas of angelic ministry, but diminish or omit the framework of their subordination to the Biblical God's will and purpose. In these stories of encounters, the angels become manifest in the consciousness when coincidence or improbability confronts the individual, as when a near-death experience causes the individual to seek explanation for otherwise inexplicably having been "saved" from catastrophe. When this surprising escape occurs, the near-victim often attributes the outcome to the work of a divine guardian angel sent to warn and protect the individual from certain harm. In some constructions of this scenario, the attuned beneficiary may receive direct communications from the angel, often through prayer or special intervention; it may happen before the crisis, or after it, when the recipient seeks to keep the spiritual relationship, and, often, to extend it to others. Many of the recent "new age" constructions offer instruction in how to learn one's guardian angel's name, how to contact and communicate with the angel, and what to do to maintain good relations. These how-to guides assume that direct communications with the angels are possible, if the individual follows the programs the books indicate. Some purport to show the reader how to become a guardian angel for others. Those who believe in such agency often develop close relationships with their guardian angels, thinking of them as partners or collaborators, although presuming that the angels are entirely selfless and only interested in the welfare of their charges. Guardian angels seemingly have no agendas of their own, except to ensure the ideal outcomes for the souls they oversee. They are invisible, inscrutable. They are beyond mortal comprehension and generally cannot be called upon at the individual's whim.

Guardian angels represent a continuing concern over the boundaries between material creation and the spiritual, among a public losing the theological distinctions of passing religious traditions. Belief in guardian angels presumes a continuity of existence beyond the material, in an afterlife, as well as a universe organized by the mind of a deity. Much of the resonance of the title and the stage imagery of Tony Kushner's *Angels in America* (stage 1993, HBO film 2003) derives from these enduring associations within American culture. In such a cosmic view, order and reason dominate over chaos, and events occur as part of a plan that is only imperfectly understood by the mortal mind. Many of the more recent guardian angel presentations involve the radical transcendence of humans who have died and become angels in order to save others. This adaptation implies a cultural need for reassurance that some use or value will attend the individual after death, and that in such "work" a degree of continued identity will be assured. The guardian angel's popularity, if it continues in this vein, may further extend the legendary American "work ethic" into its perhaps ultimate function, as a means of salvation in a self-help religion.

## WORKS CITED AND RECOMMENDED

Adler, Jerome Mortimer, and Robert Hutchins. *The Great Ideas: A Syntopicon of Great Books of the Western World.* Chicago: U of Chicago P, 1952.
Bloom, Harold. *Omens of Millennium: The Gnosis of Angels, Dreams, and Resurrection.* New York: Riverhead Books–G. P. Putnam's Sons, 1996.
Burnham, Sophy. *Angel Letters.* New York: Ballantine–Random House, 1991.
———. *A Book of Angels: Reflections on Angels Past and Present and True Stories of How They Touch Our Lives.* New York: Ballantine, 1990.
Crain, Mary Beth. *Guardian Angels: Hope, Comfort, and Inspiration for Everyday Miracles.* Philadelphia: Running P, 2003.
Freeman, Eileen Elias. *Angelic Healing: Working with Your Angels to Heal Your Life.* New York: Warner Books, 1994.
———. *Touched by Angels: True Cases of Close Encounters of the Celestial Kind.* New York: Warner Books, 1993.
Graham, Billy. *Angels: God's Secret Agents.* New York: Doubleday, 1975.
Holmes, Oliver Wendell. *The Guardian Angel.* Boston: James Osgood, 1875.
*It's a Wonderful Life.* Dir. Frank Capra. Story by Phillip Van Doren Stern. Liberty Films, 1946.
Wall, John. *Guardian Angel in the Underworld.* New York: Vantage P, 1958.
Webber, William D. "Angelmania." 30 June 2005 <www.beliefnet.com>.
*When God Sends an Angel.* [n.p.]: Publications International Ltd., 2002.

# Gun

## Michael C. C. Adams

The gun is among the most potent of American icons. Firearms ownership is ubiquitous and its ramifications permeate the fabric of American society. For many, the gun embodies core American values. Arguably, the United States has a gun culture that is unique among Western nations. Great Britain, for example, has strong firearms traditions, but it does not aspire to a gun culture. The United Kingdom is renowned for its small arms industry that has produced such classic weapons as the Enfield bolt-action rifle. The country has a proud record of competitiveness in international gun sports. But the gun also has negative mental associations in Britain; it is popularly viewed as a threat to personal safety and public order. This attitude has intensified since the Dunblane school killings of March 1996 that led to the banning of all handguns in the United Kingdom, amid a wave of public anti-gun sentiment that associated private firearms ownership with promiscuous American gun violence.

The reverse of the U.K. attitude holds true in the United States. Here, the gun is associated in many minds with personal liberty and public safety. The origins of American involvement with the mystique of the gun are complex and controversial. The frontier experience is usually seen as pivotal in the development of firearms lore. The musket was a tool for economic self-sufficiency in a wilderness where game was plentiful and hunting was essential for survival. Flintlocks also provided defense against a hostile native population, on a battlefield where regular soldiers were scarce before 1755. Historically, then, the gun was associated first with survival and then progress in the harsh American environment. Richard Slotkin, perhaps the foremost contemporary student of the American frontier as a formative force, suggests that the power of the gun to tame the wilderness and provide a haven for European immigrants from the troubles of the Old World gave Americans a strong sense of the regenerative force of violence, a theme that continues to run through American literature and drama.

The difficulty with the frontier explanation of why the gun became an American icon is that other cultures underwent the frontier experience without producing a similar firearms ethic. For instance, Canada has a hunting tradition as rich as that of the United States but experiences far fewer gun crimes, and there is no real association between the gun and national identity.

Recently, Michael A. Bellesiles has assailed the whole concept of a Colonial gun culture as pure legend. He argues that the affinity of settlers for firearms has been exaggerated, especially with regard to well-established areas where there was no longer a Native American threat. Colonials often ignored the militia provision that required all male freemen to acquire a smoothbore musket and ball ammunition; and British regular officers railed against the lack of marksmanship among provincial units. At the same time, Bellesiles's research has been attacked in turn as slipshod and understating evidence opposed to his conclusions.

Whatever the case for the colonial period, it is certainly true that by the eve of revolution, fear of a British tyranny led to the revitalization of the militia, so that on April 19, 1775, Massachusetts could put about 4,000 armed men in the field. The Revolutionary experience seems to have been crucial in constructing an American association between guns and defense of liberty against central tyranny, a strain that continued in the thinking of the National Rifle Association, the Minutemen of the Cold War era, and the private white-male militias of the 1990s. Americans did not forget that when Major John Pitcairn of the Royal Marines ordered the militia on Lexington Green to disperse, he also told them to lay down their arms. Their refusal to do so cemented an association between the bearing of arms and the preservation of liberty that is distinctly American.

Although the major fighting of the Revolutionary War fell upon the regulars of the Continental line, the folklore version held that the cause was won by untutored farmers and artisans who made up in natural virtue and superior marksmanship for what they lacked in professional training. Hence, when the new republic considered the need for a defense establishment, it put its main reliance on a well-regulated citizen militia, as embodied in the Second Amendment to the Constitution. However, the collective nature of this provision was quickly lost sight of. Perhaps this shift of vision was inevitable, given that the minuteman image was essentially individual and personal, so that the right to bear arms was soon held to be private and was embodied as such in a number of state constitutions.

The idea that American freedom depended on the individual hawk-eyed marksman was elaborated in the folklore version of the Battle of New Orleans, January 1815, which erroneously attributed American victory over the British not to General Andrew Jackson's regulars, but to the backwoods militia of Kentucky and Tennessee armed with their personal hunting rifles. The same coonskin-capped wielders of long rifles, led by Davy Crockett with Old Betsy, were purported to have laid low epic numbers of Mexicans at the Alamo in March 1836, preparing the way for another triumph of liberty. By now the American hero was, as D. H. Lawrence said of James Fenimore Cooper's hero Natty Bumpo, stoic, alone, and a killer.

America's second war with Britain enlarged the significance of the gun in a further context. Eli Whitney and other mechanics, striving to provide the fledgling U.S. army with sufficient arms for the conflict, pioneered the concept of interchangeable parts, making the mass production of weapons feasible and profitable. This groundbreaking work made possible mass production in many other areas, from farm and factory machinery to typewriters and sewing machines. Thus, Americans could proudly point to arms manufacture as a classic case of "Yankee ingenuity."

Subsequent advances in arms technology, most notably the perfection of the revolving-chamber pistol by Samuel Colt and others, along with the percussion rifled musket, coincided with the Mexican War and the further expansion of U.S. territory that, at least in American eyes, extended the area of democratic freedom. Once again, the association of firearms with liberty was reinforced.

An old Colt revolver. Courtesy of Shutterstock.

The single most significant development encouraging the growth of firearms ownership and reverence for the gun as an instrument of freedom was the Civil War. The superior ability to manufacture efficient modern weapons was material to Union success. As a result of service in the war, millions of male Americans became familiar with the use of firearms at the same time that like numbers of remaindered guns flooded the market. The result was a marked increase in gun ownership and violence. This epoch in the growth of a gun culture is memorialized by Civil War reenactors, who are amongst the most passionate believers in the gun as icon.

The ready availability of guns was coincidental with the rapid advance of the trans-Mississippi frontier. As law enforcement was often weak in the expanding West, the gun became the tool of personal justice, equalizing the odds for the common man. In this era it was axiomatic that "God created men; Colonel Colt made them equal." However, despite the popularity of the idea of the gun as an icon of equality, the concept must be accepted with caution. In legend, the cowboy was the lineal descendant of the knight errant and, like the white knight of Medieval legend, the good guy in Western myth always won the duel with the villain in black. But this justice was not necessarily true in reality, for weapons are inanimate and neutral. Outlaws usually died because society hunted them down in superior numbers, and not because they were necessarily slower with a sidearm.

Further, this was also the era of Reconstruction in the South, during which ex-Confederates systematically disarmed blacks so that they could not defend themselves against loss of civil rights and reduction to virtual serfdom. Until recently, black Americans have not had equal access to the right to bear arms, Colonel Colt notwithstanding.

Gun usage and its attendant symbolism took a jump in another postwar period, after World War I. In the roaring twenties, the snub-nosed modern revolver in the shoulder holster and the Tommy gun became symbols of cops and robbers. Roger Lane argues that gun crimes increased radically in this era partly because of the enhanced legal availability of weapons, promoted by concealed weapons laws. Also, the personal resort to violence was encouraged by contempt for a judicial system in which only 44 percent of gun crimes led to any sort of punishment. It is a continuing tenet of the gun culture that each citizen must be his own defense; the police and legal system cannot be relied upon.

As the country entered the Great Depression, Bonnie and Clyde figures came to appear as Robin Hoods, standing up to the discredited representatives of the capitalist system, the bankers and sheriff's deputies. The hoods' submachine guns became the modern equivalent of the long bow. Yet, by the same token, J. Edgar Hoover's G-Men carried the same weapons and used them to restore order. Thus the gun had a paradoxical iconic value: it was both the instigator of personal liberation and the guarantor of the status quo. The mystique of the gun continued in the film noir of the 1940s and 1950s when gritty anti-heroes like Humphrey Bogart and James Cagney further identified the snub-nosed pistol with the masculine mystique.

Bonnie Parker mockingly points a shotgun at Clyde Barrow, 1933. Courtesy of the Library of Congress.

A relatively recent addition to the gun culture is the assault weapon that features in contemporary adventure movies. Partly, the super weapon is there simply to entertain youthful audiences that enjoy heavy action more than plot nuance. But the automatic weapon is also embraced by right-wing paramilitary groups as a powerful tool in their lineup against government, and by ordinary people who feel that its destructive power restores potency to the anonymous members of the "lonely crowd." The nineteenth-century concept of the gun as leveling the playing field is now being acted out in America's schools, where children who feel slighted or bullied strike back against colleagues and teachers with deadly efficiency, desensitized to

A man shoots an AK-47 at a shooting range in Montana. Courtesy of Shutterstock.

the act of killing by thousands of violent video images, as army psychologist Dave Grossman has pointed out.

The gun as an icon has appealed to different Americans in various ways, from adherents of the Revolutionary-era black-powder musket, to the six-gun of the frontier fight, on to the automatic weapons of the twentieth century. Yet certain themes unite the various gun subcultures. The firearm is associated with personal and public identity, particularly for males (although more women are buying guns, their primary reason appears to be a pragmatic concern for personal safety rather than image or identity). For conservative white males in particular, the firearm represents personal liberty and the preservation of the republic; it is envisaged as a defense against tyranny.

There is much myth in all of this, and not all Americans subscribe to the gun culture. Polls suggest that a majority would like tougher gun control laws. It is doubtful that gun ownership makes America safer. Guns are more plentiful in the United States than, say, in Britain, France, New Zealand, Holland, or Japan, yet the gun crime rate is also much higher in America, indicating that weapons do not provide greater security. For example, in 1995 there were 409,000 privately owned firearms in the United Kingdom, which also saw seventy-seven gun killings, or a rate of 0.116 deaths per 100,000 of the population. In the same year, the United States had 222,000,000 weapons in circulation and 13,673 killings, a much higher rate of 5.25 per 100,000 citizens.

Moreover, it is doubtful that widespread dissemination of guns successfully operates as an antidote to strong central authority. Gun ownership has increased, but so has the power of the federal government. Tellingly, there has been no successful armed rebellion against central authority since the inception of the United States, including the Civil War. Nor does private arms bearing increase national security. Fantasies such as *Red Dawn* (1984), in which a group of teenagers seek to save their town from foreign invasion using their parents' private arsenals, are just that—fantasies. If the United States wished seriously to pursue the concept of a universally armed citizenry as a first line of national defense, it might follow the example of Switzerland, where every adult male is required to undergo basic training with an assault weapon that is then kept in his possession under strict rules of engagement. As it is, the U.S. National Guard is the legally designated successor of the militia, not the individual citizen who happens indiscriminately to own a weapon.

Obviously, the homage paid to the gun does not entirely depend on its actual relation to public and private security. People don't necessarily act on what is objectively true, but rather act on what they perceive as true. Whatever the reality, the gun as an icon is indelibly associated with America's commitment to personal liberty and the advance of democratic freedom. As such, it will probably retain an elevated status as icon into the foreseeable future.

## WORKS CITED AND RECOMMENDED

To read more about the gun as icon, begin with Carl Bakal, *The Right to Bear Arms* (New York: Paperback Library, 1968), a comprehensive history of the subject. Richard Slotkin studies the frontier and the gun culture in *Regeneration Through Violence: The Mythology of the American Frontier, 1600–1860* (Middletown, CT: Wesleyan UP, 1973) and *Gunfighter Nation: The Myth of the Frontier in Twentieth-Century America* (New York: Atheneum, 1992). Michael A. Bellesiles, in *Arming America: The Origins of a National Gun Culture* (New York: Alfred A. Knopf, 2000), and Joyce Lee Malcolm, *To Keep and Bear Arms: The Origins of an Anglo-American Right* (Cambridge, MA: Harvard UP, 1994), take opposing sides on the existence of a gun culture in the Colonial period. On firearms and the rise of mass production, see Constance Green, *Eli Whitney and the Birth of American Technology* (New York: Little, Brown and Co., 1956), and William Hosley, *Colt: The Making of an American Legend* (Amherst: U of Massachusetts P, 1996). Robert V. Bruce explores gun proliferation after the Civil War in *1877: Year of Violence* (Chicago: Ivan R. Dee, 1989). Roger Lane pursues the growth of gun violence during the twentieth century in *Murder in America: A History* (Columbus: Ohio State UP, 1997). Kenneth A. Stern's *A Force Upon the Plain: The American Militia Movement and the Politics of Hate* (Norman: U of Oklahoma P, 1997) analyses neo-conservative belief in the right to bear arms as a bulwark against central tyranny. Dave Grossman explores how we are desensitizing children to killing other humans in *On Killing: The Psychological Cost of Learning to Kill in War and Society* (New York: Little, Brown and Co., 1995).

# Halloween Costume

## Sylvia Grider

The American Halloween can be traced to ancient Celtic rituals honoring the spirits of the dead, which were believed to wander about on this night. Bonfires were commonly lit to keep these spirits and revenants away, and also to light the way for them as they journeyed toward the land of the dead. Halloween also has a tenuous and syncretic Christian connection because the holiday is celebrated on the evening before All Saints Day, which falls on November 1, hence the name "All Hallow's Eve" or Hallowe'en. The "Day of the Dead" celebrations of Mexico and other Latin countries draw on this same belief in the communion between the living and the dead on the night before the celebration of All Saints'. The Day of the Dead is celebrated with elaborate altars honoring the dead, pastries and sweets shaped like skeletons and skulls, and feasts in the cemetery at the graves of the deceased. Costumes are not generally part of this vernacular sacred observance. Although the trend is undergoing some dramatic changes, many of the costumes worn by both children and adults to celebrate American Halloween depict the *dramatis personae* of death: skeletons, ghosts, vampires, and mummies. Other fictional and supernatural creatures have been absorbed into the traditional Halloween pantheon, such as Dracula, Frankenstein's monster, witches, and devils.

Children costumed as fantasy creatures and other supernatural characters toting trick-or-treat shopping bags or plastic jack-o-lanterns have been an integral feature of American Halloween for decades. Costumes are essential to trick-or-treating because the protagonists must be disguised in order to beg house-to-house. At first Halloween costumes and masks were made at home by the children themselves from whatever outsized or cast-off clothing was available, resulting in a great variety of tramps, gypsies, ghosts wearing sheets with eyeholes cut out, and so forth. By the 1960s or so, however, a high percentage of children's costumes were commercially produced and seasonally marketed. Overall, these commercial costumes have proved to be more popular than the "homemade" look. In retrospect, we can see that these commercial costumes were the harbinger of the shift of the holiday away from the local and the vernacular.

Even more important than the shift from homemade costumes to commercially-produced ones has been the shift in emphasis from costumed children trick-or-treating to elaborately costumed adults cavorting in various venues, ranging from offices and businesses to shopping malls and street parades. Holiday mumming for other holidays, such as the Christmas mumming in Newfoundland, typically involves costumed and disguised adults who perform various folk dramas in exchange for drinks and food. Trick-or-treating, however, has been relegated to young children; trick-or-treating is simply not part of the emerging adult holiday activities. Regardless of the ages of the wearers or the activities, Halloween costumes have become so universally recognized, sanctioned, and enjoyed that they are accorded iconic status in contemporary American society, if only for one day out of the year.

Because of its vernacular status—that is, its lack of sanction or control by any official agency—Halloween is perhaps the most dynamic of all American calendar customs. For example, after the so-called "Candyman murders," the poisoning of a child with trick-or-treat candy in 1973, the American custom of trick-or-treating underwent major changes. After this widely publicized murder, trick-or-treating took on ominous overtones of threat and danger. In general, children are no longer allowed to roam through neighborhoods unescorted at dusk on Halloween. Instead, controlled promenades and costume contests in local shopping malls have become the norm in many parts of the country. Some churches and schools sponsor Halloween parties with such traditional but old-fashioned games as dunking for apples, as well as best-costume contests. Throughout the holiday, parents now keep a watchful eye on their costumed children, and rowdy teenagers in masks are viewed more as a threat than as a legitimate part of the holiday. Widespread concern regarding the safety of candy and treats collected by children has led to the institution of a new, technological tradition: taking the bags of treats to local hospitals and clinics to be x-rayed in order to detect any needles,

Children in costume trick or treating. Courtesy of Corbis.

razor blades, and so forth that might have been inserted into the candy. Of course the children wear their costumes during these visits, and many of the hospital and clinic personnel dress up for the occasion as well, and some even give additional treats to the visiting children.

At about the same time that costumed trick-or-treating for children was being considered so dangerous that many communities banned it entirely, national business concerns recognized a new market for costumes, minus the trick-or-treating: young adults. Accordingly, Halloween has become the second-highest grossing American holiday, following Christmas. Of course, the adult costume and party market is largely responsible for this marketing increase, in part because adults have more disposable income than children, but also because Halloween costumes for many adults are high-end purchases. Other commercially produced paraphernalia for Halloween-themed adult parties has also contributed to the increased profits during this season. Everything from special holiday greeting cards (frequently depicting ghosts and haunted houses), to house decorations, books, foods, and liquor all attempt to cash in on the lucrative adult Halloween market.

The most elaborate adult costumes are those worn to parties and street parades. In cities with a large theatrical and artistic population, Halloween costumes and masks provide a popular outlet for creativity. Some artists plan and work months ahead in order to create spectacular costumes. Sometimes whole groups of holiday revelers will dress alike and march together in choreographed units during the parades. For example, one group of gay men all dressed as Dorothy in *The Wizard of Oz*, complete with little Totos in their matching baskets. Entertainment and incongruity are the main intent of such costumed antics. However, special occasions are not the only venues for wearing costumes during the brief Halloween season. Store clerks, receptionists, and waitstaff also commonly come to work in costume on October 31, especially if Halloween falls on a working weekday. Some offices, restaurants, and stores even make a point of encouraging all employees' coming to work in costume on Halloween in the hopes of increasing business and sales. Masks, however, are generally discouraged in these settings. Costumes in general are such an integral part of Halloween that frequently little notice is taken of costumed adults in the workplace.

Adults in costume. Courtesy of Shutterstock.

Contemporary Halloween continues to drift away from traditional supernatural images and toward postmodern secularization. In some contemporary Halloween party venues for children, especially those associated with more conservative Christian churches, supernatural costumes depicting supernatural creatures associated with death and the devil have been banned. No vampires, ghosts, witches, skeletons, or mummies are to be seen in these contexts. In fact, the historical connection of Halloween with the spirits of the dead has been suppressed in so many American communities that children may not be aware of why Halloween is traditionally associated with ghosts and witches. Instead, children's costumes in these contexts tend heavily toward creatures of fantasy and the mass media.

The elaborate adult costumes associated with such popular events as Mardi Gras, especially in New Orleans, and the gay pride parades of San Francisco and other major cities have been copied and absorbed into Halloween parades and street celebrations throughout the country. Although the supernatural pantheon is still represented in some adult costumes, especially hyper-sexual vampires, political characters (frequently represented only by masks) have become more common themes. For example, during the President Clinton–Monica Lewinsky scandal, Halloween revelers of both sexes dressed in Lewinsky look-alike costumes of blue dress and dark beret, while smoking a big cigar. This topical costume was especially outrageous when worn by bearded men with unshaven legs. Other polarizing political figures such as George Bush, Saddam Hussein, and Osama bin Laden became common adult Halloween masks and costumes following the Gulf War and 9/11.

In addition to current events, the media are another source of inspiration for both children's and adults' Halloween costumes. Media tie-ins with current animated movies or television programs are evident in many commercially produced children's costumes. In 2004, such characters as Spongebob Squarepants, Shrek, Spider-Man, and Harry Potter and his friends were among the most popular costumes. Even with heavy media influence, children's costumes have consistently depicted a whole range of benign "kiddy" characters, such as princesses, gypsies, ballerinas, bumblebees, pirates, and various cuddly animals. Although cartoon-like witches and ghosts remain popular among children, other supernatural beings are less and less common. For example, today one rarely sees children dressed as devils, a popular costume in the past.

Media-influenced adult costumes cover a much wider range than children's Halloween costumes do. Popular movies and their spin-offs which lend themselves to costumes for adults include *The Matrix*, *Texas Chainsaw Massacre*, and *Friday the 13th*, as well as *Star Wars*, especially Darth Vader. Consistent with the glorification of violence in contemporary movies and computer games, more and more adult costumes depict the perverse and grotesque—the gorier the better. "Living dead" masks and other eviscerated body parts are especially popular, especially among older adolescent boys and young men. Many talented adults craft their own elaborate costumes, but others can always buy or rent the more expensive costumes which are professionally manufactured.

In mock "haunted houses" which are created as community fundraisers, the costumed actors depict the dead, dying, and grotesque in order to frighten and even disgust the patrons who are guided through the various gory tableaux which are featured in these labyrinthine seasonal parodies of fun houses. The tendency in recent years has been for the haunted house tableaux to be as realistic as possible, the best example of which are the Christian "hell houses" which depict the terrors of botched abortions, victims killed by drunken drivers, and vicious murders committed by perpetrators high on drugs. Paradoxically, the more realistic the costumes of characters in these venues are, the less they are recognizable as costumes. The main function of a costume is to disguise the identity of the wearer, not emphasize or heighten that identity.

The now iconic status of costumes at Halloween has resulted in the almost universal acceptance of costumes at Halloween in nearly every possible venue, from children's trick-or-treat and adult parties, to offices, shops, and delivery trucks. The widespread popularity and acceptance of costumes—for both children and adults—at Halloween may have weakened other aspects of the holiday, such as pranks and trick-or-treat. Although costumes depicting the dead and the evil supernaturals, such as vampires and witches, are becoming less and less common, these figures are still prominent in party decorations and media advertisements. Seasonal puns, such as holding "spooktacular" sales are depicted in newspaper, magazine, and television advertising. Perhaps relegating the pantheon of the dead to one-dimensional napkins and party favors is a symbolic way of weakening the power that tradition alleges these "creatures of the night" exert over humans. The traditional Halloween colors of black and orange, originally alluding to the flames and smoke of bonfires, are retained in party decorations and advertising. These traditional Halloween colors represent a seasonal code of instant recognition, much as green and red do at Christmastime.

In spite of all the societal pressures which are contributing to the secularization of Halloween, costumes remain the essence, the emotional core, the last vestige of traditional Halloween in America. Our society may ban trick-or-treating, but Halloween without costumes is inconceivable.

## WORKS RECOMMENDED

Grider, Sylvia. "Conservatism and Dynamism in the Contemporary Celebration of Halloween: Institutionalization, Commercialization, and Gentrification." *Southern Folklore* 53 (1996): 1–16.

Kugelmass, Jack. *Masked Culture: The Greenwich Village Halloween Parade*. New York: Columbia UP, 1994.

Magliocco, Sabina. "The Bloomington Jaycee's Haunted House." *Indiana Folklore and Oral History* 14 (1985): 19–28.

McDowell, John. "Halloween Costuming Among Young Adults in Bloomington, Indiana: A Local Exotic." *Indiana Folklore and Oral History* 14 (1985): 1–18.

O'Drain, Mary. "San Francisco's Gay Halloween." *International Folklore Quarterly* 4 (1986): 90–96.

Santino, Jack. *All Around the Year: Holidays and Celebrations in American Life.* Urbana: U of Illinois P, 1994.

———, ed. *Halloween and Other Festivals of Life and Death.* Knoxville: U of Tennessee P, 1994.

# Hard-Boiled Detective

## *Brendan Riley*

Sam Spade sits behind his desk, looking "rather pleasantly like a blond satan." His girl Friday ushers Miss Wonderly into Sam's office; hesitantly, she asks Sam to find her missing sister. Six pages later, Sam's partner is dead: shot "right through the pump" in "San Francisco's night-fog, thin, clammy, and penetrant" (14–16). Thus begins *The Maltese Falcon*, a novel whose twisting narrative and tense, realistic style unite the elements of an emerging icon, the hard-boiled detective.

The genre stands out most for its tone. Author Dashiell Hammett, acknowledged as a master of sharp, direct prose, writes in a spare style, focusing on detail and realism. But he does not write simply. Instead, he crafts careful setting and character descriptions to build emotion and environment. His "objective" style leaves the detective's motives in the dark—the hero's actions become the stuff of mystery (Marling 129–30). Hard-boiled stories also introduce several other motifs. The detective runs his own firm or works independently; he's a strong individualist with his own sense of right and wrong. He also operates in a dense, urban space (like *Falcon*'s San Francisco). Inevitably, the city abounds with criminals and officials corrupted by graft. Finally, the detective crosses paths with one or both of two kinds of women—*femmes fatales* or damsels in distress. While he tries to rescue each damsel, he must always be on his toes lest she turns out to be evil (Hoppenstand 118–20). These motifs distinguish hard-boiled detectives from their classical progenitors such as Poe's Auguste Dupin or Doyle's Sherlock Holmes. Unlike early detective stories that reinforced traditional notions of law, order, and culture, these new tales changed the genre into a distinctly American one.

While the hard-boiled detective surfaced in the early 1920s pulps (such as *Black Mask*) and novels, his most significant moment as an American figure occurs on the screen in the 1940s. John Huston's *The Maltese Falcon* (1941) captures the spirit of the novel, often translating narrative and dialog verbatim from the text. Huston shoots scenes with sharp contrast between light and shadow, making visual both the grimy reality and the emotional tenor of Hammett's novel. This deep-shadow aesthetic would come to be known by the French phrase *film noir*. More importantly, because of his everyman looks and distinctive style, Humphrey Bogart's portrayal of Sam Spade came to define the hard-boiled detective.

For example, the French "New Wave" filmmakers, whose attention to American "B" movies revitalized our own interest in them, saw Bogart as a metonym for the hard-boiled detective. Jean Luc Godard used Bogart as both the role model for the petty criminal Michel in *Breathless* (1960), and again as an inspiration for the detective Lemmy Caution in the science-fiction story *Alphaville* (1965). More recently, spoofs like Carl Reiner's *Dead Men Don't Wear Plaid* (1982) and *Murder By Death* (1976) drew on images of Bogart for their detectives.

Humphrey Bogart as Sam Spade in John Huston's *The Maltese Falcon*, 1941. Courtesy of Photofest.

Perhaps the most clear depiction of Bogart's wedding with the hard-boiled detective appears in *The Bogie Man*, a graphic novel by John Wagner and Alan Grant about an asylum resident and Bogart doppelganger who escapes and searches for the Maltese Falcon among a truckload of stolen frozen turkeys. But the hard-boiled detective has not become an American icon solely because of Bogart. Rather, he fits a niche in our collective mythos, connecting modern concerns with established ideas about the "American way."

## ROLES AND ARCHETYPES

Foremost, the hard-boiled detective brings the outlaw to the city. In "The Hard-Boiled Detective Story," Richard Slotkin explains that developments in nineteenth-century industry and urbanization shifted the focus of American adventure writers from frontier race wars to urban class wars. Two key figures in this shift were the outlaw hero of Western stories who battled against corrupt and exploitative entities of power, and the proto-detective who fought crime and unrest on behalf of corporations. Over twenty years or so, these two protagonists merged: the new character, both outlaw and detective, "acts like he could be a criminal...yet somehow...comes out on the side of the law" (99).

The hard-boiled detective's outlaw status also places him in direct opposition to classical detectives. John Cawelti explains that traditional detectives work with police to solve crimes whose clues don't make sense. The detectives have all the evidence at hand but must puzzle out how to "read" it.

Suspense in these stories comes from the movement of the detective's focus from suspect to suspect. Hard-boiled mysteries, on the other hand, work in a very different way. Instead of starting with a clear crime and evidence, they often begin with a mystery that has no crime (as with *The Maltese Falcon*'s missing sister). The detective uncovers crimes, but instead of *thinking* through them, he usually has to *track down* his solutions. In doing so, the hard-boiled detective works against police, who might suspect that he's involved in the crime. He also "finds that he must go beyond the solution to some kind of personal choice or action." This choice involves the detective's own morality, which often contradicts official justice (Cawelti 142–43). Solving the crime reveals "that behind the facades of prosperity and order the world is really run by criminal conspiracies, driven by greed, establishing themselves by violence" (Slotkin 92). These revelations invert the traditional mystery, where a single crime's solution reinforces the status quo; hard-boiled mysteries uncover a deeper social malady, one beyond a single man's means to solve. The detective settles for a small-scale solution in the shadow of a large-scale cover-up.

The hard-boiled detective's emergence as an independent investigator also bolstered an imperiled story, the Horatio Alger myth. The Alger myth—in which a disadvantaged American youth uses hard work, "pluck, and a little luck" to succeed—was threatened by the "turbulent American city of the 1920s" and the "crisis of American individualism as the political philosophy of industrial capitalism" (Dennis Porter qtd. in Walton and Jones 189). At the moment the stock market crash destabilized the myth of individual success, the hard-boiled detective emerged as a hard-working entrepreneur, someone who "reaffirms his mastery over a city out of control" (Walton and Jones 189).

Finally, it is significant that this American subgenre of the detective story reached the height of its popularity on the silver screen. Indeed, the relationship between detectives and visual media makes cinematic hard-boiled detectives nearly inevitable. Consider the possibility that the detective story has more to do with "reading the world" than with cultural mythos. Life in large cities in the nineteenth century, Robert Ray explains, left people feeling anonymous and disoriented. Publishers, aware of the unease city crowds inflicted, began releasing books called *physiologies*, which explained in a few short pages how to recognize types of people—butchers, thieves, clerks, or anyone else one might encounter. Alas, the development of photography undercut these books: every photograph captured so many errant details that the physiologies' broad descriptions were invalidated. The classical detective story answers this unease: where photography's errant details make the city hard to "read," the classical detective uses such details to restore order by using those details to solve crimes (21–23).

Maybe, then, the hard-boiled detective's emergence answers cinema's emotional effect in the same way the classical detective story answered photography. Cinema fascinates us because "the camera render[s] some otherwise ordinary objects, landscapes, and even people luminous and spellbinding" (Walton and Jones 4). This effect, dubbed *photogenie*, has always perplexed cinema scholars: how does the camera imbue the everyday with magic? Hard-boiled detective stories, rooted in visual description, emotional conflict, and "cinematic" external action, were destined to find their iconic moment on the screen. Indeed, we cannot ignore their presence at the inception of film noir where the emotional effect of cinema's photogenic quality disrupts the classical detective's clinical ratiocination. For instance, *The Big Sleep* remains famous for its lack of resolution—while Bogart's Philip Marlowe does not solve the film's mystery, the ending satisfies because cinema's "spellbinding" magic foregrounds Marlowe's journey through the treacherous night-shrouded city; the mystery becomes secondary. The hard-boiled detective thus addresses cinema's emotional effect by reshaping mysteries in terms of emotion rather than logic.

## THE DETECTIVE CHANGES

As suggested above, the hard-boiled detective's distinction as an icon derives from his role as both individualist and outsider. The stories also shift the focus of mysteries from single crimes to larger issues of culture, often creating "narratives in which lying and deceit undermine...all of the fictions sustained by respectable society" (Horsley 32). Because of its opposition to and its exploration of mainstream culture, the genre was perfect for writers seeking new spaces in which to explore contemporary issues. They accessed these spaces by changing the genre: they made the detective a woman.

In the late 1970s, while traditional hard-boiled detectives continued appearing in films like *Dirty Harry* or in books like Robert Parker's Spencer series, several authors began writing novels featuring female hard-boiled detectives (or "tough gals"). Like their male predecessors, these characters were gritty, hard, competent detectives who had to battle the "system" to get by; however, they battled not the gritty underworld of Hammett's San Francisco, but the problematic society of post-1960s America. As Priscilla Walton and Manina Jones argue, the hard-boiled mystery genre provided the ideal starting point. Its individualist, self-sufficient protagonist offered "not just an eye that sees but a voice that speaks from the margins, a voice originating in a character who both talks and behaves in an insubordinate manner" (194). Female writers produced female private eyes whose investigations explored the challenges of an America dealing with shifting gender roles. These tough gal detectives, like Sara Peretsky's V. I. Warshowski and Marcia Muller's Sharon McCone, provided a public venue through which these writers could consider a range of issues facing women in culture (Walton and Jones 1–43).

"Tough gal" writers also redeemed women in hard-boiled fiction. In early hard-boiled novels, women who are unable (or unwilling) to play "damsel" to the detective's "knight errant"—as Chandler called him—were inevitably "malicious and resourceful." These women thus become "associated...with the degenerative forces at work in the social system" (Walton and Jones 192).

The novels resent the "increased personal freedom" women of the 1920s enjoyed, making women into "dangerous contenders, able to use their sexuality to trap and weaken men" (Hamilton 33). Not surprisingly, this lack of realistic (or even reasonable) female characters led several novelists to create their own, putting "an independent working woman detective at the center of the narrative of investigation" (Walton and Jones 30).

The pioneering work of these authors has significantly changed the landscape of the detective novel. The ripple-effect of these novels shows in what might be called the "second generation" of female hard-boiled detectives, such as Janet Evanovich's Stephanie Plum or Patricia Cornwell's Kay Scarpetta. Three other developments also indicate how significantly the hard-boiled detective has changed: first, as with Sam Spade's move to cinema, descendants of the female detective have begun appearing in visual media. With her defiance of tradition and her close grappling with day-to-day issues, Buffy the Vampire Slayer clearly fits the tough gal niche; so does *Alias*'s Sydney Bristow. These heroines enact new possibilities for women because they "rely on social networks and because individual action on the part of the female...has *representational* value" (Walton and Jones 207). Second, female hard-boiled detectives have become so prominent that writers of both genders now regularly use them. In Brian Michael Bendis' noirish graphic novel *Jinx*, the title character runs her own bounty-hunting business; in Jasper Fforde's Thursday Next series, Next wrestles with love and life while solving crimes that oscillate between the "real" and the "fictional" worlds. Following the lead of female writers from the 1970s and 1980s, creators of these new hard-boiled heroines combine the inner and outer lives of their characters. Finally, the groundbreaking work done with detective fiction by Muller, Peretsky, Sue Grafton, and others suggests how the genre opens spaces for discussions of social issues. To this end, a number of "second wave" novels feature "lesbian private investigators" and "characters who are racial or ethnic minorities" (Walton and Jones 41). This genre-stretching continues to extend the boundaries of the hard-boiled detective novel wide, taking the formula to new places with characters who bring questions of race and sexuality to the fore.

## THE DETECTIVE OF THE FUTURE

Walter Ong, a famous scholar of oral and literate cultures, suggests that the detective story is *the* story of the literate age. He explains that print literacy "reaches a plenary form in the detective story—relentlessly rising tension, exquisitely tidy discovery and reversal, perfectly resolved denouement" (144). But hard-boiled detectives bring something else to the table. In particular, they bring the concerns and ideals of America. Sam Spade combines Horatio Alger's individualist ideal with the cowboy outlaw's independent morality and frontier mythos, to become a key figure representing American urban life. Bogart's regular-Joe looks and distinctive acting amplified this effect, making the hard-boiled detective iconic around the world. Finally, the hard-boiled detective represents America's ability to reconsider itself: the detective's evolution from womanizer to woman embodies America's dynamism, in particular our ongoing negotiation of gender roles.

So perhaps the hard-boiled detective *is* the perfect protagonist for modern America. Slotkin suggests that hard-boiled detectives appeal to us because "we know that on the one hand we need authority and hard lines of value, and on the other hand that authority is often corrupt and misdirected and that those lines of value are often blurry" (99–100). In some sense he is right: the genre's deep attachment to individualism and justice does provide a skeptical yet optimistic look at culture. But recent changes in the genre also suggest that culture is not about corruption so much as complexity. After all, complexity emerges when hard-boiled stories stray from the tidiness of classical detective mysteries. This complexity then mixes with skeptical optimism to create an icon who stands between them, helping America better understand itself.

## WORKS CITED AND RECOMMENDED

Cawelti, John G. *Adventure, Mystery, and Romance: Formula Stories as Art and Popular Culture.* Chicago: U of Chicago P, 1976.

Hamilton, Cynthia S. *Western and Hard-Boiled Detective Fiction in America.* Iowa City: U of Iowa P, 1987.

Hammett, Dashiell. *Dashiell Hammett: The Maltese Falcon, The Thin Man, Red Harvest.* New York: Everyman's Library–Knopf, 2000.

Hoppenstand, Gary. *In Search of the Paper Tiger.* Bowling Green, OH: Bowling Green State U Popular P, 1987.

Horsley, Lee. *The Noir Thriller.* New York: Palgrave, 2001.

Marling, William. *The American Roman Noir: Hammett, Cain, and Chandler.* Athens: U of Georgia P, 1999.

Ong, Walter. *Orality and Literacy: The Technologizing of the Word.* New York: Routledge, 1982.

Ray, Robert B. *How a Film Theory Got Lost and Other Mysteries in Cultural Studies.* Bloomington: Indiana UP, 2001.

Slotkin, Richard. "The Hard-Boiled Detective Story: From the Open Range to the Mean Streets." *The Sleuth and the Scholar: Origins, Evolution, and Current Trends in Detective Fiction.* Ed. Barbara Radner and Howard Zettler. Westport, CT: Greenwood, 1988.

Walton, Priscilla, and Manina Jones. *Detective Agency: Women Rewriting the Hard-Boiled Tradition.* Los Angeles: U of California P, 1999.

# Harley-Davidson Motorcycle

## *Wendy Moon*

When I was asked to write this entry, I requested clarification: was it the motorcycle or specifically Harley-Davidson that was the icon? The latter, editor Dennis Hall said. After all, it was "no accident that Marlon Brando in *The Wild One*, and Malcolm Forbes and Jay Leno ride Harleys... and *Easy Rider* is always in the background." Harleys, he went on, meant "quality...transgression, freedom, and fightin'." He was partially wrong in specifics—but mostly right in meaning.

Marlon Brando rode a Triumph in *The Wild One*. Forbes rode and Leno rides Harleys, but also a great many bikes of all different makes and models. In fact, one of Leno's favorite bikes is his Y2K bike with a jet airplane engine. And although the choppers in *Easy Rider* were Harleys, they were so customized the only thing utterly Davidson about them were the V-twin engines, and few Harley riders look for a fight. As to quality—there's a joke about that—there're plenty of Harley's still out there on the road... because they all broke down.

But most people make similar assumptions. A friend rides a BMW R1100, and, even though she rode it to work for years, her co-workers kept calling it a Harley, and when people ask me what I ride, they smile and nod when I say "Harley." This proves that Hall was right—Harley-Davidson is the Heinz ketchup of motorcycles. In a way, Harley is synonymous with "motorcycle" because it's the only one manufactured here—thus called "American Iron," and therefore American. But it has a far deeper meaning.

Harley became the icon of freedom and transgression in the aftermath of World War II when the new social normal became an economic model; happiness meant bigger and better buying, and stability meant cookie-cutter lifestyles with father in a 9 to 5 job and mother at home. Chain restaurants, motels, and housing developments that, in the words of the old song, "looked just the same," sprang up across the country like acne on a teen's face.

This contrast between war and peace was too discombobulating for some returning GIs, and they chose to opt out. Because many of them had been aviators in the war and motorcycling is like flying on the road, they bought Army surplus Harleys and "chopped" them—removing non-essential parts and modifying others. The result reflected the ex-GIs' mood—as design tends to do.

What society values, longs for, and fears is behind every product design—or redesign—whether subtle like Aunt Jemima's getting a politically-correct look, or overt like cars' becoming the moving fortresses we call SUVs. Motorcycles are no different. Heavy, low to the ground, and made to handle hours of moderate speeds on long, straight roads, Harleys are perfectly designed for the North American landscape.

But, even more than that, all motorcycles' basic design is the polar opposite of the automobile: it's open to the elements; the rider is exposed to view; it's fundamentally solitary; and two wheels are essentially unstable. All that makes the rider vulnerable to—well, to everything. Therefore, it was perceived as antisocial, anti-family, and anti-safety. Because the choice of vehicle is seen to be an expression of who the operator is, the motorcycle's design alone dictated the rider would be assumed to be the same, so whether they were or not, they were seen as misfits outside society's laws—therefore outlaws, though not necessarily criminal.

The Detroit-made automobile, conversely, was the epitome of everything America valued. Capacious, it could hold a growing family. Essentially stable on four wheels and protected from weather, its four walls kept unsavory others out—just as the nation sought to do. And the auto could carry more consumer goods. As a result, the car was all-American.

Those ex-GIs, however, made a profound statement—the war had "redesigned" them from their previous civilian identities, and they, too, were military surplus in a terrible way. So it was fitting they eradicated every hint of the Army origin from their Harleys; and, in a sense, creating those modifications was a way of personal redemption. They also hung around together partying and riding and partying some more—and became motorcycle clubs, but they weren't "gangs" until the media found them useful.

During the same period, the media taught society to dread the rigid conformity and repressiveness of the communists. Both too much freedom (anarchy) and too little (communism) seemed bad for America. The Soviet Union, of course, was the one villain and was symbolized by the nuclear warhead and the tank destroying everything in their paths; but the media needed its polar opposite. The motorcycle and its unruly rider were perfect and newspapers and magazines across the country demonized them—very often unjustly and inaccurately—as modern-day centaurs raping and pillaging the countryside. Papers even ran stories on biker gangs and communism side-by-side. The underlying message was that the country's safety and stability were to be found in the middle. In this way, Harleys were an essential boundary at one end of American society—this isn't freedom, it's transgression.

The Harley, however, refused to be limited to its evil incarnation. GIs weren't the only ones who felt society's "one size fits all" didn't fit them—the Beats as well as many women, racial minorities, and teenagers felt the same way. Although few women and few minorities rode them, male teens heard

Harley-Davidson motorcycles for sale at Sturgis. Courtesy of Shutterstock.

a different message in the loud pipes' roar—one of rebellion and freedom and individuality. By the late 1950s and throughout the 1960s, the entertainment industry, responding to their interest, glorified them in songs like "Leader of the Pack," and movies like *The Wild Angels* and *She-Devils on Wheels*. There's a very good reason for this dichotomy: as Matt Drutt, the editor of *Motorcycle Mania: The Biker Book*, writes, "Time and again in film, television, music, and literature, the motorcycle has appeared as both demon and savior, a Janus-faced symbol of power and coming of age" (13). America, in parallel, has a chronic identity crisis: we can't decide if we're pioneers or settlers, individualists or conformists, liberals or conservatives; we want to be in control of our lives but want the government to provide a safety net.

But any group with a strong or unilateral identity tends to be regarded with hostility and suspicion when they interact with broader society. Americanization, after all, tends to be a process of learning to prefer ketchup to salsa or chili sauce in order to be of one nation. In a period of backyard bomb shelters, social control was paramount. Freedom became associated not with literal movement or lifestyle, but with a system of government. Therefore Harley's unequivocal ungoverned identity made it icon-worthy, as a crux of resistance to ideological conformity.

The savior-demon image reveals another quintessentially American duality: we're ambivalent about liberty—we love and fear it in nearly equal measures;

we long for more of it then regulate it to make it as safe as possible; and we're willing to lose our freedoms to protect them, then quick to complain we've lost them. The motorcycle, though, cannot balance that ambivalence because freedom without risk is like a motorcycle with walls, a roof, and windows—in other words, a car. So, back then, Harleys weren't ketchup but mustard, and un-American to some. But, to others, because they thought a hot dog without mustard was no hot dog at all, the motorcycle was über-American. That brings us right back to the nation's identity conflict—there are as many diverse conceptions of what America and freedom are as there are Americans. As a result, the motorcycle embodied both core national values and anti-values, and such complexity called for response from both elders and youth, powerful and powerless; and each group was attracted or repelled for different reasons, and each group used the motorcycle as a symbol in different ways. It was and remains a potent icon because it could be used both positively and negatively to describe the same thing.

In "The Motorcycle on Screen," John G. Hanhardt explains the positive side of the resulting icon:

> [T]he biker/hero manifests a desire to control his destiny and expresses his independence from the state, invoking heroic themes that have always been a part of the mythology of the American way of life... the lone rider... was both a fearless and a vulnerable explorer, an independent hero who was confronted with problems he has to solve by himself. (99)

The biker, then, was just the latest incarnation of the early explorers, patriots, and cowboys—but, in fitting with the times, as an anti-hero. That image, however, was in the movies.

In real life, the image of the biker was, in large part, engrained in the public mind by the media's demonic portrayal, which was set by their coverage of the Hells Angels, who began as one of those ex-GI motorcycle clubs. For their part, they willingly wore the black hats in this real-life Western and related horror stories of sex and violence to gullible journalists. There was, however, no corresponding real-life Wyatt Earp in the news to balance it—even though, in reality, the wild bikers were a very small part of the motorcycling community. The Hells Angels, by the way, only rode American Iron, adding yet another layer to the motorcycle-Harley interplay and giving a specific focus to Harley as transgression.

In a very real way, then, it was the biker movies that explicitly made the connection between freedom and individuality and transgression with motorcycles. Even though relatively few saw the films, it was enough to hear about them to "get the message," and it was the terminal message that spoke positively or negatively to society. In the first biker movie, *The Wild Angels*, released in 1966, Peter Fonda says, "We want to be free to do what we want to do—to ride our machine without being hassled by the man." This manifesto became the golden standard that subsequent biker flicks ineptly and exploitingly aspired to, and they multiplied like Elvis impersonators. It was also the red flag to conservative society.

In those movies, Hanhardt explains, the motorcycle itself is "repeatedly identified as the protagonist for change" (99). The biker flicks issued the metallic voice in the wilderness calling America to return to its roots, as well as a commentary on the same themes anti-war demonstrators, civil rights activists, and feminists proclaimed on the six o'clock news—they didn't want to be hassled by the man either. The films, then, supported these great, but far more threatening, social movements.

Consequently, the scruffy, zippered black leather biker on the Harley struck terror in the general public because the image represented local mayhem and national upheaval. But it also represented the mingled hope and dread of personal freedom. Society then wanted it that way, and so do we, because they still were and we still are frontier-oriented at heart; we can pretend we're farmers, but the explorer within remains. Bikers had to play outlaws so some could feel better about circling the wagons, and others needed cowboys to rescue them. And we still need cowboys and outlaws, today, even if they're of the quasi-kind, and the motorcycle and rider still function that way.

This may be why dentists and middle managers who would be afraid to cheat on their taxes don't shave on the weekends and then, on Sunday, don their beanie helmets and leather jackets to ride their Harleys. And there is a present-day corollary although the vehicle has changed; part of the appeal of SUVs is the idea they can triumph over the most rugged terrain, thus eliciting that frontier sense of movement. Even though that ability is rarely used for more than driving over a curb to park on the lawn, it's the thought that counts: in this case, a potential freedom.

Returning to the motorcycle itself in the 1960s, motorcycle design changed to express the times; it was the heyday of the chopper—the hippie of motorcycles. The Harley's front forks were extended, the backrest rose sky-high, and the rider's position was laid back as if the biker was withdrawing even further from society. Nothing blended the hippie and the outlaw biker as well as the movie *Easy Rider*, released in 1969. It was advertised with a line that perfectly expressed the national identity crisis: "A man went looking for America and couldn't find it anywhere." In a key scene toward the end, the reason becomes clear—America had lost its distinctiveness as the land of the free and bikers had found it.

In that scene, Jack Nicholson says, "This used to be a hellava good country" and goes on to explain why society feared bikers, "They're scared of what you represent... freedom." Dennis Hopper responds, "What the hell is wrong with freedom? That's what it's all about." "Oh, yeah, that's what it's all about, all right," Nicholson says.

> But talking about it and being it, it's two different things. I mean, it's real hard to be free when you are bought and sold in the marketplace.... Oh, they'll talk

to you and talk to you and talk to you about individual freedom, but they see a free individual, it's gonna scare 'em ... and that makes 'em dangerous.

The 1960s biker flicks, then, positioned motorcycles and their riders as more fundamentally American than the automobile. The correlation between Harleys, freedom, and transgression was thus cemented in the public imagination and the icon complete.

By the mid-eighties the major civil rights legislation had passed and social furor had settled down, and Harleys were no longer needed as poster children. When bikers made a rare appearance in film or television, they were almost always the villain and their incarnate freedom was trivialized by ten-second clips on the news of half-naked biker chicks at motorcycle rallies.

The message of *Easy Rider*, however, has once again become relevant in the new age of terrorism and reminds us that there is no true liberty without risk. Once again, it frequently appears in films, television, and commercials. In this incarnation, the Harley has been left behind while the freedom, rebellion, and individuality have been retained. The new icon centers on the sleek and brightly-colored sport bike with its racetrack pedigree rather than wild child legacy. Instead of the upright cruiser or laid-back chopper, the new rider perches like a jockey, the emphasis is on speed and maneuverability, and it's the hero who rides it. As after World War II, it's the young who find meaning in the motorcycle, but no longer in the Harley; and, significantly, women often ride in front. Too, in an age of globalization, perhaps it's appropriate that almost all sport bikes are foreign imports. It remains to be seen if the motorcycle, though, has become more like the empty symbolic gesture of the SUV's off-road capabilities or is once again a protagonist of change, ushering in an era of greater personal freedom.

Even as history begins to repeat itself, the same genericization process that typed the Harley is already at work, and the media refers to sport bikes as "Ninja-style" bikes. But Ninja is a particular Kawasaki model, and not all sportbikes are Ninjas, just as all motorcycles aren't Harleys. Given the motorcycle's increasing popularity, perhaps this means that twenty years from now, Americans will assume that all motorcycles are Ninjas—after all, that's what Tom Cruise rode, wasn't it?

## WORKS CITED AND RECOMMENDED

Drutt, Matthew. "Motorcycle Mania." *Motorcycle Mania: The Biker Book*. Ed. Matthew Drutt. New York: Universe Publishers, 1998. 13–14.
*Easy Rider*. Dir. Dennis Hopper. Columbia Pictures, 1969.
Hanhardt, John G. "The Motorcycle on Screen." *Motorcycle Mania: The Biker Book* 98–107.
*The Wild Angels*. Dir. Roger Corman. American International Pictures, 1966.
*The Wild One*. Dir. Laslo Benedek. Columbia Pictures, 1953.

# Ernest Hemingway

## R. H. Miller

No single writer embodies those characteristics that constitute the iconic ideal of the American creative personage so completely as does Ernest Hemingway. His status does not even depend on judging him a great writer as Michael Reynolds argues in his "Hemingway as American Icon." In the eyes of the American public, and not just the reading public, Hemingway is without question the quintessentially American writer. No other author is automatically recognized among the public at large, nor has he or she had outdoor clothing, pens, drinks (I recommend a Papa Doble; a recipe is in *The Hemingway Cookbook*), or a line of furniture named after them.

More essential, however, to the rank of icon is Hemingway's unquestioned stature as one of the giants of American literature. His short stories and novels have earned a place in the educational canon of the American university and have received the highest awards, including a Pulitzer Prize for *The Old Man and the Sea* in 1953 and the Nobel Prize for Literature in 1954. For his time Hemingway was the American author whom we saw as a true "public figure," who hobnobbed with the rich and famous and who commanded the wealth that allowed him to be taken seriously as a famous personality. With the publication of *For Whom the Bell Tolls* (1940) he attained superstar status. No book had been published in such a large initial press run, and no book up to that point, with the exception of *Gone with the Wind* (1936), had set such sales records. For good or ill, that novel bound him over forever to the American public, and there could be no turning back.

Hemingway's "American" credentials are impeccable. He was a Midwesterner, from the heartland, just outside Chicago. Both of his parents' families had accumulated modest wealth, in real estate and in a cutlery business. His father, Clarence, known familiarly as "Ed," was a doctor, a practicing family physician and gynecologist with a large family residing in the prestigious suburban community of Oak Park, Illinois. Ernest was the second-born child and first-born of two sons. His mother, Grace Hall, was a strong, willful woman who had given up what she thought was an opportunity for a promising singing career to dedicate herself to caring for her family of six children. His name, Ernest Miller, came from the names of his grandfather and a great uncle on Grace Hemingway's side of the family.

Ernest grew up a typical American bourgeois—handsome, sports-minded, outdoorsy, surrounded by the comforts that a relatively affluent doctor's career could provide, including a summer place in northern Michigan on Walloon Lake; but he nursed a rebellious streak. He braced against the domineering ways of his mother, and he found his father to be a moral prig and a pitiful male role model, much as he loved him. His adolescence closed when, instead of going off to college, he decided to launch himself into a journalism career, much to the dismay of his parents. To that point, his life almost defines him as the artistic American *typus*, with his upper-middle-class roots, his disillusionment with his father's spineless efforts to fulfill the role of *paterfamilias*, and his rebellion at his mother's powerful grip on the family and especially on him. Reflective of his rejection of that suburban existence is his use of his mother's and father's friends' names for the characters in his sexually frank and, for the time, startling story, "Up in Michigan," which appeared in his first book, *Three Stories and Ten Poems*, published in 1923.

Deeper yet, and a distinctive mark on his artistic career, was Hemingway's growing disaffection for American life and culture, and his embrace of the American expatriate movement of the 1920s and 1930s. He tried to enlist in the army for World War I but purportedly was turned away because of vision problems in one eye. After a brief period of service in the Italian Army Ambulance Corps, during which he was seriously wounded and later decorated, he returned to the United States; but his experiences only affirmed what was a deepening disenchantment from America and from his family.

From about 1921 until mid-1961 Hemingway lived a nomadic life of self-imposed exile, with semipermanent residences in Cuba and the United States, in Key West, Florida, and Idaho. Only one of his novels, *To Have and Have Not* (1937), is set in the United States. He left America just as the poet Byron before him had abandoned England in 1816, never to return, and so become the American model of the rebellious artist. Hemingway's separation from family, nation, and culture fitted him ideally for this iconic role. While he was to return to America later, his investment in his native country remained tenuous at best.

Hemingway's creative life, which began with his journalistic career at the *Kansas City Star* and continued later with various magazines and world press organizations, effectively modeled for Americans the kind of intellectual and inspirational experience they associate with the term "famous writer." He was largely self-educated, never attended college, and even though he was deeply self-conscious and resentful about this lack, it qualified him as a genuine American natural genius. Like Mark Twain before him, who was also a self-made writer and a major public figure, he managed to capture the essence of the authentic American as no other writer had, with the exception perhaps of Twain himself. Although he was always touted as the man of action, rather than a man of thought, the facts of his intellectual life show him to have been a voracious reader and widely knowledgeable on many subjects. To many, his habit of mining literary anthologies and other sources for book titles bespoke a kind of amateurish intellectual exhibitionism (*The Sun Also Rises* from Ecclesiastes, *A Farewell to Arms* from a poem by George Peele, *For Whom the Bell Tolls* from John Donne's *Devotions*), yet his interest in intellectual matters was deep and profound.

As did Byron, he affirmed in his physical appearance a popular expectation of the self-made male artist. As a young man he was spectacularly good-looking, as the many photos of him from the 1920s show with emphasis, and he maintained his tall, robust frame throughout his life, in spite of numerous accidents, the ravages of alcoholism, and other illnesses. His voracious appetite for male activities and male-bonding experiences identified him all the more with a hairy-chested image—bullfighting, deep-sea fishing, boxing, and big-game hunting, to name a few. On the other hand, Hemingway's association with the bloodier blood sports tends often to overshadow his engagement with the finer ones like fly fishing and upland bird hunting, of which he was extremely fond. Domestically, his troubled marriages, to Hadley Richardson, Pauline Pfeiffer, Martha Gellhorn, and Mary Welsh, were in keeping with the red-blooded American tradition of the famous personality.

What marks Hemingway perhaps more than any other characteristic as an American icon is his ability to find in his own life the characters and material of his fiction, and to weld that experience to enduring "American" themes of masculine identity, courage, personal heroism, and a sense of ethics that rises high above that of most individuals. Americans have a long history of distrust of the imagined life, as Richard Hofstadter explains in *Anti-Intellectualism in American Life*. To them, fiction is akin to lying, as their Puritan forebears had warned them. As a general rule, they feel more comfortable with a kind of art that is thinly veiled reportage. Hence their appetite for books like *Uncle Tom's Cabin* and authors like Mark Twain, or their firm belief in the historical authenticity of a book like *Gone with the Wind*. So Hemingway, who found his material in his own experience, appeals all the more to that sense of authenticity.

Undated photo of Ernest Hemingway. Courtesy of the Library of Congress.

The corollary to this idea is the popular critical judgment that in his writing career Hemingway showed himself to be less and less successful artistically because, as his career drew itself out, he simply ran out of things to write about. Whether he did or not has been a subject of considerable critical debate. Nick Adams is the early Hemingway, Frederic Henry is the Hemingway of World War I, Robert Jordan embodies the values of Hemingway the NANA reporter of the Spanish Civil War, and Santiago is Hemingway in the struggle of old age, in this debate's scenario. In any case, Hemingway's appeal comes from the fact that, for example, he not only wrote about war, but he had also seen war himself. To an American, the contrary example would be Shakespeare, whose art flowed from a powerful imagination that was able to make his art truer than life, but who practiced a liar's craft, or worse yet, didn't really write all those plays, because you can't really write well about things you haven't experienced. Strikingly, the "Shakespeare claimant" controversies are almost all of American origin.

Perhaps most surprising to the discerning reader is the extent to which Hemingway's fiction works against the grain of American experience, from the disaffected Krebs in the story "Soldier's Home" to the disillusioned Santiago in *The Old Man and the Sea*. In the major pieces of fiction, of which I rank four as paramount in the Hemingway corpus (the short stories, *The Sun Also Rises*, *A Farewell to Arms*, and *For Whom the Bell Tolls*), Hemingway represents his protagonists as men disaffected with American verities, American popular philosophies, and American attitudes generally. What Sinclair Lewis's protagonist George Follansbee Babbitt is, Hemingway's heroes are definitely not. This seeming contradiction in Hemingway's writings may hold the key to his sustaining popularity: even for one who seems to manifest in his public persona the ambitious qualities that we Americans value, at the core of his writings is a strong sense that hypocrisy and corruptness lie within the avid heart of America. Hemingway's heroes, so frequently misrepresented as macho figures, are deeply sensitive and fully aware of the purer values of mutual respect, pacifism, and true democratic principles.

Such is particularly the case with Francis Macomber, in "The Short Happy Life of Francis Macomber," who sacrifices himself on the altar of American macho values; or Jake Barnes, who has fled the hypocrisies of America; or Frederic Henry, who is fed up with the violence and destruction of war; or Robert Jordan, who has given up all hope for the democratic ideal in the midst of the brutalities of the Spanish Civil War. These heroes appeal to an expatriate impulse and alienation from confident Americanism. Yet at the same time they, like the prototypical American heroes, are loners, men against the world, who possess stamina and physical prowess equal to their unmatched sense of the ethical life. They live on the edge of evil, but are not tarnished by that temptation; and even in death they make a profound statement about the value of a career dedicated to a higher sense of right and wrong.

While his fiction has received its rightful place in the canon of American literature, Hemingway's contribution to nonfiction is no less distinctive. Here we bring to mind a large body of reportage done for various newspapers and magazines that cover various aspects of geopolitics and memorable world events, and especially stories that celebrate fishing and other outdoor sports, particularly "Big Two-Hearted River," which has been called the best fishing story ever written; *Death in the Afternoon*, a heartfelt anatomy of the beauties and horrors of bullfighting; *Green Hills of Africa*, an elegiac remembrance of an Africa that is now a memory; and his literary memoir, *A Moveable Feast*. This kind of writing virtuosity also contributes to our appreciation of him as a paragon of the art, but, more to the present point, it distinguishes him as someone who has lived life in the midst of peril and who has been a witness to history in his time.

The Hemingway style likewise expresses qualities that are quintessentially American. It is "minimalist," spare, and to the point. It echoes the qualities of speech that are characteristic of the Midwest and West, and reflects a certain Midwestern distrust in language, and a stronger trust in the murky world of gut instinct, in the language of ellipsis, of what is left unsaid. The style has its origins in many sources, but its main source is the Authorized (King James) Version of the Bible, a literary source that could not be closer to the roots of American culture.

In turn, that minimalist style is thoroughly compatible with another hallmark of Hemingway's fiction: violence. The cult of violence was something that had not really been a part of American literature until the turn of the twentieth century, when it found a place in the new Realism and Naturalism, and in the "new" mystery writing called "hard-boiled." The writer Flannery O'Connor is correct when she states in various places in her essays and letters that the use of violence is essential to the artistic truth of any piece of American fiction. The incorporation of violence in fiction reflects a truth about the world of American cities and countryside: that no matter where you go, you are never very far away from violence.

Finally and sadly, Hemingway's exit from his life by suicide in 1961 befits the expectations of a public in search of an iconic identity who might have wished another outcome but who, deep in their hearts, found a sense of completion in that last self-destructive act. Like his father before him, a sister and his brother, and his granddaughter and an ex-wife after him, Hemingway took his own life, utterly demented in those last days. He chose to end it in a grand sporting manner, with one of his cherished Purdey shotguns. In that act he joined the ranks of famous personalities who have taken their lives.

Whether one of today's blockbuster authors may someday reach not only star status but also attain the level of icon is anyone's guess, but they have a long way to go to match Hemingway's grip on the American public's imagination. In that regard, no writer living or dead can touch him. He had that peculiar mix of talent, social and geographic characteristics, a life of alienation and yet one quintessentially American, a life also of high drama and tragedy, and an art that spoke clearly on issues that go to the heart of our experience, that made for his becoming an icon of our culture.

## WORKS CITED AND RECOMMENDED

Boreth, Craig. *The Hemingway Cookbook*. Chicago: Chicago Review P, 1998.

Hemingway, Ernest. *The Complete Short Stories of Ernest Hemingway*. Finca Vigía ed. New York: C. Scribner's Sons, 1987.
———. *Death in the Afternoon*. New York: C. Scribner's Sons, 1932.
———. *A Farewell to Arms*. New York: C. Scribner's Sons, 1929.
———. *For Whom the Bell Tolls*. New York: C. Scribner's Sons, 1940.
———. *Green Hills of Africa*. New York: C. Scribner's Sons, 1953.
———. *A Moveable Feast*. New York: C. Scribner's Sons, 1964.
———. *The Old Man and the Sea*. New York: C. Scribner's Sons, 1952.
Hofstadter, Richard. *Anti-Intellectualism in American Life*. New York: Knopf, 1963.
O'Connor, Flannery. *Collected Works*. New York: Library of America, 1988.
Reynolds, Michael. "Hemingway as American Icon." *Picturing Hemingway*. By Frederick Voss. Washington, DC: Smithsonian Portrait Gallery; New Haven, CT: Yale UP, 1999. 1–9.

# Jimi Hendrix

## *Joy Haenlein*

He was a tall, thin, awkward black man with unruly hair, an acne-scarred face, and a penchant for wearing feather boas, pirate shirts, and military coats. He came to us dirt-poor, motherless, and poorly educated. But James Marshall (Jimi) Hendrix did more in four years, from 1966 to 1970, to influence music and popular culture than most do in a lifetime.

It wasn't just that he had a natural gift for playing the guitar. His raw talent is evident in his records and performances at some of the legendary outdoor music festivals of the time: Monterey Pop, Woodstock, and the Isle of Wight. His long fingers made complicated guitar maneuvers look easy. His sound was unique, a conglomeration of musical styles—rock and roll, rhythm and blues, folk, soul—and guitar-driven sound effects. He could play with speed and precision. And like most good musicians, he played from his heart in a way that struck a chord in others. Hendrix's electrifying version of "The Star-Spangled Banner" at Woodstock in August 1969 has become for many the defining moment of an era, embodying in a single iconic performance the restlessness and bravado of a generation.

His devotion to his instrument also set him apart from other musicians. He got his first guitar as a teenager, and though he lost many guitars over the years and had many others stolen from him, Hendrix rarely was without his signature instrument for long. Biographers note that he slept with his guitar, even while serving in the Army, and practiced virtually around the clock, even during set breaks and for hours after the most grueling performances. Practice allowed Hendrix to perfect some of the flashy maneuvers for which he later would become famous, such as playing the guitar with his teeth or behind his back.

Guitar players have tried to emulate Hendrix in the years since his death in 1970 at age 27, and some will argue that one or two have come close to duplicating the experience of his music. But there has been no true successor, even though virtually every rock guitarist admits his profound influence. Interpretations of his work are not common—an irony because Hendrix was known for his cover versions of previously recorded songs, especially those by Bob Dylan, whom he admired. Many consider Hendrix to be the greatest

# JIMI HENDRIX

influence on the playing of the electric guitar since Les Paul built the first solid-body electric guitar in 1941. Any guitarist who has used feedback and distortion to alter and deepen sound is acknowledging Hendrix. The long guitar solos of 1970s rock and roll have their roots in his music, as do heavy metal, punk, speed metal, grunge, and practically every form of rock music developed since. Yet as much as music has changed, Hendrix's work still sounds fresh and urgent thirty-five years after his death.

He was born in November 1942 in Seattle, the first child of Al and Lucille Hendrix. The couple named their son Johnny Allen originally, but changed his name to James Marshall four years later. Marital problems, alcoholism, and deep poverty broke the Hendrix family apart and kept its members on the move. His parents signed away their parental rights to four of his five siblings in 1955. When Jimi was 15, his mother died.

Never a good or an interested student, Hendrix attended school in a racially integrated system in Seattle, where about 30 percent of the student population was black. Local black culture at that time was heavily influenced by African American and Southern white gospel music. The combination of ethnic influences in his social background might help to explain why, years later, Hendrix seemed comfortable as a black man with an essentially white audience.

His first "guitar" was a broom he pretended to play when he was 11 years old, but by age 14 a boarder his father had taken in bought a beat-up acoustic guitar for Jimi for $5. It had one string but Jimi got many sounds out of it, buzzing, twanging, and screeching. Before he got a full set of acoustic strings for his guitar, he was already dreaming of stardom. At 16, he got his first electric guitar and played with anyone in his neighborhood or school who would oblige. Like others of his generation, Hendrix listened to B. B. King, the Coasters, Chuck Berry, and Fats Domino. He saw Elvis Presley play and developed an appreciation for Muddy Waters, Elmore James, and blues musicians who appealed to his father's generation. Though his music would eventually integrate all of these influences, Hendrix's playing set him apart from an early age. He coaxed a wide variety of sounds from the guitar, just as he did from his first one-stringed instrument.

His efforts weren't always appreciated. His first band audition was at a Jewish temple; his girlfriend at the time said Hendrix was quickly cut from consideration because his playing was considered wild. This experience was Hendrix's pattern for nearly twelve years. As a guitarist, he was accomplished enough to play with anyone in the business. He didn't read music, but learned quickly, and practiced his parts until they were perfect. He had little respect for rules and convention, but he was too shy and awkward to be much of a troublemaker. Even as an adult pursuing a professional music career, he would get fired for straying from his part and playing "wild" guitar solos, or for refusing to wear the same suit or costume as the rest of the band, or for missing the tour bus.

Hendrix flunked out of school at 17, and despite his father's prodding, he never considered learning a trade. With Jimi, it was music or nothing. He was poor and hungry, owning nothing more than a guitar and an amplifier and playing any available gigs. Perhaps looking for a way out, he enlisted in the U.S. Army and made it into the 101st Airborne division in 1961, guitar in tow. While he learned to jump out of airplanes at Fort Campbell, Kentucky, the army provided him with three meals a day and a regular paycheck, which was considerably more than he had in Seattle. But his main interest was still his guitar and his music. In the service, he met bass player Billy Cox, who would become a close friend and would later play with Hendrix at Woodstock and the Isle of Wight. When their five-piece Nashville band began to get bookings in other towns, Hendrix grew eager to leave the army and perform full time. Biographers differ about his exit from the service. For years, it was said that Hendrix was given an honorable discharge after jumping from an airplane and injuring an ankle. Most recently, biographer Charles R. Cross claimed that Jimi was released after he told the army psychiatrist that he had homosexual feelings toward his bunkmates.

Through the band, the King Kasuals, Hendrix ended up touring the South from 1963 to 1965. Jimi, sometimes alone or with the rest of his band, appeared on the bill with some of the top acts of the day, including Little Richard and the Isley Brothers. A promoter told Jimi there was work in New York City, and he went to Harlem. However, audiences there were interested almost exclusively in rhythm and blues and jazz. Although he gained experience doing session work (including the background for a single called "As the Clouds Drift By" by Jayne Mansfield), he found tastes in Harlem more restrictive than in Nashville. In the South, country and rock and roll were part of his popular repertoire, but in Harlem, Hendrix felt isolated and alone.

In Greenwich Village, however, he found audiences who were more open to what had become his unique style of music—a bluesy brand of rock infused with every trick and technique he'd learned along the road from the top performers. In 1966, his group, Jimmy James and the Blue Flames, performed covers primarily, from the Troggs' "Wild Thing" and Howlin' Wolf's "Killing Floor" to "House of the Risin' Sun" and "Knock on Wood." Hendrix was a big Dylan fan and covered "Like a Rolling Stone." By this time, he was using a crude fuzz box to distort the sound of his guitar. The fuzz box, given to him by a member of another band, the Fugs, became one more element of his sound.

It all came together for Hendrix in Greenwich Village in the summer

Undated photo of Jimi Hendrix. Courtesy of Photofest.

of 1966. Audiences were primarily white and caught up in the folk music movement of that era, but Jimi played the songs they recognized *his* way. He wowed audiences with his physical tricks—playing his guitar behind his back, under his leg, or with his teeth—and the unique sounds of his guitar solos. Also, Hendrix's persona was accessible to multiracial audiences, just as the Civil Rights and counter-culture movements were coming to prominence in the late 1960s. After growing up in Seattle and playing to southern audiences with his army buddies, Hendrix was comfortable with whites, and many of his band mates in the Village were white. As important, Hendrix left behind the stiff suits and cookie-cutter looks of other bands and dressed as he wanted, in ruffled shirts and pirate jackets, feather boas, and wild colors. He might have appeared ridiculous to conventional audiences, but he appealed to white listeners in avant-garde Greenwich Village.

His reputation spread, and the top guitarists of the day came to see him play. Eventually, Bryan "Chas" Chandler, a rock and roll musician and manager from London, made it to the Village for a performance. Chandler reportedly was so overwhelmed the first time he heard Hendrix play that he dropped a milkshake down his shirt. Stunned that Hendrix was a virtual unknown in the United States, Chandler was confident that he would be a smash in Britain. He convinced Hendrix to go to London, promising him an introduction to Eric Clapton of Cream, another guitar virtuoso, and a chance for a music career. With $40 of borrowed cash in his pocket and a small bag at his side, Hendrix got on an airplane in 1966.

Although he had struggled in the United States, Hendrix was a hit in London from his very first club performance. American blues music was as popular in Britain as British music was in America at that time, and the first songs he performed in British clubs, such as the bluesy "Hey Joe," fit right in. All the great rock musicians saw Hendrix in London: besides Clapton, the Rolling Stones, Eric Burdon of the Animals, the Beatles, Jeff Beck, and Pete Townshend all came to hear Jimi play. Many guitarists and front men regarded him as a competitor, if not an outright threat, to their success, and tales of one-upsmanship between Hendrix and Townshend or Mick Jagger, for example, are numerous. Rock music, like most fields, has its petty rivalries, but there was good reason for other artists to be intimidated by Hendrix's talent. He combined so many different influences in his music—rhythm and blues, rock, soul, folk—in such a seamless way that he invented a new genre. No one seemed able to duplicate it. Not only was the music new, but Jimi designed a new vocabulary for the guitar, pushing amps to their limits to create an intense sound, and using new fuzz boxes, wah-wah pedals, and tremolo arms to distort it in various ways. In addition to playing the guitar with parts of his body, he also used his body to push and shake the amps, further manipulating the sound. These technological forays are practically required of musicians today; but they were unusual in the 1960s until Hendrix popularized the approach. The high school dropout was one of rock's first techno-geeks, laying the groundwork for all the bands that would later incorporate feedback, distortion, and tonal work into their sound: from Emerson, Lake and Palmer and the keyboard-driven bands of the 1970s, to the heavy metal and grunge guitar movements of the 1980s and 1990s.

The next two years went by in a blur for Hendrix and the two white men who were recruited in London to join the Jimi Hendrix Experience, bass player Noel Redding and drummer John "Mitch" Mitchell. "Hey Joe," the band's first single, was released to acclaim, and the group's first album, *Are You Experienced?* debuted in spring 1967, topping out just behind the Beatles at number 2 on the charts. The band gained a devoted following on their tour through Europe. But it was at the Monterey Pop festival in California in June 1967 that Hendrix captured a U.S. audience. Hendrix heard the Beatles' highly anticipated *Sgt. Pepper's Lonely Hearts Club Band* album just before the Experience was scheduled to play. He couldn't resist the urge to cover one of their songs. Along with the rest of the band, he learned the chords and put a new version together in about an hour. The Experience opened the show with "Sgt. Pepper's" and left the audience, including members of the Beatles who were in attendance, dumbstruck.

Following Pete Townshend's Who onto the stage, the Jimi Hendrix Experience delivered a blistering set that included such songs as Dylan's "Like a Rolling Stone" and several from *Are You Experienced?* His appearance probably is best remembered for his performance of "Wild Thing," during which he doused his guitar with lighter fluid and set it ablaze. Janis Joplin and other artists watched from the audience as he played guitar behind his back, under his leg, and with his teeth. From that point on, burning and smashing guitars became a regular part of Hendrix's stage show. Smashing guitars had already become a signature stage move for the Who, and members of both bands were constantly monitoring the progress and antics of the other during the late 1960s.

Working with Redding and Mitchell, Hendrix had his most musically productive years in 1967 and 1968. Three albums of new material were released: *Axis: Bold As Love* (1967), most of which was recorded at the same time as *Are You Experienced?* (1967), and *Electric Ladyland* (1968). His concerts sold out and the Experience was a top draw at the outdoor festivals, which drew tens, if not hundreds, of thousands of fans—almost all of them white. He was not the first black man to attract a largely white audience: rockers Little Richard and Chuck Berry did it before. But Hendrix ascended during the height of the Civil Rights movement, when black-white relations were being explored and, to some extent, reinvented. Though his guitar work and his sound were his gifts to the world and made him an American icon, his appeal to white audiences had a greater cultural influence for occurring at a key point in the development of race relations in this country.

He also was a figurehead in the sexual revolution and the drug culture of the late 1960s. His sexual prowess was legendary. Once he became a star, he entertained groupies and reportedly had casual sex with hundreds of women, although he also had more enduring relationships during that time. His drug use reached legendary status as well. He is said to have used everything from marijuana and cocaine to Seconal, Quaaludes, LSD, and heroin, and as time went on, drugs had an increasing influence on his performances. More than once, he either cut a concert short or failed to appear because he was unable to function.

Toward the end of his life, he seemed to be chasing a new direction, disbanding the Experience and forming loosely assembled bands with his army friend Billy Cox and other musicians. These were the groups Hendrix took with him to Woodstock and the Isle of Wight in England shortly before his death. Some recordings were made at this time, including the live *Band of Gypsies* (1970). These bands have been considered Hendrix's strongest musically, though their appeal was less commercial. Some biographers have hypothesized that prior to his death Hendrix was preparing to shelve his rock-god career and turn either toward folk music or jazz, where he could better connect with black audiences.

But it was not to be. Biographers differ about the final details. They agree that he asphyxiated on vomit as the result of a drug overdose. According to Charles Cross, Hendrix took a large dose of a German sedative called Vesparax, on top of other drugs and alcohol he had taken the night before. Some biographers have him dying in the ambulance or emergency room. Others have his body being found in the morning by a woman who slept as he choked and suffocated. He was buried in his hometown of Seattle.

Hendrix's death was the first of three to shake the rock music world over the next year. Janis Joplin died of a heroin overdose three days after Hendrix was buried. Nine months after that, Jim Morrison died of a heart attack. All were age 27 when they died, and all three became legends, at least in part because they died while they were young, while their careers still were going strong, and while 1960s counterculture was still emerging.

Although Hendrix gained stature as a musician and cultural icon because he died so young, his influence has been unique and pervasive. With Chuck Berry and Little Richard, he was one of the few black musicians of the twentieth century to be embraced immediately by white audiences, partly because he played the rock and roll that ruled the music world in the 1960s and he was accessible to white audiences. He loved to play the songs white audiences loved, covering work by Bob Dylan and the Beatles, among others. But his developments of rhythm-and-blues and soul precedents, his mastery of stage presence, and, above all, his guitar work imprint his real contributions to music. He also stands apart as a cultural touchstone for his generation. His strident individuality—reflected in his clothes, in his music, and in his lack of conventional grounding, especially as it relates to family—came together as young people in the United States and Europe were turning to those same avenues to find their own ways of exercising freedom and forging identity. His music and the lifestyle he embodied brought changes to the wider culture that continue today.

## WORKS RECOMMENDED

Bangs, Lester, and Greil Marcus. *Psychotic Reactions and Carburetor Dung.* New York: Knopf, 1987.

*The Complete Monterey Pop Festival.* Video Recording. Dir. D. A. Pennebaker et al. Monterey, CA: Pennebaker Hegedus Films–Criterion Collection, 2002.

Cross, Charles R. *Room Full of Mirrors: A Biography of Jimi Hendrix.* New York: Hyperion, 2005.

Hendrix, Jimi. *Blue Wild Angel: Jimi Hendrix Live at the Isle of Wight.* Sound Recording. Santa Monica, CA: Experience Hendrix Music Project, 2002.

Murray, Charles Shaar. *Crosstown Traffic: Jimi Hendrix and the Post-War Rock 'n' Roll Revolution.* New York: St. Martin's, 1989.

*The Official Jimi Hendrix Web site.* <www.jimihendrix.com>.

Potash, Chris. *The Jimi Hendrix Companion: Three Decades of Commentary.* New York: Schirmer Books, 1996.

Redding, Noel, and Carol Appleby. *Are You Experienced? The Inside Story of The Jimi Hendrix Experience.* London: Fourth Estate, 1990.

*The Rock and Roll Hall of Fame and Museum.* www.rockhall.com.

Shapiro, Harry, and Caesar Glebbeek. *Jimi Hendrix, Electric Gypsy.* New York: St. Martin's, 1990.

# Audrey Hepburn

## *Lucy Rollin*

Like icons in museums, admired for their beauty of design and color, Audrey Hepburn's image appeals to our aesthetic sense. Not only was she an unusually beautiful film star, but throughout her career she represented the height of fashion elegance, as she continues to do well into the twenty-first century. Her name alone conjures the simple and the ladylike in clothes. Since the virtual end of her film career in the late 1970s, however, her image has acquired spiritual meanings unusual in a film and fashion icon. She has come to represent a generosity approaching self-sacrifice—something close, perhaps, to martyrdom.

Hepburn's body combined the height and the narrow waist of the elegant model with the shapely legs and rear of the dancer—perfect for both high fashion gowns and simple sportswear. But she looked like no fashion model had ever looked, beginning with her remarkable face—its tilted, expressive eyes, long nose unusually wide at the tip, wide mouth and slightly crooked teeth. Photographer Cecil Beaton said of her, "She is like a portrait by Modigliani where the various distortions are not only interesting in themselves but make a completely satisfying composite" (Ferrer 86). She knew instinctively how to enhance her natural qualities to create an interesting look. In 1950s publicity photographs, her eyes were heavily made up while her hair looked as if it had been trimmed with nail scissors. Unsmiling, she looked sophisticated and sultry, but her wide smile was as fresh and joyful as a child's. Her tall, thin body fell into interesting poses thanks to her ballet training; her grace turned her flat chest into an asset. Photo spreads in *Life* magazine of Audrey wearing plain black capri plants with ballet flats, brief shorts and sandals, or a billowing strapless gown for the 1954 filming of *Sabrina*, made the angular *Vogue* and *Bazaar* models in their Christian Dior suits and high heels, look cold—and old.

As she became a star, Hepburn had plenty of help refining her fashion image, but she always exercised control over it. She chose French couturier Hubert de Givenchy, then only 26 years old, for her costumes in *Sabrina*—the beginning of a lifelong association; his simple lines, pure color, and elegant fabrics suited Hepburn perfectly on and off screen. By the time she made *Funny Face* in 1957, she was as much fashion model as she was actress. The film satirized those chilly Dior models and the whole business of couture, offering instead Audrey's playfulness with clothes. In it she wore everything from a simple rain jacket with jeans and loafers, to a couturier wedding gown. Her most famous film, *Breakfast at Tiffany's* (1961), launched the reign of the little black dress as a modern fashion staple. Hepburn wears at least three black dresses in the film, two short and one long. The single most iconic image of Hepburn is from this film: the head-shot of her as she looks into Tiffany's window, wearing her black gown, pearls, and big sunglasses, holding a paper coffee container.

Most of her other 1960s films capitalized on her fashion model persona, no matter what character she played. *Charade* (1963) established the pattern: distressed young woman, always wearing beautiful clothes. *Paris When It Sizzles* (1964), *How to Steal a Million* (1966), and *Two for the Road* (1967) followed this formula. Even *My Fair Lady* (1964) became a large-screen canvas for Cecil Beaton's designs, especially those in which he clothed Audrey. Hepburn in her Ascot gown and hat has become the representation of that film.

No other figure associated with high fashion has had such lasting popular appeal, for despite her haute couture image in films and *Vogue* magazine, her style is surprisingly adaptable and undated because of its essential simplicity. A slim, knee-length dress or suit, low-heeled pumps, a sleek hairstyle and minimal jewelry—this combination is the basic Hepburn look, ladylike and understated. Almost any woman young or old can achieve some flattering version of it and add her own individual touches. The editors of *In Style* magazine say Hepburn's style "continues to enchant us" for its "clean lines and restraint" (Arbetter 24). Pamela Clarke Keogh in her book *Audrey Style* (1999) asserts, "Her style is as timely as it is timeless; she is ingrained in our consciousness.... [H]er influence on contemporary style is incomparable" (14).

However, icons originated not in museums but in Orthodox churches, where their purpose is to encourage meditation and inspire faith. An icon of, for example, the Virgin and Child invites the observer not only to admire its surface beauty but also to ponder Mary's relationship with the infant Jesus, the angel's message to her before his birth, the journey to Bethlehem, her grief at his crucifixion—images and thoughts that strengthen the viewer's faith. Audrey Hepburn's appearance and her experiences have caused her image to reverberate in this way. She has become, especially since her death, a representation of purity, suffering, and self-sacrifice.

Hepburn made a total of twenty-nine films, counting two for television. Early in her career she also appeared on stage in two major productions which won good reviews for her performances: *Gigi* (New York and national tour 1951–1952) and *Ondine* (New York 1954). But Hepburn never thought of herself as an accomplished actress; her youthful appearance and manner were what she offered, and as a result, she essentially played the same role in all her work. *Roman Holiday,* her first major film and for which she won an Oscar for Best Actress of 1953, established her screen persona as a girl *almost* becoming a woman. Directors often paired her with much older leading men such as Humphrey Bogart, Gregory Peck, Gary Cooper, Fred Astaire, and Cary Grant—pairings that enhance her virginal quality. She is Cinderella forever at the ball, an image that mutes the sexual subtext of films like *Love in the Afternoon* and *Breakfast at Tiffany's.* Even in her 1960s films, those in the *Charade* mold, sexual heat is subsumed by innocent flirtatiousness; she is still more girl than woman.

In the 1950s, when Hollywood offered Marilyn Monroe and Jane Russell as representations of womanhood, Hepburn's image had a powerful appeal for girls on the threshold of puberty, and older. To girls who did not see themselves—or wish to see themselves yet—as sexual, Hepburn was a comforting alternative. In her film roles she was beautiful, fashionable, appealing, and innocent, and men fell for her completely without putting overt sexual pressure on her. Rachel Moseley, in *Growing Up with Audrey Hepburn* (2002), interviewed a number of British women of various ages about their response to Hepburn, and concludes that as a star "she offered the possibility of reconciling certain key contradictions which were significant for women... for instance in her ability to be both boyish and feminine" (128). This appeal has lasted well into the twenty-first century.

Classic Audrey Hepburn, ca. 1950s. Courtesy of Photofest.

But Hepburn brought something more to her film performances—something that was part of her deepest self and emerged through her eyes before the camera. Moseley's interviewees identified it as a kind of frailty, "like she needs looking after," while Moseley summarized it as another contradiction in her image: she represented physical fragility and psychological strength (190–91). This complex quality shows most effectively in her performance as Holly Golightly, a role for which she was remarkably well suited. Truman Capote, author of the short novel *Breakfast at Tiffany's,* wanted Marilyn Monroe to play it, casting that might have worked because Holly is apparently a call girl, but Hepburn's physical resemblance to Holly is obvious in Capote's opening pages. One of the characters is examining a photograph of a carved image of Holly: "an elongated carving of a head, a girl's, her hair sleek and short as a young man's, her smooth wood eyes too large and tilted in the tapering face, her mouth wide" (7). The bartender says she was a "skinny girl that walks fast and straight." When the narrator first sees her in person, he sees a girl in a "slim cool black dress.... For all her chic thinness, she had an almost breakfast-cereal air of health.... It was a face beyond childhood, yet this side of belonging to a woman" (13). Although she is a tough-talking girl who apparently sells her sexual favors, Holly appears innocent to those who know her. The bartender says he was in love with her, but never wanted to touch her: "I swear, it never crossed my mind about Holly. You can love somebody without it being like that" (9–10). Despite her tough exterior and sometimes crude vocabulary, Holly is sad, confused, frightened, unsure of her identity, asking for help but always just out of reach—a vulnerability that draws people to her. Along with her physical resemblance to Capote's character, Hepburn embodied Holly's vulnerability and essential purity, because they were part of herself.

In every Hepburn film, her characters at some point reveal themselves as fragile and frightened; her great eyes beg for sympathy as the camera moves in for the close-up. The clothes and makeup to which she gave such intense care were her armor, but the fear shone from her eyes. When her only armor was a nun's habit, in *The Nun's Story* (1959), her eyes became even more affecting; many believe this to be her finest performance. When she played a blind woman in *Wait Until Dark* (1967), her eyes became the focus of the film. Her thin body controlled in a dancer's posture, and the careful diction with which she delivered every line of dialogue, augmented the expression in her eyes, conveying a deep need for sympathy and understanding held under great restraint; audiences responded by loving her the way Capote's bartender loved Holly: "You can love somebody without it being like that. You keep them a stranger, a stranger who's a friend" (10).

Hepburn's son writes that sadness was an essential part of her character, beginning in her earliest life with a father who seemed incapable of close relationships, and who abandoned the family when she was 6 years old. Her mother was strong but also undemonstrative and often critical of her. Moreover, as a young adolescent she lived in Arnhem, in the Netherlands, experiencing near-starvation when the Germans occupied the town from 1939 to 1945. When the town was liberated, Hepburn was 15 and dangerously malnourished. As she regained her health, she found herself too tall and too old to realize her dream of becoming a classical dancer, but was "discovered" for films, because of the need to work rather than the desire to be a movie actress. Her thinness, and the emotional neediness she brought to her performances, remind her fans of the deprivations of her childhood and adolescence.

There were deprivations in her adult life as well. In 1954, after her success in *Roman Holiday*, she married actor-director Mel Ferrer; they established residence in Switzerland, because both preferred to remain apart from the Hollywood milieu. But as he took over the management of her career, she began to resent his decisions on her behalf; he apparently insisted that she work more often than she wanted to, especially after they had a son. She divorced him in 1969 and soon married Italian psychiatrist Andrea Dotti, effectively retiring from films, living permanently in Europe, caring for her two sons Sean Ferrer and Luca Dotti, gardening and homemaking, making only occasional public appearances. Dotti, however, was known as a playboy and continued his liaisons throughout the marriage. Hepburn finally divorced him in 1982, returned to Switzerland, and lived there with actor Robert Wolders until her death. She struggled unsuccessfully to keep her two marriages intact, sacrificing herself for husbands who did not care enough for her as a person. She never married Wolders, but he offered her the devotion she had not experienced in marriage. Hepburn appeared, in the publicity surrounding her personal life, just as she did in her films: self-sacrificing and fragile.

If she had remained in her Swiss farmhouse into her old age, enjoying the privacy she so valued, her image would probably have continued to be most associated with elegance in clothes. But at age 59 she became an ambassador for UNICEF, using her image to attract attention to starving children in places like Ethiopia, Central America, Vietnam, Turkey, and Sudan. Between 1988 and 1992 she made eight journeys to such places and appeared in other public arenas to speak about her experiences and about the great need she saw. She had an emotional investment in these experiences that few others could share, for while she offered her publicity power to help these children, she revisited her own childhood hunger. Although most photographs of her during these journeys show a smiling Hepburn, family, friends, and acquaintances said she was suffering greatly, because of her memories of Arnhem and because she felt there was so little she, or indeed any one person, could do. In September 1992 she made her last journey and the most emotionally grueling one—to Somalia, where most of the population was starving. She told her son Sean after that trip that she had "been to hell" (Paris 354). By the time she returned, she was in great physical pain. Diagnosed with terminal colon cancer, she returned to her Swiss farmhouse, where she died at age 63 the following January. There is no proof that her disease was related to her UNICEF work, but there were those who believed she had sacrificed herself for the cause (Paris 357–60).

Since her death there has been an increasing flow of books and articles about her, many with appeals for the Audrey Hepburn Memorial Fund, established by her family and administered through the U.S. Fund for UNICEF. With each book, photograph, quotation, or anecdote, her image seems to become more saintly. Her friends recall only her simplicity, generosity, dignity, warmth, and courage. UNICEF photographer John Isaac said, "Audrey had no color, no race" (Paris 346). Director Peter Bogdanovich was amazed by her fragility off screen and her strength before the cameras; he said she had "strength through vulnerability—strength like an iron butterfly" (Paris 282). Others who encountered her became even more spiritual in their descriptions of the experience. Makeup artist Kevyn Aucoin said that working with her "was like being in the presence of someone who was not merely human. She sort of had an angelic quality about her, and a sort of ethereal, rather haunting presence...an energy, a sort of light coming from within her that was just sort of overwhelming" (Keogh 230). Robert Wagner called her "a gift from God" and director Billy Wilder said, "She was just blessed. God kissed her on the cheek, and there she was" (Paris 382–83).

If the original purpose of an icon is to inspire faith, Hepburn certainly does that. Apparently millions of filmgoers from the 1950s until today believe unquestioningly that Hepburn was in life just as she appeared on screen. The young women interviewed in Moseley's study express this phenomenon repeatedly: "She's like always, like, herself"; "I mean, she seems to be *her* in all her films...she plays herself in every film...I mean it in a *good* way" (182–83). Barry Paris comments that "most people felt sincerity was her biggest asset" as an actress (Paris 376). Pamela Clarke Keogh says, "Most of all, she is honest—we believe who she is on the screen, we trust her"(18). In the midst of the cynicism that, early or late, surrounds most screen personalities, her image has remained as pure as it was in *Roman Holiday*. Now her fans' faith is rewarded. Throughout his memoir of his mother, Sean Ferrer assures his readers that

> She really was like those characters you saw in the movies: emotional, courageous, delicate, romantic....What you saw and felt when you watched her on the big screen was not only the clever presentation of characters brilliantly written, directed, shot, and edited into a performance, but a clear view of a truly magical human being who deserves the warm feelings that still transport audiences worldwide today. (xxiv)

Pamela Clarke Keogh sums up the impact of Hepburn's image today: "As an actress she embodies our hopes, our dreams, and our heartache, and reflects them back to us more brilliantly than we could ever imagine. Audrey Hepburn's beauty, her vulnerability, and her courage are instinctive, visceral, electrifying" (18). Melissa Hellstern offers an even more spiritual response in her inspirational handbook *How to be Lovely: The Audrey Hepburn Way of Life* (2004), taking various quotations from Hepburn and organizing them around ways to achieve happiness, friendship, health, and success. Says Hellstern, "It is her character that is certain to withstand the test of time...she represented all that a woman could be....May the light she shared with the world shine on in the lives of those she continues to inspire" (iv).

Hepburn herself once said: "I never think of myself as an icon. What is in other people's minds is not in my mind" (Hellstern 143). Whether her image will continue to convey such spiritual meanings to "other people's minds," no one can say. In contrast to various excesses of food, fashion, and politics, her dignified clothes, manner, and lifestyle along with her humanitarianism have inspired admiration for decades. Of course, others have led similar lives and made similar choices. But they did not look like Audrey Hepburn. All that she was, finally, is summed up in that remarkable face, an aesthetic fascination and joy. Even Hellstern's little book, which aspires to focus on what Hepburn said, is filled with pictures of her; they attract the eye more than the minimal text ever could. They are the essential Hepburn. Like Garbo's, her face continues to offer its unique beauty as an object for meditation, communicating to each individual observer more than words can convey.

## WORKS CITED AND RECOMMENDED

Arbetter, Lisa et al. *Secrets of Style: The Complete Guide to Dressing Your Best Every Day, from the Editors of* In Style. New York: In Style Books–Time, 2003.
Capote, Truman. *Breakfast at Tiffany's*. New York: Random House, 1958.
Ferrer, Sean Hepburn. *Audrey Hepburn: An Elegant Spirit*. New York: Atria Books, 2003.
Hellstern, Melissa. *How to Be Lovely: The Audrey Hepburn Way of Life*. New York: Dutton, 2004.
Keogh, Pamela Clarke. *Audrey Style*. New York: HarperCollins, 1999.
Moseley, Rachel. *Growing Up with Audrey Hepburn*. Manchester, UK: Manchester UP, 2002.
Paris, Barry. *Audrey Hepburn*. New York: Berkley Publishing Company, 1996.

# Hershey Bar

## Dennis Hall

Sister Mary Martin used them to teach us fractions, occasionally reducing a large brown wall chart into small milk chocolate squares, distributed at the end of the lesson, invariably at the end of the day. Nothing engages the attention, even the understanding, of a grammar school child like a Hershey bar. I knew the goals of learning.

One Christmas, Santa left under the tree, just for me, a whole box of Hershey bars, nestled between cartons of Lucky Strikes and Old Golds for my elder brothers. Nothing then defined indulgence like a whole box of Hershey bars (or a carton of cigarettes); it was like owning a candy store. I knew Santa loved me more than I deserved.

The vending machines at my high school and college invariably offered bars of Hershey's dark chocolate, milk chocolate, and milk chocolate with almonds, with the remaining slots filled as space allowed with Snickers, Milky Way, or Three Musketeers bars, and occasionally (this candy machine would have been an unusually big one) with such oddities as Butterfinger, Mounds, or Nutter-Butter bars. I will ever remember my dismay when a school friend, off to buy candy bars, returned, all the Hershey bars having been sold out, with a Zag-Nut bar for me. This wasn't a candy bar! Moreover, he had misapprehended my taste, my sophistication, as well as squandered my dime (still a coin of some interest in my school days) on a confection which provided no nourishment, psychic or physical. I knew then that we are, in every sense, what we consume.

When I began graduate studies, I thought, after the directives of Saint Paul, that I had put away the things of the child. But in the first meeting of English 601, the required first course in scholarly research and methods, the venerable Dr. Richard D. Altick declared that anyone who found an error in any of his work, would be awarded a Hershey bar! Not a Milky Way or the candy bar of one's choice, but a Hershey bar (as it turned out, milk chocolate without almonds). Very few Hershey bars were dispensed, but those who got them would frame them rather than eat them. To have one of Dick Altick's Hershey bars (some few actually had two of them) could make a career in English studies. I knew then, as do most Americans even now, that the Hershey bar has always borne the mark of distinction in American culture.

Chocolate has a long, well documented, and much repeated history, dating from its consumption as the beverage of the gods by Mayan and Aztec leaders, as Hernado Cortez reported early in the sixteenth century; to its widely being drunk in seventeenth- and eighteenth-century European chocolate houses, especially in England and France; through a variety of technical refinements in the nineteenth century into increasingly popular confections known as chocolates and bonbons; into the mass productions of various kinds in the twentieth century; to a revival of interest in the new millennium in craft chocolate of seemingly infinite refinement and luxury. Many devotees tend to luxuriate in this narrative nearly as fully as in chocolate itself. Readily accessible in bookstore and library, repeated continuously in the periodical press, and flowing over the Internet like dark sauce on a scoop of vanilla ice cream (see Kidd, for example), the knowledge of chocolate's progress, of the various kinds and enrichments it lends itself to, of the many, often esoteric, cultural and social and commercial uses one may make of it, serve to redeem consumption that would otherwise be thought a narrow self-indulgence. Of chocolate, there is no trivia, only information.

The Hershey bar, introduced in 1900, is the commercial offspring of Milton Hershey (1857–1945) who began his career as an apprentice candy maker in the 1870s and who, by the end of the first decade of the twentieth century, revolutionized chocolate making and icon-brand marketing in America. Moreover, he proved to be the model of the good employer, and engaged in philanthropy far earlier and far more fully than did his fellow captains of American industry. While a certain amount of hagiography is to be expected at Hershey.com, the company Web site, few are the negative utterances about Milton Hershey to be found anywhere (Brenner seems to have collected all there are; see especially chapters 9 and 10). Some entrepreneurs have complained that as a businessman he was too interested in machinery and experimenting with new and often unsuccessful products, that he neglected operations, leaving them to subordinates he thought better qualified to direct operations, and that he was insufficiently aggressive and had too little interest in profits. He is reported often to have said that "I have more money than I know what to do with." The extravagance of the Gilded Age was simply not part of his consciousness (Brenner 84). Whether by coincidence or design, he enjoyed throughout his life the reputation of a good guy in an era peopled with bad guys, particularly when compared to his principal competitor, Forrest Mars, who has been likened to "a shark in chocolatey seas" ("Candy Man Mars").

Hershey, Pennsylvania, emerged as a model company town. While Hershey's hands, to be sure, worked long and hard, the company built Hershey Park and provided a wide range of other public amenities, including affordable and good housing for workers, which were of a kind and on a scale singular for the era. He did much the same for the workers in the town of

Hershey in Cuban sugar cane fields prior to the Castro revolution. In 1909, the childless Milton and Kitty Hershey founded an industrial school for orphaned boys; in 1918, three years after Kitty's death, Hershey donated his entire estate, then some $60 million, to the school. It took five years for the public to become aware of this generosity. The endowment, now worth $5 billion, supports one of America's best boarding schools, but one serving disadvantaged students of all races and religions (Brenner 134–35). "If Hershey's philanthropy" as Carol Ann Rinzler puts it, "often made him seem the very model of a paternalistic nineteenth-century industrial type, so be it. He built houses for his workers (individually designed ones—Hershey did not believe employees should have to live in cookie-cutter cottages), created social programs, and saw to it that during the Depression of the 1930s not a single Hershey worker lost his or her job. In fact, the company created jobs throughout Hershey and the surrounding area by embarking on a program of construction—housing, halls, factories.... [H]is company continued the tradition by creating the Milton Hershey Medical Center at Pennsylvania State University" (80–81). Unless Rinzler and the many others overstate the reality by half, Milton Hershey may be the only saint in the Gilded Age.

The aura of goodness associated with Hershey *père* was from the outset transferred to Hershey *fils*—the chocolate bar. His processing of milk chocolate was a technical innovation which made use of the abundant supplies of milk in the Pennsylvania countryside and had important consequences: it made what is known as "eating chocolate" capable of mass production and distribution and relatively cheap. It made eating chocolate easy to preserve and package and so to sell in a wide variety of outlets—newsstands, lunch counters, groceries, and later, vending machines, as well as candy stores. It made Hershey bars ubiquitous. "Hershey endeared himself to the American public at large," as Wendy Woloson expresses the point, "by creating domestic chocolates that were within the reach of everyone. In fact the Hershey nickel bar, which fluctuated in size, remained the same price from 1903 until 1970" (146). For generations of Americans "Hershey bar" and "candy bar" were nearly synonymous, much as Coke stood for soft drink, or, later, Kleenex would come to stand for tissue or Xerox for photocopy.

The infusion of milk also made chocolate, at least in Milton Hershey's eyes, fit for the consumption of women and children. He insisted that his chocolate be characterized as food, be recognized as nutritious. Employees reputedly were

Photograph showing a Hershey's chocolate bar, ca. 1925. Courtesy of the Library of Congress.

instructed never to refer to Hershey bars as "candy." An early brown package, with silver raised lettering, carries the slogan

A NOURISHING FOOD
# HERSHEY'S
5¢ Milk Chocolate 5¢

For most of the Hershey bar's life, its dark brown wrapper and silver lettering was the Hershey company's only advertising. It spoke for itself with a resonance endearing to American consumers. And the basic package of the Hershey bar has stayed more or less the same, the mark of the real thing for over a hundred years, a sign of reliability and wholesomeness. When the company finally felt the need to advertise in the late 1960s, it led with nostalgia, with a jingle sung over a folk guitar accompaniment: "There is nothing like the face of a kid eatin' a Hershey bar...Hershey's, the great American chocolate bar." To this day, many parents who are appalled at the prospect of a Snicker's or some other candy bar will allow a Hershey bar.

Hershey's milk chocolate bar, indeed, rescued chocolate from its sexual and sinful associations developed throughout the nineteenth century (see Woloson, ch. 4, "Sinfully Sweet: Chocolates and Bonbons," 109–54). Chocolate was seen by friend and foe alike as making men potent and women receptive. One James Wadsworth wrote of "chocolate's rejuvenating and sexually stimulating properties":

> Twill make Old Women Young and Fresh;
>    Create New Motions of the Flesh.
> And cause them long for you know what,
>    If they but taste of chocolate. (Woloson 136)

J. H. Kellogg, of cornflakes fame, and Sylvester Graham, developer of the cracker that combined with a Hershey bar and marshmallow makes the ever popular s'mores, joined many other American voices for moral rearmament to warn against what they took to be the clear connection between "dreamy indolence and gluttony" and to describe chocolate's association with licentiousness and dissipation, especially among women and girls. "Bonbons and other fine confections" Woloson concludes, "came to be the focus of many entreaties because they were luxurious, ephemeral, and fancy items that like gratuitous sex, masturbation, and novel reading had no purpose other than to take up time and to gratify indulgences" (143). Early on Hershey sold penny portions of milk chocolate in shapes and wrappers that would appeal to children, including a whole line of chocolate cigars and cigarettes (which were a special treat, although no longer made by Hershey, when I was in grade school). "When Hershey reevaluated his products at the turn of the century, he expanded his milk chocolate line to better serve children's tastes.

His candies incorporated the logic that milk added to chocolate made it 'good' for children, in contrast to dark bittersweet chocolates, which still counted as 'real chocolate', meant for adults" (Woloson 145).

The success of the Hershey bar was such that it defined the taste and texture of American chocolate. By the 1940s Hershey was making 75 percent of America's chocolate, much of it used in the candy bars sold by other companies. "The only distinctively American taste," as Carol Rinzler points out, "was created by Hershey with its sweet, gritty dark chocolate (far too sandy for European tastes), and its milk chocolate, whose flavor derives from the special taste of naturally dried milk crumb" (59). "A serious chocolate person," she continues, "will tell you that fine dark chocolate should be smooth, without the grit or sandiness caused by sugar particles" and that fine milk chocolate ought not to have the "chewiness" created by "a relatively high proportion of milk solids and low proportion of cocoa butter" (60–61). Most Americans, however, grew up on Hershey bars and prefer their grit or chewy texture. While the proliferation of "new luxury" goods in the new millennium has led New York chocolate shops to ape Parisian *chocolatiers*, Americans still have to learn to like European chocolate. So too, there has been something of a revival of chocolate erotica, after the suggestiveness of food writers like Nigella Lawson or the explicitness of books like *Booty Food: A Date-by-Date, Course-by-Course, Nibble-by-Nibble Guide to Cultivating Love and Passion through Food*, whose eighth chapter, "Dessert's on Me," projects licentiousness and dissipation beyond the wildest fears of J. H. Kellogg and Sylvester Graham. Hershey's Kisses appeared in 1907, but, reputedly, the product was named not for the exchange of affection, but because the machine that makes them looks as if it is kissing the conveyor belt. The predominant American taste continues to favor the innocence of a Hershey's Kiss to the experience of a Perugina's *Bacio*, with its love note secreted under its foil wrapper.

The Hershey bar's aura of wholesomeness and quality and the American way is for many a matter of patriotism. The Hershey board of directors, having solicited bids, had a change of heart and recently voted (10 to 7) not to sell the company to Wrigley's or worse to Cadbury-Schweppes or worse yet to Nestle, a move that a group called the American Reformation Project hailed as a victory for "American culture, tradition, and values" (Simmermaker). This association, of course, has it roots in the Hershey bar going to war. Hershey's had provided milk chocolate bars for doughboys during World War I, after which it continued to supply the Department of the Army. As World War II loomed, Hershey's developed and was producing, by the end of 1945 at a rate of 24 million a week, "Field Ration D" for the troops, a "bar that weighed about 4 ounces, would not melt at high temperatures, was high in food energy value, and did not taste so good that soldiers would be tempted to eat it, except in an emergency" ("The Ration D Bar," www.hersheys.com). These and conventional bars were the Hershey bars that G.I.s famously gave to refugees and residents of occupied territory, making friends for the United States and for Hershey's. The shiny tinfoil in the brown paper sleeve, printed with

HERSHEY'S in sliver block letters, quickly became a sign of American culture and an international icon easily equal to that of Coca-Cola. The company jealously guards the Hershey bar's military role, as Joël Brenner demonstrates in her fascinating account of the "Bar Wars" waged between Hershey's and Mars to secure Defense Department contracts to supply heat resistant chocolate bars for operations in the Middle East (3–18). Whatever the state of corporate warfare, however, the Hershey bar remains a mark of friendship and security.

As the Hershey bar is the standard of the American taste in chocolate, it has long served at various times and in different ways, positive and negative, and with varying degrees of clarity, as a rhetorical trope. While for many people happiness is a Hershey bar, precisely these positive associations make it ripe for irony. In military parlance, for example, a Hershey bar refers to the uniform stripes indicating oversees combat service. To describe a person as a Hershey bar once indicated a person especially innocent or naive. Women in occupied territories were often said to be easily seduced by the promise of a Hershey bar and a green card. A girl in the neighborhood might be known as a Hershey bar because that's what it cost to get into her pants; so too, a very cheap prostitute. The Hershey highway is homosexual slang for anal intercourse. The green Hershey bar is a term for hashish. A Hershey bar is an acne blemish, a zit. Stan Goetz wrote a tune (on his album *Swinging at Storyville*) called "Hershey Bar."

Sometimes the rhetorical uses are more elaborate, as for example in the title, "New Highway, Same Hershey Bar," a political article on the failed promise of computer technology (Schalit). My personal favorite appears in an introduction to a symposium on aesthetic formalism: "We might say that formalism, then, is like the Hershey Bar of criticism. It's a classic. It's an archetype. It's everywhere. Everything else seems to contain a variation on its theme. As the Hershey Bar of criticism, formalism is also a creative tool, a staple ingredient of many analytical recipes. Melt it and stir it in thoroughly, chop it up and mix it into the dough in chunks, grate it into a fine powder and sprinkle just a bit of it on top. People take their formalism in many forms. But everyone likes to have at least a little bit of Hershey formalism now and then, even if they claim they can't stomach excessive quantities of it at one sitting—or can't afford to or will really pay for it later" (Gee par. 5).

While in the minds of many Americans the Hershey bar is synonymous with chocolate, it hardly seems fair to tie to its tail the host of movies, books, plays, and even operas that either nominally or substantially exploit the capacity of chocolate to attract audiences, although the Hershey bar probably does lurk in the unconscious of the readers and viewers of *Looking for Mr. Goodbar* or *Better Than Chocolate* or *Chocolat*, or *Willie Wonka and the Chocolate Factory*.

The Hershey bar is entrenched in American life and lore. The story, for example, that, when F. Scott Fitzgerald died of a heart attack in Sheila Graham's house, she had just left to buy him some Hershey bars, is entirely believable ("21 December 1940"). The Hershey bar, a defining part of the texture of American life, confers credibility on all it touches. Its many associations run deep within America's collective consciousness. Even for those of us not particularly fond of chocolate (as I confess to the astonishment of just about everyone I know), the Hershey bar serves as a medium of communication and a marker of affection and love. It is a trigger of nostalgia. And in typically American fashion, the Hershey bar is an indulgence taken apparently independent of abundance, savored all the more as a pleasure taken without apparent guilt. For most Americans, the Hershey bar can do more than Milton can to justify God's ways to man.

## WORKS CITED AND RECOMMENDED

Brenner, Joël Glenn. *The Emperors of Chocolate: Inside the Secret World of Hershey and Mars.* New York: Random House, 1999.

"Candy Man Mars." 21 July 2005 <http://www.goodbyemag.com/jul99/mars.html>.

Gee, Shaleane. "Voice, Story, Vision." Online in *Core-relations: Essays from the Humanities Common Core Curriculum* [Feb. 19, 1999]. 21 June 2002 <http://core-relations.uchicago.edu/VolumeIIpages/voiceintro.html>.

The Hershey Company. 21 July 2005 <www.hersheys.com>.

Kidd, Monee. "Chocolate FAQ." 21 July 2005 <http://www.faqs.org/food/chcocolate/faq>.

Malouf, Jacqui, with Liz Gumbinner. *Booty Food: A Date-by-Date, Course-by-Course, Nibble-by-Nibble Guide to Cultivating Love and Passion through Food.* New York: Bloomsbury, 2004.

Rinzler, Carol Ann. *The Book of Chocolate.* New York: St. Martin's, 1977.

Schalit, Joel. "New Highway, Same Hershey Bar." Online in *Bad Subjects* Issue 18, Jan. 1995. 8 Aug. 2005 <http://bad.eserver.org/issues/1995/18/schalit.html>.

Simmermaker, Roger. "Buy American Mention of the Week: A Victory for Hershey is a Victory for America." American Reformation Project. 8 Aug. 2005 <http://www.american.reformation.org/policy/BuyAmerican/HersheyVictory.htm>.

"21 December 1940." The Grim Society of Los Angeles. 23 Aug. 2005 <http://grimsociety.com/reader/grfortn.html>.

Woloson, Wendy A. *Refined Tastes: Sugar, Confectionery, and Consumers in Nineteenth-Century America.* Baltimore: Johns Hopkins UP, 2002.

# Hollywood

## Thomas B. Byers

These days, Hollywood is the mother of all icons. Of course the metaphor is a hyperbole, but how else to launch a homily to the happy home of hype? Besides, the metaphor points toward a somewhat dicey double relation of Hollywood to iconography: on the one hand, the name "Hollywood" itself carries a practically uncountable wealth of iconographic meaning. On the other hand, Hollywood is the generator, the progenitor, the mother of countless other icons that are or could be subjects of essays in this book. If you want to send a message, call Western Union—but if you want to create an icon, make movies. Hollywood has been called "the Dream Factory," but it's both the factory *and* the dream. What follows will concentrate on Hollywood itself as icon, but the icons it produces are so much a part of its meaning that they will keep creeping in.

The first problem is one of definition. What is Hollywood? Of course, everyone knows it's a town in California—except that it isn't: it is a district of the city of Los Angeles. In any case, these days what we associate with the name is only rarely located in the geographical place. Hollywood is the name of an industry—a complex of industries, really (not only movies, but television, popular music, and music video, and so on)—whose products, taken together, are one of the United States's leading exports. Hollywood is also, more particularly, the name for the industry, the medium, the art form, and the style of mainstream American movies. But more than that, it's a cultural site—a fantasyland. It's where the stars live the lives that are so much richer, so much more romantic, so much *more* than our own. The fact that almost none of them live there, and that most of their work is not done there, only adds to the fantastic, phantasmatic, magical quality of the word.

In order to try to give some manageable shape to the meanings that sprawl out from the Hollywood sign, I'll discuss them under four major rubrics: sex, politics, ambition and class, and America. In each case, we will find that Hollywood embodies multiple, often contradictory meanings and tensions, and indeed that the contradictions and tensions themselves are iconic for some of the deepest splits and most relentless struggles in U.S. culture.

## SEX

Sex is the subject of perhaps the most obvious category, and probably the most fun to talk about. Some simple lists of names may get us started; here's a sampling of those who are commonly identified as stars and as sex symbols (which don't always amount to the same thing, but they do more often than not): Rudolph Valentino, Mae West, Clark Gable, Jean Harlowe, Lena Horne, James Dean, Marilyn Monroe, Brad Pitt, Julia Roberts and, of course, Rock Hudson. Some of them come in brilliant pairs, some meteoric, others enduring: Douglas Fairbanks and Mary Pickford, Tracy and Hepburn, Bogart and Bacall, Fred and Ginger, Liz and Richard, Ron and Nancy, Tom Cruise and Nicole Kidman. Other names carry whiffs of shame and scandal, sometimes forgiven, sometimes not: Ingrid Bergman, Errol Flynn, Lana Turner, Charlie Chaplin, Fatty Arbuckle, Roman Polanski, Michael Jackson. Then there are the great gender benders—among them Marlene, Madonna, and (in their fashion) Jack Lemmon and the Tonys: Curtis and Perkins.

But the names are only foreplay. The money shot is that Hollywood says sex, and means it. It is where Americans, and many others around the world, learn what sex is and how to do it, what sexuality is and how to have it, what sexy is and how to be it. Think how much more, and more varied, experience we all have of romance on screen than we have of it in our lives. Hollywood is the home address of eros and the hotbed of, well, hot beds. Where sex is concerned, it is a Fantasyland far beyond Walt Disney's imagination—though for many of us, his films contain our first such fantasies, or at least our first conscious, shared, social ones. Whether our fantasies are of everlasting love and happily-ever-afters, forbidden passions and secret trysts, or wanton orgies and Richter-scale orgasms, Hollywood is the place where sex is the more that we all want it to be.

Of course, sometimes it is too much. Hollywood is also a place where innocence goes to be destroyed, where the bright-eyed young girl finds that the road to starletdom crosses the casting couch, where predatory men commit statutory rape, where the tabloids find their fodder of both heartbreak and scandal. These in turn feed the darker fantasies of the minions of morality, from Will Hays, Joseph Breen, and the Legion of Decency (or their sisters in the Ladies of the Law and Order League in John Ford's *Stagecoach*), to Dan Quayle, Bob Dole, and more extreme right-wing critics. For those of this persuasion, Hollywood is and has long been at best sexually irresponsible and immoral, and at worst a latter-day Sodom. For example, consider the words of William Donohue, President of the Catholic League, speaking on MSNBC: "Hollywood likes anal sex....I believe in traditional values and restraint. They believe in libertinism" ("Scarborough Country for Dec. 8," 6 September 2005 <http://msnbc.msn.com/id/6685898>).

In sum, whether its connotations are ameliorative or pejorative, whether it is imagined as a place of erotic freedom and possibility, or one of temptation and damnation, Hollywood stands for sex.

# HOLLYWOOD

## POLITICS

Charges of immorality and corruption link sex to politics, libertine to liberal, corrupter of youth to communist conspirator (after all, they are all body snatchers). In politics as in morals, right-wingers from the House Un-American Activities Committee in 1947, through Dole and Quayle in the 1990s, to today's cultural conservatives, have seen Hollywood as standing for the radical extreme to Middle America's traditional, conservative mean.

That there have been various strains of left-wing or left-leaning sentiment, commitment, and activity in Hollywood, from Communist Party membership to New Deal left populism and contemporary liberalism, is unquestionable. However, Hollywood's iconic status as leftist other seems a bit odd, given that all of the most prominent Hollywood figures who have actually made the transition from show business to politics, from Shirley Temple to Arnold Schwarzenegger, are Republicans, and among the most famous are such intensely conservative leaders as Ronald Reagan and Charlton Heston. Moreover, perhaps the most popular of all male Hollywood stars, John Wayne, not only was personally conservative but remains a conservative icon of heroic proportions. And as for the movies themselves, though they express a range of political positions (from Rambo's to Oliver Stone's), they generally tend toward the middle and marketable rather than the radical or even politically thought-provoking.

Nonetheless, in the popular imagination, and certainly in the ideology of the right, Hollywood is coded leftist, as the place not of Dutch Reagan and Duke Wayne but of Marlon Brando, who sent Sacheen Littlefeather to decline an Oscar for him because of Hollywood's treatment of Native Americans, and Jane Fonda, who notoriously went to North Vietnam during the Vietnam War. More recently it is identified with Susan Sarandon and Tim Robbins and their opposition to the second Iraq war, and with Barbra Streisand and Steven Spielberg and their support for liberal causes and candidates.

The prominence of the latter two in current attacks on liberal Hollywood—and particularly in charges that it is "anti-Christian"—points to an issue that is always either lurking beneath the surface or rearing its ugly head: partly because Jewish moguls from Louis B. Mayer, Sam Goldwyn, and Harry Cohn to Michael Eisner, Michael Ovitz, Rob Reiner, Spielberg, and Streisand have become rich, powerful, and exceptionally visible in Hollywood, it has long been, and remains, a lightning-rod for anti-Semitism. Even a very brief session of Web browsing will uncover the current virulence of this phenomenon. For example, William Donohue, quoted earlier as saying that "Hollywood likes anal sex," said in the same MSNBC broadcast that "Hollywood is controlled by secular Jews who hate Christianity in general and Catholicism in particular. It's not a secret, okay? And I'm not afraid to say it." And hence by association the pro-anal sex, anti-family "libertines" (that is, in code, "the queers") either are, or are under the control of, Christian-hating Jews. Of course Donohue represents an extreme, paranoid reading, but he only echoes the earlier views of Joseph Breen, who ran the Production Code Administration, the official Hollywood censor of the 1930s and 1940s. Theirs was only the extreme of an interpretive disposition whose more mainstream versions are nonetheless quite suspicious of Hollywood. As a political icon, particularly in our moment, Hollywood connotes a bastion of communism and liberalism, Jews and gays.

## AMBITION AND CLASS

Hollywood's connotations are, in general, a good deal sunnier in this area than they are in politics. Indeed, it is an iconic setting for the playing out of the American dream—a place where, by dint of determination, pluck, and luck, an "average" Joe or Jane may make, or fall into, a fortune. It's a place where one may go to succeed—as indeed many of the early moguls themselves did, along with many other children of immigrants, like Frank Capra. More even than New York, it's a magnet for aspiring actors, and a place full of beautiful, eager, young people on the rise (and on the make). It's also a place where your life may turn in an instant, where you may strike gold out of the blue—where simply drinking a Coke at the right time in the right place (say, after school in a little shop across from Hollywood High) may turn you into Lana Turner. And it's the last hope for fame and fortune of many people out there at their computers (formerly, typewriters), thinking that surely they can write a screenplay or television script for a show better than all the crappy ones they've sat through.

Yet even this fantasy has its darker side, just as the American success story, from Ben Franklin's *Autobiography* onward, is always shadowed by the failures who embody the threat that gives it meaning. For every Lana Turner there is a Judy Garland or Frances Farmer, as well as countless nameless would-be starlets used up and thrown away by the disposable, superficial culture of Tinseltown. If, for some, Hollywood Boulevard leads to Rodeo Drive, for others it turns into the Boulevard of Broken Dreams. In one par-

The famous Hollywood sign. Courtesy of Corbis.

ticular version of this (always cautionary) tale, Hollywood is specifically the ruination of the serious artist: easy money, vulgar taste, crass commercialism, and hedonist dissipation destroy the self-discipline that genius requires to bloom. This is the Hollywood of the F. Scott Fitzgerald legend, one of the reasons why, as Fitzgerald himself once famously said, "there are no second acts in American lives."

What makes the dream so attractive in spite of these caveats is that the potential gains are so great. Hollywood's version of the American dream, like just about everything else about the place, is extreme, heightened, superlative. It's not just the money (though one has the sense that the place is rolling in it), not just the pleasures of sensuality or celebrity in themselves. It's something even beyond the glamour, though that's certainly part of it. It's the notion that success in Hollywood bestows on its achievers something as close to the aura of royalty as our middle-class democracy has to offer. And it's also the notion of self-transformation—of ceasing to be Betty Joan Perske and becoming Lauren Bacall, casting off Archibald Leach and putting on Cary Grant, leaving Norma Jean Baker behind and waking up as Marilyn Monroe. It's not only making it to Hollywood, but making it there from Marion, Indiana (James Dean), or Helena, Montana (Gary Cooper), or a tobacco farm in Brogden, North Carolina (Ava Gardner), or even from Thal, Austria (Arnold Schwarzenegger). It's ceasing to be nobody, and becoming somebody bigger than life. It's actually ending up as one of those people you grew up seeing, and wanting to be, and thinking you could never touch in a million years.

## AMERICA

Hollywood is more than just a site of, or an icon of, the American dream. Finally, it is an icon, or a dream (or in fact many dreams) of America itself. In its simplest versions, this notion might refer to the misunderstandings of twentieth-century foreign visitors to the United States who thought they were coming to the Old West of the Western, complete with cowboys, stagecoaches, Indian attacks, and so on. Their misconceptions were naïve, but nonetheless symptomatic. For most of the world's people (and peoples), their conceptions of the United States are formed as much from the Hollywood products they consume as from any other source.

Moreover, in this regard, Americans themselves are not all that different. The movies, Pauline Kael once said, are "our national theatre." Not only do we get many of our pictures of different regions from their cinematic and televisual representations, but we get many of our overall conceptions of the "essence" of Americanness from Hollywood as well. The Old West not only is over, but in fact it never quite existed in the first place—but it is an inextricable, and politically influential, part of our conception of America. Similarly, the America of Bedford Falls in *It's a Wonderful Life* is largely gone; far more Americans live in cities than in small towns, and even more of us live in suburbs; and small-town life wasn't exactly Bedford Falls anyway. Yet Bedford Falls is still part of what we think of as distinctly American. If, for nearly a century, Hollywood has been the mother of American iconography, it has particularly been the mother of our iconography of America and Americans.

Finally, though, Hollywood doesn't only make our icons of America; it is itself such an icon. It means *us*. There is a certain mathematical proportion to this phenomenon; in terms of culture, as America stands relative to the world (and particularly to old Europe), so Hollywood stands in relation to America: it is richer and brighter, more vulgar and meretricious, more glittering and glamourous and meteoric and hedonistic. It is at once more materialistic and technological, while more idealistic and dreamy, more staked on risk even as it is utopian. It is a place we look down on, and yet it is where we all want to end up. And in a peculiar way, we have. In our postmodern times Hollywood is, more and more, where we live.

## WORKS RECOMMENDED

Biskind, Peter. *Easy Riders, Raging Bulls: How the Sex-Drugs-and-Rock 'N' Roll Generation Saved Hollywood*. New York: Touchstone, 1998.
Bukowski, Charles. *Hollywood*. New York: Ecco–HarperCollins, 1998.
Fitzgerald, F. Scott. *Love of the Last Tycoon*. Ed. Matthew Bruccoli. New York: Scribner, 1995.
Gabler, Neal. *An Empire of Their Own: How the Jews Invented Hollywood*. New York: Anchor–Random House, 1989.
Levy, Frederick. *Hollywood 101: The Film Industry*. Los Angeles: Renaissance Books, 2000.
Miller, Toby et al. *Global Hollywood 2*. London: British Film Institute, 2005.
Navasky, Victor A. *Naming Names*. New York: Hill and Wang, 2003.
Phillips, Julia. *You'll Never Eat Lunch in This Town Again*. New York: New American Library, 2002.
Schulberg, Budd. *What Makes Sammy Run?* New York: Vintage, 1993.
Sylvester, Christopher, ed. *The Grove Book of Hollywood*. New York: Grove, 1998.
Thomson, David. *The Whole Equation: A History of Hollywood*. New York: Knopf, 2004.
Tolkin, Michael. *The Player: A Novel*. New York: Grove, 1997.

# Horse

## Barrett Shaw

Seabiscuit, Secretariat, Smarty Jones—periodically a rare race horse transcends the subculture of the track and engages the imagination of the American people en masse. For a few weeks in the spring, the country thrills to the notions of speed, heart, and victory. Particularly if the animal comes from a relatively humble background, it seems to epitomize many aspects of the American dream. Then, by mid-June, especially if, as in recent decades, the third jewel is not set in the Triple Crown, the horse fades back into our collective memory.

*Equus* couldn't be more American. Its earliest ancestor, little dog-sized, multi-toed eohippus, inhabited the jungles of what is now the United States 50 million years ago; its remains have been found in Utah and Wyoming. Later, mesohippus crossed a land bridge to Europe. When jungles turned to grassy plains, the horse adapted, growing in size, developing hooves from the central toe, moving in herds. It spread into South America and across the northern land bridge to Asia, Europe, and Africa.

The native horse disappeared from the Americas around 8,000 years ago, along with other large prehistoric animals. No one knows exactly why, but one speculation is overhunting. A few thousand years earlier, Paleo-Indians, spreading through the hemisphere after crossing from Asia, had begun using spears.

The horse made a triumphant return to its homeland on the vessels of the Spanish conquerors. There was apparently no collective memory of it then, certainly not as domesticated. Some of the Central American natives at first thought the riders were centaur-like gods. With sixteen horsemen, Cortez was able to subdue a civilization.

In Europe and Asia, the horse had been refined as an instrument of war. The Mongols had swept across Asia on their tough little mounts, and in medieval Europe the heavy horses of the north had borne the weight of armored knights. In the Crusades the northerners confronted the light, swift steeds of the Middle East and North Africa, and the merger of the two types brought about the development of most modern breeds. Spain, in particular, produced the epitome of the war horse. Today's dressage and *haute école* developed from maneuvers learned for battle.

Key to conquest, horses were brought over in larger numbers and multiplied rapidly. Some were abandoned on less successful excursions into what is now the American Southwest; they quickly readapted to their old territory and wild herds began to spread. These mustangs—from the Mexican Spanish *mesteño*, or stray—were the source of many American breeds such as the Quarter Horse, Appaloosa, and Paint. The native peoples at first thought they were large super-dogs and revered them, developing with the animals a relationship of partnership rather than subjugation.

Meanwhile, settlers from more northern European countries, especially England, brought horses with them to the East Coast. Though many died in dark ships' holds, bodies cast overboard in the "horse latitudes," enough remained to become indispensable in establishing agriculture and enabling exploration of the new territories. The image of the horse is an inextricable part of the history of the westward development of our nation: pioneers crossing the Cumberland Gap on horseback into the wilds of Kentucky; teams pulling covered wagons over the plains; the circuit rider; the cavalry versus the Indians; the Pony Express carrying the news.

The horse in America also served its traditional function in war. As always, the commanders and officers had the best mounts; the cavalry were the elite soldiers; sturdy, less glamorous horses dragged the artillery and supplies; and the common infantryman slogged on foot. That hierarchy goes back through the middle ages to ancient civilizations and illustrates how the position and use of the horse have always mirrored social stratification.

But for a while the horse became fairly universally used in America, particularly in the West, where the spaces that had to be covered were so vast. It found its deepest niche in the American psyche herding cattle on long drives and carrying the law in pursuit of rustlers. Horses like these were the colleagues of the heroes America grew up with in the mid-twentieth century, in movies and later television: Roy Rogers and Trigger, Hopalong Cassidy and Topper, Gene Autry and Champion, the Lone Ranger and Silver. The rodeo preserves the activities of those days with its team roping and penning competitions. And the bucking bronco epitomizes one treasured aspect of what the horse symbolizes for us—freedom, wildness, defiant refusal to be tamed.

It wasn't long, though, before technology began displacing the horse, first telegraphy and the railroads, then the telephone, radio, and the automobile—the power of which, of course, is still measured in comparison to horses. By the second decade of the twentieth century, carriages, horsecars, and freight wagons were swiftly disappearing from the urban landscape, and working horses held on only a few decades longer in rural areas. Horses changed from middle-class necessities to upper-class luxuries.

The pampered performance or pet horse of today is the inverse of the wild mustang. It has become totally dependent on human care, kept in artificial

Drawing of stagecoach, covered wagons, cowboys, and horses on the Oregon trail, ca. 1930. Courtesy of the Library of Congress.

circumstances that cut it off from its natural way of living, and bred for certain traits sometimes to the detriment of its overall well-being.

It is not cheap to keep a horse. Race or show horses require special feed and supplements, shoeing and medications, tack and equipment, training and exercise. Competitors in each different discipline must wear certain traditional kinds of clothing, boots, and headgear. Sports such as fox hunting, polo, steeplechase, and high-level horse shows are inevitably connected in the public mind with wealth. In the show ring or on the racetrack, the owners who can afford the best-bred animals and the most successful trainers get the most wins.

Horse racing is often called the sport of kings. The American version is directly derived from the English, as is the American Thoroughbred from its British forebears. For generations the racing scene was dominated by names like Mellon, Phipps, Whitney, and Vanderbilt; in recent years they've been joined by Arab sheiks. The epicenter has been the bluegrass region of Kentucky, the limestone fields of its fabled farms producing the bluebloods of the breed.

But anyone who visits the backside of a racetrack sees that racing encompasses poverty as well as wealth. The microcosmic world of this particular equine industry clearly mirrors the socioeconomic structure of the larger society. The owners pay the bills and have the bragging rights. The trainers have to serve and please them. Below them, the grooms muck stalls and try to keep the horses happy. And at the bottom are the hotwalkers, who lead the horses to cool them down after they exercise or race. Those at the lower levels may bunk on the backside in concrete-block barracks or even on a cot in a tack room, while those at the top have star-studded Derby bashes at their mansions.

The horses, too, are divided hierarchically, but by their levels of ability. Like other athletes, not all are elite. (The apparent key to Secretariat's dominance was a heart more than twice normal size.) The best run in stakes races, the kind the public is most familiar with. Then there are allowance races for solid but not exceptional horses. And the rest, the great majority especially at smaller tracks, are claiming races. Any horse entered can be bought, or claimed, out of the race by any owner or trainer for a preset price that keeps the horses racing against comparably skilled animals; they have to run against peers to make it a horse race. At this level it literally doesn't pay to get attached to an animal; it's a commodity.

Because racing has immemorially been a gambling enterprise, it above all equine pursuits is subject to corruption. Even with plenty of scrutiny and oversight, with so many workers living in or near poverty, and with so much money at stake, it doesn't take a lot to bribe someone to influence the outcome of a race. Sad to say, horses are sometimes overdrugged or raced with injuries. Those with little speed might be turned into riding horses or jumpers, but many others get passed from hand to hand and may end up neglected and starving or sent for slaughter.

Down the final stretch they come... Courtesy of Shutterstock.

Still, the Thoroughbred is born to run—I've seen one less than a day old, at a full-tilt, gangly, all-legs gallop along a fence, bang head first against the crossrail at the end of the field, fall over, get up, turn around, and start back as fast as he could go, mama cantering at his side. He might not win the prize for smarts (he collided with the fence a second time but had figured out about brakes by the third try), but he certainly should get points for heart and instinct.

Horses, as a rule, like to work and like to have a job. That's why we can get away with how we use them. When we make them perform to the absolute limits of their physical capacities, as in racing, we can say, "But they love to run. They love to win." When we make them leap six-foot jumps, or scramble miles across country over horrendous hurdles, or whiz around barrels, or trot with their legs so lifted and their neck so arched that their knees practically hit their nose, or stand on their hind legs and leap into the air from there, we can say, "But they enjoy it." And, thank goodness, they usually do. But we have to remember that they're just doing it because we're making them. They'd much rather be hanging around grazing all day with an occasional dash around the pasture with their buddies just for fun.

By making the horse dependent on us, we have assumed responsibility for it. Most horses were just chattel, overworked and routinely subject to abuse, before post-industrial sensibilities were awakened in the late nineteenth century by Anna Sewell's *Black Beauty*, the horse's *Uncle Tom's Cabin*. To this day, little girls weep over Beauty's tribulations on his downward slide through British society. (When I was seven and had surgery for a crossed eye, my mother came into my hospital room and found me with bandage pulled up, reading *Black Beauty*. Her exasperated response: "Well, at least it could have been something you hadn't read before!") Now there are associations supporting animal welfare and laws to punish abusers.

The loving hearts of little girls are another world where horses dwell, quite apart from the more macho realms of racetrack and rodeo. As much as cowboys and soldiers and lawmen have been associated with horses, their largest and truest contingent is no doubt young females. They may start with a rocking horse and carnival carousel or pony rides (remnants our society has kept so all children can at least be exposed to the cultural memory of being on horseback). Then they pore over Walter Farley's Black Stallion and Island Stallion books, Marguerite Henry's classic *King of the Wind* and *Misty of Chincoteague*, and their reams of successors. From My Little Pony to Pony Club, they dream of a perfect four-legged, maned companion, and the lucky ones whose parents can afford it or are willing to make the sacrifice get to realize their dream. They transfer their nurturing instincts from dressing and coifing Barbie to grooming and tacking up their mount. Whatever type of riding they do, their pony, and his larger successors as they grow, teaches them poise, confidence, discipline, responsibility, trust. He carries them into adolescence, where some abandon him for boys and others manage to balance the two attractions. Many who leave the stable find themselves compelled to return later in life.

A popular image of this bond is the medieval fable of the unicorn and the maiden. Hunters could not catch this elusive horselike beast by force. But irresistibly attracted by the presence and scent of a virgin, it would approach and lay its single-horned head in her lap and fall asleep. Then the men could close in and capture it. The phallic symbolism is obvious; but there is more to be learned from the tale about why women do so well with horses and why there has lately been a plethora of books about the nature of this relationship, such as *She Flies Without Wings: How Horses Touch a Woman's Soul* by Mary D. Midkiff and *The Tao of Equus: A Woman's Journey of Healing and Transformation through the Way of the Horse* by Linda Kohanov.

Women tend to relate to horses with intuition rather than force. They try to understand them as individuals, be supportive when they are afraid (which, with their herbivore heritage, they are quite frequently). Men are not immune to this approach; in fact, "horse whisperer" trainers like John Lyons and Monty Roberts are cashing in big time with their videos, books, and clinics, teaching methods based largely on observing and interacting with horses' natural herd behavior and body language. And more power to them. Their popularity means that far fewer horses will be subject to harsh, dispiriting training regimens.

But most people who say they are animal communicators or psychics are women. Many would dismiss their claims as New Age hot air, but there is anecdotal evidence that horses actually communicate with some degree of telepathy. Riders are taught to look where they want to go and the horse will go there, and it works. No doubt the rider, consciously or unconsciously, aligns her body and gives subtle signals to support that aiming, but the looking does seem to help focus the horse. In this context, the animal can be seen as a direct contact with nature, instinct, intuition; this aspect is the yin to its concurrent yang of force, speed, work, sport, and war.

It is ironic, then, that one of the newest uses we have come up with for horses is "farming" the urine of pregnant mares for estrogen for hormone replacement therapy. Every year thousands of mares are impregnated, then stand shoulder-to-shoulder in stanchions in barns, urinating into strapped-on bags connected by tubes to underground collection tanks, unable to walk, run, graze, play, turn around, or lie down flat for months, so human females can avoid hot flashes and other natural effects of aging. Thus, too, thousands of mostly unwanted foals are produced each year, many of which will be sold abroad for meat.

But those are uses we don't like to talk or think about. On the whole, the fashionable yin view of the horse has given it a growing popularity as a leisure-time distraction from the stresses of contemporary life. More and more people want to be able to possess the paradox of wildness tamed, to link back to the Native American's connection with this swift, powerful, beautiful, mysterious Native American.

You can even adopt a real mustang through the Bureau of Land Management for a few hundred dollars. But then you are responsible for it. And it may or may not choose to bond with you.

## WORKS CITED AND RECOMMENDED

Budiansky, Stephen. *The Nature of Horses.* New York: Free P, 1997.

Hendricks, Bonnie L. *International Encyclopedia of Horse Breeds.* Norman: U of Oklahoma P, 1995.

Kohanov, Linda. *The Tao of Equus: A Woman's Journey of Healing and Transformation through the Way of the Horse.* Novato, CA: New World Library, 2001.

Smiley, Jane. *Horse Heaven.* New York: Random House, 2000.

Swift, Sally. *Centered Riding.* North Pomfret, VT: Trafalgar Square, 1985.

# Indian Scout

## Tom Holm

Charles Alexander Eastman was perhaps the most well-known Native American of his day. A Wahpeton and Mdewakanton Dakota, Eastman, whose Dakota name was Ohiyesa (the Winner), was born in 1857 and grew up steeped in the traditions of his people. At fifteen he was sent to Alfred Riggs' Santee Indian School. He proved to be an able student and later attended Knox College, and Dartmouth, and eventually graduated from the Boston College School of Medicine. Eastman started his career as the physician on the Pine Ridge Oglala Lakota reservation in South Dakota. He treated the survivors of the massacre that took place at Wounded Knee in 1890. He left the Indian Service in 1893, entered private practice for a time, lobbied for the restoration of Santee treaty rights, translated Dakota surnames into English for the Indian Office, served as the physician at the Crow Creek Sioux agency, worked for the YMCA, and established a girls' camp at which he taught "Indian lore" (Wilson).

Eastman gained greater fame, however, as a writer; between 1902 and 1917 he published ten books and numerous articles in most of the popular magazines of the early twentieth century. In addition to his autobiographical and philosophical monographs, he wrote several children's books aimed primarily at extolling the virtues of living life close to nature. As a physician, he was wrapped up in the sanitation and health movements of the period and firmly believed in the notion that hiking and camping were both physically and spiritually beneficial. He was one of the many philosophers of the era who tied human well-being to the conservation movement and the preservation of wilderness areas. Eastman's work with the YMCA, and as a teacher of Native life to the youths who vacationed at his girls' camp, led him to endorse the Boy Scout and Camp Fire Girl organizations. Most of his books targeted young people and paid special attention to converting that which whites viewed in Native life as pure savagery into something positive. He was at his best in doing so with the publication of *Indian Scout Talks* in 1914.

Eastman's main thrust in *Indian Scout Talks* was to take the contemporary image of the Native American warrior as the antithesis of white American

# INDIAN SCOUT

manhood and recast it as the actual prototype of the white ideal. Eastman's ideas were seemingly Cooperesque in that he always supported the romantic and nostalgic side of the conservation movement. But instead of thinking of conservation as a method of saving America's natural resources for future use, Eastman viewed conservation as something much more meaningful in a spiritual sense. The underlying theme of most of his many monographs hinged on the notion that the same things that were jeopardizing the American pioneering spirit—urbanization and industrialization—were the same things that were putting Native Americans' physical and spiritual health at risk (Eastman, *Soul of the Indian*; "The Indian's Health Problem").

*Indian Scout Talks* essentially outlines the ethos of warriorhood, an ethos that was very likely an underlying foundation of youthful male behavior in nearly every cooperative, traditional society that owed its particular identity to a specific place or territory. Eastman's scout was in many ways an Edward Curtis photograph depicting a handsome young man in profile looking out over a vast landscape with his right hand planted on his brow, shading his eyes from the sun. But more importantly and accurately, Eastman's scout was not only far-seeing in every sense of the word, but also self-sufficient, knowledgeable, resourceful, proud, athletic, indispensable to society, caring, and absolutely trustworthy. The Indian scout's duty was patiently to seek out both the game animals and the enemies of the people. The scout had to report honestly where the food resources were and on the movements of the enemy; the safety and the prosperity of the people rested directly on the shoulders of the scout. He also had to be a hunter as well as a warrior.

Eastman expanded on the positive side of the image of the Indian scout in his work. He was not, however, its inventor. The stereotype of the Indian scout not only is long-standing but also has become a true American icon. The image of a Native warrior gazing fixedly into the distance (with one hand shading his eyes), or walking with head bent and eyes to the ground searching for signs of game or the enemy, or lying prone staring at an approaching enemy on the crest of a hill, is easily recognizable and needs no further explanation as to the warrior's occupation. The terminology "Indian scout" is equally recognizable and conjures up in the American mind these same vivid images. In short, the image and term are fixed and inseparably connected.

The icon is nearly as old as the European invasion of the Americas, but by and large it held a negative connotation for most of the 500-odd years of Native-white contact. European and Native American warfare could not have been more dissimilar. European warfare was aggressive, confrontational, and intended to slaughter an enemy's military forces in a decisive battle. Native American warfare, on the other hand, was ritualized, restrained, and did not usually result in a high mortality rate on the battlefield. What made the Native American way of war so repugnant to Europeans was that Natives typically avoided decisive battle and limited warfare to smallish raids and even smaller ambushes. Much of Native warfare emphasized the taking of

A European man standing among four Indians scouts, 1907. Courtesy of the Library of Congress.

captives to replace deceased members of the tribe or to frighten the whites away from sacred places or out of their national domains.

In order to conduct surprise raids or to set up an effective ambush, a military force had to effect surprise and concentration of force at the correct time and place. This unit (whether raiding party or ambushing force) would need to have a good idea of an enemy's movements and a correct assessment of the enemy's strength. The scout had to be able to deliver a detailed picture of the enemy's strengths and weaknesses. During the seventeenth and eighteenth centuries, whites called Native scouts "spies" and dubbed Native methods of combat the "skulking" way of war, terms far more negative in the European mind than "warrior" or "restrained warfare." The skulking way of war was supposedly an anathema in contrast to European methods of combat. Europeans stood their ground and fought face-to-face battles; Indians hid behind trees and attacked from ambush. When defeated in a pitched battle, European officers surrendered their swords honorably; Indians simply ran away, living to fight another day. Europeans treated prisoners of war according to certain well-established rules; Indians scalped or tortured their captives. Europeans met on a field of battle; Indians raided unsuspecting settlers. Europeans were soldiers, implying that they followed orders and were well-grounded in a strictly defined code of honor; Indians were warriors and, thus, savages without honor (Malone; Starkey).

The problem was that whites were caught in a dilemma. Although they disliked Native tactics and stealth, they also realized that to fight in the New World required them to adapt to the terrain and to Native combat in general.

# INDIAN SCOUT

To do so the whites employed Native auxiliaries in the New World, recruiting them by exploiting traditional enmities between two or more Native nations. Moreover, the British developed a colonial militia system that utilized the woodcraft of the white hunters in warfare, and Native American tactics served the Americans well during the Revolutionary War. By the nineteenth century the term "scout" was primarily used to describe the function of white frontiersmen who operated with the American armed forces, militia or regular, against Native enemies, the British, and others. And when the wars erupted between Natives and whites in the far west, the Indian scout became increasingly essential to the opening of the gold fields, the range cattle industry, and the railroads. In 1866 for the first time ever, Congress passed an act that allowed the U.S. Army to recruit, arm, and enlist Native Americans in the newly created Scouting Service. No longer would the United States rely on Indian allies to fulfill the military roles of scouts; Indians would be part of the American military service in a special branch (Dunlay).

After the Scouting Service was established, four Native units in particular became especially famous. The first was the Pawnee battalion that served under the leadership of Colonel Frank North. The Pawnees essentially fought their traditional Lakota and Cheyenne enemies, and by doing so protected the laying of the first transcontinental railroad. The Seminole-Negro scouts were enlisted against the Apaches, Comanches, and Kiowas in Texas. On the northern plains the Crow and Arikara scouts led the Army against the uprising of the Lakota and Cheyenne in 1876. Crow scouts warned Custer against attacking the Lakota at the Little Big Horn River but he, headstrong as ever, refused to heed their caution. Several Arikara scouts died in the sanguinary battle that was ultimately Custer's last folly. The Apache scouts were perhaps the most famous of all the Indian scouting units. They were, of course, the main force that tracked down and cornered Geronimo, and for many years they were called to and from active duty. Some of the Apache scouts, without whom it might be said Arizona could not have become a state, were actually incarcerated due to the fact that they were Apaches and potentially hostile to the United States. However, when General John Pershing led an American expeditionary force into Mexico in 1916 to hunt down Pancho Villa, he enlisted a group of Apache scouts. When the United States entered World War I the next year, Pershing, as the commander of the American forces, took the Apache scouts with him to France (Holm, "Stereotypes,...").

The Army Indian Scouting Service was not disbanded until 1943, and the last Apache scout, Sergeant William Major, retired from the Army in 1948. But its exploits were legendary in the military service, and when the Army Special Forces was formed during World War II it adopted the crossed-arrow insignia of the Scouting Service as its own. In many ways the "Green Berets" view their highly trained unit as the direct descendent of the Indian Scouts. During its seventy-seven years of life, the Indian Scouting Service received more decorations for valor per capita than any other Army unit. Sixteen Native

An engraving from *Harper's Weekly* of Indian scouts on Geronimo's trail during the Apache War. Courtesy of the Library of Congress.

American members of the Scouts won the Medal of Honor (Holm, "Scouts"; Downey and Jacobson).

Perhaps more important was a lasting image of the Indian Scout in the non-Indian military mind: the Indian scout was the ultimate primitive warrior, so in tune with the natural environment that he could determine whether or not an enemy was present in the area by a bent blade of grass or an overturned rock. Supposedly the Indian scout could track an opposing force and tell from the circumstantial evidence of its spoor how many individuals were in it, what weaponry it carried, how long ago it had passed, and where it was heading.

In my study of Native American Vietnam veterans conducted by both questionnaire and interview over several years, I found a single combat experience common to a majority of the men who had experienced combat. This particular practice was known as "walking point." In this tactical maneuver, a single person, or perhaps two people, are sent out to walk in advance of a main unit on the move, or of a small patrol. The point man was essentially a scout who was expected to detect and report immediately the presence of the enemy. Not only was the position dangerous but also it required a good deal of stealth, knowledge, and a certain awareness of one's surroundings. Whole units of long-range reconnaissance personnel existed in Vietnam, and apparently a number of Native Americans were assigned to them (Holm, *Strong Hearts, Wounded Souls*).

Several of the veterans surveyed and interviewed stated flatly that they were assigned to perform reconnaissance duties or walk point because they were Indians. What I have called the "Indian Scout Syndrome" has infected non-Indians for a considerable period of time. During World War I, *The Indian's Friend*, a newsletter dedicated to the assimilation of Native peoples into mainstream American society, proudly but more than a bit ironically reported: "Indians in the regiments are being used for scouting and patrol duty because of the *natural instinct* [emphasis added] which fits them for this kind of work." After the United States entered World War II, the media exploited the Indian Scout Syndrome for propaganda purposes. Harold Ickes, the

# INDIAN SCOUT

Secretary of the Interior under Franklin Roosevelt, in the popular magazine *Collier's* touted "the fact that [the Indian] is one of our best fighters":

> The inherited talents of the Indian make him uniquely valuable. He has endurance, rhythm, a feeling for timing, co-ordination, sense perception, an uncanny ability to get over any sort of terrain at night, and better than all else, an enthusiasm for fighting. He takes a rough job and makes a game of it. Rigors of combat hold no terrors for him; severe discipline and hard duties do not deter him. (58)

Little wonder that when many Natives reported to their units in Vietnam they quickly encountered the syndrome. One Native veteran was told to walk point because his platoon commander reasoned that Indians had "grown up in the woods" and would therefore be familiar with the forest (jungle) terrain of Vietnam. Although he had tried to explain to his platoon commander that he had in fact been brought up in an urban area, he was nevertheless assigned the point position. A Navajo veteran was caught up in the same dangerous predicament because, as he described, he was "stereotyped by the cowboys and Indian movies. Nicknamed 'Chief' right away. Non-Indians claimed Indians could see through trees and hear the unhearable. Bullshit, they even believed Indians could walk on water" (qtd. in Holms, *Strong Hearts, Wounded Souls* 152).

In short, the supposed virtues of the "Indian scout" have been indelibly imprinted on the American mind. On the other hand, bravery in battle, stealth, and a tenacious fighting spirit are equally the dubious qualities of the savage Indian warrior. A scout/warrior dialectic might be the more appropriate terminology to apply in discussing this iconology. Be that as it may, the icon certainly has led to some negative outcomes. For example, the scout stereotype undoubtedly placed very real Native Americans in extremely perilous positions. Whether infiltrating German lines during World War I or walking point on patrols in Vietnam, Native Americans faced the dangers of being killed, captured, or wounded perhaps to a greater extent than their non-Indian comrades in arms. Native Americans have, on a per capita basis, suffered more casualties in war than any other American ethnic group. Whether or not this casualty rate correlates with taking on highly dangerous duties as a result of commanders' applying a stereotype to war-making remains to be investigated. It would certainly be an interesting study.

The continued "Indian mascot" controversy has elements of the scout/warrior dichotomy. When defending the retention of these harmful and degrading stereotypes to promote various sports teams at the high school, college, and professional levels, most people normally and without hesitation stipulate that they are honoring American Indians for their battlefield virtues. In essence, they are utilizing the Indian scout icon as model of valor, honesty, and tenacity, and very likely believe that they are truly idolizing Native American people (King and Springwood). In fact, they are twisting the icon into a celebration of warfare and the conquest of the Americas.

The scout icon establishes the idea of "savage virtue" in combat. The word "Indian" is, of course, an invented term; and because Europeans were its inventors, they have defined it in any way they pleased (Berkhofer). The "Indian" represented the wilderness that was to be overcome. The Indian scout/warrior was seen as a savage foe who abducted "helpless" women, murdered white babies, treacherously ambushed stout-hearted soldiers, and toasted hapless frontiersmen over bonfires. In that sense the Indian scout/warrior was an especially dangerous enemy because he knew his environment. That he was stealthy and tenacious as well simply confirmed in the American mind that the conquest of America was a vast blood sacrifice. Conquering both the Indian as the icon of the wilderness and the Indian scout as the embodiment of "savage virtue" in battle is part of the American identity. When Americans honor the mascots, which are of course simple stereotypes of the Indian scout, they are glorifying their own military prowess and celebrating the American frontiersman's sacrifice to civilization. They are engaging in a dialectic that makes no sense except in the colonial discourse on the right of conquest.

## WORKS CITED AND RECOMMENDED

Berkhofer, Robert F. *The White Man's Indian*. New York: Knopf, 1978.
Downey, Fairfax, and Jacques Noel Jacobson, Jr. *The Red Blue Coats*. Fort Collins, CO: Old Army P, 1973.
Dunlay, Thomas W. *Wolves for the Blue Soldiers*. Lincoln: U of Nebraska P, 1982.
Eastman, Charles A. (Ohiyesa). *Indian Scout Talks*. Boston: Little, Brown, 1918.
———. "The Indian's Health Problem." *The American Indian Magazine* 4 (Apr.–June 1916): 139–45.
———. *The Soul of the Indian*. Boston: Houghton Mifflin, 1911.
Holm, Tom. "Scouts." *The Encyclopedia of North American Indians*. Ed. Frederick E. Hoxie. Boston: Houghton Mifflin, 1996.
———. "Stereotypes, State Elites and the Military Use of American Indian Troops." *Plural Societies* 15 (1984): 265–82.
———. *Strong Hearts, Wounded Souls*. Austin: U of Texas P, 1996.
Ickes, Harold. "Indians Have a Name for Hitler." *Collier's Magazine* 113.1 (15 Jan. 1944): 58.
*The Indian's Friend* Jan. 1918: 1.
King, C. Richard, and Charles Fruehling Springwood, eds. *Team Spirits*. Lincoln: U of Nebraska P, 2001.
Malone, Patrick M. *The Skulking Way of War*. Baltimore: Johns Hopkins UP, 1991.
Starkey, Armstrong. *European and Native American Warfare 1675–1815*. Norman: U of Oklahoma P, 1998.
Wilson, Raymond. *Ohiyesa: Charles Eastman, Santee Sioux*. Urbana: U of Illinois P, 1983.

# Martin Luther King, Jr.

## *Ricky L. Jones*

Many contend the true legacy of slain American civil rights icon Martin Luther King, Jr., must be continuously revisited and reevaluated as we settle into the twenty-first century so that the true mission of his life is preserved. Of course, the same is also true of titans such as Frederick Douglass. It is so, according to some, because on that fateful day in Memphis when King was killed a man died and a misleading image was born. At the instant King the man died from the impact of an assassin's bullet in 1968, a facsimile, an imitation, a deformed "it" was constructed and has been sold to the American public until this day. To be sure, it is difficult, if not impossible, to reconcile the two. Instead, we should remember the liberating man, and destroy the oppressive myth.

Let me be clear at the outset. When I speak of destroying a myth, I am not advocating sullying or denouncing King in any way. To the contrary, I love King. As a student at Morehouse College, I walked by King's statue which towers in front of King Chapel on our campus daily. There he stood, that bold, proud Morehouse Man from the Class of 1948 with outstretched hand—pointing the people towards freedom. Here is the man whom Morehouse Men still consider the best the school has ever produced (and Morehouse has graduated many great men). He is our model, our standard, our torch bearer, our candle in the dark. Therefore, I affirm without hesitation that this man was no oppressor of the people, but the dominant image of him most often encountered today most certainly is. I cannot make this point better than Michael Eric Dyson does in *I May Not Get There with You: The True Martin Luther King, Jr.*:

> Since his death, we have made three mistakes in treating King's legacy.
>
> First, we have sanitized his *ideas*, ignoring his mistrust of white America, his commitment to black solidarity and advancement, and the radical message of his later life. Today right-wing conservatives can quote King's speeches in order to criticize affirmative action, while schoolchildren grow up learning only about the great pacifist, not the hard-nosed critic of economic injustice.

Second, we have twisted his *identity* and lost the chance to connect the man's humanity, including his flaws, to the young people of today, especially our despised black youth.

Finally we have ceded control of his *image* to a range of factions that include the right, the federal government and its holiday, and even the King family themselves, who have attempted to collect a fee for nearly every word the great man gave the world. (ix–x)

The appropriation of King by the religious and political right, inside as well as outside the race, has resulted in a repackaged effigy that is used to anaesthetize the people whenever trouble comes and resistance tactics beyond increasingly ineffectual protest marches, sit-ins, and emotive but nonsubstantive prayers are proffered. Disturbingly, the passive image of King has been adopted by many who do not have the best interests of oppressed people at heart. These people, not all of whom are white, are quick to trot out this portrait of King when the dispossessed rightfully protest their treatment in increasingly conservative America. At these times, "image pimps" across lines of race disapprovingly admonish the weary masses, "Remember the Dreamer—he would not have approved of this."

Sadly, some of the worst exploiters of King are today's black ministers. The very ones who should reinforce King's ideals are now exploiting them without any real commitment to the construction of a truly egalitarian society. It is not unusual to go into black churches whose conservative ministers routinely invoke King's name, but have very little dedication to progressive sociopolitical agendas of the sort which King sacrificed his life defending. In their churches one may find newsletters and magazines entitled "The Dreamer" or "The Drum Major" which remind us of King, but do not continue his mission. These men demand consistent tithing and offerings from their members and guests to sustain lavish personal lifestyles, while never acknowledging that King unselfishly only took a salary of one dollar a year from the SCLC, which he helped found following the historic Montgomery bus boycott. Unfortunately, many

Martin Luther King, Jr. delivering a speech at Girard College, Philadelphia, 1965. Courtesy of the Library of Congress.

ministers do not stop there. A good percentage of them are now all too ready to jump on the right-wing, self-help bandwagon which blames blacks for their own suffering.

Ironically, many of these men, who often lead comfortable lives as a result of the financial contributions of their usually struggling black flocks, now admonish blacks to "pull themselves up by their own bootstraps." They forget, do not know, or will not acknowledge, that King commented on such an ideology in one of his lesser known sermons, "Remaining Awake through a Great Revolution":

> Now there is another myth that still gets around: it is a kind of overreliance on the bootstrap philosophy. There are those who still feel that if the Negro is to rise out of poverty, if the Negro is to rise out of slum conditions, if he is to rise out of discrimination and segregation, he must do it all by himself. And so they say the Negro must lift himself by his own bootstraps.
>
> They never stop to realize that no other ethnic group has been a slave on American soil. The people who say this never stop to realize that the nation made a black man's color a stigma; but beyond this they never stop to realize the debt that they owe a people who were kept in slavery 244 years.... It's all right to tell a man to lift himself by his own bootstraps, but it is a cruel jest to say to a bootless man that he ought to lift himself by his own bootstraps. (271)

Since King's death, black religious leadership has become, in many respects, disproportionately strong in the black community. While some religious leaders do commendable work in certain areas, many have also developed an infectious, arrogant aversion to question and challenge, which black communities, more often than not, support. Critiques of black ministers are difficult to levy, because followers fear—and ministers often threaten their critics with—damnation. If the case involves misbehavior on the ministers' part, pleas for forgiveness—accompanied by reminders that some of God's favorites (including Moses, David, and, yes, King) were also flawed—are submitted. Without ever seriously addressing the concerns of the community, use of such emotive tools to diffuse accusations of ministerial malfeasance is powerful. The sad cases of the adulterous behavior of former National Baptist Convention President Henry Lyons and Rainbow/Push leader Jesse Jackson, and black people's general reluctance to hold them accountable are examples of this indulgence.

Of course, a large part of black ministers' power is a result of the historical reality of black suffering itself. It makes perfect sense that a race which has endured such a drudgerous existence would develop the idea that a better life awaits after death as a coping mechanism. In this progression, the black minister has come to be regarded as the unquestioned intermediary to God, and to challenge him is simply not acceptable. It is undeniable that far too many ministers have given Marx's observation that religion is the "opium of the masses" some modicum of validity.

King's impact on black people has also paved the way for a number of other realities which are rarely connected to him. While black ministers have always been powerful in the black community, King's feats moved their places to even more solid ground. For many in black America, having the title Reverend precede one's name is a prerequisite for leadership. It is also an almost absolute assurance of the unquestioned submission of the masses. A number of rather crafty fellows have parlayed this free reign in the community into small empires of which they are lord and master.

The best example of this phenomenon is the black religious-business hybrid—the mega-church. We see the rise of such entities in cities where there is a black population large enough to sustain them. Unfortunately, along with size, power, and influence, mega-churches (like any other business) also carry with them voracious appetites for economic resources which must be fed. Over time, the mega-church extends itself to the point that tithes and love-offerings can no longer sustain it, and outside support must be sought. While business (fundraising, institutional expansion, etc.) has always been an aspect of the black church, in many ways black mega-churches *are* businesses and their leaders, therefore necessarily, become businessmen. Once such a transition is made, these ministers often lose the authenticity and sincerity of their external place as moral critics because they enter the fray for money and power which sustains the capitalist state. Smaller church ministers are often critical of their colleagues' behavior, but many of them would jump at the opportunity to join their ranks if it were possible.

A good percentage of the African-descended population in America acknowledges that, unlike King, many ministers have become little more than demagogues who prey on black suffering without substantive defiance from the masses. A few black ministers have even been able to follow the leads of Billy Graham and Jim and Tammy Faye Bakker by transforming themselves into traveling entertainers or nationally viewed television personalities. They use their television shows, more often than not, as mediums to peddle video and audio tapes and to advertise the location of their next "road show" stop. The meteoric rise of Bishop T. D. Jakes and his marketing empire is the best example of this. Jakes is certainly not alone. While no minister may be quite so popular, Fred Price, Creflo Dollar, Eddie Long, and others enjoy varying degrees of regional and national success.

Unfortunately, most of these men provide a hyper-frenzied brand of entertainment rather than education. More importantly, they do not promote any type of liberatory theology which powerfully addresses hegemonic sociopolitical structures, in the tradition of Albert Cleage, James Cone, or Martin Luther King, Jr. Contrarily, not only do they not push radical agendas, they are often staunch conservatives in the vein of Clarence Thomas, Ward Connerly, Alan Keyes, and Armstrong Williams. Unlike Thomas, Connerly, Keyes, and Williams, black ministers are able to mask their conservatism in religious rhetoric with God supposedly giving it his stamp of approval. The messages of former National Baptist Convention leader Joseph H. Jackson and Opportunities Industrial Centers founder Reverend Leon Sullivan are examples of this trend.

In this madness, the real Martin Luther King, Jr., is lost. He has been reduced to a few utopian, out-of-context words taken from the "I Have a Dream" speech of 1963. Lost is the intellectual King who studied Marx, Neibuhr, Hobbes, Plato, Aristotle, Hegel, Thoreau, Nietzsche, and Ghandi and could engage their theories cogently and clearly. Lost is the rational, critical King who saw undirected emotionalism in the church as counterproductive. Lost is the warrior King who got angry and screamed that he was tired of marching and fighting for rights which should already be his. Lost is the political King who proclaimed that America had become the world's most intrusive imperial power. Lost is the revolutionary King whom the U.S. government considered the most dangerous black man in America, before Malcolm X presented a more radical variation on the same theme. Lost is King the lover of the people who died working for the rights of sanitation workers, not building a new wing onto his church or laundering Republican grant money through a 501c3 development corporation! What we are left with now is a false image of King which cripples and confuses.

To add fuel to this fire, as we begin the twenty-first century, many of our political and civil rights leaders continue to be little more than black preachers painted onto different canvases. While ministers like King have a long legacy of participating in the black freedom struggle beyond the walls of the church, the current crop is akin to traveling showmen who get paid well for their performances. Most of their appearances usually amount to little more than taking the sermonical tone and tactics used in the pulpit to secular venues. In the final analysis, most of these people deliver no serious challenge to the hegemonic structures which continue to oppress people of color and the poor. It is difficult to deny that men like Jesse Jackson, whom many in the black community correctly label "opportunistic," continuously travel to different sites of trouble, give stirring speeches/sermons, and may even lead a march or two.

Incredibly, in the midst of the crises which summon them, they always seem to have time to take healthy financial offerings from the masses that come out to be encouraged. Ultimately, these men offer little, if any, viable instruction or support for the organizing of sustained oppositional struggles by the people. Maybe the title of one of Jackson's books, coauthored with his son, says it best when questions are raised concerning many of these new-age ministers' primary motivation—*It's About the Money!* Where is Martin when we need him?

If we are to move forward with any liberatory sociopolitical agenda, we must always remember that it is detrimental to allow the greatest men and women America has given the world be used against us, and that is exactly what is happening to King. The sooner we rediscover the *real* King and reject his oppressive, posthumous doppelganger, the better.

## WORKS CITED AND RECOMMENDED

Dyson, Michael Eric. *I May Not Get There with You: The True Martin Luther King, Jr.* New York: Free P, 2000.

*A Guide to Research on Martin Luther King, Jr., and the Modern Black Freedom Struggle.* Stanford, CA: Stanford U Libraries, 1989.

King, Martin Luther, Jr. *The Autobiography of Martin Luther King, Jr.* Ed. Clayborne Carson. New York: IPM–Warner Books, 1998.

———. *The Movement: 1964–1970.* Comp. Martin Luther King, Jr., Papers Project. Westport, CT: Greenwood, 1993.

———. *The Papers of Martin Luther King, Jr.* 5 vols. Berkeley: U of California P, 1992.

———. "Remaining Awake through a Great Revolution." National Cathedral, Washington, DC. 31 March 1968. *A Testament of Hope: The Essential Writings and Speeches of Martin Luther King, Jr.* Ed. James Melvin Washington. New York: HarperSanFrancisco, 1986. 268–78.

———. *The Speeches of Martin Luther King.* Videocassette. MPI Home Video, 1990.

# Evel Knievel

## *Randy D. McBee*

Extreme sports—skateboarding, inline skating, BMX riding, surfing, wakeboarding, and freestyle motorcycle riding—have taken the country by storm over the past few years. The intricate twists, flips, and gravity-defying stunts and jumps competitors perform no doubt help explain the sports' growth and popularity. But that inexplicable need to push the body to unimaginable limits, that incomprehensible desire to flirt with danger, are not as new as some enthusiasts may have assumed. Extreme sports, which began with motorcycle jumping, date back to at least the 1960s and early 1970s; and only one man is generally identified with the sport—Evel Knievel.

Knievel's first public jump took place in 1965 as part of a publicity stunt to increase sales of Honda motorcycles at his dealership in Moses Lake, Washington. As the story goes, Knievel attempted to jump a distance of forty feet over two mountain lions and a wooden pen filled with rattlesnakes. Knievel fell short of the 40-foot mark, and the motorcycle smashed open the pen of snakes, which sent them slithering towards the frightened spectators. During the decade and a half after his less than spectacular start, Knievel would attempt more than 300 jumps, spend countless numbers of days in the hospital recovering from his often near-fatal injuries, but also thrill and captivate millions of men, women, and children across the country and around the world.

The excitement and energy of motorcycle jumping, the thrill of the spectacle, and the never-ending potential for a deadly outcome all contributed to Knievel's popularity. But his fame was as much a product of his behavior off his bike as it was a reflection of his daredevil stunts. Between the time when Knievel first attracted national attention until his retirement, U.S. involvement in Vietnam would escalate sharply, the Civil Rights Movement became overshadowed by Black Power, and the gay and women's liberation movements spread across the country. Never one to shy away from conflict, Knievel quickly became embroiled in the controversy surrounding these movements, and in some cases bitterly attacked them. While his comments often attracted the scorn of the media, they also help explain his popularity as growing numbers of Americans shared his concerns about the changes taking place. The 1970s may have been a decade when Americans, consumed by disillusionment, despair, and distrust in national leadership, walked away from the social and political movements of the preceding decades in search of their own individual fulfillment. But the decade of the 1970s was not without its own energy and enthusiasm, and for some its own heroes. In this case their hero was not a politician or an activist but a man who wore a leather jumpsuit and made his living performing death-defying motorcycle jumps.

By 1967 Knievel was working full time as a stuntman, and he was beginning to attract national attention. During that year he attempted to leap over the fountains at Caesar's Palace. Knievel cleared the fountains but botched the landing. The resulting crash and injuries sent him to the hospital where he slipped into a coma for twenty-nine days. It was also in 1967 that Knievel set a new record by successfully jumping over fifteen cars at the Ascot Park Speedway in Gardena, outside Los Angeles, which ABC's Wide World of Sports filmed and aired a few weeks later. ABC's Wide World of Sports established a format that featured the unusual mix of high-profile boxing championships and other typical sporting contests with less traditional events like arm wrestling, rodeos, demolition derbies, ski jumping, and even chess. Knievel's daredevil antics fit well with the show's format; and throughout his career, he often appeared on ABC. In fact, his 1975 jump over fifteen Greyhound busses at Kings Mills, Ohio, remains Wild World of Sports' highest-rated broadcast in the show's history.

After Knievel attracted national fame, he began showing up on talk shows and on magazine covers, and imitators became all too common. By the early 1970s, other men and some women were joining the ranks of the motorcycle daredevil, and Knievel's claim to fame as the greatest was increasingly difficult to sustain. Men like Super Joe Einhorn, Wicked Ward, Gary Wells, and even Debbie Lawler, the single female stunt cyclist to attract national attention, became serious contenders, and in some cases surpassed Knievel's best efforts. To the dismay and alarm of parents, many of their children also began attempting their own daredevil stunts, generally with a makeshift ramp constructed out of wooden boards and bricks. The resulting injuries ranged from the minor cuts and bruises to more serious broken bones, lacerations, and concussions, causing parents and politicians alike to campaign to ban Knievel's stunts from being aired on television. Knievel's influence was so profound that one biographer claims that the slogan "don't try this at home" was coined in response to the scores of children attempting to impersonate Knievel.

By the early 1970s, manufacturers also began to produce toys based on the wily stuntman. In 1973 Knievel paired up with Ideal Toy Corporation and produced an Evel "Movable Figure" and a wind up "Stunt Cycle." The Evel figure stood seven inches high, had a hard plastic head and a removable plastic helmet, and came with a red, white or blue outfit. The "Stunt Cycle" was wound up with what was called a "Gyro-Powered Energizer." Before

# EVEL KNIEVEL

Evel Knievel jumps over six Mack trucks at dragway 42 in Cleveland, Ohio, on May 28, 1974. AP/Wide World Photo.

long, Knievel was blasting across kitchen floors and down driveways and sidewalks in houses and neighborhoods across the country. The Evel "Figure" and "Stunt Cycle" quickly became one of the hottest toys on the market; its sales even surpassed those of the famous GI Joe. Other Evel-inspired toys started showing up on store shelves across the country, including the Knievel "Scramble Van," the Canyon Sky Cycle, a Stunt and Crash Car, a Formula One Dragster, the Escape From Skull Canyon play set, and the Evel Knievel Artic Explorer set.

Knievel's popularity, however, was not simply the product of his ability to jump great distances or his being the first stuntman to appear on the national stage. He attained his fame, in part, because he survived and because of his ability to endure the pain and violence of motorcycle jumping. By the early 1970s, Knievel was fighting to maintain his title as the greatest stuntman alive, but many of the individuals who surpassed him had either been killed or physically incapacitated. Knievel not only continued to jump, but also his crashes and the injuries he sustained became the focal point around which the myth of Knievel took shape. Stories about Knievel's daredevil stunts routinely focused on his hospital exploits, often on the quality of the food he found at hospitals and the quality (or looks) of the nurses assigned to his care, but including specific details surrounding his injuries and the difficulty doctors had faced putting him back together. Throughout the 1960s and 1970s Knievel was routinely compared to a host of personalities and fictional characters like Elvis Presley, Liberace, Paul Bunyan, Captain Ahab, Robert Mitchum, Jack London, Paul Newman, Steve McQueen, and Jesus Christ, to name a few. But he was also known as the man of steel or referred to as Superman, attesting both to the degree of complication surrounding his injuries and his ability to withstand any kind of punishment. In fact, no sooner had Knievel crashed onto the scene, than the myth of breaking every bone in his body surfaced. Knievel's critics dismissed the claim as preposterous, and by Knievel's own count the number of bones he broke was thirty-seven. But the myth of breaking every bone in his body was such an integral part of the public's consciousness about Knievel that it survived.

Knievel was also politically brash and provocative. Knievel often referred to himself as a modern day P. T. Barnum and dismissed the idea that he was nothing more than a stuntman. He was a pioneer, a frontiersman, pushing man and machine to new heights regardless of the risks involved and the potential for injury. Yet Knievel was simultaneously looking backwards. Knievel came to prominence against the backdrop of the gay and women's liberation movements and amidst growing opposition to the war in Vietnam, and he was never shy about making his opposition apparent. His interviews, press conferences, and the speeches he gave before and after attempted jumps were laced with numerous references to religion and God, involved plenty of flag-waving and appeals to patriotism, and included tirades against drugs and support for "law and order." By the early 1970s, Knievel was also becoming known for his verbal attacks against Jews, Native Americans, Italians, Poles, gays, lesbians, and especially feminism, which in 1974 he described as a "bunch of horseshit." Indeed, as growing numbers of American men and women were asking pointed questions about men's behavior, Knievel was routinely boasting about his taste for Wild Turkey Bourbon, his love of hunting and other dangerous sports, his penchant for violence and his various brawls with other bikers, hippies, and an occasional reporter, as well as his numerous sexual exploits, which he claimed involved over six hundred women.

The controversy surrounding race in the late 1960s and 1970s also shaped the public's adoration for Knievel. During this period, the press frequently made comparisons between Knievel and Muhammad Ali, comparisons that led to debates about which one had the larger ego, who was the loudest braggart, whose respective box office draw was the most significant, and which of the two deserved the claim to fame as "the greatest." Comparisons became so common that a savvy promoter picked up on the controversy and attempted to organize a fight between Ali and Knievel. The promoter, who remained anonymous, was prepared to offer a $10 million, winner-take-all prize for the match, if Evel and Ali agreed to a genuine fight. The pair would be allowed to establish their own ring rules, although the promoter felt that a bare-knuckle fight would be better than gloves and that kicking should be allowed to offset Ali's boxing skill, even though Knievel had described himself as an expert in street fighting. Knievel had apparently agreed to discuss the match, but Ali refused to take the idea seriously.

Comparing Knievel to Ali undoubtedly reflected Ali's status as the heavyweight champion, a status that for decades had stood as the ultimate expression of sporting talent, brute strength, and stamina. Yet Knievel's rise to fame coincided with whites' growing fears about the African American male athlete, who by the 1960s had become a dominant force in major league sports and who was openly challenging the racism he faced as an athlete and as an American; the most notable example was Ali, who attracted national scorn for his opposition to the Vietnam war and for joining the Nation of Islam. These growing concerns led white Americans to search for an explanation for this athletic supremacy, and to begin what appeared to be a renewed search for a "white hope." Knievel's claim to greatness and the constant comparisons with Ali were not simply a challenge to Ali as a formidable athlete. They were a challenge to Ali as an African American man who had boldly defied his station in society, and ultimately a challenge to the values Ali represented to other African American men and women across the country, during a time of intense divisiveness over race and over the meaning of equality in the United States.

Knievel's popularity did have its limits, however, and those limits were exposed when he tried to jump a little-known canyon in Idaho in 1974. During the late 1960s, Knievel first began to talk about jumping over the Grand Canyon. That jump would never materialize because of opposition from the federal government, forcing Knievel to settle for Idaho's Snake River Canyon. The jump would eventually take place in September 1974; and, instead of a motorcycle, Knievel attempted the jump on what became known as his Sky Cycle. The Sky Cycle was a steam-powered rocket that in theory was expected to shoot to a height of 3,000 feet at nearly 400 miles per hour. Once it reached this height, Knievel was supposed to pull a lever and release the parachute system, which would gently float the Sky Cycle to the ground and to the other side of the Canyon. Unfortunately for Knievel, the parachute prematurely released before the rocket cleared the tower. The rocket only reached a height of about 1,000 feet and then floated down into the near side of the Canyon, barely missing the river below. Knievel emerged only slightly bruised (except perhaps for his ego) and with only superficial scrapes to his face. Knievel had failed to complete his jumps on numerous previous occasions; despite those failures, there had been little doubt that he had given his best and that the jump and his intentions were genuine. Press reports about the Snake River Canyon jump were largely negative, and the jump was dismissed as a rip-off.

The fiasco at the Snake River Canyon marked the beginning of the end of the golden age of motorcycle jumping. By the mid 1970s, Knievel was beginning to have trouble finding promoters, and the public was quickly losing interest in these daredevil stunts, despite Knievel's best efforts to tantalize them. In the latter 1970s, for example, he proposed to jump between the towers at the World Trade Center, and came up with the idea of jumping out of a plane at 40,000 feet without a parachute (or a motorcycle) and then landing into one of thirteen hay bales.

A number of reasons might explain the public's waning interest in Knievel. But Americans were growing tired of Knievel just as they were losing interest in the need for someone like Knievel. In other words, fascination with the stuntman was beginning to dissipate just as the political and social movements that helped define Knievel's public persona were subsiding or seemingly disappearing altogether. Knievel was not necessarily a product of these movements. But his popularity coincided with these struggles, and his anti-drug rhetoric, his patriotic style, his respect for the law, and his anti-gay diatribes and attacks against women's libbers and hippies spoke directly to a public growing frustrated with the pace of social and political change. That historic controversy and Knievel's daredevil antics left an indelible mark on the 1970s and help explain his enduring appeal as an icon.

## WORKS RECOMMENDED

Gorn, Elliott J., ed. *Muhammad Ali: The People's Champ*. Urbana: U of Illinois P, 1995.

Kazickas, Jurate. "Evel Knievel Talking About His $6 Million Leap." *San Francisco Examiner* 5 July 1974.

Lyle, David. "Cup of Anguish." *Esquire* Jan. 1969: 89+.

Mandich, Steve. *Evel Incarnate: The Life and the Legend of Evel Knievel*. London: Sidgwick & Jackson, 2000.

Miller, John J. "Memo from John Miller." *San Francisco Chronicle* 22 Sept. 1974.

Schulman, Bruce. *The Seventies: The Great Shift in American Culture, Society, and Politics*. New York: Da Capo P, 2000.

Twombly, Wells. "Knievel's Projected Leap the Last Great Youth Orgy." *San Francisco Examiner* 5 Sept. 1974.

# Kodak Camera

## *Richard N. Masteller*

Consider disposable cameras. They have names like the Kodak "Fling" and "Fun Saver." You can find them almost anywhere: in racks for impulse buying at grocery store checkouts, in pharmacies, in gas stations, in the caverns of big-box retailers selling everything from headphones to refrigerators, in fast-food restaurants at the beach, in "convenience" stores, hotel gift shops, and airport shopping malls. Disposable cameras became popular late in the twentieth century, and they all promised, in essence, what George Eastman first promised late in the nineteenth century: "You press the button, we do the rest." In the twenty-first century, disposable digital cameras now appear beside disposable film cameras at drug store checkouts.

Over the decades between the first Kodak in 1888 and its most recent digital manifestation, billions of images have been framed and hung in "family rooms," enshrined in photo albums, and stuffed into shoeboxes. The twenty-first-century equivalents of shoeboxes are digital memory cards, computer harddrives, and CD-ROMs. Given a variety of "storage media" and a glut of imagery, "disposability"—the option to "delete"—seems increasingly not only a convenience, but a necessity.

George Eastman's Kodak camera first enabled this mass production of image-making: it brought popular, personal photography to the masses by enabling everyone—even a child—to become his or her own image-maker. As an icon of popular culture, the Kodak camera in fact helped to define that culture by certifying particular occasions as especially worth photographing: "Vacation Days are Kodak Days," ran one advertising slogan. But we also learned that almost any event could be a "Kodak moment" or a "Kodak occasion"; on its Web site the Eastman Kodak Company now urges us to "Share Moments. Share Life."

Briefly tracing the dissemination of Kodak cameras across the cultural landscape of twentieth-century life will indicate the extent of its diffusion and suggest its impact on taste-making. The iconic nature of the Kodak is apparent in books produced for avid collectors (Coe, Gilbert, Lothrop), as well as in numerous Web sites devoted to collecting and displaying various Kodak cameras, advertisements, and other ephemera. But the primary cultural significance of the Kodak camera goes beyond the sheer number of different models that have carried the Kodak name for over a century and propelled the success of a major twentieth-century corporation. Because the Kodak as popular artifact spurred the act of photographing, the result was another popular artifact—the ubiquitous amateur photograph.

Tracing the Kodak camera as an icon leads inevitably, then, to questions about the iconic act of photography and to reflections about the significance of the billions of images that result—each the product of a single act, but each also resembling so many other photographs taken by the masses of largely untutored record-makers, who today can carry in their pockets sleek cameras no larger than a cigarette pack, and in some cases approaching the size of a credit card. Throughout its history, the Kodak camera has functioned on a variety of levels: as an aid to entertainment, as a means of fashioning memory, and even as a fashion statement itself. As Susan Sontag has argued in *Regarding the Pain of Others,* the past is more likely to come alive for us these days not through stories we hear or read, but through photographs we see (89). The Kodak camera and counterparts produced by competing corporations gave millions of people a means of capturing a trace of reality beyond the lens, but they were also able to edit and revise that reality in ways that reveal and fulfill their own desires. Ostensibly a device for recording reality, the Kodak is equally significant as a tool of the imagination.

When George Eastman announced his Kodak camera in 1888, he stressed the simplicity of the photographic process: "you press the button, we do the rest." The Kodak was easily portable; it could be held in one's hand and weighed about 1½ pounds. It was bought already loaded with a roll of film that would take 100 circular photographs 2½ inches in diameter. When the roll was fully exposed, the camera was returned to the factory, where the photographs were developed and printed on cards roughly 4 × 5 inches and where the camera was reloaded with fresh film before being returned to the owner. The Kodak camera, together with its first roll of film, cost $25; processing the exposed film and loading new film cost another $10.

George Eastman, 1926. Courtesy of the Library of Congress.

In her excellent *Kodak and the Lens of Nostalgia,* Nancy West has suggested that this initial Kodak was too expensive to democratize photography. The cost, she suggests, was roughly equivalent to $400 in early-twenty-first-century prices, and only a little over 10,000 Kodak No. 1 and No. 2 cameras were manufactured from 1888 through 1890 (23–24). But innovations were rapid and ongoing. The production of the $5 Pocket Kodak announced in 1895 led to production runs of 25,000 a year from 1895 to 1900, and the Folding Pocket Kodak of 1898, weighing only eight ounces and selling for $10, could literally be pocketed, thus anticipating by a century the portability of the latest digital cameras (24, 51). By the turn of the last century, Kodak had produced some thirty-five different camera models for public consumption.

As West suggests, to promote amateur photography Eastman Kodak marketed its invention as a toy. While production figures increased each year during the 1890s, it was the Brownie camera of 1900, marketed explicitly to children and their parents, that accelerated and assured the democratization of photography. Costing $1 and recording six pictures on a roll of film that cost fifty cents to buy and develop, over 150,000 Brownies were sold within the year in England and America (75). In "The Wizard of Photography," a television documentary tracing the career of George Eastman, one commentator suggested that Eastman well knew what he was doing with the Brownie campaign: he hoped to capture the young and turn them into full-fledged Kodak junkies as they grew up. The success of the Brownie was crucial, not only because it enhanced the dispersion and influence of the Kodak name and helped promote the Kodak habit, but also because it put the practice of photography into the hands of the masses.

Ancillary industries and marketing mechanisms accompanied this democratization. The Montgomery Ward catalog of 1900 contained an ad for photo belt buckles, photo watch charms, and photo garter belts, announcing, "It is now quite a fad for the ladies to wear the picture of a favored one on her garter" (Masteller 1209). Whereas personal albums in the nineteenth century were frequently leather-bound, gilt-edged tomes with brass corners and

A young girl takes a picture of her doll with a new Kodak camera, 1917. Courtesy of the Library of Congress.

elaborate clasps, containing stiff ornamented pages with specially designed cut-outs for the insertion of standard size cartes-de-visite and cabinet photographs made in the photographer's studio, by the early twentieth-century albums were simpler and cheaper: on pages commonly black, one could use photo corners to arrange and attach rectangular photos of various dimensions and could buy additional pages to expand the album as photographs accumulated. In short, the democratization of photography occurred at the same time that companies like Sears and Montgomery Ward were learning the techniques of mass marketing and were seeking to create a public oriented toward consumption.

An ongoing, astute advertising campaign responding to current events throughout the twentieth century kept the Kodak habit in public consciousness. During World War I the small Vest Pocket Kodak was advertised as "the Soldier's Kodak." In the United States and in England soldiers heading to the battlefields of Europe were encouraged to "Make your own picture record of the War" (Coe and Gates 34). During the jazz age of the twenties, Kodak enlisted the talents of the prominent industrial designer Walter Dorwin Teague to create the "Vanity Kodak" camera, essentially a Vest Pocket Kodak embossed with gold diagonal lines, dressed up in one of five fashionable color schemes—Bluebird (blue), Cockatoo (green), Jenny Wren (brown), Redbreast (red), and Sea Gull (gray)—and supplied in a matching carrying case lined with colored silk. Given the fickle fashions of the flapper, these streamlined Kodaks were not especially profitable items. By the mid-1930s Kodak reverted to predominately, always tasteful black, although Teague went on to design more successful "modern" looking cameras for the firm, notably the Baby Brownie of 1934, a camera molded of black plastic that sold for a Depression-era price of $1, the same price as the original Brownie of 1900 (Coe and Gates 38–42).

In addition to competitive pricing and both cosmetic and substantive design innovations, Kodak used other strategies to keep its product in the public consciousness. Frequent ads appeared in popular magazines throughout the twentieth century. Young girls and women were particular targets, and the "Kodak girl" in her distinctive striped dress became a recurrent motif in Kodak ads from the first decade of the twentieth century into the 1970s (West 114–35). In the teens and twenties ads targeting boys suggested that learning and performing the operations of photography were particularly appropriate for future men of business and industry (West 101–4). From 1914 through 1932, Kodak published its own periodical *Kodakery*, containing the latest product news, advice for taking successful photographs, and examples of the work of amateur photographers. In the mid-1920s, Kodak sponsored a radio show titled *The Kodak Hour*.

An especially ingenious advertising campaign marked the fiftieth anniversary of the company in 1930. Kodak announced that it would distribute 500,000 free cameras to the "children of America" as a "nation-wide gift," and it was explicit about the two motives behind its munificence. One was "*sentiment*": the gift was to serve as "a token of appreciation to the grandparents and parents who for fifty years have played so important a part in the development of amateur picture-taking in America." The Company wanted "to place in the hands of their children and grandchildren an...important educational and character-building force." The other motive was "*business*": the campaign was "a means of interesting hundreds of thousands more children in picture-taking.... For as amateur photography increases in popularity, the use of Kodak products will naturally increase with it." The Company enlisted Mrs. Calvin Coolidge to explain further the higher goals of this campaign: "Instead of coming together to play games and eat ice cream and cake...each guest" at this anniversary party would receive a gift enabling him to "satisfy and develop his appreciation of the beautiful things of nature and make lasting records." Thus, she explained, "he will be a guest at that delightful sort of party which never ends; and as the years pass he will be united with the other guests in a common interest" (Eastman Anniversary Camera).

Mrs. Coolidge's testimonial, no doubt ghostwritten by an employee in Kodak's advertising department, highlights some of the ideals that recurred throughout Kodak's advertising campaigns in an effort to elevate the product beyond the status of a mere toy, ideals which help explain its popular appeal. A Kodak camera will elevate the sentiments by teaching one to appreciate beauty. It will document reality. It will arrest that reality, giving it longevity beyond the moment. Finally, "as the years pass"—indeed, despite the passage of years—it will reinforce community. Similar ideas appeared in the first user's manual in the 1880s: "Photography is...brought within the reach of every human being who desires to preserve a record of what he sees. Such a photographic note book...enables the fortunate possessor to go back by the light of his own fireside to scenes which would otherwise fade from the memory and be lost" (Newhall 64). An idyllic ad from the 1950s reiterated the point more succinctly. It depicts mom in her tennis shoes standing on a lakeside dock photographing the rest of her nuclear family (father in the rowboat with his fishing rod, her two sons cheerfully holding up the catch of the day). The main caption reads, "With snapshots, the sun never sets on boyhood" ("Brownie Ads...").

The Kodak became an icon in American culture, in short, not because the Eastman Kodak Company promoted a product, but because it promoted an idea—the idea of photography (West 25). The company's astute advertising campaigns and promotions suggested that the act of photography could play—and even needed to play—a crucial role in a wide variety of activities. To that end Kodak worked to align their cameras with a panoply of events that constituted American life and leisure. Family occasions such as birthday parties, graduations, weddings, and anniversaries were obvious candidates for photographs. But even the earliest ad campaigns linked the camera with other leisure activities: camping, bicycling, and especially the burgeoning tourist industry. We were encouraged to evaluate a scene as a potential photograph, to judge it "as pretty as a picture," including any "picturesque" or "exotic" inhabitants thereof. By the middle of the last century, the ubiquitous role of the camera and the zeal with which Kodak promoted the idea of photography led the Company to this summary advice: "take your camera with you everywhere—for that's where great snapshots are."

The Kodak as icon fostered the iconic act of photography and created the photograph as artifact—a surrogate reality that was, in Kodak's worldview, pleasant, worth remembering, and above all useful for establishing and reinforcing ideas of harmony, good fellowship, and community. At the turn into the twentieth century, the Kodak enabled the masses to create their own selective versions of reality, guided by Kodak's advertisements. The assumption was that an innocuous world was ready for recording, and thousands of "family albums" seem to confirm that assumption. Of course, the serene idea behind Kodak's campaigns—that "great snapshots" were "everywhere"—precluded certain kinds of images, and as the century and the practice of photography evolved, people began to create more personal albums and to record more carnivalesque moments that pushed against the boundaries or conventional norms of middle-class propriety (Holland 148). A "Kodak moment" more broadly conceived might include Mardi Gras in New Orleans, homecoming weekends in the fraternity, or snapshots of an annual reenactment of *The Rocky Horror Picture Show*.

These days, amateur snapshooters once again include soldiers-in-arms, and while the iconic act of photographing pleasant events continues, the definition of pleasure is apparently evolving. The evidence from Iraq's Abu Ghraib prison has once again reminded us of the predatory, aggressive language that permeates the photographic act: "capturing" the subject, "aiming" the camera, taking the shot. How can these images be understood as recording anyone's "pleasant" moment? The photographic act here does more than document; it dehumanizes both the subjects and their captors, and one can speculate whether, over time, such images might also dehumanize their viewers, making them as callous as the photographers who posed their victims.

Such iconic images seem far removed from the sunlit world of mid-century Kodak advertisements or from contemporary ads touting digital cameras as fashion accessories. It appears that every moment can now indeed be a Kodak moment. But the array of imagery now so effortlessly available—you press the button, pixels do the rest—extends far beyond the conventions of decorum and decency that Kodak fostered when it promoted its first cameras. At the turn into the twenty-first century, as Kodak refashions itself and its cameras for the digital age, it and its contemporary competitors—Canon, Minolta, Nikon, Olympus, Panasonic, Sony—continue to sell cameras as aids to entertainment, aids to memory, and as fashion accessories in a culture of leisure and conspicuous consumption. The act of photography is deemed a natural act—easy, spontaneous, as necessary as breathing. The snapshot continues to show us ourselves as we fashion ourselves for the camera. We may now easily dispose of these selves—deleting whatever versions fail to please us. On the other hand, we may replicate them, worldwide, more quickly than ever before. The digital Kodak as icon—and its cousins from other corporations—have made it easier than ever to fashion surrogate selves, or to capture fragments of the realities before us, or to give vent to the desires of our unfettered imaginations. But the evidence of the resulting images generates increasing distrust: can what we see in these images really be? Can we any longer believe our eyes? Is this really who we are? Can we—should we—dispose of the evidence?

## WORKS CITED AND RECOMMENDED

"Brownie Ads and Posters 1900–1963." *The Brownie Camera Page*. 31 Jan. 2005 <http://www.brownie-camera.com/posters/pages/074_1953.shtml>.

*The Brownie Camera Page*. Ed. Chuck Baker. 31 Jan. 2005 <http://www.brownie-camera.com>.

*BoxCameras.com*. 31 Jan. 2005 <http://www.boxcameras.com>.

Coe, Brian. *Kodak Cameras: The First Hundred Years*. Stillwater, MN: Voyageur P, 1988.

Coe, Brian, and Paul Gates. *The Snapshot Photograph: The Rise of Popular Photography, 1888–1939*. London: Ash and Grant, 1977.

The Eastman Anniversary Camera. Advertisement. 31 Jan. 2005 <http://www.brownie-camera.com/anniv.shtml>.

Gilbert, George. *Collecting Photographica: The Images and Equipment of the First Hundred Years of Photography*. New York: Hawthorne Books, 1976.

Hirsch, Marianne. *Family Frames: Photography, Narrative, and Postmemory*. Cambridge, MA: Harvard UP, 1997.

———, ed. *The Familial Gaze*. Hanover: UP of England, 1999.

Holland, Patricia. "'Sweet It Is to Scan...': Personal Photographs and Popular Photography." *Photography: A Critical Introduction*. Ed. Liz Wells. 3rd ed. New York: Routledge, 2004. 113–58.

*The KodakGirl Collection*. Ed. Martha Cooper. 31 Jan. 2005 <http://www.kodakgirl.com/index.htm>.

Lothrop, Eaton S., Jr. *A Century of Cameras from the Collection of the International Museum of Photography at George Eastman House*. Rev. and expanded ed. Dobbs Ferry, NY: Morgan and Morgan, 1982.

Masteller, Richard. "Photography as Popular Culture." *The Greenwood Guide to American Popular Culture*. Ed. M. Thomas Inge and Dennis Hall. Vol. 3. Westport, CT: Greenwood, 2002. 1199–1237.

Newhall, Beaumont. "How George Eastman Invented the Kodak Camera." *Image* 7.3 (Mar. 1958): 59–64.

*The Norwood Teague Kodak Brownie Collection*. California Museum of Photography at the University of California, Riverside. 31 Jan. 2005 <http://photo.ucr.edu/cameras/brownies>.

Sontag, Susan. *On Photography*. New York: Farrar, Straus, 1977.

———. *Regarding the Pain of Others*. New York: Farrar, Straus, 2003.

West, Nancy Martha. *Kodak and the Lens of Nostalgia*. Charlottesville: U of Virginia P, 2000.

"The Wizard of Photography." *The American Experience*. Videocassette. Green Light Productions, Inc. for WGBH/Boston. PBS Home Video, 2000.

# Las Vegas

## Lawrence E. Mintz

As an American icon, Las Vegas has an identity that is as clear and definitive as any. Las Vegas is about "sin," most evidently about gambling, sex, and self-indulgence in food, alcohol, and entertainment. Gambling, or as the industry euphemistically but ironically and correctly calls it, "gaming," is not about accumulating wealth; it is about playing, and play itself in the American cultural tradition is "sinful" enough. Sex, too, is playful, in Las Vegas. It is more about the show, the quasi-public striptease than about actual sex. With the unlimited availability of good food and drink and good middlebrow entertainment, gaming and sex represent a focus on pleasure that superbly supports an escape into an underworld that visitors covet, but understand explicitly and completely as temporary and isolated. The careful, expensive, and exquisitely crafted environment for this safe and controlled descent into heavenly hell is truly one of the wonders of the modern, or postmodern world.

While the iconic theme of Las Vegas is unambiguous, the motifs that make up the environment of tourist Las Vegas are complex, and they represent an identity crisis that would make the members of the American Psychology Association salivate. While its current manifestation can be traced to the middle 1940s, Las Vegas has banked on a "wild west" image of "everything goes," of excessive cash in search of adequate reward for the risk-taking, rough-living, dangerous, and onerous labor associated with prospecting and ranching. Cultural analysts as early as Mark Twain understood that the struggle for finding treasure in the new west had lawlessness and the pursuit of forbidden pleasure built into its cultural matrix. Town was an oasis into which hard-living fortune seekers slipped for recreation, if not rest, and the ethos of prospecting shaped their activities there just as it did in the wilderness.

The notorious Bugsy Siegel, universally credited with dreaming up the twentieth-century version of Las Vegas, grasped this historical concept whether or not he realized or articulated it. With his background in the criminal underworld, he was able to realize that gambling, sex, alcohol, and an unabashed pursuit of and acceptance of pleasure was perfectly situated in this western town. His resort hotel started Vegas's first identity as an oasis in opposition to the natural "desert"—in terms of pleasure—which most of the visitors inhabited when they were outside this manufactured environment. First-generation resorts like the Sands, Dunes, Sahara, and Aladdin offered a place with pools and palms and available food and drinks and "dates," in more than one sense of the word, to those adventurous travelers willing to risk the journey and to make an investment in a managed level of risk. These resorts provided excitement and enjoyment as a consolation prize in the event of failure at the slot machines and gaming tables.

The reality of the greater American social climate clearly dictated that the lawlessness and sin had to be brought under control and reinvented as a *simulacrum* or *hyperreality*, to use the terms of Jean Baudrillard and Umberto Eco, respectively. Just as American society would not accept polygamy, even if it was to be confined to the bordered and controlled space of the Mormons, it demanded that the real criminal elements be forced out of Las Vegas, that government supervision be installed, and that actual free-flowing sin be replaced by an artificial, closely managed and supervised environment. But we must remember that simulacra and hyperrealities are not mere imitations, replicas, or reproductions. Rather, they are entities unto themselves, real in their own original conceptualization, creating and maintaining unique, if artificial, landscapes and features.

So Las Vegas embraced the quest for themes that would contain the "sin" within more palatable, acceptable cultural borders. First it was necessary to create the sense of a special, man-made world in which normal concepts of time and all of the senses could be suspended and replaced with a boldly, unashamedly artificial place. The place had to support the visitor's self-perception that the visit was just that, a temporary excursion that did not correspond to nor carry over to what she or he might do, how he or she might live, outside "the oasis." In the 1960s, Caesar's Palace was a brilliant, pioneering gambit to establish just such an ambiance. Its Roman setting was perfect. Libertine pursuits of gambling and consumption could be indulged in an environment clearly marked as not of the real worlds of the players. It was framed in the ancient past, connected with myths of Roman cavorting, and in a structure that was self-consciously fake, almost to the point of parody. Female employees who wore strange costumes that showed generous hints of breast and butt represented sex; however, these servants of food and drink entirely avoided inviting anything but decorous, professional interaction—look but don't touch. The contemporary Caesar's Palace has installed incredibly unreal animated spectacles that at specific times and places in the hotel reinforce the idea that the visitor can play-act in the fantasy, but not lose sight of its artificiality. Expensive but familiar and within reach, the shopping and other trappings of "class" in the hotel's appointments further reinforce the idea that time spent in Caesar's Palace is a luxury and "an experience," but not a way of life that might ensnare the vacationing pilgrim.

The success of Caesar's Palace proved that creating themed environments and suggesting luxury was the way to go. It also established another vitally

The famous Neon cowboy on the Strip in Las Vegas. Courtesy of Corbis.

important principle: Las Vegas has to have attractions that are spectacles in and of themselves, places to be seen, photographed, talked about, and visited for reasons other than the overt themes of gambling and self-indulgence. Visitors have to be reminded that they are tourists, not gamblers or sinners. Several devices work to maintain this crucial illusion. Actually it is not an illusion, but we need to remind ourselves that Vegas is what it is; that is, a place designed to be visited, gawked at, and experienced, just as much as it is a place to play slot machines, craps, and blackjack and to overindulge in food and drink. The mature actualization of Las Vegas early on discovered the power of bright lights, colorful and lively signs, and the transformation of a highway into the Strip, multiplying in an almost hypnotic or dizzying sense of "otherness," of a special place. The signs and lights actually reference Broadway, but because Broadway is also a simulacrum, the reference supports rather than challenges Las Vegas's status as a special, boundaried space.

And size matters. A crucial step was to make the resort hotels very big. This bulk adds to the spectacle, the reason to visit and to talk about the trip. Size also adds to the sense of the space as special, as extraordinary. Following Caesar's Palace, large hotels like the MGM Grand, among many others, were deliberately created as cavernous environments embracing many restaurants, shops, theaters, lounges, and, of course, the immense casino floors that characterize just about all Las Vegas resort hotels. The use of the disorienting exotic themes was for many years less pronounced, at least compared with Caesar's and in such hotels as The Riviera or MGM Grand, but it is now nearly always a part of the package. The huge Mirage has a theme, of course, but theme is overwhelmed by size and spectacle, most notably the nightly eruption of the famous man-made volcano. The basic Las Vegas hotel is a self-contained city that typically includes—regardless of the hotel's theme—Italian, French, Chinese, and steakhouse restaurants, a coffeehouse or two, and a buffet. The all-you-can-eat buffet is another Las Vegas performance that signifies excess, but it also provides a rationalization for going to Vegas, for these buffets are typically low priced and often "comped" for hotel guests. The buffet feasts are in the minds of many part of the "good deal" that is to be had in Las Vegas in addition to the one dealt one at the blackjack table.

Following the notion that people come to Las Vegas for the simulated sin but need to think of themselves as seeking spectacle and entertainment led to one of the few questionable decisions in the history of the town's self-invention. Perhaps with an eye to the Disney theme parks' success, Vegas moguls decided to feature family fun and mega-theme environments in their next identity incarnation. Hotels like Circus Circus, Excalibur, and Treasure Island jack up the visibility of the theme park ambiance and seek to accommodate families with children, hoping that the total package will attract the crowds, and that at least one member of the family can be counted on to drop the Strip-average $500 or more at the tables and machines. The problem was that blatant promotion of family values changed the town's iconic projection, and Las Vegas began to seem, to many, like just another theme park or vacation place, rather than a unique and special site for licensed sinning. To be fair, the planners were facing competition from Native American and "riverboat" (read riverbank with an emphasis on *bank*) casinos, and they were facing a charge that Las Vegas was stuck in a 1950s or early 1960s past of rather lame, post-vaudeville shows, pedestrian buffets, and fraying environment. As Vegas began to seem more like Atlantic City, it was losing the interest and enthusiasm of the baby boomer with post-family disposable income, and failing almost entirely to attract a younger clientele, DINK (dual income, no kids) couples and partygoers made rich in the new economy.

So Las Vegas had to rereinvent itself. Once again, size mattered, but now it was allied with "class" and "hip" to attract the younger men and women who have the money it takes to do Las Vegas right. The first step was to follow the lead of the Mirage and use size and luxury to appeal to a sense of distinctiveness. In a way hotels like Bellagio, Luxor, Paris Las Vegas, New York–New York, the Venetian, and Mandalay Bay, among others and including some mega-works in progress, recall Caesar's Palace in their projection of escape via theme to an obviously manufactured fantasy world and play land through their use of size and luxury. A feeling of "class" is created in these hotels by the expense and devotion to detail in their physical plant, by the quality of their buffets (still a bargain but now featuring gourmet options rather than merely all the shrimp and crab legs one can consume)

Treasure Island and Bellagio's reflecting pool, Las Vegas. Courtesy of Shutterstock.

and their shows (bringing in headliners other than those associated with the nightclubs of the 1950s or casino-special lounge acts with no entertainment credibility outside the traditions of Vegas and Atlantic City), and their shops such as Hermes, Ralph Lauren, Calvin Klein, Prada—familiar, accessible, but a retail step well above the department store. The themes here are much better realized than at Caesar's (which remains my favorite Las Vegas hotel—camp should be proud or not at all). Like "The World Showcase" at Walt Disney World and "The Old Country" at Busch Gardens in Virginia, Bellagio's and Venice's invocation of Italy, Paris Las Vegas's representaion of Paris, and the other Vegas theme creations are not advertised as substitutes for European travel. Vegas's New York–New York is not supposed in any way to provide a "New York" experience-west. Ironically the themes piled on top of one another visually say "Las Vegas" loud and clear.

These themed environments remind you that you are in a place of self-invention, an oasis that does not have to and does not correspond to the rest of the world. Fabricated as the reason to go to Las Vegas, they serve those who want the gambling and other pleasures, but need to convince themselves and others that this is a temporary indulgence rather than a slide into depravity. Indeed one of the reasons that most visitors are not deeply unhappy or angry when they lose their calculated grubstakes is that they can write it off in their minds as "gaming," a part of the entertainment package and as the just wages of sin and far less expensive than in our traditional teaching.

For the younger visitors, today's Las Vegas is more openly and defiantly a place where sinning is celebrated. Hotels like the Palm and Hard Rock court the hip, Gen-X fun seeker with lively lounges, rock music, and a cleverly promoted image as "the in place" to see celebrities from the sports and entertainment worlds. Much of the new resident entertainment in Las Vegas, notably Cirque de Soleil's three shows, The Blue Man Group and Penn and Teller, among others, openly appeals to hip, postmodern, somewhat esoteric tastes. To be sure, Wayne Newton still packs the house, and impressionists, traditional night club standup comedians, and Elvis impersonators are welcomed here as nowhere else. Vegas entertainment still has a few of the seminude, flashy reviews, and while the formula seems tired, the strip clubs seem to me to be ripe for the new vaudeville and new burlesque performance theater that is experiencing renaissance in New York, Los Angeles, and San Francisco these days. Some

A group of people plays poker in Las Vegas. Courtesy of Corbis.

vestiges of family entertainment will no doubt survive, but it is not likely that it will be too heavily promoted from now on.

In keeping with this current iconic reinvention, Las Vegas has a new, very successful advertising tag—"What happens here stays here," a slogan dear to Las Vegas mayor Oscar Goodman. While technically honcho of the downtown, but not of the Strip, he is a colorful figure and self-appointed spokesman for the city. He has even threatened to legalize prostitution, a possibility in Nevada but a long shot in Las Vegas given its brand of sinning. Goodman either misses the point of *controlled* sinning, of temporary transgression without fear of serious, permanent repercussions, or he thinks that the next generation of visitors does not share the fears of the present generation of visitors or the fears of those who actually have to live in Las Vegas. Actually, my guess is that he knows perfectly well that legalizing prostitution in Vegas can never happen and would hurt rather than help Vegas's appeal, but he is smart enough to know that just talking about it contributes to the iconic projection that makes the resort work.

In these early years of the twenty-first century, Las Vegas is hotter than ever, and that is not referring to the summer desert temperatures. More than a dozen current television shows reference it, some in fictions located there, others in documentaries, Vegas-located poker tournaments, and Food Network and Travel Channel specials. Films that use the locale are being churned out regularly. The classic overhead shot of the Strip at night, lights blazing and cars cruising past the familiar hotels has become ubiquitous. A recent cover story in *Time* magazine trumpets, "Its Vegas, Baby!" and a *New York Times* editorial frets that Las Vegas "has gone awfully mainstream." However it is not likely that the culture war between the forces of permissiveness and the guardians of traditional moral values will be won so quickly and decisively that Las Vegas will become the American norm. If that were to happen, it would lose its special appeal. Las Vegas has more to fear from "sin" becoming commonplace in America than it does from its gaming competition on the Mississippi and on the Native American reservations. Its iconic value is invested in representing a sacred space in which the rituals of licentiousness can be celebrated and kept within the mega-resort cathedrals.

## WORKS CITED AND RECOMMENDED

Baudrillard, Jean. *Selected Writings*. Stanford, CA: Stanford University, 1988.
Eco, Umberto. *Travels in Hyperreality*. San Diego: Harcourt, Brace and Jovanovich, 1986.
Gottdiener, Mark. *The Theming of America: American Dreams, Media Fantasies, and Themed Environments*. Boulder, CO: Westview, 2001.
"Its Vegas, Baby!" *Time* 26 July 2004: 22–35.
"Leaving It in Las Vegas." *New York Times* 7 June 2004: A26.
Urry, John. *The Tourist Gaze: Leisure and Travel in Contemporary Societies*. London: Sage, 1990.

# Rush Limbaugh

## Thomas A. Greenfield

Radio historians are passionate about benchmarks and turning points in radio history. A handful of dates and accomplishments have survived the rigors of radiophile debate to emerge as landmarks of the medium: the first "official" commercial radio broadcast (1920), the birth of the first radio network (1926), and Orson Welles's "War of the Worlds" mock Martian invasion (Halloween 1939) stand out as highlights. When the definitive histories of twentieth-century broadcasting are written, many historians will be arguing—not all of them happily—for the inclusion of August 1988: Rush Limbaugh brings his radio program to national syndication.

Limbaugh (b. 1951), the most well known, most listened to, and most influential American radio personality in the last fifteen years, completely reinvented American talk radio to accommodate his jovially abrasive on-air personality and uncompromising animosity toward liberalism. In the process, he elevated the talk format from innocuous low-rated late night programming to a top-rated national platform for a new kind of mass media star: the conservative broadcast political attack artist. Talk-radio icon Limbaugh yet keeps his audience loyal and large with a blend of homespun right-wing moralizing, impish humor, "radio outlaw" antics, and just enough antisocial malice to whet the attention of the establishment media he abhors.

Leaving college after one year to pursue a radio career, Limbaugh had a lackluster first decade as a rock and top 40 disc jockey in the 1970s. Fired from several radio stations for offending listeners, callers, sponsors, and pillars of various communities, Limbaugh eventually realized that the music he was playing on the air was interfering with his self-admitted talent for insulting people in an engaging way. Landing his own talk show and the support of conservative management on KFBK in Sacramento, he honed the "right wing attack machine" style that made him, as he describes in his trademark mix of congenial self-inflated hyperbole and in-your-face bravado, a broadcasting phenomenon: "[I am] destined for my own wing in the Museum of Broadcasting" (McManus).

# RUSH LIMBAUGH

Like most mass-media innovators in the last half of the twentieth century, Limbaugh used established techniques and traditions in fashioning an approach to radio broadcasting that was altogether new. In the mode of radio pioneers from Walter Winchell to Edward R. Murrow, Limbaugh developed aural cues and signatures that resonate with his listeners and have become uniquely the property of Limbaugh and his audience (the most famous of these being the interactive "dittos" that his fans, self-proclaimed "dittoheads," use to affirm their allegiance to him moment by moment and point by point). While delving almost exclusively into political content, he brought a front-porch sage guy-at-the-corner-bar sensibility to political talk and in so doing drafted a blueprint for countless on-air imitators, disciples, and Rush "wannabees." In the 1990s many neighborhood restaurants and taverns boosted daytime revenues by opening Rush Rooms where the local clientele would bond in political solidarity over Limbaugh's show.

In a throwback to radio's pre–World War II "golden era" Limbaugh rejected the modern broadcast editorialists' self-imposed ban on reading commercials—a practice widely seen in contemporary broadcasting as compromising one's integrity as a broker of political information. Like the pioneer news commentators of the 1930s and 1940s, Limbaugh moves effortlessly between pitches for weight loss systems or home improvement services and straightforward program content, be it allegations of treason on the part of liberal politicians or gasps of emotion as he recalls the videotaped execution of an American citizen by Iraqi insurgents.

While not the first political or conservative broadcast personality, Limbaugh is the first to successfully wed the upbeat, "full-tilt boogie" patter of the drive-time rock DJ with the call-to-action invective of the propagandist pamphleteer. Limbaugh on the air is often angry but never "down." He is high-energy, high volume, and, no matter how dire the conditions or how roused his ire, rarely more than ten seconds from a witty putdown or irreverent quip at the expense of a Democratic politician or left-leaning journalist. It is, in fact, his irrepressibility and phenomenal on-the-air energy that powers his personal connection to his adoring audience. Even his political enemies openly, if begrudgingly, acknowledge Limbaugh's astonishing skills as a broadcast personality and communicator.

Conservative commentator Rush Limbaugh gestures while speaking during the National Association of Broadcasters convention in Philadelphia, 2003. AP/Wide World Photos.

Limbaugh's appeal, however, goes far beyond his skillful merging of traditional radio gimmicks, DJ glibness, and hard-edged conservative ideology. While declaring himself a voice of mainstream America, he is actually a groundbreaking iconoclastic radio "bad boy," demolishing long-standing traditions of broadcast gentility and sponsor-friendly inoffensiveness. Like his contemporary, "shock jock" Howard Stern who introduced new levels of sexual content to big time radio, or 1960s "outlaw" FM disc jockey Wolfman Jack who dropped more than casual allusions to the pleasures of illegal drugs into his on-air patter, Limbaugh rewrote the rules of political engagement in joyous, unapologetic, spectacular fashion. Prior to Limbaugh's arrival on the national scene, traditional political broadcast talk, with some isolated exceptions, tended toward restraint and tastefulness: issue-oriented and only mildly personal by today's standards. In many markets the sports talk shows were nastier. The traditional talk also tended to garner meager public service level ratings to match.

Not so in the Limbaugh era. While eschewing the sour personality of modern conservative broadcast predecessors Joe Pyne or Morton Downey, Jr., Limbaugh's attacks are notoriously personal and often jovially cruel. In his ability to convert his political animus to amusing mockery and harassment of his political enemies—Democrats and liberals in politics, the media, and elsewhere—he developed a new kind of interactive mass radio audience which quickly evolved into an important and heretofore unknown force in American electoral politics.

By 1992, four years after his national debut, the number of stations carrying *The Rush Limbaugh Show* had grown from its initial fifty-six outlets to several hundred with weekly audience numbers well in excess of 5 million. By the mid to late 1990s that figure would exceed 10 million, and some current estimates go as high as 15 to 20 million. Limbaugh had already stunned observers with his ability to rally his "dittoheads" on any given issue to flood politicians' offices with enough phone calls, faxes, and e-mails to shut down normal operations for days at a time. However, the broadening of his interests from high-energy political talk into direct advocacy for candidates and legislation began in earnest with the 1992 presidential campaign of Clinton-Gore versus Bush-Quayle, and peaked with the historic 1994 off-year Republican conservative "sweep" of the Senate and House of Representatives.

A number of factors contributed to Limbaugh's gravitation toward establishment political power-brokering. As Philip Seib points out, during the 1992 campaign candidate Bill Clinton was using his pop culture savvy to reach young voters and control his media exposure in a way he could not through standard media outlets—the legendary "wailing saxophone" television appearance on the self-consciously hip *Arsenio Hall Show* being the most memorable of these forays (191–92). The Bush-Quayle campaign took notice of the power of alternative media and courted favor with Limbaugh, who broke his long-standing ban on in-studio guests and brought on both President Bush and Senator Quayle for separate on-air appearances. These broadcasts identified Limbaugh as an apologist for the Bush-Quayle campaign rather than a completely "independent," or at least unaffiliated, conservative voice (Fallows 61–66).

While Clinton's impressive victory over an incumbent president was not going to dampen Limbaugh's ardor, Clinton's postinauguration honeymoon period might well have diminished, if only temporarily, the influence of diehard Clinton bashers. But Clinton seemed bent on ending his honeymoon quickly and Limbaugh was more than happy to capitalize on the moment. Clinton's clumsy out-of-the-gate advocacy of gays in the military ("don't ask, don't tell") immediately galvanized the conservative base against him, giving Limbaugh an ideal platform for two of his high-card plays: anti-gay humor and fear of liberal social engineering.

Adding to this postelection bounty, Clinton presented Limbaugh with a badly managed federal healthcare initiative presided over by Hillary Clinton. Healthcare would have been a serviceable left-wing target for Limbaugh's right-wing shots, but having Hillary Clinton center stage made it almost too easy for Limbaugh to rally conservative troops to action. Right-wing visceral disdain for Hillary Clinton, the self-declared "co-President," combined with her own early missteps in fashioning the image of the "new breed of First Lady" she aspired to be, gave Limbaugh plenty of hot burning fuel for his pre-election 1994 broadcasts.

Perhaps the most significant conduit between Limbaugh and the 1994 Republican election effort proved to be the flamboyant, media-wise Speaker of the House, Newt Gingrich. As the Clinton presidency faltered early, Gingrich gained power and visibility as the White House's principal political nemesis. As "point man" for the 1994 Republican congressional election effort, he designed for his candidates a powerful campaign rhetoric that mirrored Limbaugh's daily radio broadsides: demonize the opposition with small details, cast them as cultural aliens out-of-step with real American values, stigmatize the word "liberal," and ridicule the opposition into irrelevance. By November Limbaugh had become an important and visible operative in the Republican victory, which also served as a coming out party for the neoconservative political movement. Observed Republican strategist-turned-commentator Mary Matalin: "Rush is a major reason for the 1994 sweep. When you look at the data, 44% of the voters say they got their news primarily from radio. That's Rush" (*Rush Limbaugh: Always Right*). No broadcast personality before or since has exercised this magnitude of direct influence over national electoral politics. As Limbaugh himself would say, it was quite an achievement for "a boy from Missouri who just wanted to be on the radio" (*"The Rush Limbaugh Show" Official Website*).

Although Limbaugh's radio show flourished after 1994 with Clinton-bashing remaining his stock and trade, his identity as a Republican party operative and insider receded somewhat. Gingrich, the politician with whom Limbaugh was perhaps most closely identified, lost public favor for high-handed political tactics. The dead-on-arrival 1996 presidential candidacy of the decidedly uncharismatic Republican Senator Bob Dole offered little temptation for the high voltage, success-driven Limbaugh. New conservative media outlets and stars had emerged, making Limbaugh the top dog in a large pack but no longer the only one. Of course, in the late 1990s nothing in the realm of standard party politics could match the appeal to conservative broadcasters of White House intern and presidential paramour Monica Lewinsky and other events leading up to Clinton's impeachment hearings.

Limbaugh's daily on-air hounding of Bill Clinton (counting each day of his presidency as a day of America held hostage, thereby invoking press coverage of the 1980 capture of fifty-one American hostages in Iran) brought scrutiny to Limbaugh's inexhaustible creativity for attack humor. While normally trafficking in boilerplate insults of the "other side's" intelligence, patriotism, honesty, or physical attractiveness (he once referred to President Clinton's teenage daughter as the "White House dog"), Limbaugh's appeal and iconic stature owe much to his occasional forays into groundbreaking levels of cruelty and insensitivity. In 1994, without ever affirming its accuracy, Limbaugh broadcast a rumor that Clinton friend and White House attorney Vince Foster, who by all official accounts had committed suicide in a Washington, D.C. park, had been murdered in an apartment owned by Hillary Clinton—presumably with some unspecified level of complicity on the part of the Clintons. Although Limbaugh was neither the first nor only conservative commentator recounting variations of this rumor (which still surfaces occasionally in right-wing media circles), the clout of his radio program kept the Vince Foster murder story in the public dialog for weeks. Writing years later in his memoir *My Life*, Bill Clinton cited Limbaugh by name as the principal force in advancing the murder rumor, asserting by this example that those who attacked him personally were guilty of harming innocent bystanders—in this case Foster's family (587).

While normally glorying in the outrage he engenders in his victims, Limbaugh on rare occasions crosses an unspecified line of acceptable malice and finds himself on the defensive. Such an example occurred in May 2004 when he made comments trivializing U.S. soldiers' mistreatment of prisoners during the American invasion of Iraq. Major news outlets worldwide had broadcast a series of photographs showing American troops, in clear violation of the Geneva Convention, sexually humiliating and physically torturing prisoners at Iraq's Abu Ghraib prison. Domestic and international protest was so strong that the normally unrepentant President George W. Bush and Secretary of Defense Donald Rumsfeld offered public statements of contrition for the troops' actions.

Limbaugh would have none of that. On his May 6 broadcast Limbaugh attempted to counter the cries of outrage: "This no different than what happens at the Skull & Crossbones initiation [a fraternity-like secret society of undergraduates at Yale University].... I'm talking about people having a good time.... You ever heard of needing to blow some steam off?" (*"The Rush Limbaugh Show"*). Although Limbaugh was not the only conservative commentator or politician to assert that public outrage over the photographs had been overblown for political purposes, his statements alone made sustained national news. He became *the* icon of downplaying the Abu Ghraib controversy, completely overshadowing U.S. Senators James Inhofe and Zell Miller among others who took nearly identical public positions.

Public revulsion over the photographs, however, was so deep that even Limbaugh's conservative base could not forcefully rally to his cause, and Limbaugh had to backpedal. While not apologizing for his remarks, Limbaugh offered public clarifications (he did find some of the photographs troubling and had said so on the air) and counterattacks (the liberal media had taken his words out of context) to explain away one of his few pronouncements that seemed not to be resonating with many of his admirers. He even gave an interview to *Time* magazine to get out from under the criticism—a rare instance of Limbaugh using a forum which he does not control, much less a nonpartisan one, to get his message out.

Limbaugh's "bad-boy" persona has also inoculated him against fallout from other potentially career-killing scandals and missteps. In an industry notorious for expelling talent for a single on-air breech of decorum, Limbaugh, like the old-time radio hero Superman, has "powers and abilities far beyond those of mortal men." His radio program and political influence have survived, and even prospered, in the face of formidable challenges to his honesty and integrity—any one of which would have torpedoed the career of almost any other major broadcast personality.

- For years Limbaugh has simply brushed off numerous documented cases of his factual errors, fabricated evidence, and serious misrepresentation of data—routinely dismissing corrections and contravening evidence as politically motivated attacks;
- In October 2003, during a stint as a television commentator on sports channel ESPN, Limbaugh asserted that pro football quarterback Donovan McNabb was receiving unmerited favorable press owing to the sports media's penchant for hyping African American quarterbacks. Public protests along with McNabb's performance statistics and elegantly understated retort ("It's sad that you've got to go to skin color. I thought we were through with that....") drove Limbaugh from the television program. But his radio ratings and sponsor support showed not even a dent. For several days thereafter Limbaugh railed on the air about how the ESPN episode was a case of the establishment media's efforts to censor him.
- In 2004, Florida authorities charged him with illegally obtaining prescription drugs to support a self-admitted addiction. Excoriating the Democratic district attorney prosecuting his case, Limbaugh used the arrest and prosecution efforts to advance one of his show's signature themes: liberals are obsessed with silencing him.

Limbaugh's ratings and mystique flourish in the face of these eruptions, so much so that one can hardly imagine Limbaugh surviving long without them—or wanting to. This presents a paradox in assessing his legacy in broadcasting and popular culture. To the unquestioned good of the medium, he redesigned the landscape of American daytime radio. By transforming talk radio from a marginal, largely local nighttime format to a staple of daytime programming nationwide, he discovered and cultivated a new, massive national audience for the medium. By declaring and then proving he could be the first talk-show host in radio or television history to carry a full-length daily talk show without guests or co-hosts, he expanded the definition of what a radio personality could do. By becoming a major political power broker through his broadcasts he expanded the boundaries of what a modern radio performer could be.

However, Limbaugh has also created an entertainment program that serves millions of listeners as their primary source for daily news. Limbaugh has no bonds to the journalism profession's standards for factual accuracy ("I am an entertainer") nor traditions of civility ("This is a program about what I think"). But his audience has conferred upon him the stature of a newsman, and the rest of the medium has taken notice. His success has emboldened other news outlets, most notably Fox television news, to engage in advocacy journalism and *ad hominem* political commentary. Critics of mass media note that even mainstays of journalism—the old-line major television networks and newspapers—are feeling competitive pressure to incorporate "populist" journalism and modified advocacy in their reporting, an issue complicated exponentially by the problems of covering the post-9/11 "War on Terror" and American military actions in Afghanistan, Iraq, and elsewhere.

Just how the American mass media will face the challenge of defining and delivering news to the twenty-first century audience lies well beyond Rush Limbaugh's influence. To do so successfully, however, the media will have to keep up with the evolving demands and expectations of that audience. No one—absolutely no one—has done more to mold, sculpt, and empower that audience than has Rush Limbaugh. And no one understands it better.

## WORKS CITED AND RECOMMENDED

Anderson, Kurt. "Big Mouths." *Time* 1 Nov. 1993: 60–66.
Clinton, Bill. *My Life*. New York: Knopf, 2004.
Fallows, James. "With Talent on Loan from the GOP." *Atlantic Monthly* May 1994: 61–66.
Franken, Al. *Rush Limbaugh Is a Big Fat Idiot and Other Observations*. New York: Dell, 1996.
Limbaugh, Rush. *"The Rush Limbaugh Show" Official Website*. 1 Aug. 2003 (transcript from fifteenth anniversary radio program) and April–July 2004 <http.www.rushlimbaugh.com>.
———. *The Way Things Ought to Be*. New York: Pocket Books, 1992.
McManus, John F. "Establishment Dittohead." *The New American* 1.14 (10 July 1995) <http.www.thenewamerican.com>.
Randall, Steven et al. *The Way Things Aren't: Rush Limbaugh's Reign of Error*. New York: The New P, 1995.

"Rush Limbaugh: Always Right." *Biography*. Television segment. Lisa Zeff, Executive Producer. ABC News and A&E Network, 1995.

"The Rush Limbaugh Show." WHAM 1180 AM, Rochester, NY. April–July 2004.

Seib, Phillip. *Rush Hour: Talk Radio, Politics, and the Rise of Rush Limbaugh*. Fort Worth, TX: The Summit Group, 1993.

Zolgin, Richard. "10 Questions for Rush Limbaugh." *Time* 7 June 2004: 17.

# Charles A. Lindbergh

## Roger B. Rollin

The airplane was silver, with sleek lines. Its pilot looked like a hero: tall and slender, unruly hair, boyish good looks. An early friend said he was "the most perfect man I have ever known" (Davis 157). The first good look the American public had of both plane and pilot came after they landed at Curtiss Field, Long Island, on May 11, 1927. Photographs of these newest entrants in the race to fly from New York to Paris, taken that day, appeared on May 12 in newspapers all over the United States.

Those news photographs show the 25-year-old pilot, Charles A. Lindbergh, still in his flying gear (he had just flown from St. Louis to New York), standing somewhat uncomfortably at the nose of his airplane. Behind him we see his Ryan New York-to-Paris's (NYP) hammered aluminum spinner encasing a two-bladed duralumin propeller. Behind the prop, protruding from the engine cowling, are the business-like exposed cylinders of the mighty Wright "Whirlwind" J-5C engine, rated at 223 horsepower. It was then one of the world's most reliable aircraft engines, and it would have to be. The monoplane's name, *Spirit of St. Louis,* is also visible behind Lindbergh, emblazoned on the engine cowling. (The flyer was an airmail pilot, based at Lambert Field in St. Louis, and his financial backers were from that Missouri city.)

In the photographs, the man and the airplane almost become one. Soon, in the man's mind, as he flew over the forbidding Atlantic, he and the machine would indeed become one. After he landed in Paris, in various statements he referred to "we." Who do you mean by "we," he was asked; after all, you flew alone. What he meant, he explained to the earthborn, who had never experienced the bond that can develop between an aviator and his airplane, was he and the *Spirit of St. Louis.* He entitled the book he wrote about his epochal flight, *"We."* In a sense Lindbergh was the first "cyborg," a machine-supplemented human being.

There is no evidence that the Wright Brothers, those bicycle-shop-owning geniuses, ever felt the psychological connection with their aircraft that Lindbergh did with the *Spirit of St. Louis.* Midway through his 1953 account of his flight he writes, "Now . . . I'm taking a favor from my plane. It makes the *Spirit of St. Louis* seem more a living partner in adventure than a machine of cloth and steel" (210). Even the great World War I aces—Lufbery, Fonck, Ball, Bishop, von Richtofen, Rickenbacker—did not seem to identify with the frail, primitive aircraft that could just as easily kill them as transport them to fame and glory. But Lindbergh was of a later generation as an aviator, and the *Spirit of St. Louis* was an aircraft much advanced from those that did battle in the air in World War I. Early on, Lindbergh and the *Spirit of St. Louis* were as merged in the public mind as they were in the pilot's. He was the most famous man in the world, the Ryan NYP the most famous airplane. No one ever flew it except him. The man was the greatest hero of the young twentieth century, the plane the aircraft that had done what no other had done—fly the Atlantic and land safely, almost routinely, at its destination, Le Bourget Field, Paris.

Today, when thousands daily fly across the ocean in jet-propelled airliners, it is difficult to imagine a time when a young American and a small single-engine prop plane could become international icons for doing that very thing. But in 1927 airplanes were still relatively primitive and few of them had the fuel capacity to fly non-stop even a thousand miles, much less 3,600. Aircraft engines were far less reliable than today, the weather over the Atlantic Ocean was notoriously unreliable, and even transoceanic weather forecasting was only slightly more reliable than informed guessing.

Furthermore, good men had died trying to fly the Atlantic. In 1926 France's leading ace of the Great War, Rene Fonck, crashed on take-off in New York, and two of his crew perished. In April 1927 Navy fliers Noel David and Stanton Wooster died test-flying their huge Keystone Pathfinder, the *American Legion*. The famous aircraft designer and manufacturer Anthony Fokker crashed his own big tri-motor aircraft, injuring himself, the equally famous American hero Commander Richard E. Byrd, and renowned flyer Floyd Bennett. Another French icon of World War I, Charles Nungesser, who shot down forty-five German planes and was seventeen times wounded, set off from France for the United States on May 8, 1927, in his single-engine *L'Oiseau Blanc*, and, along with his navigator, François Coli, was never seen again. All six deceased flyers were well known and highly experienced, with serious financial backing.

By comparison, Charles Augustus Lindbergh was a kid, 25 years old but looking younger. In the great trans-Atlantic race, an underdog. He had been flying for only five years. He had been a barnstormer, one of those free spirits who flew from town to town, pasture to pasture, in World War I surplus training planes, selling rides and giving aerial exhibitions. Although he already was a skilled pilot, in 1922 he joined the United States Army Air Service and learned to fly the military way. He graduated at the top of his cadet class, but the peacetime Army had its quota of aviators and released Lindbergh from active duty. So he signed on to fly the airmail, at that time one of the most dangerous jobs in the world.

Lindbergh was no stranger to danger. In 1923 alone, eighty-five of his fellow barnstormers were killed in crashes and another 162 injured (Nevin 60). He had crashed in the middle of a small town in Texas, in a Kansas field, and in a Minnesota swamp. During a formation-flying exercise in the Army he had a mid-air collision, one of the most deadly of all airplane accidents, but managed to parachute to safety. Flying the airmail, he was twice forced to bail out of his aircraft. After his trans-Atlantic flight he would be called "Lucky Lindy," and luck he did have. But he was above all a superlative pilot and a dreamer who also happened to be a meticulous planner.

It was while he was flying his airmail route that Lindbergh began to consider going after the Orteig Prize—$25,000, a handsome sum in 1927—for flying non-stop New York to Paris or Paris to New York. (The *Spirit of St. Louis* itself would cost only a little more than $10,000, and it was designed and built especially for Lindbergh.) The Atlantic had in fact already been crossed by airplane. In 1919 two former British military fliers, John Alcock and Arthur Brown, flew a Great War twin-engine bomber from a remote meadow in Newfoundland to crash-land in an Irish bog. The two of them, in a huge military aircraft, had flown but half the distance Lindbergh, in his single-engine private plane, intended to fly alone. Alcock and Brown were hailed in England as the heroes they were, and were knighted; but they never became icons like Lindbergh. For one thing, Sir John Alcock would die in a plane crash only a half year after his historic flight, and Sir Arthur Brown would never fly again. Charles A. Lindbergh was a survivor.

The mythology of the aviator-hero usually accords to him or her an element of the daredevil, and it would take a daredevil to attempt to fly the

Charles Lindbergh standing alongside his airplane, the *Spirit of St. Louis*, 1927. Courtesy of the Library of Congress.

Atlantic alone. But Lindbergh was also efficiency itself in rounding up financial backing, in actively participating in the design and construction of the *Spirit of St. Louis*, and in planning his route of flight, from the details of navigation to the management of his plane's fuel. Before takeoff, the press labeled him "The Flying Fool"; he was, in fact, anything but.

The Lindbergh Story was a mass media dream. Against all odds, the young, good-looking aviator, after an almost sleepless night, barely lifted his overloaded plane—a flying fuel tank, a bomb waiting to explode—into air, ahead of his older, more experienced, well-heeled rivals. They staggered through the air, only laboriously gaining altitude—and to a flyer altitude is life. Heading northwest from New York he crossed his first patch of the Atlantic to hit Nova Scotia only six miles off course, a navigation error of merely 2 percent (Nevin 92). Planning! The last sighting of the *Spirit of St. Louis* in North America was over Newfoundland. The small plane disappeared over the monstrous Atlantic.

Another monster the hero must fight is sleeplessness. He had been awake for forty-eight hours, eighteen of them piloting an overloaded aircraft (Nevin 93). He would nod off, then jerk awake: sleep is death. He encountered towering clouds and the *Spirit of St. Louis* began to ice up. Ice also kills, adding weight to an aircraft and making it less controllable. Lindbergh descended to warmer air near the surface of the roiling Atlantic. He began to hallucinate, then to doubt his ability to carry on. In desperation he stuck his head out of the open window into the bracing, frigid air. Anything to stay awake!

Then, after twenty-six hours of flying, fifty-five hours without sleep, the young aviator caught a glimpse of fishing boats, the first sign of human life since Newfoundland. *Now* he was awake, alert, and when Dingle Bay, Ireland, came into view this master navigator, after flying alone the equivalent of New York to California, was only three miles off his intended course. By nightfall he had followed the River Seine to Paris, circled the illuminated Eiffel Tower, and felt his way to Le Bourget. After thirty-three and a half hours in the air, he made what he concluded was a respectable landing on the sod of that unfamiliar and largely dark airfield. Into fame. Into glory. Into history.

Tens of thousands of nearly hysterical Parisians surrounded the *Spirit of St. Louis*, seized its emerging pilot, and exuberantly passed him over their heads until he was rescued. So frantic was the moment that Lindbergh later noted he was afraid that his machine, his other self, might be "injured" (Lindbergh, *The Spirit of St. Louis* 496).

In the next few days, merely by making brief appearances and briefer speeches, young Charles Lindbergh conquered France and Belgium. The next Lindbergh conquest was England, with more honors, more medals, more accolades. Then the President of the United States sent a U.S. Navy cruiser to bring "The Lone Eagle" home. (Although Lindbergh had felt that it was "beneath the dignity" of his machine to be disassembled and shipped back to the States, it went back with him on the warship [Lindbergh, *The Spirit of St. Louis* 483]). Four and a half million New Yorkers gave him one of the biggest ticket-tape parades yet seen. President Calvin Coolidge awarded him the Medal of Honor and jumped Reserve Lieutenant Lindbergh through four Army ranks to Colonel. In the gushing prose of U.S. Ambassador to France Myron T. Herrick, reflecting the near religious hysteria of the masses, Lindbergh becomes almost Christ-like: "No flaw marked any act or word, and he stood forth amidst the clamor and the crowds the very embodiment of a fearless, kindly, cultivated American youth—unspoiled, unspoilable" (Lindbergh, "*We*" 110). "Gods," observes Kenneth S. Davis, "are created by those who worship them...created through the very act of worship; and Lindbergh, by the end of June, 1927, was worshiped" (227).

Lindbergh spawned an industry of buttons, posters, sheet music, anything that could be emblazoned with his portrait and pictures of the *Spirit of St. Louis*. Separately, jointly, theirs were the most recognizable images in the world. This iconic status was to an extent enhanced by what could be regarded as Lindbergh's self-promotion. By popular demand and with the backing of the Guggenheim Foundation, he exhibited the *Spirit of St. Louis*—and himself—in all of the forty-eight states. Inevitably, wherever he landed he was cheered by hero-worshiping throngs, but he hobnobbed chiefly with the rich and powerful. He stayed in the news, and in the newsreels, with goodwill flights to Mexico and Latin America, with his public promotions of the struggling airline industry, and by allowing the forerunner of Trans-World Airlines to call itself "The Lindbergh Line." Hollywood, naturally offered him stardom—which the hero rejected (Telotte 71).

A myth, in the truest sense of that term, is a kind of public dream, expressing fundamental human aspirations and fundamental human fears. In Lindbergh and the *Spirit of St. Louis* the Dream of Flight, of achieving transcendence of the earthly; the Dream of Technology, of achieving transcendence of human limitations; and the universal Dream of the Hero, of achieving personal perfection; all met. In time it would seem that the burden of those dreams, of incarnating an American myth, would become too much for the man to bear.

To complete the myth-cycle of the Hero, the son of a maverick U.S. congressman meets the Lady, a daughter of the U.S. Ambassador to Mexico. Anne Morrow was gifted, shy, and pretty. The gifted, shy, handsome flyer, who heretofore had had no recorded romantic relationships—though American womanhood swooned at the sight of him—quietly married her less than two years after they met. To the media it was nothing less than a royal wedding: "The Eagle Meets his Mate;" "Anne Morrow Makes It 'We Three.'"

But the Lady was also thoroughly modern: Anne learned to operate a radio, to navigate, and earned a pilot's license. She accompanied her husband on a widely publicized flight to Central America. Then, on her twenty-fourth birthday, Anne bore Charles Augustus Lindbergh, Jr. This joyous event would, in less than two years, begin to transform the Romance of the Lone Eagle into the Tragedy of Charles A. Lindbergh. When the baby was under two years old, he was kidnaped and subsequently murdered. Both events, of

Charles Lindbergh on a podium on the Washington Monument grounds during his reception in Washington, D.C. Courtesy of the Library of Congress.

course, made international headlines, as did the arrest, trial, and execution of the man accused of the terrible crimes, Bruno Richard Hauptman.

The relentless attention that had focused upon Lindbergh led over the years to his increasing alienation from the very media that had transformed him into an American icon. The death of his child and its aftermath were the final straws. With bitterness, the Lindberghs left their country to live in seclusion in England. Nonetheless, Lindbergh subsequently accepted an invitation to visit Germany, where he and Anne consorted with the Nazi high and mighty. Unbeknownst to the public, a part of which was uncomfortable with Lindbergh's lending his prestige to the Third Reich, his inspections of German aircraft factories and Luftwaffe bases on this and later trips resulted in intelligence reports he made to the U.S. government, including the Chief of the Army Air Corps, Major General H. H. Arnold.

Unfortunately, so impressed was Lindbergh by the progress of German aviation, which was then producing the most technologically advanced aircraft in the world, that he began to feel that the Nazis were unstoppable. He concluded that the United States should stay clear of the oncoming war in Europe and began to make isolationist statements in public appearances and on the radio. He seemed oblivious to the viciousness of Nazi Germany and its Japanese allies. Blatant racism and anti-Semitism, shocking even for the 1930s, pervaded his speeches and publications.

It is "The End of the Hero" (Davis 383ff.). At a time when President Roosevelt was risking his presidency to aid France and Britain, Lindbergh's indifference to fascist aggression and tyranny appalled many. Disenchantment with "The Lone Eagle" grew, then rapidly increased when he enlisted in the "America First" movement, a coalition of isolationists and pro-Nazis. Even when his country was attacked at Pearl Harbor by the Japanese and declared war upon by Hitler, Lindbergh did not repudiate his pro-Axis statements—and never would, seemingly retaining an "invincible confidence in his own rectitude and infallibility" (*The American Experience* 13). To historian Arthur Schlesinger, "he was a man who very much misconceived the nature of the great struggle of the 20th century, [that] between democracy and totalitarianism" (*The American Experience* 1).

Yet Lindbergh did attempt to join the war effort. President Roosevelt personally quashed that. Finally Lindbergh did manage to wangle a position as "civilian aviation consultant" and headed for the war in the South Pacific. Before that war would be over he would—quite illegally and at an advanced age for fighter pilots—fly on fifty combat missions and shoot down Japanese aircraft in dogfights. More importantly, the expert in transoceanic flight instructed pilots half his age how to manage their aircrafts' fuel and thus increase the range of their combat operations by five hundred miles—an enormously significant contribution to the war effort. He cannot help but be the Hero.

All of this, however, was top secret. As far as the general public was concerned, the greatest American icon of the first third of the century had disappeared into well-deserved oblivion. Eventually, though, his past obtuse arrogance began to fade in the public memory. President Eisenhower promoted the aging Colonel Lindbergh to Brigadier General in the U.S. Air Force Reserve. Then Lindbergh was awarded the Pulitzer Prize for his magnificent account of the flight, *The Spirit of St. Louis*. A movie of the same title was released in 1957, on the thirtieth anniversary of the mythic flight. It starred one of Hollywood's most popular actors, Jimmy Stewart, himself a real-life pilot-hero who flew bombing missions over Europe in World War II. It is also, arguably, the best aviation movie ever made. Though a critical success, it was a box office failure. Although the Lone Eagle had been publicly rehabilitated he was, it seems, to the public no longer an icon. Icons command attention, and the attention that Lindbergh had both sought and shunned was no longer accorded to him.

He became an avid proponent of conservation and moved his family to Hawaii. It was in Maui that Lindbergh spent his final days, dying of cancer on August 26, 1974. In accordance with his explicit instructions, only a few hours after his death his body was garbed in work clothes, wrapped in an old blanket, laid in a plain wooden coffin, and put into the earth.

The grave of Charles A. Lindbergh is obscure, but his *Spirit of St. Louis* to this day hangs in a place of honor in the world's most visited museum, the National Air and Space Museum in Washington, D.C. It is viewed daily by thousands of people. Some of them know the Lindbergh story; a few of them may think of it as the Lindbergh tragedy. The silver monoplane's pilot may be gone and largely forgotten, but the *Spirit of St. Louis*, the most famous airplane of all time, is very much with us, suspended from the great museum's ceiling as if it were still flying, as if it were still "we."

## WORKS CITED AND RECOMMENDED

*The American Experience: Lindbergh*. Public Broadcasting System. Enhanced transcript produced for PBS Online by WGBH (Boston), 1999 http://www.pbs.org/wgbh/amex/lindbergh.

Berg, A. Scott. *Lindbergh*. New York: Putnam's, 1998.

Davis, Kenneth S. *The Hero: Charles A. Lindbergh and the American Dream*. Garden City, NY: Doubleday & Company, 1959.

Grant, R. G. *Flight: 100 Years of Aviation*. New York: DK Publishing, 2002.

Lindbergh, Charles A. *The Spirit of St. Louis*. New York: Charles Scribner's Sons, 1953.

———. *"We."* New York: G. P. Putnam's Sons, 1927.

Nevin, David. *The Pathfinders*. Alexandria, VA: Time-Life Books, 1980.

Telotte, J. P. "Lindbergh, Film, and Machine Age Dreams." *South Atlantic Review* 64.4 (1999): 68–83.

# List

## Dennis Hall

The word "listomania" entered my mind, without my consciously having heard or read the expression before, as a result of the work Susan Grove Hall and I have done on American icons. We became acutely aware of the power and resonance of lists as we struggled to develop a list of over a hundred icons to be included in this collection. People we discussed the list with quickly moved from the indicative to the imperative mode; our list invariably generated not only conversation but sometimes heated argument, revealing gender and generation differences, among many other cultural investments. While we talked about icons a great deal, we tried to avoid discussing the lists of them with our fellow iconomaniacs.

But I suppose that deep down I knew "listomania" must have been circulating "out there" for a long time and not in punning allusion to the nineteenth-century popular passion for Franz Liszt or Ken Russell's 1975 flop on the same theme. You see, I still own and have often perused, if not exactly read, both editions of the immensely popular *People's Almanac* (1975, 1978), and the twenty-fourth chapter of each edition is devoted to lists. Moreover, I seemed to have forgotten that David Wallenchinsky, Irving Wallace, and Amy Wallace, in both editions of the also very popular *Book of Lists* (1977, 1980) freely use the terms "listomania" and "listomaniacs" to describe the abiding interest, if not a consuming passion, that they share with all but the most passive of human kind. As H. Allen Smith (in Wallenchinsky et al., *Book of Lists* xvii), Louis Menand—citing Aristotle or was it Parmenides? (in *The New Yorker*)—and others have pointed out, the human being is less accurately defined as an animal capable of reason or able to use language or given to laughter than as a list-making animal, a creature apparently incapable of survival without making lists of one kind or another.

Indeed, lists are everywhere to be found, not only in the many books of lists (David Wallechnisky is not alone in the economic exploitation of this human propensity) but also from the poetic catalogs of Walt Whitman to the comic routines of David Letterman's "Top Ten" lists (and its many predecessors and imitators) to the top ten lists that flood the press at New Year's to the "all time" lists of the top 25 or top 100 or top 1,000 movies, books, plays, record albums, celebrities, best- and worst-dressed people, children's names, roses, breeds of dogs, and the like which periodically feed a voracious popular press. Moreover, the World Wide Web has fueled this human passion for lists with an unprecedented technical leverage and democratic spirit. "Catalist," for example, is a Web site list of Listserv lists. One may find several lists of phobias—hundreds of them from ablutophobia to zoophobia. The Web has transformed the "who's who" phenomenon from a relatively narrow interest within distinct professional groups into what we now call "networking," with someone offering lists of people involved in every industry and occupation, diversion, and perversion known to humankind. Virtually every specialized periodical from *Accounting Today* to *World Trade Magazine* publishes a list of the 10 or 50 or 100 of the most powerful or most influential or "best" or "top" or "important" people in its realm of interest. At a recent Popular Culture Association convention, a heavily attended session focused on each speaker's list of the best A western movies ever, the best B westerns, and the best TV westerns; the session generated more discussion and dissension than any other I attended at the meeting. Some of us are old enough to recall seeing on TV Joseph McCarthy holding up a piece of paper and declaring that he had in hand a list of known communists working in the government or to recall Richard Nixon's enemies list. I remember seeing (and exactly what it looked like is seared into my mind's eye) the National Legion of Decency's list of current movies posted on the bulletin boards of my Catholic grade and high schools, with the list of "condemned" movies providing sure-fire recommendations.

My desk and yours are crowded with lists of "things to do." Many, perhaps most of us, at least enter the grocery store with a list, make packing lists for trips, compile Christmas lists, maintain lists of birthdays and anniversaries to remember. Cathy Guisewite's comic strip "Cathy"—particularly its run up to the title character's recent wedding—could not function without play on lists and list-making. Some of us, after the precedent of George Washington or Jay Gatsby or Mother Theresa, may even make lists of things we ought and ought not to do. Many of us suffer under the direction of such lists, while making others suffer under the direction of lists we impose. Nothing good or bad or important is without its list; nothing indifferent, however, warrants a list. No human activity or interest or fear or desire of any significance is without its list in the household, the interest group, the workplace, the neighborhood, the political party, the country, or beyond.

The entries for "list" in an unabridged dictionary (nine in *Webster's Third International*) provide better dictionary reading than do most words, as we make our way through such earlier but related senses of the word as *to gratify* and *inclination*, *to pay attention*, *edge*, and *border*, and *field of competition* before getting to such more familiar senses of the word as *roster*, *index* or *catalog*, *to enumerate*, *to categorize* or *classify*, or *to declare to be*.

It may be objected, of course, that a list is not sufficiently visual to be a genuine "icon," that it remains too abstract, is not sufficiently concrete, is too much a verbal and mental construct to keep company with such human icons as George Armstrong Custer, Marilyn Monroe, or Babe Ruth, or Elvis Presley or with such artistically created icons as Whistler's Mother or Micky Mouse or Rosie the Riveter—with which we are more familiar and comfortable—or even with such iconic things as the Golden Gate Bridge, or the Hershey bar, or the Ford Mustang.

But we all do know what a list looks like, recognize it as a visual object. We recognize its fundamentally vertical rather than horizontal character, its pattern reflecting a paradigmatic rather than syntagmatic construct. The success of Microsoft's PowerPoint program, I am convinced, is owing in large measure to the ease with which it allows the visual presentation of a wide variety of "bulleted" lists and so legitimates the avoidance of syntactical structures (see Tufte).

Clearly, all icons are not created equal; some are more powerful, more salient, doing more cultural work than others, and often doing a different kind of cultural work. But the list, *qua* list, for all of its individual variation, I want to argue, rises to the level of popular culture icon, standing many, if not all, such tests of popular iconography as these: surviving change over time, stimulating use in ritual behavior, embracing contradictions, triggering memory and nostalgia, reflecting generational differences, prompting disagreement about meaning, and, perhaps most importantly, exhibiting rich metonymic resonance—that is, embodying associated ideas that allow a list, simply by virtue of its being a list, to deliver meanings into the contexts in which it appears, meanings beyond the simple utilitarian functions of a roster or an enumeration of items. The list delivers meaning quite apart from what it nominally contains.

The list, of course, has a long history, from the Code of Hammurabi and the Ten Commandments to the Anglo-Saxon Chronicle, the genealogies of royals and commoners to the lists of the celebrated and the damned, ancient and contemporary. There are significant pleasures in these simple texts. Lists mediate between the abstractions of law, history, family, and fame and the concrete particulars of adultery, Black Death, King Henry, and William Shakespeare or the names on the Vietnam memorial wall, and the names and faces on the playing cards that circulated among soldiers in Iraq. This play between the abstract and the concrete is reflected in some of the common associations, teaming with contradictions, that any list bears: authority, definition, hierarchy, description and prescription, order and direction, among I suspect others.

The list suggests authority. The makers of lists either legitimately possess the authority to do so or assume the authority to do so. Parents, for example, have the authority to make a list of prohibited behaviors for their small children, but a brother will view his sister's making such a list as a usurpation of power. And lists also confer authority, as when we make the honor roll or the promotion list or appear in the organizational chart. Or they deny it, as when we do not. Some lists, of course, specifically condemn, as do the annual tax delinquency rolls or the lists of America's most wanted criminals or the lists in fashion magazines (invariably photo-illustrated) of notorious fashion victims. Not to make some lists can be both a pleasure and an achievement. Indeed, the resonance of authority in a list is sufficiently great that it tends to shift the burden of proof from the maker of the list to the challenger of the list itself or of an item on the list. The list of prohibited items of dress in a high school, for but one example, may set students to objecting to not being allowed to wear rags or baggy trousers or low rise jeans and so allowing the whole question of a school dress code to be begged. So too, a bulleted list of twelve outcomes measures for English majors—or neighborhood beautification or city recycling or air pollution control or responsible stock investment—very often inverts the axiom that they who assert must prove, shifting the burden to those who object. Hence the affection for lists among the powerful.

But this very authoritative quality includes, in good Derridian fashion I suppose, the very seeds of its own displacement. The number of elaborate jokes that depend upon the rhetoric of the list, as is clear to readers of Jonathan Swift and of the humor pages on the Web, is legion. Undermining these associations of authority is in large part responsible for the success of Letterman's Top Ten list routine. There is something subversive about presenting a list of ludicrous causes or effects or characteristics with such authoritative fanfare. The power and authority of the list is, at least in current practice, unstable; it is very often kept in play.

Lists define far more effectively, if not more efficiently, than do manipulations of genus and specific difference and accounts of typical characteristics. An enumerative definition seems to be the real thing, while a genus and species definition feels like an escape we make when we are overwhelmed by too many things to count. The gratifications of something solid and affirming in lists, no amount of abstract taxonomy can replace. I count the people in my tribe, my friends and enemies; I can only hope to define by characteristics the citizens of my nation, or those likely to be my friends or enemies. Richard Nixon found comfort in an enemies list, not in an understanding of the characteristics of his enemies. The primitive satisfactions of lists defy philosophy, which may help to account for their ubiquity in American popular culture. Such lists, of course, do not so much define realities as present alternative realities, and they expose many, perhaps all of us, to the tender mercies of the growing profusion of lists.

Related to this defining quality is the list's capacity to establish the existence, the sense, as the *Third Unabridged Dictionary* puts it, of list as *to declare to be*, the list as creating word. "Let there be light" in Genesis is the first item in a not terribly long but crucial list. When people, places, and things have been listed, they and the categories to which they belong are culturally constructed. A place on the roster of the church or club or team or school or corporation or professional association goes a very long way toward establishing one's identity, one's reality. To have one's name stricken from the Book of Life is to cease to exist. But this central principle also motivates the profusion of lists, at least in American culture. There is a list somewhere for everyone. They are like T-ball trophies or university service awards or entertainment industry honors; anyone can get on a list; some people get on them even as they try to avoid them.

One's place within lists points to the nearly inescapable association of lists with hierarchies and values. Lists, a lot like modern dictionaries, are both descriptive and prescriptive constructs. Often a list purports only to describe what exists, to provide an enumeration of reality; but no sooner than it appears, the list is taken as prescription, used to construct reality and evaluate it. Hard upon the concern about even being on a list follows the anxiety about place on a list. Whether one is concerned about one's self or children or friends or one's favorite movie star or saint or cultivar or baseball team or brand of beer or college or university or contestant for Miss America or any of the innumerable possibilities—place on a list is important, a matter of value and, as a consequence, a matter of contention. The more arbitrary the criteria for placement on a list, it seems, the more intense the struggle for place. The less arbitrary the criteria, the greater the claims that they are capricious by the lowly placed or (shudder) the displaced. Lists seem to have an axiological imperative all their own. Indeed, so great is the power of a list to impose hierarchies of value that we explicitly go to extreme lengths to impose order of appearance or alphabetical order or some other principle of organization upon lists in order to avoid such judgements. The effort is to no avail, for the Cole Porter Principle prevails: if "You're The Top," you are the best no matter what principle put you at the top.

Here again, the proliferation of lists undercuts this association. If one does not like one's place in a list, then one may with relative ease create a new list in a new category; the situation is like the ubiquitous characterizations of bridges or mountains or buildings; everyone of them seems to be at or near the top of a list of longest or highest or biggest of its kind or circumstance: "This bridge is the second longest suspension structure east of the Mississippi, constructed of steel made of scrap iron."

Lists can deliver order and direction, as many can attest who resort to lists of things to do in a particularly confusing week or use checklists to assure that important routines are met. A list can provide for one's self and for others a sense of an ending and a basis for evaluation. A list can be a powerful stimulus to dialogue and reflection, alone or in the company of others. And lists I think—at least those self-created ones—are predominantly a middle-class passion, for the very poor with little or no control over their environments and the very rich with a great deal if not total control, have relatively less need of lists, as of other kinds of assurance and insurance. The vast middle of America employs lists in an effort to control self and, to the degree possible, environment, and thus engages the list as an agent of self-definition, of identity formation. The penchant for lists is exhibited by Robinson Crusoe and Moll Flanders, by George Washington and Jay Gatsby and Bill Clinton in their youth, in the Boy Scout handbooks and in the whole range of self-help literature from Charles Atlas and Norman Vincent Peale to Alex Comfort and the latest accounts of the five, ten, fifteen, or twenty-five habits of successful people. These lists, however, tend to define what is valued more clearly than to explain how to achieve it; they have their eye more clearly focused on prizes than on processes, all their claims to the contrary notwithstanding.

The American passion for instrumental knowledge, the sheer bulk of "how to" discourse, particularly in American popular culture, collapses enumerations of what counts for pleasure or success or happiness or influence or whatever end is desired, into an undifferentiated mass. Too many lists, of course, can create disorder and misdirection, as those many people who spend more time on making lists of things to do than on getting things done can attest. All the paraphernalia that attends getting and being organized often enriches Office Depot and Staples at the expense of one's control of self and environment. The resort to simplistic lists of steps in many, perhaps most, self-help books, is often a sign of indeterminancy, if not confusion.

Lists, I submit, are a kind of intellectual comfort food. We enjoy lists because we associate them with agents of direction and environmental control, authority, definition, clear value, and the like dispositions that Americans continue to hold in high esteem. But lists provide the pleasures of taxonomy and axiology without many—in some cases any—of the demands of rigorous analysis, whether we make and use our own lists or employ the lists of others, whether these lists attend to the trivial or the profound. Lists, particularly in their popular manifestations, are very often masks, convenient and satisfying substitutes for those very dispositions and disciplines we admire.

Lists also tend to oversimplify likeness and difference in an interesting way. Lists emphasize likeness and overlook difference within their own boundaries, and tend to overlook likeness and emphasize difference outside their boundaries. To be on a ten best (or worst) dressed list—or a list of the town's outstanding volunteer workers or the state's most wanted criminals, or a list of the top 100 albums of the decade or the twenty-five worst shows in the history of television or the university's list of the ten best teachers or the student government association's list of the ten worst teachers—foregrounds quantitative likenesses and backgrounds, and often even erases qualitative differences. Lists appear to fix the flux, and as a consequence are, in many respects, a modern rather than a postmodern tick; and I think the current passion for them is yet another in the long (dare I say) list of modernist responses to postmodernism.

Ironically, however, a proliferation of lists contributes to the very instability of meaning that this impulse seeks to counteract, and so contributes to the condition of postmodernity. Lists traffic in associations of security that are in high demand in a climate of intellectual and political insecurity. To employ distinctions John Cawelti applies to popular artifacts, lists are more formula than form, more conventional than inventional, more reassuring than challenging ("Concept of Formula"). That said, their profusion contributes to the climate of cultural insecurity.

Function as a mediating device is, I think, central to understanding all icons, and is the source of their resonance. Lists, as do all icons, perform their mediating function because they foreground the material; in this case, that typographical, vertically formatted, roster of nouns or phrases or sometimes even whole sentences. Moreover, lists, despite their being made up of words, perform much, perhaps most, of their work in a way more like the non-verbal functions of icons than the symbolic functions of language; that is, they attempt to forge relationships and understandings that cannot be expressed adequately in the conventions controlled by syntax. They seek a resonance of association—inclusion or exclusion, degrees of proximity and remoteness, likeness inside a category and difference outside of a category—that either cannot be expressed in the acts of predication that syntax demands, or cannot as adroitly or efficiently be expressed in syntax. This characteristic may account for the intense interest in icons in contemporary American culture, as it grows increasingly disaffected with niceties of conventional language, especially predication.

The list, then, I take to be a cultural space for play, and in play, a venue that is not entirely free of language but does not fully engage language. To put the point in other terms, lists engage the uses and gratifications of language in a sufficiently satisfying way, without entangling either the list maker or the list consumer in the complexities or personal, intellectual, or cultural demands of a fuller exercise of language.

The list, I submit, is a cultural venue especially suited for the exploration, for the reaffirmation, and for the destruction of relationships. While differences in degree, of course, may be very great, lists are in kind paradigmatic in their function; that is, they put existing relationships, the realm of the syntagmatic, into play and present the maker of the list and the consumer of the list with a structure of possible relationships, the realm of the paradigmatic. The list allows, even compels, one to explore possible utterances, possible stories, possible lives, possible identities, even multiple identities. Any list, for all of its associations of authority and definition, is open to challenge by an alternative list, by the relatively simple and widely accessible means of inclusion and exclusion. Relatively simple, that is, compared to exercises of syntax.

The list is a signally loose cultural artifact, despite all of its "modernist" associations of determination, definition, and authority. By virtue of its profusion, it helps to sustain "postmodernism." Once remarkably unified in its meanings and associations, the list has slipped into the very condition of postmodernity that many felt resort to the list might resist. Moreover, the list has become fragmented and contingent, pointing less to structures of actual meaning, to fixed relationships, or to determinations, than to structures of possible meanings, to sets of contingencies, to indeterminations.

Every person is now his or her own maker of lists, participant in the struggle for authority and determination in the culture. While this democratization of list-making is not the equivalent of the Gutenberg revolution, it is akin to it. The list, like so very many popular icons, materially signs the schizophrenia of the postmodern condition.

## WORKS CITED AND RECOMMENDED

"CataList: The Official Catalog of Listserv lists." 13 Sept. 2004 <http://www.lsoft.com/catalist.html>.
Cawelti, John. "The Concept of Formula in Popular Literature." *Journal of Popular Culture* 3.3 (Winter 1969): 381–90. Rpt. in *Popular Fiction: An Anthology*. Ed. Gary Hoppenstand. New York: Longman, 1998. 730–36.
Menand, Louis. "Best of the 'Best'." *The New Yorker* 1 Jan. 2004. Posted online 5 Jan. 2004.
Tufte, Edward R. *The Cognitive Style of PowerPoint*. Cheshire, CT: Graphics Press, 2003 [1–27].
Wallechinsky, David, and Irving Wallace. *The People's Almanac*. New York: Doubleday, 1975.
———. *The People's Almanac #2*. New York: Bantam Books, 1978.
Wallechinsky, David, Irving Wallace, and Amy Wallace. *The Book of Lists*. New York: William Morrow, 1977.
Wallechinsky, David, Irving Wallace, Amy Wallace, and Sylvia Wallace. *The Book of Lists #2*. New York: William Morrow, 1980.

# Log Cabin

## *William J. Badley with Linda Badley*

In the mid-1970s, I (or, rather, we) built a log cabin near Bouchette, Quebec, about two hours north of Ottawa, Ontario. At the time a resident of Louisville, Kentucky, I had been in Ottawa visiting a former college friend I had helped desert from the U.S. Army during the Vietnam War in 1969. As he was interested in buying property as a way to gain "landed immigrant" status, we went camping in Quebec to inspect a lot for sale that a Canadian friend had told him about. Like many American males in their twenties, I felt confronted with the alternatives of staying in the United States (with a good probability of ending up in Vietnam) or to going to Canada. Buying land in Canada offered a "backup" position.

Land in Quebec was cheap, with few strings attached. The two lots, with roughly 140 feet of shoreline and 150 feet to the back, were $999.00 each or U.S.$2,000 (which I paid in monthly installments, without interest), there being at the time no objection to Americans buying land. For a graduate student with virtually no savings, the deal seemed miraculous, and I put money down on two lots on a narrow, stony peninsula densely overgrown with spindly trees and surrounded by Lac Rond (Roddick Lake). I was, in the words of Canned Heat, "Goin' Up the Country," an American dream that (paradoxically) included leaving the United States behind. The dream blended a righteous civil disobedience with a fantasy of self-sufficient "living off the land," a combination that couldn't have been more stereotypically American. As for phrases like "getting back to the basics," which we used unblushingly in those days, what we meant was modeled on Thoreau's decision "to front only the essential facts of life" (2, par. 16). To me as an American living in downtown Louisville, as for many of my generation (and as for Thoreau) the land represented a garden that had been promised and long since lost.

Living in the woods, as I realized at the time, had emotional ties to the pilgrimages of my own childhood. My family left the sweltering July heat of Oklahoma City and drove to Alexandria, Minnesota, for a two- or three-week vacation in crude two-room cabins on Lake Victoria. The journey always seemed like moving from the desert to a land of tree-covered estates.

# LOG CABIN

Even more so the log cabin, our eventual summer homestead, was a nostalgic gesture and a quintessentially American dream. Soon after my wife, in-laws, and I began making summer camping pilgrimages, we discovered two hand-hewn log cabins, one completed, nestled among the pine trees on the picturesquely rocky point of the peninsula, and the foundation of the other started in the lot next to ours. These structures led us to young Canadians on "our" peninsula who shared our ideals, and offered their skills and knowledge as well. The fellow who had completed his cabin led me to the man who had sold him his logs, a local French-Canadian farmer named Floribert Bastien, a man of the nineteenth-century values of frugality and personal trust, values that America had once laid claim to. Monsieur Bastien spoke as little English as I did French but agreed to cut logs in the fall, debark them for seasoning, and deliver them to the worksite. When I told him that I had no money but would be paid for teaching in the fall, he said, "Send it at Christmas; I'll need it then." We shook hands, and it happened.

Just as our log cabin was not strictly speaking "American," Thoreau's on Walden Pond was not, strictly speaking, made of logs. But, with the legendary borrowed ax, it was rough cut and hand-hued from "arrowy white pines" on the pond for joists, studs, and rafters and "shanty" wood that Thoreau bought for $4.25: "the walls being of rough, weather-stained boards, with wide chinks, which made it cool at night." Even so, it seemed ethereal, even Olympian: "To my imagination it retained throughout the day more or less of this auroral character, reminding me of a certain house on a mountain which I had visited a year before. This was an airy and unplastered cabin, fit to entertain a travelling god, and where a goddess might trail her garments" (2, par. 8).

Thoreau moved into his cabin on "Independence Day, or the Fourth of July, 1845" (2, par. 8). I started building mine in the bicentennial year of 1976. I ordered 120 logs of poplar, red pine, white pine, and oak: sixty for the side walls to measure eighteen feet on the interior and sixty logs for the front and back to measure fifteen feet on the interior. These plus the sill logs, purlins, ridge pole, and planed lumber for the floors, purchased at a rural sawmill, cost about $2,400. Other "incidentals" included twenty bags of cement, nine Sona tubes that were twenty inches in diameter, nine-inch and twelve-inch spikes, a load of sand, a fifty-gallon drum of water, and two books on building log cabins. As Thoreau borrowed an ax, we borrowed a cement-mixing box (metal sheet on the bottom, surrounded by two- by-eight-inch wood). Because we had no electricity, all of the nine Sona tubes were filled with hand-mixed concrete, from bedrock to heights of two inches to six feet. Our tools included a Craftsman twelve-inch chain saw (the piston had to be replaced), an ax, two hammers, two compasses, a cement hoe, a fifteen-inch bow saw, a carpenter's crosscut saw, a level, a plumb bob, a lantern, and a propane camping cook stove with two burners.

Thoreau says that "If you have built castles in the air, your work need not be lost; that is where they should be. Now put the foundations under them"

(18, par. 5). M. Bastien and I built a "castle in the air" with our handshake, and the foundation began with the back-breaking job of mixing cement. The nine pillars on which the cabin now proudly sits had little in common with T. E. Lawrence's *Seven Pillars of Wisdom*. As a matter of fact, the wisdom learned was that large rocks can be used to partially push into wet cement so that it can "tie" this portion with the next day's cement. Other wisdom learned was that wetting the rocks for the cement leads to separated finger flesh when skin oil is leeched out, that hand mixing cement changes the arms and upper body, and that touching logs after two weeks in cement and sand is like being reborn because it is touching something that was once alive.

From the earliest times, trees have been sacred and mysterious. The process of working with the logs—that is, building the cabin itself—had a noble simplicity as well as a good amount of tedium. For the basic design, we referred to the Lincoln Logs we had played with as children and stacked matches to simulate the process. Because M. Bastien delivered the logs to the top of the hill, the logs had to be hauled to the working site, about one hundred yards. At peak periods, "we" included five or six men and women who hoisted the logs in concert between our legs, lifting and pushing them down to the site a yard at a time. After getting the sill logs and subfloor down, the process of notching and placing the logs began. Using a compass to measure the depth of the log on which the new log would sit and then to draw a semicircle on each side of the log to be cut, we made five "watermelon" cuts across the log. Then we used an axe to knock out the slices of wood. Then came the process of setting the log on the one below. Because each log was different, we had to flip it several times, using the chain saw and axe to "flatten" and match the sides of both logs. Once the logs were sufficiently close to each other, after sealing the notch with oakum (étoupe), we reset the logs, and drove a twelve-inch spike down each corner to hold the joint. This process went on for the sixty-six logs, each one treated individually as if still a living thing. The positive side was that when we made mistakes, we could fix or "hide" them; the logs were forgiving of our lack of knowledge.

Thus we did not worry about exceedingly fine details, as working with logs meant accommodating their natural shapes, and we extended the principle to trees on the land, which we worked around rather than cut down. Instead of cement, we chinked the logs with oakum, a far more provisional substance. The windows were discards obtained from local farmers and shop dealers, usually after extensive negotiations, and therefore of different sizes, shapes, and conditions. Bestowing windows on the cabin meant remaking it to fit them. Eventually it sported a large front deck and a nine-foot dormer that turned the sleeping loft into something resembling a second floor.

This monument to self-sufficiency invariably became, at several crucial points, a cooperative process much like the community barn raisings of prairie settlers. Friends from the United States and several like-minded local Anglophone and French Canadians, some of whom had bought a farm collectively, worked to raise the rafters and put on the roof and to celebrate afterwards. In fact, as it took shape, in this meticulously planned yet invariably haphazard fashion, our cabin, like Thoreau's, gave material form to several contradictions at the heart of American values. It was the culmination of our dream of "getting back to nature," yet its fundamental purpose was to protect us from the elements. (And so, while we scorned the amenities at first, as it grew it accommodated a second floor, larger families, electricity, a hot shower, and a flush toilet.) It represented freedom from traditional restraints and requirements while remaining a symbol of traditional values. As something we had made with our hands and that, as we often remarked in awestruck voices, would probably (barring fires, floods, and Armageddon) outlast us all, it was a symbol of permanence. Yet it was a shelter raised quickly from available natural resources that were destined to be destroyed. It was built in opposition to all the values associated with American capitalism, and yet the simplicity of construction that made it a monument to the "do-it-yourself" ethos and American ingenuity also made it infinitely capable of rapid and rabidly patriotic mass production. We wanted Walden too, and reproduced it in our fashion—and so, as we have subsequently found, has everybody else.

In today's culture, the log cabin similarly includes nostalgia for simplicity and tradition while cultivating equally the desire for affluence intrinsic to a consumer culture. The "log home" that preserves and projects "traditional values" forward (and therefore expands exponentially outward) for the next generation is featured in ads in every medium. Thus, in a culture that is continuously in hyperdrive for change, the American log cabin is associated with conservation—with stability; continuity of past, present, and future; and the "real" as opposed to the "plasticity" of manufactured, modern culture. At the same time, it represents the opposite of such values, belonging perhaps more accurately with Thoreau's advocated practice of traveling light and burning or "busk[ing]" some possessions as was the custom of the Mucclasse Indians (1-E, par. 4). This is another side of American tradition—the cut-trees-plant-crops-leach-the-land-and-leave-for-more-land mentality. It can be seen in razing any building that stands in the way of progress and can be seen in the symbolic destruction of cities in American cinema (*Independence Day* and natural-disaster flicks like *The Day after Tomorrow*).

While sold nationally and internationally for their association with American frontier and traditional values and permanence, most of today's log homes are "vastly different" from those of yesteryear. Eric Fulton, communications manager of the Log Homes Council, the national organization of log home manufacturers and part of the National Association of Home Builders, notes that "When log homes were first built, they were generally one or two rooms...stripped by hand...finished as best they could and filled with chinking" (qtd. in Xiong, F3). Today they tend to be large, often two or three story "estates" with great rooms, large windows, and even indoor swimming pools.

These "dream homes," which "you" design, are almost invariably (according to the ads) constructed from prefabricated "kits." Conversely, most

A modern-day log cabin provides an alternative to traditional houses. Courtesy of Shutterstock.

home building kits are log cabins. After a few solar and other manufactured home kit sites, Google finds under "home kits" Web site after Web site advertising log or "timber" homes. Kits pretend to combine the American ideals of consumerism and freedom of choice with self-reliant do-it-yourself-ism in that one selects and seemingly designs one's dream home from the ground up—if usually without lifting a finger. Despite their obvious mass production—the logs come from manufacturers pre-cut, numbered, and ready to be assembled—most log home kits are advertised as American "originals." For a conspicuous example, the Original Lincoln Logs, Ltd.: Authentic American Homes site advertises two "systems." The "Classic Solid Timber" homes offer a choice of several packages of bleached, uniform, and uniformly notched logs and a choice of several wood "species" of pine and cedar; the "Thermo-Home Panelized Wall System" on the other hand offers the "beauty of a log home *and* the unlimited finish options of a conventionally framed home" by attaching a log facade to the outside of a traditionally framed home. The latter is touted: "Best of all, this building system is delivered partially constructed. This means that [as in the days of community roof raising] building is fast and easy" (The Original Lincoln Logs, Ltd.).

In the above instance, these modern, mass produced versions of the do-it-yourself (or communal) simplicity that made the log cabin a natural in the first place are opulent adult variations on one of childhood's great pleasures. True, Original Lincoln Logs, Ltd., have taken both name and concept from "Honest Abe" Lincoln, the president most often identified as being born in a log cabin—in fact, their "frequently asked questions" feature is labeled "Ask Abe." But boasting a history far longer than Original Ltd., and obviously their true source of inspiration, are the "Classic Since 1916!" children's toy sets with the same "Original Lincoln Logs" name. Emphasizing their "Real Wooden Logs," their home page features commemorative models such as the "Conestoga Homestead" set that promises: "Rediscover the Wild West…. Enjoy hours of creative fun building a homestead, a covered wagon and settling on the new frontier!" ("Nostalgia: Collectors' Sets"). Tabs prominently displayed at the top of the page advertise two distinct types: the "Nostalgia" models, which feature the "rich, deep color," rugged look, and all-wooden parts that "Mom's" generation would want to share, and the "Classic" models, which offer smooth-textured, light tan logs and a large variety of plastic parts that allow one to provide the same sorts of amenities as modern adult "kits" afford.

Emblazoned on yet another homepage claiming to be "The Original Log Cabin Homes" are the words: "Adventure, Dream, Imagine, Spirit." The hot button "An American Original" pronounces log-home living "an intensely personal experience." Thanks to "computer-assisted design and manufacture," one can return to nature and have the comforts afforded in modern "estate" homes, "Designing the Dream" assures. The site's boasted commercials for Log Cabin Homes are on three television programs: *Outdoor Moments*, *The American Outdoorsman*, and *Best of America By Horseback*.

Abraham Lincoln's log cabin. Courtesy of the Library of Congress.

The advertisements' range exemplifies crosscurrents of television, Internet, and magazine publishing, with some publishers printing several log cabin magazines sold at Lowe's and other hardware stores, and supermarkets. But the big news is that TV star "Grizzly Adams" Dan Haggerty has joined the Log Cabin Homes, Ltd., Team as its "international" spokesman: "We're excited about Dan joining our team. His portrayal of Grizzly Adams truly depicts the lifestyle of Americana that we desire for our worldwide marketing and sales efforts" ("Trump Elegance Inspires Grizzly Adams").

A *Grizzly Adams* wilderness cabin lifestyle can also be purchased through Bison Log Cabin RV/Park, an Original subsidiary that ingeniously marries the ruggedness and stability of the log home with the mobility of the recreational vehicle, Thoreauesque aesthetics with the Thoreauesque tradition of "busking": "Beauty, simplicity, and quality natural materials has [*sic*] been brought up to date with the latest in technology and design" (*Bison Log Cabin RV/Park*). Although Bison Log Cabin RVs are in actuality not as "mobile" as some might dream, they are prefabricated, easily erected and taken down, and moved. At the bottom of the Bison home page, below rusticized representations of the RV Park, is a miniature of Tom Verse, President and Founder, dressed like a forest ranger. Behind him, a herd of bison graze, and behind them is an evergreen forest.

Not only are log cabins more mobile than one might have thought; long associated with populist values, they are just as often claimed by Republicans. The Log Cabin Republicans, a group fighting from within the Republican Party for inclusion of gay and lesbian Americans, in its name refers to the first Republican President of the United States, Abraham Lincoln, who "built the Republican Party on the principles of liberty and equality" and who believed the party "should return to its roots." The group considers Ronald Reagan a hero for opposing attempts to ban gays and lesbians from teaching; their motto is "Inclusion Wins" ("A Proud History"). The icon brings positive associations for politicians of all kinds, however. Elsewhere, "The Political

Graveyard" idealizes politicians born in log cabins, twenty of whom were Democrats, nineteen Republicans, one woman, six Presbyterians, two Baptists, two Methodists, and two Confederates (Kestenbaum).

Log cabins are for sale internationally, for rent in Georgia and Big Bear Lake, Californa, for adults or for "Little Tykes," the brand name of backyard log cabin for the kids. The ads are usually, if not universally "white." One can "work at home" to earn money for a cabin at wealth.DukeCityAdvertising.com, or learn how to get money to bid quickly on eBay to get a cabin at auctionsniper.com. A Google search of 0.14 seconds provides 1.3 million hits for "log cabin." If only, thirty-odd years ago, I had known what I know today: Thoreau's American dream lives on in various and sundry, populist and elitist, national and international—and increasingly mobile and mass-produced—forms.

## WORKS CITED AND RECOMMENDED

*Bison Log Cabin RV/Park*. 2002. 2 July 2005 <http://www.bisonlogcabins.com/>.

Kestenbaum, Lawrence. "The Political Graveyard: Politicians Born in Log Cabins." 10 Mar. 2005. 28 June 2005 <http://politicalgraveyard.com/special/born-log-cabin.html>.

"Nostalgia: Collectors' Sets." *The Original Lincoln Logs*. 2005. 8 July 2005 <http://lincolnlogs.knex.com/nostalgia.php>.

The Original Lincoln Logs, Ltd.: Authentic American Homes. 2005. 8 July 2005 <http://www.lincolnlogs.com/buildingsystems.html>.

The Original Log Cabin Homes. 2003. 2 July 2005 <http://www.logcabinhomes.com/>.

"A Proud History." *Log Cabin Republicans*. 2004. 8 July 2005 <http://online.logcabin.org/about/history.html>.

Thoreau, Henry David. *Walden*. 1854. 2001–2005. 8 July 2005 <http://eserver.org/thoreau/walden00.html>.

"Trump Elegance Inspires Grizzly Adams." *PRNewswire* 22 Feb. 2005. 8 July 2005 <http://www.logcabinhomes.com/pressreleases.html>.

Xiong, Nzong. "Lure of a Log Home." *The Daily News Journal* 24 Apr. 2005: F3, col. 4.

# Lorraine Motel

## Thomas S. Bremer

The Lorraine Motel in Memphis, Tennessee, is less an iconic place than an iconic moment. In April 1968 the world awoke to a photograph, now indelibly etched in the collective American consciousness, of three men on a motel balcony pointing urgently upward across the street while another crouches down with a dying Martin Luther King, Jr. Just outside Room 306 of the Lorraine Motel about six o'clock on the evening of April 4, 1968, an assassin's bullet had struck down the indefatigable leader of the American Civil Rights Movement. The nondescript motel façade, with the metal railings of its narrow second-story balcony and the large drapery-covered windows, instantly became in that terrifying moment the place of martyrdom for one of America's most heroic, and most controversial, leaders.

Like other American sacred places, the Lorraine Motel quickly became, and remains today, a site of conflict. The motel still looks today as it did on the fateful day in 1968, serving as a poignant façade to the National Civil Rights Museum. For some, it stands as an ugly and embarrassing reminder of America's worst moment, a scar carved by the ruthless hatred in America's long history of racism and division. For others, the Lorraine Motel is a shrine to the legacy of Dr. King, and to the immeasurable sacrifice that he and others involved in the Civil Rights Movement offered to the highest ideals of American democracy. But even among those who agree that the site should honor the memory of Dr. King and what he stood for, differences abound. A place of collective memory; a pilgrimage destination that honors the life and martyrdom of Martin Luther King, Jr.; an educational center focusing on the history of the Civil Rights Movement; a site for carrying on the work of Dr. King through social activism; a tourist attraction that bolsters the local economy—the Lorraine Motel encompasses all of these and more.

The motel became the Lorraine in 1942 when Walter and Loree (short for Lorraine) Bailey bought the business and changed its name. Under their ownership it became a favorite lodging house for prominent African Americans visiting Memphis in the segregated South; as Kenneth Adderley notes, "it was one of the few places in Memphis where African-Americans could get a room for the night" (27). Over the years such luminaries as Nat King Cole, B. B. King, Aretha Franklin, and Jackie Robinson all stayed at the Lorraine. But, Walter Bailey explained to reporter Lloyd Shearer, their most special guest was Martin Luther King, Jr.; they always reserved for him number 306, a double room that he preferred, and never charged him for it (4).

Just hours after Dr. King's assassination, Loree Bailey suffered a stroke and fell into a coma; she died five days later, the same day as Dr. King's funeral. Her husband was at a loss as to what to do with the motel. He continued operating it on his own, believing, as Shearer reported in *Parade* magazine, that he had "a potential goldmine"; Bailey knew right away that with thousands of people driving by every week to see the place where Dr. King had fallen, the Lorraine Motel "by all rights should become a hallowed shrine." Bailey told Shearer, "I honestly think that Room 306 will go down in history as the most famous motel room in the world" (4).

Bailey contributed to the room's enduring fame by establishing a shrine there in memory of Martin Luther King, Jr., and Loree Bailey. He glassed in the portion of the balcony where Dr. King fell, and inside Room 306 he collected, in the estimation of reporter Paul Turner, "a rather amateurish arrangement of photographs, newspaper clippings and plaques recalling the life and death of the civil rights leader" (A1). But the goldmine Bailey envisioned never materialized. As he sank further into debt, he looked for a buyer who would respect the hallowed ground where Dr. King had given his life.

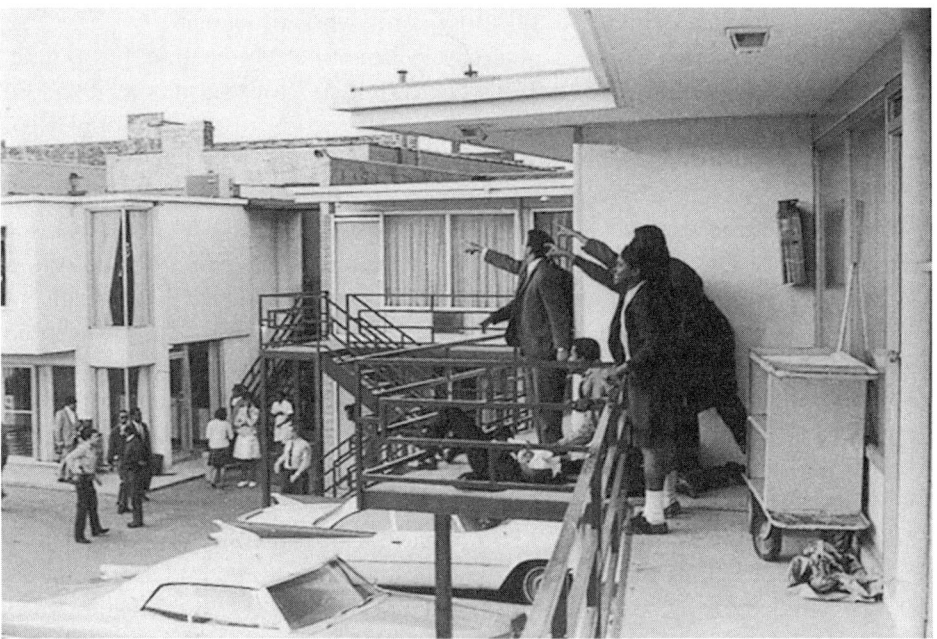

The now-famous picture of the assassination of Martin Luther King, Jr. Joseph Louw/Time & Life Pictures/Getty Images.

## LORRAINE MOTEL

The deteriorating condition of the Lorraine Motel caught the attention of local attorney and civil rights activist D'Army Bailey (no relation to the motel's owner). In a 1979 editorial he complained that "leaders in the black and white communities have not done much to preserve the world-famous King assassination site at the Lorraine. It is one of the key places that concerned visitors to Memphis want to see.... [S]ome of those who visit are surprised and disappointed by what they see" (Adderley 31). D'Army Bailey went on to organize the Lorraine Civil Rights Museum Foundation that first acquired the motel property at a bankruptcy auction, and then sought government funding to establish the National Civil Rights Museum at the site. In 1987, the Foundation transferred ownership of the property to the state of Tennessee, but agreed to take continuing responsibility for operating the education center and museum there (Adderly 49).

With allocations of $8.8 million from state and local governments, the Lorraine Civil Rights Museum Foundation was able to build a full-scale, professional museum that, according to the mission statement on their Web page, "chronicles key episodes of the American civil rights movement and the legacy of this movement to inspire participation in civil and human rights efforts globally, through our collections, exhibitions, and educational programs." The museum preserves the façade of the Lorraine Motel that includes the balcony where Dr. King was shot. But the rest of the motel building and complex were removed to make room for the new museum building. Inside, visitors can view temporary exhibitions on display in a special gallery just inside the main entrance. Next is a small auditorium where a short introductory film begins the tour of the museum. The galleries follow a chronological walk through African-American history and the Civil Rights Movement. Beginning in 1619 with the earliest African slaves in England's American colonies, visitors learn along the way about such topics as the Civil War; Jim Crow laws; the *Brown v. Board of Education of Topeka* case in the U.S. Supreme Court; the Montgomery Bus Boycott; Freedom Rides; the March on Washington in 1963 and Dr. King's famous "I Have a Dream" speech; and finally, the sanitation workers' strike in Memphis that brought Dr. King to the city in 1968 where he met his fate at the hands of an assassin. The various exhibits include life-size, interactive displays, such as a Montgomery city bus with the driver insisting that Rosa Parks move to the rear; protesters seated at a lunch counter with a couple of thugs looking on in a threatening pose; and a jail cell like the one in Birmingham where Dr. King wrote his famous letter.

The museum tour culminates with a solemn viewing of the shrine to Martin Luther King, Jr., in the reconstructed Room 306 of the Lorraine Motel. According to the museum's Web site, "The emotional focus of the Museum and the historical climax of the exhibit is the Lorraine Motel, where Dr. King was assassinated. Dr. King's room can be viewed as it was on April 4, 1968." Visitors can also peer out a window onto the balcony at the very spot where the slain civil rights leader fell, and look across the street to the small window at the back of the rooming house where the assassin fired from.

Leaving the somber experience of gazing into Dr. King's disheveled room as it was at the moment he died (reconstructed for the benefit of visitors), the path leads down a flight of stairs and into the museum gift shop. Since 2002, visitors can continue their visit across the street where they pass through a ground level tunnel that enters the former rooming house from where the assassin fired his deadly shots. This new section of the museum focuses on "Exploring the Legacy," and, according to the museum's Web site, its exhibits ask, "What happened after Dr. King's death? What happened to the Movement, did it die in Memphis? Are we any closer today to the life that Dr. King dreamed of than when he was assassinated 34 years ago?" The expansion of the museum includes the reconstructed room where convicted shooter James Earl Ray stayed and the bathroom from where the fatal shot was fired. The multimedia displays include conspiracy theories about the assassination as well as exhibits about the progress of the Civil Rights Movement since 1968. The tour ends with a film about nonviolent protests around the world and the international progress of civil rights. Again, visitors exit into yet another gift shop.

"Exploring the Legacy" responds to complaints about the original museum presentation of the Civil Rights Movement as static, depicting the assassination of Dr. King as the end of the movement. Mabel O. Wilson notes how the former museum "unwittingly denies its public the possibility of articulating their own meanings and associations. Thus, the endeavor to memorialize encourages, albeit unintentionally, a static interpretation of African-American history" (17). Wilson goes on to suggest that freezing the moment of Dr. King's death by making the reconstructed setting of the assassination the emotional focus of the museum "preempts the possibility of imaging the event from a contemporary perspective. Entering the museum, visitors become passive consumers of an image the media have made iconic" (18). However, the new, expanded version of the museum attempts to take visitors beyond the definitive moment of the killing and into contemporary perspectives on the legacy of the movement that Dr. King gave his life for.

But D'Army Bailey, now a Circuit Court judge in Memphis and estranged from the museum's Board of Directors, regards the new addition as "an abomination." He told Beryl Lieff Benderly that it "takes a beautiful story of the civil rights struggle that covered everybody, every little person in the fields of Mississippi, diverts attention away from them, and sends people through a tunnel chasing the death and assassination of King and all kinds of conspiracy theories." Rather than working actively to overcome the pernicious realities of racial inequality that continue to exist in American society, the new part of the museum, he feels, offers little more than "just sort of general rhetoric" about how far we have come (Benderly 33–34).

Other critics go further than Judge Bailey in objecting to the museum's mission. Ever since her eviction from the motel in March 1988 to make way for the new museum, Jacqueline Smith has kept up a protest on the sidewalk in front of the site. For nearly two decades she has been there, talking to visitors, distributing literature, and vociferously objecting to the whole idea of a museum on the site where Dr. King was killed. Her protest Web site, *Fulfillthedream.net,* describes the National Civil Rights Museum as

> a Disney-style tourist attraction, which seems preoccupied with gaining financial success, rather than focusing on the real issues. Many people have criticized the "tone" with which information is portrayed—Do we really want our children to gaze upon exhibits from the Ku Klux Klan, do we need our children to experience mock verbal abuse as they enter a replica bus depicting the Montgomery bus boycott? Do we have so little imagination, that we need to spend thousands of taxpayers dollars recreating a fake Birmingham jail, to understand that Dr. King was incarcerated?

She concludes, "All in all, the greatest criticism of the Museum is that it dwells heavily on negativity and violence." Moreover, Smith regards the museum as an insulting displacement of the very people that Dr. King most wanted to help, low-income African Americans who once lived in the vicinity of the Lorraine Motel but have been forced out of the neighborhood by redevelopment around the museum. The new businesses, Smith told Benderly, offer "a diet of croissants and cappuccino" that the former residents could scarcely afford (35). Benderly reports that Smith would rather see a homeless shelter or medical clinic for the poor instead of a museum appealing to tourists at the Lorraine Motel; in a more appropriate tribute to the ideals of the Civil Rights Movement, the goal would be to "help the least among us, just like Dr. King did when he came to help the garbage men strike for better working conditions and better pay. They were considered the lowest of the low" (Benderly 33). In a tradition of protest pioneered by Martin Luther King, Jr., Jacqueline Smith calls for a different engagement with the past from her sidewalk vigil across from the museum.

The protests of critics like Smith and Bailey urge visitors to the museum and the American public in general to move beyond the iconic moment of the King assassination and continue the struggle for freedom. Their dissenting voices remind us that the great accomplishment of Martin Luther King, Jr.'s life was more a matter of process rather than a particular achievement. Certainly, the fight against racial inequality and the pervasive injustices of political and economic disenfranchisement did not cease with the fateful gunshot that ended Dr. King's life. The iconic moment of the Lorraine Motel's notoriety stands as a stark reminder of how distant the prize of equality still remains, how difficult the challenges that still lie ahead, how great the price we have already paid and are yet to pay again.

On the other hand, the fallen King lying on the motel balcony remains a momentous image in the history of the nation. In that instant we witness a martyrdom and the apotheosis of Martin Luther King, Jr., himself as well as the ideals for which he fought and died; from his repose beside Room 306, King rose to the realm of national deity, assuming his place among other great figures of American democracy, standing beside the likes of George Washington, Thomas Jefferson, and especially Abraham Lincoln in the imagination of the American people. To the extent that Room 306 remains a shrine to Dr. King and his legacy, it serves as a memory place of the American experience, at once both tragic and hopeful.

## WORKS CITED AND RECOMMENDED

Adderly, Kenneth Roger. "Monument on the Mississippi: Background, Development and the Rising Significance of the National Civil Rights Museum." MA thesis. University of Memphis, 1997.

Benderly, Beryl Lieff. "Heartbreak Motel." *Preservation* 55 (2003): 30–35.

*Fulfillthedream.net.* 29 July 2005 <http://www.fulfillthedream.net/index.htm>.

National Civil Rights Museum. 2003. 29 July 2005 <http://www.civilrightsmuseum.org/>.

Shearer, Lloyd. "The Lorraine Motel...Moneymaker, Memorial to Martin Luther King, Jr. or Both?" *Parade* 30 June 1968: 4.

Turner, Paul. "Drab Motel Is Sad Memorial to Important Man." *Commercial Appeal* (Memphis) 28 May 1982: A1.

Wilson, Mabel O. "Between Rooms 307: Spaces of Memory at the National Civil Rights Museum." *Sites of Memory: Perspectives on Architecture and Race.* Ed. Craig Evan Barton. New York: Princeton Architectural P, 2001. 13–26.

# Jessica Lynch

## *Anna Froula*

The story of Army PFC Jessica Lynch is a narrative that riveted the nation in the beginning of the second Iraq War. In writing about the compelling features of this story, we are not evaluating or maligning one woman soldier or any other soldier. Rather, we are interpreting and examining the American cultural and mythic significance of the media's representations of women at war.

In April 2003, Jessica Lynch smiled bravely from magazine covers as the ideal embodiment of America at War. Her dramatic rescue by America's best—Navy SEALs and Army Rangers—and her subsequent celebrity eclipsed media coverage of the deaths of other soldiers and Iraqis, and destruction of Iraq's infrastructure. Furthermore, amidst criticism that the invasion could likely devolve into another military quagmire, her sensational liberation transformed the lingering Vietnam-War trope of America *fighting* itself into America *rescuing* itself. At stake in her story—more marketable than those of other soldiers injured or killed in the firefight—is that Lynch symbolized how the United States would present and represent itself in all wars. Image-makers from the Pentagon to *People* and *Newsweek* seized upon this pretty, blue-eyed blond to fashion an inspiring damsel in distress who served her country in the military yet fit within normative patriarchal gender roles. Manipulating the details of her ordeal, the U.S. administration would subsequently portray the war through the captivity narrative, a genre that Sacvan Berkovitch calls "auto-American-autobiography: the celebration of the representative self as American, and of the American self as the embodiment of a prophetic universal design" (136). This paradigm of understanding American experience dates from the seventeenth-century Indian wars and interprets the capture and rescue of a white hostage held in an alien culture. American studies professor Melani McAlister initially recognized how Lynch's story modeled the genre in which "the captive (an ordinary, innocent individual, often a woman) embodied a people threatened from outside. The captive confronted dangers and upheld her faith; in so doing, she became a symbol, representing the nation's virtuous identity to itself," thus confirming the settlers' presence in the New World as John Winthrop's "city on the hill," from his 1630 sermon to his fellow Puritans *A Modell of Christian Charity*.

Promoting Lynch as an emblematic captive, the media images varied little—the shining blond hair, the brave smile, the ideal face of America abroad as victim, rather than invader. "If Lynch had been an ugly white woman," writes Charles Mudede, "the mission wouldn't have been as impressive or celebrated. In order for the plot to work, the men of Special Forces had to be seen saving a beautiful white woman" (par. 8). The story Mudede notes advances the cultural archetype of America at war, saving the captives from the wilderness and bringing the dark, savage captors to justice. The captivity narrative comprises much of the first American literature, with its metaphors used by ministers such as Cotton Mather—himself a quintessential mythmaker—as morals to guide colonists away from the temptations of "Indian" life and to exemplify the Puritan mission as a beacon of God's goodness in a wilderness of corruption (Johnson 17). The trope of rescuing the innocent victim from the vicious tyrant in many fiction genres—such as Westerns like *The Searchers* (1956)—recurs as well in our patriotic legitimizations of attacking other nations, most recently in the Balkans, Afghanistan, and Iraq. Berkovitch explains that the success of a myth lies within its adaptability. Via her own debilitating captivity, Jessica Lynch unquestionably fit the role of the innocent captive, particularly when night vision cameras captured her rescue in mass-produced images of her frightened face nestled in an American flag.

As Richard Slotkin explains, the captivity allegory "allows only two responses to the Indian and to evil, either passive resignation or violent retribution in the name of a transcendent and inhuman justice" (141). Legitimating this mythic dichotomy necessitates forgetting the less savory ambiguities of its seventeenth-century precedents. In one of these, Mercy Short returned to Boston in 1693 as a war orphan after eight months with her Abenaki captors. Destined for a life of servitude until she demonstrated symptoms of demonic possession, as a ward of Cotton Mather, she helped to convict and execute Sarah Good for witchcraft. In another, in 1697 Hannah Dustan stole hatchets from her Abenaki captors and killed four adults and six children in the dead of night; later she traded their scalps for bounty in Haverhill, Massachusetts. Historians' revisions of Dustan's story veer from Cotton Mather's celebration of divine motherly instincts to Nathanil Hawthorne's

Jessica Lynch makes remarks from a wheelchair to hundreds of journalists who were in attendance to report Lynch's first public words since her ordeal, 2003. AP/Wide World Photos.

castigation of the "bloody hag's" violent behavior (Weis 46). Even Mary Rowlandson of Lancaster, Massachusetts, who published her own captivity narrative in 1682, complicates the rescue of the good white woman when she uncomfortably realizes that her capacity for evil equals that of the "black creatures of the night" after she steals food from a small English child (71).

These incidents of women as agents of violence complicate the myth of heroic rescue. The accounts that praise Hannah Dustan justify her gruesome brutality by explaining it as a mother's rage, because the intruders had bashed her newborn's head against a tree during their attack. As Mather manipulated both Dustan's and Short's captivities, in similar story management, Pentagon sources not only planted a false story about Lynch "fighting to the death" and, later, being tortured by her captors, but refused either to correct the record or to release the full version of the filmed "rescue." The "official" shaping of Lynch's story responds to a nationalist desire to see the Iraqis as evil, to see them victimize Lynch as they would all of America with the then-presumed arsenal of WMDs. Furthermore, this fictionalized image of her shooting until cornered establishes her as a neat personification of America's often-invoked "resolve." Such a heroic narrative easily subsumes ambiguities and fictions within women's purported pacifist nature. Whether concocted by Mather or the Pentagon, iconization requires eliding these more troubling facts of the stories, as well as other details such as the accounts of Lynch's fellow troops.

The death of the first woman killed in Gulf War II, PFC Lori Piestewa, received comparatively little press coverage independent of Lynch. A Hopi, she was the first Native American woman killed in combat wearing a U.S. uniform. Her lack of media attention reenacts the stereotype of the Indian maiden who sacrifices herself for the white woman's survival, an integral subplot of many Westerns and early dime novels. This mythic tradition recasts Piestewa as a spiritual force of the wilderness who would strengthen the white heroine before stepping aside, nobly and tragically, for the restoration of the innocent woman to the Paradise of America, as in such films as *My Darling Clementine* (1946) and *High Noon* (1952). Had Piestewa survived— linked as she was to the Iraqi captors by her dark skin and mythic associations to savage nature—her image could have provided the dark background on which to project the contrastingly white Lynch. The mythic narrative of conquest, of saving the white maiden from the wild, insists that the white woman remain sexually pure, and thus discounts an experienced woman such as Pestiewa—a single mother of two—for her evident sexuality.

Unlike Piestewa, Spec. Shoshana Johnson survived the firefight and her subsequent captivity. Still, the Pentagon's and the mass media's reluctance to figure the nation and its mission in Johnson's image speaks more to negative stereotyping of the single African-American mother and the racist underpinnings of nationalism, than to the bravery and sacrifice of soldiers who do not fit into America's official self-image. The Black Entertainment Television network chose her as its 2003 Woman of the Year, and indeed, she has a vaguely recognized name. However, American forces found the ex-POW "by accident" nearly three weeks after Lynch's "liberation" (Mudede par. 5). Though images of her weary, scared face had proliferated in the televised coverage of the capture, Johnson returned not to the book and film deals but to a difference of $600–$700 in monthly Army disability payments, even though she and Lynch had received similar incapacitating injuries. Mudede explains how the Pentagon understood that rescuing Johnson would lack the political and cultural currency of saving Lynch, but "also, saving Johnson would have immediately presented the American public with ambiguities: Not only was she dark-skinned, like the 'enemy,' but a single mother too" (par. 5). The preferred picture of a helpless Jessica Lynch wrapped in the stars and stripes allowed the United States to appear at war with Iraq to save itself.

In contrast to the patriotic appeal of Lynch, the internet explosion of controversial photographs of PFC Lynndie England, one year later, raised troubling questions about the cultural premises and myths that would have allowed us to envision ourselves at war as both savior and victim—as Special Forces and Jessica Lynch, mythic hunter and maiden captive, rather than invader and torturer. Embedded within these myths reside American assumptions of sexuality and gender roles. Cynthia Enloe has demonstrated that "militaries need men and women to behave in gender-stereotyped ways." Women should be maternal and need men's protection. More crucially, the military needs men to believe that their masculinity depends on fighting and generally supporting, even desiring, that their nation go to war (Turpin 16). Like Lynch, England most obviously violated these conventions by serving not simply in the military but in a combat zone. Even more dangerously, she violated cultural assumptions of how and why we go to war. Not only did England invert the basic premise behind the captivity narrative of our nation's beginnings, she also rendered woman's traditional, home-front role in war outmoded.

General Robert H. Barrow argued in 1981 that women's participation in combat "tramples the male ego. When you get right down to it, you've got to protect the manliness of war" (qtd. in Enloe 154). From Penelope fending off suitors during the twenty-year absence of Odysseus to Wilma Cameron (Cathy O'Donnell) patiently tending to her paraplegic veteran fiancé in *The Best Years of Our Lives* (1946) to Julie Moore (Madeleine Stowe) tending to other military wives as they wait for their husbands in *We Were Soldiers* (2002), Western war culture abounds with popular images testifying to women's inherent role in war: to wait, to nurture, to sanctify the veteran tainted by the violence and atrocities of war. Joshua Goldstein summarizes, "Women collectively, then, serve as a kind of metaphysical sanctuary for traumatized soldiers, a counterweight to hellish war" (304), a sanctuary corrupted by the threatening figure of Lynndie England.

The 2004 media spectacle of England revealed the sexual nature of American war. As Elliott Gruner explains, the mass media emphasizes "the abuse of women in enemy captivity while it seldom foregrounds American 'Top Guns' who gang rape or a 'Major Dad' who commits incest" (50).

Major General Antonio Taguba acknowledged at least one photo of an MP "having sex with a female prisoner" in Abu Graib (Ridgeway par. 1), yet stories of U.S. servicemen raping women do not garner the kind of media attention England has attracted. The public image of England holding a leash attached to a naked Iraqi—not to mention the *New York Post*'s reports of unreleased photos cataloging her "sexcapades" through Abu Graib—and the subsequent shock felt around the world threaten our gender and military system. If a woman displays enough sexual power, she not only may achieve a level of sexual dominance that could potentially surmount woman's age-old subordinate position to man, but also may become the war rapist. If women provide a sanctuary for military men, then images of England desecrate this haven by redefining her as the weapon in the torture room, by her not merely possessing but becoming the phallus, a powerful symbol of masculinity.

Equally unsettling to American culture is how the Abu Graib photos undermine our mythic and racist ideology of sex. In her examination of how Hollywood has perpetuated this ideology, Ella Shohat invokes "the sexual politics of colonialist discourse" to understand how "the sexual interaction of Black/Arab men and White women can *only* involve rape" while "the sexual interaction of White men and Black/Arab women cannot involve rape" (682). Inasmuch as American popular culture normalizes the vision of a lascivious dark man overcoming a protesting, terrified white woman, the "official" statement that Jessica Lynch had been raped legitimates our continuing occupancy of Iraq. Yet the pictorial odyssey of Lynndie England exposes the sexualization of such international conquest. The infamous photos depict a short, white woman simulating forced sex with captive and feminized Arab men, images that subvert conventional ideology about wartime rape and peacetime sex roles. England's initial torture hearings provided images of a pregnant soldier and produced the further visual oddity of military garb as maternity wear.

Various online media outlets accused England of intentionally getting pregnant in order to project a more nurturing Madonna image and restore her maidenhead via the social currency of motherhood. Though the paternity of Spec. Charles Graner, Jr. is uncontested, unreleased photos of her simulating and having sex with the prisoners, as well as the actual pictures of her impish gazes at their genitals, ironically suggest that she could have raped a detainee into fathering her child. Even the suggestion that Lynch was raped, combined with the reality of her injuries, fortifies her as a icon for America that, for many people, instills the idea that the vitality and future of the nation are at stake in Iraq. But then Lynch serves as the idealized metaphor that England subverts. The images of England's allegedly raping male prisoners coupled with her pregnant body grant her a dangerous agency, but present her as too richly fertile, out of patriarchal control, and potentially an actual source of enemy combatants. Hence many media representations of England attempt to separate her from us, to depict her as a backwoods anomaly rather than a "real" American. But although they would, in effect, lynch England, they cannot erase the irony that—amid her service in a country that the United

States is violently occupying—England figures the America not in need of protection that Lynch personified, but the sort of rogue nation against which America should defend itself. Thus contemporary American war narratives reiterate our past, aided by the media deployment of national myths that continue to shape our national identity with a simplified story. These illusory tales gratify our collective desire to believe that our heroes are unambiguous and we are unequivocally right(eous) in kind.

## WORKS CITED AND RECOMMENDED

Berkovitch, Sacvan. *The Puritan Origins of the American Self*. New Haven, CT: Yale UP, 1975.

Enloe, Cynthia. *Does Khaki Become You? The Militarisation of Women's Lives*. London: Pluto, 1983.

Goldstein, Joshua S. *War and Gender: How Gender Shapes the War System and Vice Versa*. New York: Cambridge UP, 2001.

Gruner, Elliott. "Forgetting the Gulf War POW." *Journal of American Culture* 17.1 (1994): 47–51.

Johnson, Cynthia Brantley. "Hawthorne's Hannah Dustan and Her Troubling American Myth." *The National Hawthorne Review* 27.1 (2001): 17–35.

McAlister, Melani. "Saving Private Lynch." *New York Times* 6 Apr. 2003, late ed., sec. 4: 13.

Morris, Vincent, and Deborah Orin. "Leash Gal's Sex Pix." *New York Post* 13 May 2004. Online edition. 15 Jan. 2005 <http://pqasb.pqarchiver.com/nypost/>.

Mudede, Charles. "Soldier Girls." *The Stranger.com* 13 May 2004. 28 May 2004 <www.thestranger.com/2004-05-27/policebeat.html>.

Ridgeway, James. "Rape at Abu Ghraib." *The Village Voice* 25 May 2004. 6 Sept. 2004 <www.villagevoice.com/news/0421,mondo2,53784,6.html>.

Rowlandson, Mary. *The Sovereignty and Goodness of God, ...a Narrative....* 1682. Ed. Neal Salisbury. Boston and New York: Bedford–St. Martin's, 1997.

Shohat, Ella. "Gender and Culture of Empire: Toward a Feminist Ethnography of the Cinema." *Film and Theory: An Anthology*. Ed. Robert Stam and Toby Miller. Malden, MA: Blackwell, 2000. 669–98.

Slotkin, Richard. *Regeneration Through Violence: The Mythology of the Frontier, 1600–1860*. Middletown, CT: Wesleyan UP, 1973.

Turpin, Jennifer. "Many Faces: Women confronting War." *The Women and War Reader*. Ed. Lois Ann Lorentzen and Jennifer Trupin. New York: New York UP, 1998. 3–18.

Weis, Ann-Marie. "The Murderous Mother and the Solicitous Father: Violence, Jacksonian Family Values, and Hannah Duston's [*sic*] Captivity." *American Studies International* 36.1 (1998): 46–65.

# Loretta Lynn

## Don Cusic

Loretta Lynn became an icon to many women beginning in the late 1960s through her songs about a troubled marriage. All marriages have their difficulties, but some marriages are more difficult than others and that was certainly the case with Loretta and Mooney Lynn. While Loretta articulated the concerns and frustrations encountered in a marriage where the husband drank and ran around on his wife, she also became an icon for those struggling in poverty and obscurity. Loretta Lynn was a living example of someone who could come from a dirt poor background, a "nobody" on this earth, and become a "somebody" whose singing put her in the spotlight in front of millions of adoring fans.

The background of Loretta Lynn before she achieved fame in country music is as impressive—and colorful—as her story of achieving fame. Born Loretta Webb on April 14, 1934, in Butcher Hollar, Kentucky, to Melvin "Ted" Webb and his wife, Clara, Loretty, as her mother called her, was the second in a family that would include eight children—four boys and four girls. The family lived in a four-room house in the coal mining area of eastern Kentucky and Ted Webb worked in the coal mines.

On December 10, 1947, Loretta sang in a talent show at a church and, after the show, there was a "pie bidding" contest. A young man who had just gotten out of the Army, known locally as "Mooney" Lynn, bought Loretta's pie for $5—a princely sum in that part of the country. The pie was not particularly good; Loretta had used salt instead of sugar in the recipe.

Loretta was 13 years old at the time but she and Mooney soon began courting. It was a quick courtship; on January 10, 1948, Oliver Vanetta Lynn and Loretta Webb were married by a judge at the courthouse in Paintsville, about twenty miles away from her home. Loretta was three months away from being 14 years old at the time. Soon, she was pregnant with their first child and remembers that "I never knew where babies came from until it happened to me" (Lynn, with Vecsey 21).

The marriage was rocky from the start; Mooney had been in love with a young lady before he left for the service; during his time away, she had married. However, after his marriage to Loretta, Mooney began seeing this young lady again—threatening the marriage. Loretta, pregnant with their first child, moved back in with her parents. When she found out about the "other woman," Loretta sat down and wrote a letter to the girl; Mooney found out about the letter and confronted Loretta, saying, "If I ever had any love for you, I lost it today" (Lynn, with Cox 38).

Although that encounter broke Loretta's heart, she managed to get back with her husband before their child was born. In 1950, Mooney, Loretta and their young family moved to Custer, Washington, near Bellingham, where they stayed on the farm of two bachelors, Bob and Clyde Green. Mooney worked in manual labor—as a mechanic and heavy equipment operator. Loretta stayed home and took care of their four children. In the evenings, Mooney was often out drinking and on many occasions, he was not faithful to her.

On Loretta's eighteenth birthday, in 1952, Mooney had bought her an inexpensive guitar from Sears. She learned a few chords and enjoyed singing around the house and to her children. Mooney noticed she had a good voice and encouraged her to work on learning the guitar and singing; she did and learned some songs.

On their tenth anniversary, in January 1958, Mooney told her he wanted her to perform in public at a local bar; at this point, Loretta had never even been in a barroom or sung in front of an audience. However, they visited a club where Mooney badgered the bandleader to let Loretta sing. Instead, the bandleader invited them over to his house for an audition that week; Mooney and Loretta went over, her singing impressed the Penn Brothers, leaders of a group called The Westerners, and soon Loretta was singing with their group.

Loretta Lynn sings during a solo concert at the Washington County Fair, 2004. © AP/Wide World Photos.

Loretta Lynn called her husband "Doolittle" and always admitted that "the singing career was Doolittle's idea...without Doo and his drive to get a better life, there would have been no Loretta Lynn, country singer" (Lynn, with Cox 66).

The bar where Loretta first sang was filled with people dancing and drinking. "They wasn't really listening," said Loretta. "I was glad about that." Loretta admitted that, when she sang, she looked at her feet; "I wouldn't raise my head to face the crowd. But I knew they were there, just a few feet away. I could hear them." After each song, "I turned my back to the crowed. I just couldn't face the people. I was so scared, I didn't even want to walk through the crowd to use the bathroom. Also, I was embarrassed to think people would know what I was doing" (Lynn, with Cox 67).

After a few months of working with the Penn brothers for $5 a show, Loretta started her own band. Loretta's group included her brother, Jack, who was living near them by this time, and they called themselves "Loretta's Trail Blazers" and landed a job at a local tavern, playing six nights a week (Lynn, with Cox 69).

Buck Owens had a television show in Tacoma, Washington, and played at a club there. Owens hosted a talent show where singers were invited to perform for a prize. Mooney decided that Loretta should be on that show, so he and Loretta drove over to Tacoma and went to the club where Buck was performing. Mooney repeatedly asked Owens to let Loretta sing; Owens finally relented and let her sing one song and "he must have liked it because he let me sing another," said Loretta. "Finally he came over and sat down with us and said we should really stay over for his amateur television show on Saturday night. Doolittle decided maybe we'd better manage it somehow" (Lynn, with Vecsey 108). On that talent show, Loretta sang "My Shoes Keep Walking Back to You" and won the contest; the prize was a wristwatch (108).

The show reached across the Canadian border into Vancouver, British Columbia, where Norm Burley was watching. Burley, a wealthy man from the lumber business, had just lost his wife. He contacted Doolittle and Loretta and offered to help them; Burley owned a record label, Zero Records.

Loretta Lynn started writing songs around 1960 after she bought a copy of *Country Song Round-Up*, a magazine that printed the lyrics to country songs. "I figured it looked so simple," said Loretta. "Since everyone else was writing songs, I might as well, too. There was nothing to it, really. I'd think up a title first, then write some words, then pick out a tune on my little old rhythm guitar."

One of the first she wrote was "Honky Tonk Girl," which was "mostly about a girl I used to see in Bill's Tavern drinking beer and crying. I don't think she recognized that song was about her" (Lynn, with Vecsey 109). Burley liked the song "Honky Tonk Girl" and gave them some money to go to Los Angeles and record it. On that session Loretta recorded four songs: "Honky Tonk Girl" with B-side "Whispering Sea" would be their first single.

Doolittle had taken up photography so he took a picture of Loretta and they mailed that picture and a short bio with the records to 3,500 radio stations on a list they had obtained. Radio stations began playing the record and soon retailers began demanding copies to sell.

Norm Burley agreed to give them money to drive across country, visiting radio stations on the way to Nashville. Burley was a kind man who said to Loretta "one of the kindest things" she had heard. Burley told her that he thought she

> had a lot of talent and he wanted me to learn as much about the business as I could. And he said that if I ever got a chance to go with a major recording

company, he would release me from our contract. He said he never wanted to stand in our way. (Lynn, with Vescey 111)

Doolittle and Loretta loaded up their old Mercury and drove down the West Coast, sleeping in their car and eating baloney and cheese sandwiches as they visited radio stations. When they came near a station, Loretta would get in the back of the car and change into her dress for the visit to the station. "I'd stay in those radio stations as long as they let me talk on the air," said Loretta, while Doolittle sat in the car, listening to the interview on the radio and "getting burned up if I said something dumb" (Lynn, with Vescey 112).

In 1961, Loretta and "Doo" arrived in Nashville. Her song, "Honky Tonk Girl" was a hit on country radio and led to her appearance on Ernest Tubb's "Midnight Jamboree" radio program, held at the Ernest Tubb Record Shop, across Broadway from the Ryman Auditorium, after the Grand Ole Opry's show was finished.

Although Loretta Lynn's first trip to the Grand Ole Opry came soon after she and Doo arrived in Nashville when they scraped together their money for two tickets, her next visit to the Opry was when she performed "Honky Tonk Girl." Soon, she was appearing regularly on the Grand Ole Opry as a "guest."

Doolittle instinctively knew that he did not have the connections or know-how to further Loretta's career once they got to Nashville. He met the Wilburn Brothers and agreed to let them manage and book Loretta as well as publish all of her songs. It was a lifetime contract—one which no artist with a good lawyer would have signed. But the Lynns were naive and struggling; they felt they had to take whatever opportunity they could get.

There were four Wilburn Brothers: Teddy, Doyle, Leslie, and Lester. Teddy and Doyle were "The Wilburn Brothers" who recorded for Decca and appeared on the Grand Ole Opry. Leslie and Lester took care of business. The Wilburn brothers publishing company was Sure-Fire Music and their talent agency was Wil-Helm Talent, co-owned by Don Helms, the former steel guitar player for Hank Williams.

Doyle Wilburn took a demo of Loretta singing "Fool Number One" to Owen Bradley, head of Decca Records in Nashville and the producer of Kitty Wells, Ernest Tubb, Patsy Cline, Brenda Lee, and other talent on the Decca roster. Bradley did not want to sign Loretta as an artist; he thought she sounded too much like Kitty Wells, and Kitty was already on the label. But he wanted the song, "Fool Number One" for Brenda Lee. Wilburn held out, insisting Loretta should be signed as an artist. Finally, Bradley relented, agreeing to sign Loretta Lynn to Decca if Brenda Lee could record "Fool Number One." (Brenda Lee's recording of "Fool Number One" reached number three on the pop charts at the end of 1961.)

Loretta Lynn's first recording session for Decca was in 1961 and she had top-ten records on Billboard's Country Singles Chart for the next five years—but none that she wrote. However, beginning in 1966, she emerged as the first major female singer-songwriter in country music, telling the story of her life and marriage—and articulating the thoughts and feelings of women all across the nation—in songs like "Don't Come Home A'Drinkin' (With Lovin' On Your Mind)," "What Kind of a Girl (Do You Think I Am?)," "Fist City," "Your Squaw Is On the Warpath," "To Make a Man (Feel Like a Man)," and "The Pill." She wrote her life story in a song, "Coal Miner's Daughter," which became a best-selling book, then a movie starring Sissy Spacek.

Her two most controversial songs were "Rated X" and "The Pill." In both of these songs, she addressed issues confronting women in the early 1970s. In "Rated X," she speaks about the stigma of being a divorced woman; in "The Pill" she talks forthrightly about birth control.

By 1970, it was apparent that Loretta Lynn had outgrown the Wilburns; however, she had signed a lifetime contract with them for management, booking, and publishing. The Wilburns' television show had ended by this time and they were no longer actively touring. Teddy Wilburn moved to California and Doyle was drinking heavily. When Loretta requested an end to her management contract, they balked but she signed with David Skepner, a former executive in the Los Angeles office of MCA Records, her record label, as manager. She and Conway Twitty formed "United Talent," which became their booking agency. The Wilburns sued her for $5 million; it was a lawsuit that would drag on for eleven years. In the end, Loretta was allowed to keep her income from booking and management, but the Wilburns owned the publishing on her most successful songs.

"The 1960s was a time I wrote more than ever before or after," remembers Loretta.

> I did it out of loneliness and love and there ain't no better songwriting inspiration. There wasn't nothing else to do after a show. If Doo wasn't with me, I missed him. If he was, all he done was get drunk at the show and pass out on the bus or in the motel room. On the bus, I'd write to the whir of the wheels. In a motel I'd write with the "background music" of people partying and raising cain out in the halls. Loneliness turned into a pile of hit songs. (Lynn, with Cox 113–114)

During the early 1970s, Loretta Lynn reached the height of her fame in country music. In 1970, Music City News named her "Country Female Artist of the Year" and the year ended with the release of her album *Coal Miner's Daughter*, which would climb to number four the following year.

The year 1971 was a year of awards from the Academy of Country Music, *Music City News*, the Grammies, *Billboard*, and BMI. In 1972 Loretta Lynn became the first female to win the Country Music Association's Entertainer of the Year Award. In addition to her "Entertainer of the Year" award from the

CMA, she was also voted "Female Vocalist" and "Vocal Duo" with Conway Twitty by that organization.

By the end of 1972, Loretta Lynn had been a Decca recording artist for ten years, had twenty-five top-five records on the Country Singles Chart in *Billboard*, including six number ones as a solo artist and two more number ones as duets with Conway Twitty. But all was not sugar and spice; on the night she accepted the CMA's Entertainer of the Year Award from Chet Atkins and Minnie Pearl, her husband was not there. Doolittle had elected to go hunting instead of accompanying her on the biggest night of her career. Adding to this heartbreak was the fact that she did not know whether he was hunting two legged or four legged "deer."

"Doo not showing up for the biggest night of my career hurt me as much, maybe more, than anything he ever done," said Loretta, who admits that she "cried because Doo wasn't there with me" (Lynn, with Cox 132). Instead of savoring the sweetness of the accomplishment, Loretta climbed in her pickup truck alone and drove home after the show.

Loretta continued her string of awards into the early 1980s, but by 1976, her writing had pretty much stopped, a result of the frustration with the Wilburns lawsuit, her busy performing schedule, and an increasingly hectic lifestyle.

Still, she remained a spokesperson for women through her country songs, mostly written by other songwriters but expressing Loretta's views. "My shows are really geared to women fans," she said

> To the hardworking housewife who's afraid some girl down at the factory is going to steal her husband, or wishing she could bust out of her shell a little bit. Those are things most women feel, and that's who I'm thinking about and singing to during my shows. And the girls know it. (Lynn, with Vecsey 115)

She was in the right field. "Country music is real," she said

> Country music tells the story the way things are. People fall in love and then one of 'em starts cheating around, or both of 'em sometimes. And usually there's somebody who gets hurt. Our country songs are nothing but the truth. That's why they're so popular. (Lynn, with Vecsey 127)

In 1988, Loretta Lynn was elected to the Country Music Hall of Fame. This was the height of her professional career, but her personal life remained tumultuous, a result of a hard-drinking, unfaithful husband. But when her husband contracted diabetes, she remained with him, taking care and nursing him. Mooney Lynn also had open heart surgery, and during the final years of his life he required almost constant care; Loretta provided it.

On one hand, Loretta was a liberated woman, refusing—in her songs—to accept a double standard. Yet, in her life, she was a faithful wife to an unfaithful, abusive husband. That seems to be a double standard, but it is a conflict many women deal with every day. To Loretta, "marriage" meant forever, staying together through thick and thin. If she found her husband cheating, she was determined to win him back; if her husband was drunk, she accepted him and continued to love him; if her husband was abusive, well, she could fight pretty good herself—and struck a few blows on her own.

Loretta Lynn is an icon in country music because she spoke for the women in the country music audience. She spoke articulately and eloquently, in songs and in concerts, and gave women strength, hope, and empathy. Loretta was always transparent; she always let her audience know that things were not always perfect in her life, but she was determined to speak her mind and keep her man. Those songs still give many women moral support and a voice to express their feelings when they need it most.

## WORKS CITED AND RECOMMENDED

Bufwack, Mary K., and Robert K. Oermann. *Finding Her Voice: Women in Country Music.* Nashville: Vanderbilt/CMF P, 2003.

Guterman, Jimmy. Liner notes to *Honky Tonk Girl: The Loretta Lynn Collection.* Geffen Records, 1994.

Kingsbury, Paul, and Alan Axelrod, eds. *Country: The Music and the Musicians.* New York: CMF/Abbeville P, 1988.

Lynn, Loretta, with Patsi Bale Cox. *Still Woman Enough: A Memoir.* New York: Hyperion, 2002.

Lynn, Loretta, with George Vecsey. *Coal Miner's Daughter.* New York: Warner Books, 1976.

# MAD Magazine

## Charles Hatfield

*MAD* magazine was the single most important influence on American graphic humor, and arguably on popular satire, in the second half of the twentieth century. Conceived as a bracing contrast to the staid mainstream culture of the Eisenhower era, it became a signpost in the landscape of American adolescence, one that has endured for more than fifty years—a sort of cynical yet oddly affirmative landmark between youth culture and the strictures of adulthood.

The creators of *MAD*—starting with editor-writer-cartoonist Harvey Kurtzman, who dreamed up *MAD* for publisher EC in 1952—understood that making fun of common things is a way of bringing people together, of striking up relationships. Parody is a bridge, a means of establishing rapport, almost conspiratorially, with one's audience, for it assumes a relationship between parodist and audience based on shared knowledge of the material being mocked—a logic as clear in, say, Cervantes or Lewis Carroll as it is in *MAD*. In short, parody is a way of ingratiating yourself to the audience. In the case of *MAD*, as with Carroll's *Alice in Wonderland* or Looney Tunes cartoons, the audience being flattered is mostly young, bemused, and frustrated by the constraints of adult society, and prone to take a subversive low-angle view of all things serious, pious, and inflated. And, like *Alice*, *MAD* at its best went (occasionally still goes) beyond mere humorous imitation of cultural artifacts, into genuine satire based on an incisive understanding of the ideological precepts embedded in those artifacts.

So, for example, Kurtzman and artist Wallace Wood understood that the granddaddy of comic books, the early *Superman*, was a fable of beleaguered masculinity—the story of the closeted hero who couldn't get the girl—and, accordingly, made their parodic response, "Superduperman" (*MAD* No. 4), into an acid satire both of the cringing milquetoast Clark Kent and of his hyper-masculine counterpart Superman. This satire revolves around Kent's hapless desire for the Lois Lane character and, in the end, her contemptuous spurning of *both* his identities, wimp *and* hero. Similarly, Kurtzman and Wood's "Woman Wonder" (No. 10) nastily punctured *Wonder Woman*'s feminist subtext, consigning the superheroine to a life of housewifely drudgery and sexual domination. Among the sharpest of such examples, Kurtzman and artist Will Elder's take on *Robinson Crusoe* (No. 13) satirized Defoe's Protestant work ethic, colonizing zeal, and empire-building hubris, climaxing with Crusoe's Frankenstein-like construction of a female mate using the brain of his man Friday. While *MAD* would only occasionally rise to the political fury of contributor Max Brandel's Vietnam-era satire (for example, Brandel's pitiless photo-collage of political corruption and violence set to the Preamble of the U.S. Constitution), its best parodies grow out of a bitter understanding of the cultural myths implicit in the originals.

The style of humor pioneered by *MAD* had everything to do with the graphic and rhythmic possibilities of the comic book page. Creator-editor Kurtzman, who essentially scripted and laid out everything in the early issues, possessed a metronome-like sense of visual rhythm, and sought, through painstaking page layout, to control the pace of the reader's movement through successive images. This quality was not unique to *MAD*, but also distinguished the other EC titles edited by Kurtzman: the war comics *Two-Fisted Tales* and *Frontline Combat*, revered by many for their unparalleled attention to verisimilitude, their ironic, Stephen Crane–like questioning of wartime heroism, and, above all, their gemlike formal perfection, most readily appreciated in their thumping, verbal/visual cadences. Again and again Kurtzman constructed pages that guided and disciplined the reader by manipulating the relative size, shape, and positioning of panels in sequence. Each page was a paragraph, an indissoluble unit of narrative design, and each panel within it a sentence, both crystalline in its architecture and inextricably tied to everything else on the page and in the story. Characteristic was the shifting between two-panel, three-panel, and four-panel rows, or tiers, and especially the exploitation of the three-panel tier—the Kurtzman triptych—with which he would parse action into deliberate increments: one, two, three.

In other words, the essence of Kurtzman's work was timing; prerequisite to his various comic effects was the precise control of cadence. What *MAD* added to the formula established by Kurtzman's war comics was, first of all, the exaggeration of the cadence, of the build-up, yielding a peculiar comic persistence and stridency, and second, the inevitable rim shot, a comic deflation after the prolonged buildup, which made every pretentious passage collapse in on itself. *MAD*'s original modus operandi was remarkably similar to that of the war comics—the deflation of pretense, the bracing disclosure of hard truths, the crowning of absurdity—but with that added rim shot, that surprising abruption, which distilled and perfected the formula. Not only was this, formally, a highly readable and endlessly fascinating approach, but it also fit with the thematic and ideological agendas of Kurtzman's humor, by setting up every sacred cow for demolition. *MAD*'s humor was not simply screwball, but mock-pompous, always walking hand-in-hand with the overheated cadences of pulp and the fatuous self-importance of officialdom; it was delivered by means of emphatic, almost incantatory repetition and rhythmic control. Simply put, Kurtzman wanted to "set up" his readers, then shock them into recognition.

At least this was one part of the formula. But playfully at odds with Kurtzman's control of rhythm was the abundance of background detail in *MAD*'s panels: a surplus of visual gags and comic asides, delivered via unnamed background characters, graffiti, billboard-like sloganeering, et cetera, all of it adding up to a lovingly rendered graphic excess. This surfeit of detail, what artists and readers came to call "chicken fat," gave each and every page of *MAD* a potential for surprise, a quality that could slow down the expectant reader's eye and inspire an even greater appreciation for the precisely delineated images. Kurtzman tried to drive the reader forward, but, in concert with the *MAD* artists who did the final renderings—none more so than Will Elder, a longtime chum of Kurtzman's and the man who gave "chicken fat" its name—Kurtzman would also give the eye plenty to linger over. Vintage *MAD* pages by such artists as Elder and Wood teem with detail, all of it organized around Kurtzman's unfailing panel rhythms but nonetheless endlessly inviting to the eye. (It helped that Elder was a master mimic, unerringly imitating the styles of countless artists: visual homage and parody became essential to the humor.) Thus *MAD* was not only a linear reading experience; it was a *gazing* experience, and the graphic asides that occupied the "backgrounds" were often as hilarious as the foregrounded action.

The cover of *Mad* magazine, October 1972. Courtesy of Photofest.

This was the basic template for *MAD* the comic book, which was the earliest and most seminal of *MAD*'s several incarnations. It originally included Kurtzman, Elder, Wood, John Severin, and the wonderfully versatile Jack Davis (who would become one of the most recognizable commercial illustrators of the late twentieth century). A slicker magazine format, though still short of the newsstand "slicks" of the day, followed in 1955, after the comic book industry's adoption of a self-censoring, frankly authoritarian "Comics Code" nudged EC publisher William (Bill) Gaines toward getting out of the comic book business altogether. A brief flirtation with post-Code comics came to no good—these were too constrained, one suspects, to satisfy either Gaines or his readers—after which *MAD* vaulted to larger size to evade the suffocating Code. In short, *MAD* became a "magazine," still under Kurtzman's direction but with a notably different look. Typeset text replaced the old hand-lettering; black-and-white replaced the comic book's original pulpy color. Also, mascot Alfred E. Neuman (the "What, me worry?" kid, modeled on a folk character far predating *MAD*) stepped from the margins to front and center, starring in a long and mostly unbroken series of covers that continues even now. Along with all this came a ratcheting up of content, as the freewheeling and gleefully adolescent parodies established by Kurtzman and others mingled with satire reminiscent of hipster humorists such as Lenny Bruce and Mort Sahl; in fact *MAD*, for a brief period, featured work by such well-known absurdists as Ernie Kovacs and Bob and Ray. (Sahl would later contribute to Kurtzman's *Help!*, while Bob and Ray, Kovacs, Steve Allen, and Sid Caesar all wrote forewords for early *MAD* compilations.) Some of the comic book's original high-spiritedness was replaced by a new attempt at classiness, a certain cultivated élan that was frankly more collegiate than adolescent in tone. But *MAD*'s graphic flamboyance and penchant for snot-nosed truth-telling remained.

An important rupture took place in 1956, when Kurtzman's failed bid for a controlling financial stake of *MAD* led to his firing by Bill Gaines. Kurtzman went on to create the short-lived *Trump*, then worked on *Humbug* and *Help!* before settling into his tenure with Will Elder as creators of *Playboy*'s smarmy strip *Little Annie Fanny*. At *MAD* he was replaced by longtime EC writer-editor (and Gaines' good friend) Al Feldstein. Against the odds, Feldstein consolidated Kurtzman's successes and drove the magazine forward to ever-greater visibility and clout.

Feldstein, though at first preserving his predecessor's sophistication, decoupled the magazine from Kurtzman's singular, highly personal approach. Feldstein's long tenure, likely never to be surpassed, established the parameters of today's *MAD* by making movie and television parodies an institution and establishing a diverse and frankly ill-matched stable of artists ("the usual gang of idiots"). This group included, incongruously enough, the staid Dave Berg, whose realistically-rendered "Lighter Side" strips expressed a bemused middle-class response to contemporary fads and controversies; the antic Don Martin, whose slaphappy cartoons were all big-footed, hooked-nosed grotesques; Antonio Prohias, the Cuban émigré whose pantomime strip *Spy vs. Spy* endlessly rehearsed the Cold War as a series of elaborate but graphically minimalist gags; Al Jaffee, whose "daffynitions," curious inventions, and "fold-in" covers were often surprisingly ingenious (he could have designed incredible pop-up books); and more conventionally trained illustrators such as George Woodbridge and Mort Drucker, the latter blossoming into a master caricaturist who was often called upon to do movie parodies and the like. Various prolific writers filled out the mix, such as associate editor Nick Meglin, ace versifier and song parodist Frank Jacobs, movie and advertising parodist Dick DeBartolo, and others who, like DeBartolo, came from and/or went on to writing careers in standup and television comedy: Stan Hart, Larry Siegel, Arnie Kogen, Lou Silverstone. This wild mix continued past Feldstein's retirement from the editorship in 1985 (he was initially replaced by co-editors Meglin and John Ficarra, the former retiring in 2004, the latter continuing as of 2005).

Even as Feldstein and his "gang" set the now-familiar *MAD* formula, codifying the magazine's agenda and style, *MAD* began to take effect in other media. Its first notable spinoff into performance media was *The MAD Show*, a successful musical comedy revue that premiered off-Broadway in 1965, with a script by *MAD*'s Larry Siegel and Stan Hart, a score by Mary Rodgers (daughter of Richard Rodgers), and innovative staging by director Steven Vinaver. Its hectic, non-stop humor, both verbal and visual (including comics-inspired devices such as word balloons), has been credited as an influence on TV's seminal *Laugh-In*. Much later, after *MAD*'s failed flirtation with a *National Lampoon*-like endorsement of a crass film comedy (*Up the Academy*, 1980), the Fox television network launched, as if in tribute to *The MAD Show*, its series *MAD TV* in 1995. (A previous *MAD* television pilot had failed in the early seventies.) However, *MAD TV*, a sketch comedy/variety show, seemed to have only a nominal connection to the magazine (aside from the occasional animated take on *MAD* strips, most notably *Spy vs. Spy*). Rather, it was a revue formatted much like the familiar *Saturday Night Live*, but without *SNL*'s legendary star-making capacity. Though never a huge hit, and of scattershot quality, *MAD TV* persists as of this writing (2005). In a sense *MAD TV* has been a victim of *MAD* magazine's success, for by 1995 *MAD*'s influence had become pervasive, bubbling through *Saturday Night Live*, David Letterman's late-night comedy, and *The Simpsons* (to name a few obvious examples), so much so that *MAD TV* never had a chance to seem fresh and innovative. By then even the magazine itself had been surpassed, in satiric boldness, by rather more adult publications such as Paul Krassner's cult classic *The Realist* (1958–1974, 1995–2001) and the more commercially visible *National Lampoon* (1970–1998).

After Bill Gaines' death in 1992, *MAD* underwent gradual changes as it was more thoroughly absorbed into its corporate parent company, Time Warner, Inc. Until then Gaines had retained control over *MAD*, despite selling the magazine in the early 1960s to the Kinney National Company (later to become Time Warner). In 1994 *MAD* became, in essence, an imprint of DC Comics (another Warner Bros. Entertainment brand); then, in 2001, *MAD* began to take outside advertising for the first time. This was widely regarded as newsworthy, and in some quarters as a blatant sellout, because *MAD*'s reputation for satiric independence had made ads a no-no since 1955. Along with ads, and presumably financed by advertising revenue, came increased use of color. Finally, the post-Gaines era has seen the induction of younger artists into the "gang of idiots," notably cartoonists who already had reputations with comics fans, such as Drew Friedman, Peter Kuper, and Bill Wray. Such artists, associated with alternative comics, have given the magazine a fresh infusion of graphic energy while chipping away at its classic,

Feldstein-era look. Yet *MAD*'s formula for humor has, in essence, remained the same.

This formula, institutionalized by Feldstein and perhaps best represented by television-minded writers like Debartolo, Siegel, Hart, and Kogen, and by caricaturist Drucker, was a far cry from *MAD*'s first incarnation. Feldstein and Company departed widely from the deliberately-timed humor of Kurtzman, and, over the years, the jokes became rather more direct, almost hectoring, in tone. The movie and television parodies began baldly declaring the ridiculousness of their source material without adopting matching styles, that is, without engaging in the kind of subversive mimicry that made the original *MAD* so disarming. In late-period Feldstein, dead-on celebrity caricatures and large, overbearing dialogue balloons—precisely rectangular balloons, linked in long strings across the page, a technique started by Kurtzman but now carried to the nth degree—were used to make wisecracks and to assert, rather flatly, the stupidity of the material being mocked. The approach taken was based less on inversion, less on a deep understanding of the ideological and psychological subtexts of the original material, and more on put-downs and quips. Kurtzman's rhythmic lures, his comic buildups and deflations, were deemphasized in favor of derisive taunting. (A Drucker parody would often begin with a roll call of celebrity faces, each making caustic remarks about the proceedings.)

Increasingly, the writing stood *outside* of the material being mocked, rather than parodying it from within. The kind of corrosive self-reflexivity that Kurtzman had shown at his most cynical (for instance, "Julius Caesar" in *MAD* No. 17, which was, in essence, a self-mocking treatise on how to do a *MAD* parody) became the norm: the characters were very aware of being in a *MAD* parody, and would often discourse on the parody as well as on the material being spoofed. Thus some of the delicacy, some of the spirit of ironic homage that animated the original *MAD*, was lost—what remained was the kind of sarcastic humor one might hear from David Letterman or in the opening monologues of *Saturday Night Live*. While *MAD* has always given pride of place to pop-culture satire, in recent years the humor has stemmed less from knowing inversion and more from the assumption of a hipper-than-thou attitude—the attitude of the disaffected adolescent consumer, armed with cynicism though still vulnerable to the same old commercial hard-sell that *MAD* began ridiculing more than fifty years ago.

By now *MAD*, for all its snottiness and reflexive self-deprecation, is an institution. Given its familiar formula and shameless marketing to young readers, the magazine is unlikely to sally forth into untested satiric waters. Though on occasion it still ventures a political barb (with, for example, a few post-9/11 takes on terrorism and war), *MAD* continues to give strictest attention to movies, television, and pop culture in general, making it, inadvertently, a time capsule of bygone fads, ephemera, and celebrity gossip. For long-time readers, the few surprises in it have to do with renegotiating the boundaries of the permissible: what is just crass enough, versus what is just too crass (in this sense *MAD* serves as a barometer of changing tastes and tolerances). Yet, if the *MAD* formula has dulled with time, there is something perennially reassuring about the magazine's iconic familiarity and relative consistency. *MAD* is the low-brow humor magazine *par excellence* for American consumer society, a pinprick of satire against the constant, suasive pressure of a culture that encourages young people simply to buy, buy, buy. That its satire should have become so aggressively commercial—one more thing to buy—is perhaps the bitterest irony, but the magazine still succeeds, often, in being knowing, graphically playful, and funny.

## WORKS RECOMMENDED

DeBartolo, Dick. *Good Days and* MAD: *A Hysterical Tour Behind the Scenes at* MAD *Magazine.* New York: Thunder's Mouth P, 1994.

Elder, Will. *Will Elder: The Mad Playboy of Art.* Seattle: Fantagraphics Books, 2002.

Evanier, Mark. MAD *Art: A Visual Celebration of the Art of* MAD *Magazine and the Idiots Who Create It.* New York: Watson-Guptill, 2002.

Jacobs, Frank. *The Mad World of William M. Gaines.* Secaucus, NJ: Lyle Stuart, 1972.

Reidelbach, Maria. *Completely* MAD: *A History of the Comic Book and Magazine.* Boston: Little, Brown, 1991.

Von Bernewitz, Fred, and Grant Geissman. *Tales of Terror: The EC Companion.* Timonium, MD, and Seattle: Gemstone Publishing and Fantagraphics Books, 2002.

# Madonna

## Diane Pecknold

Robert Christgau once wrote that Madonna "regards celebrity as her art," and indeed her fame is so far-reaching that it is difficult even to measure (201). Try to count, for example, the number of magazine covers she has graced around the world. In 1993, the popular literature on her was so great that scholar David Tetzlaff equated reading it all to "mapping the vastness of the cosmos" (239). "Cut Madonna," *Time* magazine quipped in 1991, "and ink comes out" (Tresniowski 75). Nearly any poll of the biggest, greatest, or best in popular culture includes her name: in 2003, VH1 viewers voted her the greatest female pop culture icon ever; Discovery Channel viewers voted her one of the top 50 "greatest Americans" in 2005; that same year, the Guinness British Hit Singles and Albums book ranked her the fifth most successful recording artist of all time. In March 2005, a month during which she released no new material of any kind, she was the most Googled celebrity in the U.S. Her claim to distinction as "the world's most famous woman" seems to require no defense (Sexton). She even changed the English lexicon. *Time* coined the term "wannabe" in 1985 to describe the legion of teenage girls who imitated Madonna's style and attitude (Skow 74); and the title of her first feature film *Desperately Seeking Susan* produced a new idiomatic phrase (consider the 2005 newspaper headlines "Desperately Seeking Boredom," "Desperately Seeking Style," and "Desperately Seeking Ratings"). With typical hubris, she acknowledges that her cultural significance extends far beyond mere pop music stardom in the title of her official fan club magazine, *Icon*, which in her case apparently requires no limiting modifier.

Many contemporary observers contended that from the very beginning of her career, Madonna's main ambition was to become an icon, and that pop music simply provided the most convenient avenue for attaining that goal. It was a sensible choice of venue in the early eighties, when the advent of MTV made popular music a visual medium to an unprecedented degree. Individual television appearances—by Elvis and the Beatles on *The Ed Sullivan Show*, in particular—had become cultural events and ensured superstardom prior to MTV, but the cable video channel changed the way the music business operated, making visual presence a prerequisite for launching a major new artist. It also provided a format in which an artist could set multiple interpretations of a song against one another and make them accessible 24 hours a day. As a white artist (early MTV discriminated heavily against black artists) performing black music for a teen audience, and one who was exceptionally adept in front of the camera, Madonna was the MTV ideal. Her video image of a sexy, independent, streetwise vamp electrified her relatively innocuous dance pop and resulted in sixteen consecutive top-five hits—a record bested only by Elvis (another white artist playing black music for a teen audience). Her ubiquity on MTV, and the highly sexualized and controversial uses she made of it, reached its apex with the forty-eight-hour Madonnathon surrounding the 1992 release of the video for "Justify My Love." The station declined to air the video because of its explicit depictions of sadomasochism, homosexuality, and group sex, but ran the Madonnathon nonetheless. Along with Michael Jackson, Madonna proved the power of the new music video format.

By the late 1980s, Madonna had become what cultural studies scholar E. Ann Kaplan labeled the "Madonna phenomenon"; she was not only an omnipresent figure but a polarizing one (131). More than once she appeared in the top five of *Rolling Stone* reader polls for both best and worst artists in the same year. In 1993, she was the subject of the *I Hate Madonna Handbook* and the following year the inspiration for *I Dream of Madonna*, a compendium of the ways she figured in the collective unconsciousness as seen through the dreams of ordinary women.

Madonna, 2003. Courtesy of Photofest.

The fact that not only her work but her person was open to multiple interpretations contributed to the rise of Madonna studies, a cottage industry of academic writing that heralded and hastened the development of American cultural studies. For most of the twentieth century, American scholars subscribed to the idea of an objective and universal canon, a system of aesthetic assessment that ranked art hierarchically from avant-garde high art to degraded commercial mass culture. Madonna's pastiche of pop culture references, her use of avant-garde techniques such as camp, and her self-proclaimed affinity with high art figures such as photographer Cindy Sherman, typified the increasingly blurry boundaries between high and mass culture, and also accorded with intellectual trends that examined popular culture as an important medium for everyday resistance against power. By the early 1990s, academics were applying to Madonna the same sophisticated textual readings once reserved for great literature. Moreover, because so many of her fans pilfered her image to create their own identities and cultural products, she was an excellent vehicle for analysis of the multiple meanings and pleasures readers can take from texts, another hallmark of cultural studies. She became part of the curriculum as no other pop star had before.

Critics, however, maintained that such writing about Madonna was not representative of an important new discipline, but instead merely a symptom of "contemporary academics' attempts to counteract their own marginality by making desperate forays into popular culture" (Harris 790). By applying theoretical pyrotechnics to simple texts, detractors argued, intellectuals demonstrated that they had not been able to take popular culture seriously on its own pedestrian terms. Thomas Frank complained that such analyses obscured the real power relations of popular culture by presenting Madonna as a gender-breaking (or race-breaking, or Protestant-capitalist-breaking) revolutionary, a conclusion, he noted, that could have been derived "directly from a Madonna press kit," and that "uncritically reaffirmed the mass media's favorite myths about itself" as a force for cultural protest (153–54).

Although she was a canvas upon which commentators inscribed American discourses about race, ethnicity, religion, and money (to name only the most prominent themes), Madonna garnered the most attention as a sexual and gender rebel. The juxtaposition of her name with her sex-kitten visual style challenged the virgin/whore trope that dominates Western cultural representations of women, and she further undermined this discourse by playing such an exaggerated version of the whore that she reduced it to a caricature. Her famous cone bra, men's suits with breast slits, and ironic evocation of past icons of blonde bombshell femininity, such as Marilyn Monroe, created a similar tongue-in-cheek burlesque that denaturalized gender roles by drawing attention to their superficial, performative nature. She also invoked elements of gay culture to destabilize heterosexual norms. Her connection with the gay male club scene, her flirtations with Sandra Bernhard, the simulations of lesbian sex in her 1992 book *Sex*, and even an unusual moment as post-motherhood provocateur in which she French-kissed Britney Spears on the 2003 MTV Video Awards, all illustrated an engagement with gay and lesbian cultures that some viewed as legitimizing and others viewed as appropriation.

Madonna's whorishness was perceived in cultural and economic terms as well as sexual ones. Her pop commercialism was seen as a prostitution of authentic rock; and in her incarnation as Material Girl, she became a symbol of excess, greed, and acquisitive capitalism that captured, for many, the moral bankruptcy of the "me decade" during which she became popular. Yet for all of her good-time-girl posturing, Madonna's work ethic—exemplified by her obsessive dedication to remaking her body through a rigorous workout regimen—contradicted her invitations to sexual rebellion and indulgence. "There's a grim, aerobic, almost Protestant strenuousness to the Madonna spectacle," observed Simon Reynolds and Joy Press (321).

Characteristically, she was embraced and scorned by both feminists and anti-feminists for her gender theatrics. Feminists welcomed her as a symbol of female independence and power, but cringed at video images of sexual submissiveness and worried that Madonna substituted "apathy and masturbation" for meaningful social change (Conniff 212). Post-feminist critic Camille Paglia argued by contrast that Madonna's unabashed sexuality exposed "the puritanism and suffocating ideology of American feminism" (168). For "pro-sex" critics like Paglia, Madonna's libidinous abandon offered a much-needed antidote to what Katie Roiphe later described as the helplessness and frigidity of "victimization feminism." Madonna's ambiguous relationship to feminist ideology, moreover, influenced a generation of female musicians, who extended contradictory elements of her explorations of femininity. She is widely regarded as a progenitor of the post-punk "riot grrrls"—whose girl-power aesthetic also dealt with the marginalization of women in music and with the relationship between power and sexuality—as well as a new generation of teen pop idols such as Britney Spears and Christina Aguilera, whose sexualized marketing strategies evince none of the irony or self-reflexivity of Madonna, and so seem to bear out feminists' worst fears about objectification.

For many years Madonna's name served primarily as an ironic counterpoint to her provocative exploration of sexuality and her vamp burlesque. When she announced the impending birth of her first child, Lourdes Maria Ciccone Leon, she fulfilled the prophecy of her name and became a highly contested symbol of motherhood. Some fans posted online messages suggesting that the pregnancy was conveniently timed to resuscitate her flagging career, promote the U.S. theater release of her film *Evita*, and revise her image in the wake of *Sex* and *Erotica*. "What better way to prepare the public for a kinder, gentler Madonna than a baby," one such message ran, predicting that magazines would be "full of photos with Madonna and baby, therefore burying the image of Madonna as sex-obsessed pop star from the *Erotica* era" (Manners 85).

If Madonna-watchers imagined her motherhood as, finally, one career maneuver that would not provoke consternation, they lacked imagination. Echoing the scandal surrounding her video *Papa Don't Preach*, which generated controversy for its anti-abortion message, her decision to have a child out of wedlock intersected with discourses about welfare, work, and social reform, and her pregnancy occasioned fraught discussion of values and economics. By 1996, even the Clinton administration enthusiastically promoted legislation aimed at discouraging the formation of single-parent families. The rhetoric of welfare reform castigated irresponsible breeders and enshrined a new commitment to promoting the married, two-parent household as the normative family. In this atmosphere, *Newsweek*'s open letter encouraging Madonna to marry the baby's father ("the next wave is restoring the family, and with it, the country itself. Ride it, Madonna") came as no surprise (Alter); even if *People* sanctioned her decision by featuring approving comments from the father's parents (Schneider 51). Other responses to Madonna's pregnancy evoked anxieties about the high cost of balancing family and work that emerged in the wake of second-wave feminism's collapse. Where once Madonna's business savvy and drive had been a source of admiration that seemed to give the lie to her air-headed boy-toy image, her identity as a powerful professional woman now seemed to threaten her maternal fitness. The question of whether a former pop tart could be a good mother was subordinated to whether an obsessively driven businesswoman of Madonna's magnitude could become anything other than a Mommie Dearest.

Since Lourdes's arrival and the subsequent birth of her half-brother, Rocco Ritchie, however, Madonna's maternal image has become her controlling identity; *Ladies' Home Journal* recently ran a fifteen-page spread on her home life in which she explicitly repudiated the outrageous sexual exploits that defined her through the mid-1990s. Indeed, conservative essayist Mary Kenny lauded Madonna as an example of a woman matured by motherhood who promotes "firm concepts of right and wrong, and proper standards of manners and morals" (20). Such an assertion suggests not only that Madonna's image has undergone yet another radical transformation, but that fundamental understandings of the nature of that image have shifted. Analyses of Madonna's earlier personas presented even the most intimate revelations as part of a self-conscious performance rather than as a window onto any "real" Madonna, a paradigm that was particularly apparent in discussions of the documentary of her Blonde Ambition tour, *Truth or Dare*. Yet the public portrayal of her home life today is generally accepted as the truth about Madonna. The chameleon who once served as poster-girl for postmodern indeterminacy and ambiguity has become firmly fixed as mother and wife.

Madonna's relationship to the religious dimension of her name has changed as well. Once she personified the 1980s obsession with getting and spending; now she signals the preoccupation with religion and spirituality that has increasingly shaped American culture and politics since the attacks of 9/11. Her identity as a Catholic was always central to her persona, but for many years it functioned primarily as the repressive foil to her campaign for sexual liberation and guilt-free personal indulgence. Her 1998 album *Ray of Light* introduced her as a "post-Catholic, anti-material/antimatter Indian princess," an image which, however much it reinforced Orientalist stereotypes of eastern spirituality, represented religion as an avenue to enlightenment and inner peace rather than as a source of shame and corruption (Tata 91). Her flirtation with Hinduism turned out to be fleeting, but her study of Kabbalah, a Jewish sect for which she is now the leading celebrity spokesperson, has solidified her status as a mystical, rather than material, girl.

In the new millennium, Madonna has also become an icon of American identity. The rags-to-riches story of her rise from Midwestern working-class girlhood to unimaginable wealth and cosmopolitan celebrity always qualified her as one incarnation of the American Dream, and that narrative was further enriched by her marriage to British noble Guy Ritchie in 2000. But even before she adopted the conservative English country lifestyle, she began to represent both the imperiousness and the embattled defensiveness of American national identity in an international context. When Madonna was cast as Evita Peron in the film version of *Evita*, Argentinian outrage was a response partly to the notion that a self-styled notorious slut would be portraying a national saint, but also to the widespread perception that America was gobbling up yet another chunk of its neighbors' patrimony as grist for the global pop culture mill. Since the movie was released, Madonna's new pan-European accent has been the subject of popular derision, in part, no doubt, because it exposes longstanding cultural insecurities during a period of heightened nationalism. Her more recent work has also directly questioned America's materialism and imperialism, particularly in her 2003 album *American Life*, and the video accompanying the first single from that album. Ironically, given her more reflective awareness of her uniquely national nature, her explorations of American identity have been more popular abroad than at home, and she now inspires the same kind of daily news coverage in the United Kingdom that she once garnered in the United States.

Boy toy, sexual rebel, material girl, spiritual mom, ugly American. Madonna's fame seems due not so much to her own creativity, though she remains prolific, as to the creativity of her admirers and critics; not so much to her ability to reinvent herself as to her ability to be continually reinvented by her audiences, whether they love or loathe her. More than anything, Madonna's career has been about creating and maintaining herself as "a container for a multiplicity of interests" (Sante 141).

## WORKS CITED AND RECOMMENDED

Alter, Jonathan. "Get Married, Madonna." *Newsweek* 29 Apr. 1996: 51.
Christgau, Robert. "Madonnathiking Madonnabout Madonnamusic." *Desperately Seeking Madonna: In Search of the Meaning of the World's Most Famous Woman*. Ed. Adam Sexton. New York: Delta, 1993. 201–7.
Conniff, Ruth. "Politics in a Post-Feminist Age." *Desperately Seeking Madonna* 210–13.
Frank, Thomas. "Alternative to What?" *Commodify Your Dissent: Salvos from* The Baffler. Ed. Thomas Frank. New York: Norton, 1997.
Harris, Daniel. "Make My Rainy Day." *The Nation* 254 (1992): 790–93.
Kaplan, E. Ann. "Madonna Politics: Perversion, Repression, or Subversion? Or Masks and/as Master-y." *The Madonna Connection: Representational Politics, Subcultural Identities, and Cultural Theory*. Ed. Cathy Schwichtenberg. Boulder, CO: Westview, 1993. 149–66.
Kenny, Mary. "The Making of a Female Mullah." *Spectator* (London) 16 Nov. 2002: 20.
Manners, Marilyn. "Fixing Madonna and Courtney: Sex Drugs Rock 'n' Roll Reflux." *Reading Rock and Roll*. Ed. Kevin J. H. Dettmar and William Richey. New York: Columbia UP, 1999. 73–92.

Paglia, Camille. "Madonna—Finally, a Real Feminist." *Desperately Seeking Madonna* 167–69.

Reynolds, Simon, and Joy Press. *The Sex Revolts: Gender, Rebellion, and Rock 'n' Roll.* Cambridge, MA: Harvard UP, 1995.

Sante, Luc. "Unlike a Virgin." *Desperately Seeking Madonna* 140–48.

Schneider, Karen S. et al. "And Baby Makes Three." *People Weekly* 29 Apr. 1996: 46–52.

Sexton, Adam, ed. *Desperately Seeking Madonna: In Search of the Meaning of the World's Most Famous Woman.* New York: Delta, 1993.

Skow, John. "Madonna Rocks the Land." *Time* 27 May 1985: 74.

Tata, Michael Angelo. "East Is Hot! 'Madonna's Indian Summer' and the Poetics of Appropriation." *Madonna's Drowned Worlds: New Approaches to Her Cultural Transformations, 1983–2003.* Ed. Santiago Fouz-Hernández and Freya Jarman-Ivens. Burlington, VT: Ashgate, 2004.

Tetzlaff, David. "Metatextual Girl: → patriarchy → postmodernism → power → money → Madonna." *The Madonna Connection* 239–63.

Tresniowski, Alexander. "A Look at the Books on Madonna." *Time* 16 Sept. 1991: 75.

# McDonald's

## *Betsy Beaulieu*

It has long been the American way to like things big: big cars, big houses, big shopping malls, big-screen televisions. And so it is no surprise that as fast food became increasingly popular in the latter half of the twentieth century, both fast-food portions and the size of those consuming the portions grew. McDonald's, unquestionably the most high profile of the many fast-food franchises that dot the American (and, indeed, international) landscape, is known not only for burgers but also for the super-sized fries and soft drinks that are the inevitable accompaniment to the burger. In the 2004 documentary *Super Size Me*, director Morgan Spurlock charts his month-long experiment eating nothing but McDonald's fast food, examining the fast-food phenomenon and putting his own health at risk.

When the documentary premiered at the Sundance Film Festival on January 17, 2004, it garnered a great deal of international attention. Spurlock was inspired by a 2002 lawsuit filed by two Bronx teenagers alleging that McDonald's was responsible for their obesity and related health problems. In casting the spotlight squarely on questions of nutritive value, marketing strategies (especially those targeted at children), and consumer awareness, *Super Size Me* challenged McDonald's corporate responsibility. In March 2004, just weeks after the film's debut, McDonald's announced that they were planning to phase out their super-sized fries and soft drinks in U.S. outlets, and on April 15, 2004, the corporation launched a "comprehensive balanced lifestyles platform" in response to the Department of Health and Human Service's call for more attention on obesity and physical fitness in America (McDonald's Corporation Site). The new initiative is designed for both children and adults, emphasizes healthier food choices, and educates about the importance of physical fitness. It seems, at the beginning of the twenty-first century, that McDonald's is actively distancing itself from "super-sized" portions of high-fat convenience food, promoting instead food that fits in with the current national agenda concerning health and fitness.

## McDONALD'S

In spite of menu makeovers, however, McDonald's remains the leading fast-food outlet in the United States, accounting for forty-three percent of the American fast-food market. It is estimated that McDonald's feeds more than 46 million people a day, with 20 million of those living in the United States. More than 30,000 McDonald's restaurants are presently in operation in over 100 countries. Indeed, the sign of the Golden Arches is one of the most familiar symbols worldwide, whether off an exit ramp in the midwestern United States, in the center of Paris, or in Indian or Israeli cities.

Ray Kroc is commonly believed to be the founder of McDonald's, but in fact the fast-food restaurant had its origins as McDonald Brothers Burger Bar Drive-In. Opened in San Bernardino, California, in the early 1940s by Richard and Maurice McDonald, the restaurant was extremely successful but eliminated the car-hops in 1948; at that time the brothers pioneered "Speedee Service System," introducing the concept of self-service to the dining out experience. Hamburgers (sold for fifteen cents apiece) were cooked on an enormous custom-made stainless steel grill, and condiments were dispensed by a machine that could dress six buns a second. Customers walked up to a counter, placed their orders, and received inexpensive but freshly-prepared food within minutes. Initially favored by workers with limited time for lunch, the restaurant soon became popular with families who enjoyed the picnic-like atmosphere of informal food and service.

Ray Kroc, a salesman with a shrewd combination of opportunism, creativity, ambition, and thirst for risk, was selling milkshake mixers in 1954 when he met the McDonald brothers and immediately saw the potential for franchising their restaurant. He persuaded the brothers to sell him the right to license the restaurant and recognized early that site selection would be key in spreading the chain across the nation. Kroc was extremely successful in establishing the chain, but he wanted more. In 1960 he paid $2.7 million to the McDonald brothers to purchase McDonald's outright. He immediately began an effort to modernize and publicize the establishment, launching what has been described as the most expensive and aggressive ad campaign in American corporate history. Kroc's empire grew from approximately 250 restaurants in 1960 to 3,000 in 1973, to about 30,000 worldwide at the end of the twentieth century. Kroc turned McDonald Brothers Burger Bar Drive-In into an American icon through expansion and marketing. His success became our success as Americans all across the country sat down together over a meal of burgers and fries, living Ray Kroc's version of the American Dream.

A number of factors contributed to Kroc's achievement, among them the growing American car-culture and the increasingly fast pace of life. These two factors combined not only to enable consumers to eat in their cars but also actually to encourage it. McDonald's and other fast-food chains capitalized on postwar prosperity and Americans' love of the automobile by providing food that could be obtained quickly, eaten with one hand on the steering wheel, and in wrappings easily disposed of. Additionally, with more women working

The familiar golden arches of McDonald's. Courtesy of Shutterstock.

outside of the home, Kroc saw another market to be capitalized upon and marketed McDonald's meals as an excellent substitute for home-cooking. He insisted that the American flag be flown above all his restaurants, implying that the chain embraced wholesome family values, values that were transferred through the food that a working mom could proudly feed her family.

Indeed, as Kroc took over and McDonald's spread across the country, a certain ethos came to be associated both with the chain and with the food it served. Kroc tapped into a need for comfort and security by offering a menu that was consistent and familiar no matter which restaurant in the chain a customer stopped at; he tapped into a growing demand for convenience to accommodate a hectic lifestyle by providing food that was easy to purchase, to consume, and to clean up after. The products were inexpensive and popular; soon burgers and fries became a cultural norm signifying a casual, easy-going, wholesome lifestyle. There was also an element of community built into a McDonald's meal; families who went to McDonald's for lunch or dinner were likely to encounter families like themselves, whether they were dining in their hometown or traveling across the country.

Although initially workers on their lunch breaks were the most reliable patrons of McDonald Brothers Burger Bar Drive-In and Kroc's first franchised restaurants, more than anything McDonald's came to be associated with families. This change occurred in large measure due to Ray Kroc's marketing genius. His target consumers were children, not workers. He believed, rightly, that every child who wanted to eat at McDonald's would bring along at least one paying adult, and he also counted on the fact that a lifelong loyalty would develop that would keep the children returning to McDonald's with their own children once they were parents themselves. Much of McDonald's advertising over the decades works to evoke a sense of nostalgia for the childhood experience of eating a fun meal in a familiar place, surrounded by loved ones—both parents and characters.

According to Joe L. Kincheloe in *The Sign of the Burger: McDonald's and the Culture of Power*, "McDonald's removes food from the context of cooking and presentation, as it focuses consumers' attention on the 'McDonald's experience,'...mak[ing] food a dramatic spectacle" (88–89). Most of what Kincheloe refers to as "spectacle" is aimed at the child consumer;

he lists the McDonaldland characters, the playgrounds, the Happy Meals (complete with toy), the colorful environment where the food is prepared in plain view as though on a stage, the process of unwrapping one's hamburger as if it were a holiday gift, as enticements for children who skillfully persuade their parents to spend money on food-as-entertainment. And by the time they have children of their own, nostalgia for the experience is so deeply ingrained that they want it for their children as well. Coupled with the convenience, the inexpensive cost, and the chain's ubiquity, it is hard for most Americans to stay away from McDonald's. Kroc's genius was anticipating and cultivating this type of loyalty; he trained the American palate to locate it under the Golden Arches in the form of a burger and fries. And then he trained the world.

Eric Schlosser says in *Fast Food Nation: The Dark Side of the All-American Meal* that Kroc "liked to tell people that he was really in show business, not the restaurant business" (41). Eventually, Kroc was not satisfied with producing the show only in America, and he launched an initiative to spread McDonald's across the globe. At the beginning of the twenty-first century McDonald's operates about 17,000 restaurants in more than 120 countries outside of the United States, and opens approximately five new restaurants a day, at least four of which are abroad. Schlosser argues that McDonald's now "ranks as the most widely recognized brand in the world" (229). The Golden Arches, symbol of opportunity and prosperity, is one of America's most popular and easily-recognized exports. A source of comfort for Americans traveling abroad (who among us hasn't hungered for a familiar meal in the midst of a grueling trip or when visiting a foreign country with children in tow?), McDonald's has also been more recently viewed as a tool of cultural imperialism for the ways in which the corporation co-opts national identity and replaces a country's traditional values and practices with America's capitalist hegemonic philosophy, embodied by the ubiquitous hamburger and the accompanying fries and soft drink. The emphasis on uniformity and standardization that established the foundation on which McDonald's the phenomenon rests has led to what some call the "McDonaldization" of the planet, a notion that the corporation's international slogan seems to confirm: "One Taste Worldwide."

Kroc began introducing McDonald's to the overseas market in 1970, and he faced numerous challenges. According to John F. Love in *McDonald's: Behind the Arches*, McDonald's "was attempting to export something that was now endemic to American life but totally foreign everywhere else. Quick service food was uniquely American" (418). Europeans in particular were accustomed to full-service dining, usually without children. Thus the McDonald's corporation had to figure out how to introduce a casual dining environment and new food items to their target middle-class consumers who were not in the habit of dining out with the family one or more times a week.

Initially McDonald's introduced local specialties to their menu, but this proved less than popular and McDonald's International soon concluded that they would be more successful in changing local eating habits than incorporating local cuisine into their restaurants. " 'McDonald's is an American food system,' reasons Steve Barnes, chairman of McDonald's International. 'If we go into a new country and incorporate their food products into our menu, we lose our identity' " (qtd. in Love 437). They learned the same thing in terms of architecture; after several "experiments" in redesigning their restaurants to mimic local tastes and culture (Love mentions, for example, a Munich "beer hall" McDonald's), the corporation returned to the familiar Golden Arches yellow and red theme for all of their restaurants. Clearly part of the appeal for international consumers is to participate vicariously in the American lifestyle that McDonald's has come to represent in the global community.

Fast-food corporations have undergone increasing scrutiny in the latter half of the twentieth century, and McDonald's, as the most dominant fast-food enterprise, has received much of the criticism. The industry has been indicted for a multitude of sins: labor activists point to the tendency of fast-food chains to rely on lower class, unskilled workers who are easily exploited; environmental activists are concerned with the amount of litter generated by disposable wrappings and also with the impact of fast-food production on the meatpacking and other agricultural industries. Health experts warn of an epidemic of obesity and related health problems that can be directly tied to American's fondness for high-fat, high-sodium fast food. Advocates for children worry about the impact not only of diet but also, in an age when Ronald McDonald is as familiar to most American children as Santa Claus, of intense advertising pressure on the susceptible young as well. Fast-food chains threaten local independent businesses, and, in a climate where corporate ethics are viewed with suspicion, McDonald's is keenly aware that it must acknowledge its responsibility to the world it wishes to feed. Hence the corporation eliminated its use of polystyrene containers in the early 1980s, refused genetically altered potatoes for its french fries in 2000, and introduced more healthy alternatives to its menu in the wake of *Super Size Me*. Critics, however, insist that these changes are not sincere and do not reflect an adjustment in corporate philosophy but merely have been enacted to counter negative publicity.

Nevertheless, America continues its love affair with fast food, which may well be the national cuisine. McDonald's remains the American standard for fast food at home and abroad. The days of the 15-cent burger and the 12-cent fries are over, but today's consumer still seeks comfort and convenience and a meal that is as familiar as a home-cooked one under the Golden Arches. The slogans, although they have changed over the years, reflect the corporation's commitment to provide its customers with the best: "We do it all for you" (suggesting that you don't have to do anything other than come to McDonald's and enjoy a meal); "You deserve a break today" (insisting that only at McDonald's will you get the respite you need from the stress of modern life); "My McDonald's" (implying the personal nature of the dining experience you'll have at your home-away-from-home), to the most recent catch-all, democratic, upbeat testimony "I'm lovin' it!" For many who fancy a burger and fries, there's much to love about McDonald's. For others, it is difficult to overlook the perils presented by the fast-food industry, and McDonald's in particular. Regardless, though, of the views an individual may hold, it is hard to dispute the fact that McDonald's is truly a super-sized American icon.

## WORKS CITED AND RECOMMENDED

Boas, Max, and Steve Chain. *Big Mac: The Unauthorized Story of McDonald's*. New York: E. P. Dutton, 1976.

Kincheloe, Joe L. *The Sign of the Burger: McDonald's and the Culture of Power*. Philadelphia: Temple UP, 2002.

Kroc, Ray. *Grinding It Out: The Making of McDonald's*. New York: St. Martin's, 1977.

Love, John F. *McDonald's: Behind the Arches*. New York: Bantam, 1986.

*McDonald's Corporation Site*. McDonald's Corporation. 1 Aug. 2004 <http://www.mcdonalds.com>.

Ritzer, George. *The McDonaldization of Society: An Investigation into the Changing Character of Contemporary Social Life*. Thousand Oaks, CA: Pine Ridge P, 1996.

Schlosser, Eric. *Fast Food Nation: The Dark Side of the All-American Meal*. New York: Houghton Mifflin, 2001.

*Super Size Me*. Dir. Morgan Spurlock. The Con, 2004.

# Mexican-American Border

## Susana Perea-Fox and Iván Figueroa

A reform plan proposal called the Guest Worker Program has created a heated debate within American society about a topic that has long eluded the minds of many: the matter of undocumented immigrant workers who continue to arrive through the southern border, and the possible ways to protect the Mexican-American border, which has become an icon for the conflicted attitudes about immigration among a nation of descendants of immigrants.

The great majority of Latin immigrants cross into the United States via the Mexican-American border. Its 1,952 miles form one of the most differentiated borders of the world. It extends from San Diego–Tijuana, at the Pacific coast, to Brownsville-Matamoros, at the Gulf of Mexico. About half of its length is run by the Rio Grande-Bravo and the other half by the Sonoran desert. The border was set in 1848 with the signing of a treaty that ended the Mexican-American War and gave control to the United States of about one-third of what had been Mexican territory, from New Mexico to California.

The problem of how to protect the border is as large and difficult as the border itself. Homeland Security—encompassing the former Immigration and Naturalization Agency—hopes to deport 460,000 people by 2009. Yet, and in spite of all efforts, it is almost impossible to stem the flow of people across the border. There were approximately 9 to 10 million illegal immigrants in the United States in 2003, and it was predicted that about 3 million would enter in 2004. In the past, the main ports of entrance were the surrounding areas of towns such as Laredo–Nuevo Laredo, El Paso–Ciudad Juarez, or the river, for example. But with an increment of patrols in those areas, the route shifted to the Arizona desert. This route, however, has proven dangerous and deadly, even more deadly than the treacherous river, where many people have drowned. Since 1995, 3,500 people had died crossing the border. Two years ago, 200 people lost their lives as they tried to cross the border from Mexico into Arizona. They died from dehydration in the 120–130° heat of the Sonoran Desert (Ufford-Chase 20). In 2004, just from January to May, 30 people died making the trek through the desert, but according to Robert Bonner, the commissioner in charge of the border patrol, the worst was yet to

The barb-wired international border separates a truckload of Mexico's Groupos Betas, the Mexican government–sponsored group that tries to discourage migrants from crossing and aids those stranded in the Sonora Desert, 2004. AP/Wide World Photos.

come: 80 percent of the deaths in a year happen between May and August (Eagan 1).

However, agents feel confident that immigrants choosing the desert route also would fail to cross because of the increment of agents and resources in this area. In an interview with Carrie Kahn for National Public Radio (NPR), agent Johnny Bernau said that by June 2004, "a full complement of 260 agents will be in place along with four more helicopters and several unmanned surveillance drones." Because the new equipment is ultra-sensitive to movement, the agents expect to make record arrests.

Immigration is not a foreign concept to most American citizens. The vast majority in one way or another are either immigrants or descendants of immigrants. And yet, most Americans have little sense of the real situation of Latinos who are drawn to cross the border. Many citizens do not want more immigrants let into the country. A poll conducted by NPR, the Kyser Family Foundation, and Harvard's Kennedy School of Government from May 27 to August 2, 2004, showed that even though most Americans are not negative about immigration, 41 percent said that legal immigration to the United States should be decreased, and 59 percent said that illegal immigrants have hurt the national economy (Rosenbaum 1).

Others think that immigrants want to sign up for welfare programs and to get free medical services. But Alexander Monto, a health inspector of labor camps in California, observes that the idea of Mexicans using public services is a misconception. During his tenure as inspector, he was appalled by the conditions under which immigrants lived. He thinks that the great majority of immigrants do not come with the goal of becoming welfare recipients: "[N]ot only is that stereotype untrue—their utilization of such services is lower than that of the native-born population, and many are not even eligible for such programs" (Monto xv).

Moreover, the jobs immigrants are taking are the jobs that very few American unskilled workers take. As a matter of fact, Massey, Durand, and Malone found that as societies become more industrialized, at least part of the jobs become highly skilled and better paid. These are the jobs favored by the natives of the country, while the "bad" jobs, the jobs that receive lower wages, are filled by immigrants. However, and most importantly, if there is not demand for their services, if the natives would do these jobs, "immigrants, particularly those without documents, would not come, since they would have no means of supporting themselves" (145). In other words, there is immigration of unskilled workers to the United States because there is a demand for these types of workers.

To aggravate the problem, some American companies that require middle-skilled factory workers, such as *maquiladoras*, have been moving to other countries for economical reasons. At the beginning they moved just across the border into Mexico, pulling north many people who would not have tried to move there otherwise. Ten years ago, 1,600 plants brought more than 750,000 new jobs; but in the last two years "more than 500 of those plants have closed [relocating into Asia], taking with them a quarter of a million jobs" (Fleeson 24). The displaced workers, having already moved north and being unable to find employment in other places, now look to the United States as their new source of jobs. Some of them will become nannies, housecleaners, hotel maids, or restaurant cooks; but others may compete for medium-skilled jobs, such as the ones they just lost.

Immigration is a long-standing problem for the United States and Mexico. Most years the presidents of both countries meet to discuss a series of bilateral issues, mostly associated with immigration. But stopping illegal immigration is so impossible to achieve that in 2004, the year of U.S. presidential elections, while Hispanic communities were pushing for immigration reforms, neither one of the major presidential candidates stepped up to address the issue. Instead, the U.S. government increased border patrol and security against the terrorist threat. It is true, as Robert Leiken of the Nixon Center pointed out, "with the exception of the Oklahoma City bombing, all terrorist attacks in America had been carried out by immigrants—that means that immigration has a real national security dimension" (Geyer). Yet, one can see that there is a great distance between Latin American immigrant workers and foreign terrorists who want to harm the United States.

One of the reasons that the problem of illegal immigration has persisted for so long is rooted in the deep poverty in which many of the immigrants live in their own countries. Most of them look toward the United States as the solution to their problems. Their dream is to get to the United States, work hard, and send or save money to take back to their families. According to a poll sponsored by the Inter-American Development Bank, nearly one Mexican in five regularly receives money from relatives employed in the United States, making this country the largest repository of such remittances in the world (Thompson). One can see why the government of Mexico would not try hard to stop the flow of emigrants to the United States. These workers not only send money back and help the Mexican economy; they also serve as an escape valve for unemployment and discontent there. These emigrants are desperate to make a living and are willing to risk their lives in order to do so. But little do they know about the treacherous journey.

While in the process of getting to the United States, immigrants learn the full meaning of modern immigration: *coyotes*, *cholos*, *la migra*, drug traffickers, the Mexican police, and white supremacist groups. Every immigrant will come into contact with at least one or two from this nefarious cast. The *coyotes* are the people who know the border well. They will charge an average fee of $2,000 to smuggle people into the United States. In 1990, Barich reported, "*Coyotes* will lead a migrant across, store him in a safe house, and then refuse to release him until his relatives in the United States cough up a ransom" (77); and the same problem persists today. Legally, this tactic is nothing less than kidnapping. Unfortunately, there is no one to whom the migrants can go for help. When the family of the kidnapped person goes to the authorities and the authorities make arrests, not only is their loved one deported back to his or her country, but also they themselves run the risk of having their status reviewed.

*Cholos*, or young hoodlums, are others who take advantage of the migrants. Shorris in "Borderline Cases" claims that most of the killings at the border are done by *cholos*. Whenever *cholos* need money, or are bored and looking for fun, they hunt immigrants who stay in burrows in the hills (68). The police find hundreds of bodies along the border every year. Nobody knows for sure how many people have been killed by *cholos*.

Certainly the border patrol agents do not protect illegal immigrants either. They themselves have been guilty of abuses. To solve the problem, some years ago the Immigration Agency started to hire agents of Mexican-American origin, but this policy did not decrease the abuses. These new agents were eager to prove their loyalty to their employers by brutalizing their own people (Shorris 72).

However, abusive treatment of immigrants also comes from other groups. There are many white supremacist groups or other xenophobic individuals who think that Latins are here to take over their country and their jobs, or that they are bandits or drug traffickers. When interviewed by Chavira, a member of one of these groups tried to clarify: "We have nothing against Mexicans,... many of them are hard workers. A lot of the others don't come to work. They steal, break into people's homes, bring drugs" (12). Unfortunately, to the regular citizen, drug smugglers, bandits, and innocent people all look alike.

Latin American immigrants have done all types of work. They have cleaned tables at restaurants, worked with hazardous wastes, labored as roofers and hod carriers, wrecked their backs and knees picking lettuce and tomatoes, cleaned sewers, and have been willing to do everything. It is not a secret that many farm owners use immigrants as cheap labor. Farmers can get away with not paying their workers minimum wage, not paying them benefits nor providing proper working conditions according to law. Some employers take even greater advantage of the illegal immigrants by turning the workers over to authorities one day before payday (Barich 89).

When immigrants are deported back to Mexico or are on their way north, another danger awaits them: the Mexican police. Although most savvy Mexicans know how to deal with the police, many rural Mexican peasants and Central Americans do not, and thus are more susceptible to their abuses and attacks. Shorris points out that "The danger is real. By the time they get across the border into the United States, most of the immigrants will have been robbed, beaten, extorted, or raped by bandits or Mexican police" (75).

The Immigration Act of 1986 provides a special section that can be used to help solve some of these problems: The H2 Workers. This section requires an employer "to apply to the Secretary of Labor no more than 60 days in advance of needing foreign workers, and then requires the employer to try to recruit domestic workers for the jobs that need to be filled" (228). If these jobs are not filled with domestic workers, then an employer could go to the border and legally hire temporary help. This way, both the employer and the worker will have more protection. The worker will not face the dangers of crossing the border illegally.

One problem that started the implementation of this act was the widespread exclusion of Latin American–looking people. Because the employer had to pay a fine for using illegal workers, the easiest way to avoid being fined was not to employ any "brown skins" and people with Latin names and accents ("Employing Immigrants. No Brown Skins" 42). Prospective employers did not differentiate among legal immigrants, longtime residents, and illegal workers, and probably forgot that up to 1853 the states of California, Arizona, New Mexico, Nevada, Utah, and Texas, and portions of Wyoming and Colorado, were part of Mexico. When the United States annexed this area its inhabitants remained there; hence a large number of Hispanic-looking people still live there.

U.S. President George W. Bush and Mexican President Vicente Fox have agreed that the system was not working and that there was a necessity for modification of the Act of 1986. They called for a reformed immigration policy—the Guest Worker Program—that would (1) open borders to legal travel and trade while shutting them to drug traffic, criminals, and terrorists; (2) serve the economic needs of the United States while providing fair income and legal protection for working visitors; and (3) offer incentives for immigrants to return to their country of origin (Ufford-Chase 20). But up to this day, these ideas have not been implemented because of political pressures and because there seems to be confusion in differentiating between honest workers and criminals.

Drug trafficking, terrorism, and illegal immigration are separate problems; but they have become collapsed in American consciousness, and signed in the Mexican border. The United States government wants to protect its border from illegal drugs and terrorists, but at the same time it wants to stop illegal immigration. While governments of other countries are likely to cooperate to fight drugs and terrorism, they are less likely to involve themselves with illegal immigration, a problem they see as mostly internal to the United States. However, a simple solution is to grant more work visas so that the U.S. government could allocate all the economic resources and agents to combat drug trafficking and terrorism.

Another important point that must be addressed is the need to modify the quota of visas for Mexicans. It is inequitable that Mexico with its much larger population and closer cultural ties receives the same number of work visas as each other Latin and Caribbean country. For example, in 2002 the Dominican Republic with its 8.2 million inhabitants received 20,000 visas—the same number as Mexico with its 100 million people. An increased number of Mexican visas would assure that these workers would hold legal jobs, would pay taxes and social security, and would buy medical and vehicle insurance; this change ultimately would save the lives of many people. Historically, it has been proven that, given the opportunity, illegal immigrants would choose to enter legally. In the late 1950s a similar provision granted 450,000 *bracero* visas annually, reducing undocumented immigration to near zero (Massey et al. 159).

Current immigration projects fail to reach the heart of the issue. To make real progress, drastic changes are necessary to avoid more violations to the basic human rights of these people. Immigrants cross the border moved by hunger and in search of a better life, and that it is why the efforts by Homeland Security to stop them have been and will be unsuccessful. These immigrants, legal or not, are citizens of the world and have basic human rights that everyone should respect and protect. They need protection against *cholos*, *coyotes*, drug traffickers, and white supremacist groups. While the United States must make and carry out laws governing immigration, it has an even greater responsibility to protect the human rights of those immigrants who in fact provide valuable services to the United States. The United States always has been a powerful advocate for the implementation of human rights policies. It is important for the government, and for the American people who elect it, not to forget their own backyard in this regard.

## WORKS CITED AND RECOMMENDED

Barich, Bill. "La Frontera." *New Yorker* 17 Dec. 1990: 72–92.
Chavira, Ricardo. "Hatred, Fear and Vigilance." *Time* 19 Nov. 1990: 12–20.

Eagan, Timothy. "Border Desert Proves Deadly for Mexicans." *New York Times* 23 May 2004, late ed., East <http://80gateway.proquest.com.argo.library.okstate.edu/openurl?url>.

"Employing Immigrants. No Brown Skins." *The Economist* 314 (3 Feb. 1990): 42.

Fleeson, Lucinda. "Leaving Laredo." *Mother Jones* 28.5 (Sept./Oct. 2003): 24–27.

Geyer, Georgie Anne. "Immigration Reform Group Marks 25 Years of Uphill Battle." *Tulsa World* 10 Oct. 2004: G5.

"Immigration Act of 1989." *Congressional Digest* Oct. 1989: 225–30.

Kahn, Carrie. "New Efforts to Prevent Illegal Immigrants from Crossing Mexican Border into Arizona." *All Things Considered*. NPR, Oklahoma State U. 19 May 2004. Transcript. 29 June 2004 <http://gateway.proquest.com/openurl?url_verZ39.88-2004>.

Massey, Douglas S., Jorge Durand, and Nolan J. Malone. *Beyond Smoke and Mirrors: Mexican Immigration in an Era of Economic Integration*. New York: Russell Sage Foundation, 2002.

Monto, Alexander. *The Roots of Mexican Labor Migration*. Westport, CT: Praeger, 1994.

Rosenbaum, Marcus D. "Immigration in America." *All Things Considered*. NPR, Oklahoma State U. 7 Oct. 2004. Transcript. 7 Oct. 2004 <http://www.npr.org/templates/story/story.php?storyId=406205>.

Shorris, Earl. "Borderline Cases: The Violent Passage Across the Río Grande." *Harper's Magazine* Aug. 1990: 68–78.

Thompson, Ginger. "A Surge in Money Sent Home by Mexicans." *New York Times* 28 Oct. 2003, late ed., East: A14.

Ufford-Chase, Rick. "Dying to Get in." *The Christian Century* 121.16 (10 Aug. 2004): 20–23 <http://80gateway.proquest.com.argo.library.okstate.edu/openurl?url>.

# Miami

## Gary Harmon

A city, even a contemporary American city, carries a wealth of signification, like that of ancient Byzantium and the sacred icons that filled its churches and households. Miami, stretching along the beaches of south Florida's Atlantic coast, evokes a range of meanings. It plays various roles in the lives of those who travel there in the flesh or, perhaps more commonly, those who explore the possibilities it represents in their minds. American cities, unlike their Old World counterparts, have commonly offered their visitors and newcomers and even their longtime residents a sense of what may be. In the colonial era, New York and Boston and Philadelphia and Charleston; in the era of westward expansion, St. Louis and San Francisco and Los Angeles; in the emergence of the New South, Atlanta and Charlotte and Dallas; in the era of industrialization, Chicago and Pittsburgh and Cleveland and Detroit, among many others, offered opportunity for wealth or pleasure or progress that life on the land, for all the promise of the legendary "territory ahead," could not. America, the land of opportunity, has been and continues to be a city.

In the first decade of the twenty-first century, the "city on a hill" of America's seventeenth-century founders has been replaced by the city on the beach, which retains many, perhaps, most of their aspirations in new millennial dress and in post-colonial practices of integration and diversity. Today's Miami contributes to the development of a new American mythos. It stands as an icon of American ideas, beliefs, and values for millions of people—hinterland Anglo-Americans avoiding lousy weather or pursuing economic profit in the fastest growing state in the union, Jews pursuing community on vacation or in retirement, Cubans escaping and expelled by Castro, Haitians retreating from poverty, Europeans seeking an informal sophistication, Latinos from across Central and South America fleeing economic and political turmoil, among many, many others. The melting pot, a concept lost to most of America in the 1960s and 1970s, is alive and well in Miami, but with a postmodernist embrace of diversity. This city enjoys a drawing power cutting across age, gender, race, and class as well as ethnic boundaries. Miami is not just another city on the American map or the world map; it holds a special place in the minds of millions. Miami is now and has been for some time hot, hot, hot.

Apart from such data-driven mental disciplines as physical geography and economics, it is almost impossible to think about Miami, to get one's head around this city, without reference to the ads that promote it or sell other goods in a play on its associations; without images of its fashions in clothing, food, and architecture that we experience directly or vicariously; without the movies and novels that exploit it as a resonant setting, and without the tourist literature and guide books describing its exotic pleasures—all of these reveal Miami as the siren of South Florida's Gold Coast. By extension, Miami has come to represent, for very many people, all of Florida, particularly for those who do not actually live in Miami or in Florida.

Many of the guidebooks seek to render Miami a palatable, predictable place. From them we learn that Miami is the "Cruise Capitol of the World," the "Crossroads of America," or the "Magic City." A Fodor or Frommer guide offers an ordered summary of features, a catalog of tame adventures available to anyone who has the time or the money to visit. The guidebook Miami eventually enters the consciousness of millions, either as first-hand experience or as told-to-experience, and frequently moves one-time visitors to stay. Their function seems to be to tame the icon, to put a sober constraint on our imagined hopes and dreams about Miami.

Miami, of course, is not a single entity. The city proper is a mere 375,000 people. But as one quickly discovers, this great city consists of a web of interconnected subcities, including the American Riviera of Miami Beach; the style-setting South Beach; the horseracing burb of Hialeah; the upscale sanctuary of Coral Gables; Cocoanut Grove with its art-crowd and night spots; the thriving hotel capital and business hub of central Miami; the elite Key Biscayne; and the sedate North Beach. More Americans have a greater awareness of, often even detailed knowledge of, the exurbs and suburbs of Miami than of any other American city: Bal Harbor, West Palm Beach, Coral Springs, Pompano Beach, Coral Gables, Homestead, Del Ray Beach, and Boca Raton, among others, register in the consciousness of people living in New Hampshire, Ohio, Minnesota, and Arkansas. Moreover, the ethnic communities of former outsiders and exiles from other countries and states color neighborhoods and suburbs with their architecture, activities, foods, style, and vigor to delight and sometimes frighten the uninformed tourist.

While technically Miami can trace its history to the early sixteenth century and Ponce de Leon, this polyglot of ethnicities and suburbs as a practical matter gets underway after the Civil War, not terribly long even by American standards, but it is a history with remarkable vigor, especially in the twentieth century. Miami is in every sense a modern American city.

Mild winters and the warm ocean attracted visitors to the Miami area, first Indians and then northerners in the late 1800s. Julia Tuttle, from Cleveland, settled on the north bank of the Miami River in 1891 and began to plan a city. Her first step was to entice railroad magnate Henry M. Flagler to extend

Winter bathing at Miami Beach Casino, March 1923. Courtesy of the Library of Congress.

a line south to the tip of the Florida peninsula. Flagler had built a line to St. Augustine and then in 1893 to Palm Beach, but he was not interested in extending it another sixty-six miles to tiny Miami. In the winter of 1894–1895, however, a freeze destroyed most of the citrus crop, but the cold did not reach Miami, where oranges still blossomed. Tuttle, legend holds, sent Flagler a single orange blossom, and he quickly changed his mind. In April 1896, Miami's 300 residents greeted the train and a new era, promoting itself as "America's sun porch."

In the early twentieth century, roads were cut and swamps were drained, beginning the demise of the Everglades. Waves of warmth and sunshine seekers wanted to move to Miami, and developers obliged by carving the farmland into subdivisions in the early 1920s. And rum-runners had a field day during Prohibition, followed by a phalanx of mobsters who operated with virtual immunity from the law. Miami's vice took an early place in the American imagination. With the development of Coral Gables by George Merrick, the nation's fascination with Miami erupted into a real estate boom, but it began to fade in 1925. In September 1926 nature burst the speculative bubble with a major hurricane. Many fled smashed houses and destroyed businesses, leaving Merrick bankrupt. But in the next decade, tourism picked up, especially in Miami Beach, where over 500 hotels, apartments, and businesses were constructed in the "modern" Art Deco style. Tourists again flocked to Miami for warmth and sophistication and the services flourishing gangsters could provide. In the 1940s, the war killed tourism. When a German U-Boat torpedoed a tanker in full view of the Florida coast in 1942, hotels emptied. But the war sparked another kind of development. By the end of 1942, the department of the army turned 147 hotels into barracks and many hotels into temporary hospitals for wounded soldiers. GIs trained in Miami, and German prisoners of war were interned in Homestead. After the war, ex-soldiers returned to Miami, many becoming students on the GI Bill at the University of Miami. A new housing boom arose, as farms became suburbs. Arthur Godfrey broadcast his famous television show from Bal Harbour. With this national exposure, gargantuan hotels sprouted on the beaches, buildings made habitable in the summer months by air conditioning, which would soon become an American addiction. The future looked rosy, albeit suffused with gang activities and ethnic conflict.

In 1959 Miami took a major turn in its course. Fidel Castro deposed Cuban dictator Fulgencio Batista, declared himself a socialist, confiscated property, and nationalized many businesses. Cubans by the thousands fled to Miami. Overnight entire neighborhoods were transformed into islands of Spanish-speaking language and culture. After the failed CIA-led Bay of Pigs invasion, thousands of political refugees fled Cuba on "freedom flights" to Miami and by 1973 the Miami Cubans numbered over 300,000. The effect of these influxes was a squeeze on jobs held by Miami's African American community. The city's first race riot erupted in 1968 in Liberty City when Richard Nixon gave his acceptance speech at the Republican National Convention in Miami Beach. In the 1970s drugs brought in big money; a new, distinctly different underworld replaced Miami's Prohibition-era crime, as people from throughout the country sought to satisfy their demand for illegal narcotics.

One of the streets in Miami Beach, 1939. Courtesy of the Library of Congress.

The Cuban community prospered by building successful businesses, and the city prospered; by the end of the decade international banking interests brought in more money from Latin America, and a rapid transit system revitalized Miami's downtown.

In 1980, blacks and disadvantaged Miamians rioted after a Tampa jury acquitted a white policeman of murdering a black man. Haitian "boat people" were landing in great numbers on South Florida beaches, and Fidel Castro permitted anyone who wanted to leave Cuba to do so, including inmates of Cuba's prisons and mental institutions. The 125,000 new "Marielito" refugees tarnished the city's reputation among tourists. South Beach, where many of them settled, became a near-slum, prompting whites from other parts of Miami to leave for Broward County, just north. Drug dealers injected over $10 billion into the economy, and handgun sales soared, as did the murder rate; with 621 violent deaths in 1981, Miami assumed another nickname, "Murder Capital, USA."

Despite this turmoil the mid-1980s brought another building boom, and the city's romantic image was repaired, as was its image of adventure with the premiere of television's *Miami Vice* in 1984. A new Bayside Marketplace attracted tourists, and the Pope visited in September 1987, just before Miami Heat basketball arrived. These international events joined in the public imagination with the University of Miami football team's winning the national championship three times, the new Joe Robbie Stadium where the Miami Dolphins hosted Super Bowls in 1989 and 1995, and the roar of race cars through downtown in the Miami Grand Prix.

Those 1930s Art Deco buildings underwent transformation from housing Jewish retirees to become hotels, artist's lofts, fancy restaurants, oceanfront cafes, art galleries, and theaters. International celebrities spangled South Beach with their iconic presence. The city became a landing place for visitors from Brazil, Columbia, and the Caribbean as well as Germans, Brits, and Scandinavians. Even 1992's Hurricane Andrew, which destroyed much of Key Biscayne, or the killing, in 1993, of nine foreign tourists did not long dampen tourism or arrest Miami's economic expansion. Entering the new millennium, Miami challenges New York's claim to be the most cosmopolitan of American cities, as the complicated mix of races, cultures, and ethnicities has become an asset in attracting millions in investment and millions of tourists annually.

Miami, a place unusually rich in diversions, stands for America's passion for play. If offers a wider range of sports than perhaps any other American city. There are the Miami Dophins, the Florida Marlins, the Miami Heat, the Florida Panthers, jai alai, stock-car racing, horseracing, parasailing, snorkeling, wind surfing, tennis, golf, biking, coral reef diving, jet skiing, boat racing, sky diving, and fishing, among others.

Miami is the city of "attractions" in a state that seems to have invented this distinctly American diversion. We can watch Lolita the killer whale somersault and dine on fish morsels from a maiden's hand at the Miami Seaquarium; visit the Monkey Jungle or the Gold Coast Railroad Museum; taste jelly at berry farms; glide over swamp waters of the Everglades just a short drive away; take a cruise from the world's largest cruise port; visit architectural marvels by I. M. Pei or Philip Johnson; gawk at wild animals at the Miami Metrozoo or the parrot jungle and gardens; enrich our minds at the Lowe Art Museum, the Florida Pioneer Museum, the Museum of Science, the Goombay Festival (the world's largest African-American festival of art, music, and culture); the Miami Film Festival world premieres, the Holocaust Memorial, the Hispanic theater festival, the orchid show, the Cocoanut Grove Playhouse, the Redlands Fruit and Spice Park covering thousands of acres, an alligator farm, the Weeks Air Museum, or the Bass Art Museum, and even a wine festival, to name a few. We can ogle the Coral Castle created by a Latvian immigrant, Ed Leedstainen, who spent twenty-eight years building a strange coral structure that some compare to Stonehenge. These allure visitors with a sense of security and predictability. The prospect of seeing them all is numbing, but to have visited a few of them carefully tucks Miami into our imaginations through experiences at once familiar and exotic, safe and adventuresome.

As a resort of the celebrated, Miami itself becomes an attraction. Robert Frost not only visited but owned seven acres in Miami. Robert De Niro, Lana Turner, Cher, and Sylvester Stallone made news in Miami. Liv Ullmann, Janet Reno, and Jack Nicklaus live there; so did Jackie Gleason and Isaac Bashevis Singer. Gianni Versace brought worldwide fashion fame to Miami and Muhammed Ali extended his legend there (1961–1964), and Shaquille O'Neal moved there to lift the Miami Heat into NBA title contention. Edward Albee retired there—even getting caught on Miami Beach early one morning while air bathing in the dawn. These and hundreds more spark our imagination to the firing point.

Miami has a rich fantasy life, something like New Orleans, but with a New World rather than an Old World flavor, as much a taste of freedom to do as escape from. Miami's fantasy is reflected in the gritty but colorful detective series *Miami Vice*, in which a cross-racial pair of hard-boiled cops pit the powers of instinct and inductive reasoning against the forces of death and destruction. Out of the chaos wrought by the city's under life, the detectives outwit the bad folks and bring order to the steamy nightspots and engaging neighborhoods of multiracial Miami.

While *Miami Vice* may be the most widely known version of the Miami fantasy, a horde of novelists turn out forests of mystery and detection books focused on Miami's ambiguities, perhaps its largest literary industry. A few titles from recent popular books disseminating the mythic Miami may surprise for their consistency of impression. There's Marshall Frank's *Dire Straits*; Dirk Wylie's *Medical School is Murder* or *Biotechnology is Murder*; Tom Coffey's *Miami Twilight*; Dave Barry's humorous *Big Trouble* mystery; Ana Veciana-Suarez's *The Flight to Freedom* and *Cuba Confidential: Love and Vengeance in Miami and Havana*; Carolina Garcia-Aguilera's *Bitter*

Present-day Miami Beach at night. Courtesy of Corbis.

*Sugar: A Lope Solano Mystery*; Barbara Parker's *Suspicion of Betrayal* and *Suspicion of Malice*; Edna Buchanan's *Garden of Evil*, *The Ice Maiden*, and *You Only Die Twice*; Jilliane Hoffman's *Retribution*; Heather Graham's *Picture Me Dead*; Max Allen Collins's *Florida Getaway*; Michele McPhee's *Mob Over Miami*; James Grippando's *Last to Die* and *Beyond Suspicion*; Lisa Miscione's *The Darkness Gathers*; Elmore Leonard's *Pronto*; and Michael Gruber's *Tropic of Night*. This genre, the most prolific of all novel genres to feature Miami, again and again underscores the allure of mystery, suspicion, getting away, death, or looming doom. Miami's iconic fantasy rises here as a place of exotic, even erotic adventure, a place of lurid and troublesome passions frothing amid its orderly urban streets and neighborhoods.

New York and Los Angeles once dominated the mystique for American metropolitan edginess, but Miami is making a strong bid for the "naked city" franchise, as *CSI: Miami* has become a very popular TV drama. The color palette for Miami alternates between the dark geometries of the crime lab, where top cop David Caruso and his assistants apply high-tech instruments to pillow cases, glasses, carpets, steering wheels, or the like, and the lush warmth of Miami with its modern architecture, beaches, and neighborhood palms and palmettos. Questions of crime and punishment give way to the mysteries of discovery.

Probably nothing rivals the films shot on Miami locations for expressions of the fantasy Miami. Joe Buck, the "midnight cowboy," was taking Ratso Rizzo on the bus to a fantasy Miami, so he could experience before he died the heat and beaches in the company of wannabe models with sculpted buttocks, voluptuous 36Cs, wearing leopard skin bikinis as he frolicked with them on the Florida sand. But then, there's Marilyn Monroe, Tony Curtis, and Jack Lemmon who escape death in New York to reach Miami's beach in *Some Like it Hot*. The list of films set in Miami is long: *Goldfinger*, *Big Trouble*, *Snow Dogs*, *Bad Boys II*, *Far from Heaven*, *Miami Blues*, *The Crew*, and *Any Given Sunday*.

Miami is, as Carl Hiassen suggests, a place where things happen that you cannot make up. The Miami of the imagination is a place for getting away, for finding sensuality, spontaneity, wildness, and unpredictability, but it is also a place to find safety and a new home. As do most icons, Miami embraces contradictions rather than resolves them.

## WORKS RECOMMENDED

Buchanan, James E., comp. and ed. *Miami: A Chronological and Documentary History, 1513–1977*. Dobbs Ferry, NY: Oceana Publications, 1977.

Egendorf, Laura K., ed. *Urban America: Opposing View Points*. Farmington Hills, MI: Greenhaven P, 2005.

Grenier, Guillermo J., and Lisandro Pérez. *The Legacy of Exile: Cubans in the United States*. Boston: Allyn and Bacon, 2003.

Hollingsworth, J. Rogers, and Ellen Jane Hollingsworth. *Dimensions in Urban History: Historical and Social Science Perspectives on Middle-Size American Cities*. Madison: U of Wisconsin P, 1979.

Krabbendam, Hans, Marja Roholl, and Tity de Vries, eds. *The American Metropolis: Image and Inspiration*. Amsterdam: VU UP, 2001.

Mohl, Raymond A., ed. *The Making of Urban America*. Wilmington, DE: Scholarly Resources, 1997.

Nash, Eric P., and Randall C. Robinson, Jr. *MiMo: Miami Modern Revealed*. San Francisco: Chronicle Books, 2004.

Rishel, Joseph F. *American Cities and Towns: Historical Perspectives*. Pittsburgh: Duquesne UP, 1992.

Schultz, Stanley K. *Constructing Urban Culture: American Cities and City Planning, 1800–1920*. Philadelphia: Temple UP, 1989.

# Mickey Mouse

## M. Thomas Inge

There is no more widely known an iconic figure out of American culture in the world at large than Mickey Mouse. So successful have been the marketing strategies of the Walt Disney Company, so widely distributed have been the films and comics, and so strongly appealing is the image of the mouse to children and adults alike that there are few small corners of the earth where Mickey is not instantly recognizable, if by nothing more than a set of round ears. Crude reproductions of Mickey and his girl friend Minnie Mouse appear on the walls of bus stops and telephone booths in remote African villages, and children everywhere decorate the walls of their nurseries and schools with their images. In China the folk figure of the Monkey King has been known to appear with Mickey's face, and a 2003 exhibition of postmodern Russian art in Moscow featured a bronze statue by Alexander Kosolapov of Lenin with the head of Mickey Mouse. In Italy he is known as Topolino, in Sweden Musse Pigg, in Spain Raton Miguelito, in China Mi Lao Shu, and in Vietnam Mic-Kay. His admirers have included Sergei Eisenstein, E. M. Forster, William Faulkner, Charlie Chaplin, Franklin D. Roosevelt, John Updike, Maurice Sendak, Andy Warhol, Roy Lichtenstein, and George Lucas.

For socialists and left-leaning intellectuals, Mickey represents American capitalism and cultural imperialism at its most unscrupulous. For conservatives and those to the right, he represents the sweet success of free enterprise and capitalism at its most admirable. For ordinary people, however, Mickey is a symbol of what's good about America and its culture. Gentle but self-confident, sentimental but not maudlin, and naïve without being foolish, Mickey epitomizes a kind of character whose appeal cuts across class and national boundaries.

Stories about the creation of Mickey Mouse are legend and contradictory. Walt Disney had been producing a series of successful animated films for Universal Studios about a character called Oswald the Lucky Rabbit. When Disney traveled to New York from Hollywood to renew the contract in 1928, he discovered that the distributor, Charles Mintz, had hired away most of his staff and intended to produce the films at a lower cost with or without

Disney. Although created by Disney, the figure of Oswald had been copyrighted by Universal. Disney refused to cooperate with Mintz. At this moment he probably promised himself never again to work on a property over which he did not exercise control and to be sure that his own intellectual property was protected to the full extent of the law.

In search of a character for a new series, one story has it that Disney remembered a pet mouse that visited the young aspiring cartoonist's drawing board in Kansas City. Another was that he dreamed up the character and sketched him out on the train on his way back from the dispute over Oswald. He wanted to call him Mortimer, but his wife suggested that a better name was Mickey. The likely truth is that like all of his creations, it was a matter of consultation and collaboration, mainly with his friend and talented artist Ub Iwerks, who had remained faithful and refused to leave Disney for Mintz.

It may partly have been a simple process of elimination. While no one in particular had decided that anthropomorphism was to be the order of the day in animation, it has worked out that way, from Gertie the dinosaur to Ren and Stimpy. The cat had already been used most famously by Otto Messmer in Felix the Cat, as well as by Disney himself in a Felix look-alike named Julius in the early Alice comedies produced before the Oswald films. Dogs were being used by Max and Dave Fleischer in the *Out of the Inkwell* series, specifically in Bimbo and his canine girlfriend Betty (before she metamorphosed into a girl as Betty Boop). Oswald had cornered the market on rabbits for a long time, until Bugs Bunny came along. What they were left with were rats and mice, largely indistinguishable in how they were drawn in animated films. They had already been used by Disney and others as frequent background characters, except for that singular mouse Ignatz who threw bricks at the love-struck Krazy Kat but who never made a successful transition to the screen from his comic strip existence. If one examines the rodents who cavort in the Alice comedies, one can see Mickey in an early form not unlike the way he would appear in *Plane Crazy*, the first of the Mickey shorts to be drawn. (See especially *Alice Rattled by Rats* of 1925 where dozens of proto-Mickeys play music, dance, and cause chaos in the household. They even have rounded ears, and as in the case of *Alice the Whaler* in 1927, wear small pants.)

The idea may have been Disney's, but likely the physical form of Mickey is attributable to Ub Iwerks. In the operation of the studio, Disney had already turned over to Iwerks the painstaking art while he focused on plots, gags, and technical and business matters. Disney would remain strongly attached to and closely identified with Mickey all of his life, doing the voice of the mouse for the films and defending him against all criticism. In fact, many would view Mickey as Disney's alter ego, and on one occasion he made the oddly revealing statement, "I love Mickey Mouse more than any woman I've ever known" (Grant 23).

If the power of Mickey Mouse as an image is as important to his popularity as his character, then Iwerks remains equally responsible for his success. An incredibly rapid artist, Iwerks had finished work almost single-handedly on

*Plane Crazy* and *The Gallopin' Gaucho* when Disney was inspired to use in the third film sound and music, which he saw as the wave of the future. Thus *Steamboat Willie* was the first animated film to be drawn in full synchronization with previously selected pieces of music. Then music had to be added to the first two, although the third was the first to be released to the public on November 18, 1928.

It was not until *Steamboat Willie* that Mickey began to assume in full his traditional appearance. In the first film he wore no shoes and had a head more in the shape of a real rodent, except he had the round ears and wore pants. In the opening scene on the steamboat, Mickey is wearing the large round shoes that would become his trademark, adopted from what was known as the "big foot" school of cartooning in the comic strip world, and he has the large circular head that would remain with him. Like Felix, Bimbo, Oswald, and most of the animated film characters who preceded him, Mickey had a black body and head, large white eyeballs, and a white area around the mouth—all characteristics of African Americans as portrayed stereotypically in cartoons, illustrations, and advertising of the time and based on the image of minstrel-show performers in black face. When white gloves were added, Mickey moved even closer to his sources. None of these characters retained, however, any of the language or cultural nuances of black life, although Mickey has sometimes been thought to retain some of the free-swinging style of the hipster and trickster. Mickey then may be "black" in more than one sense of the word.

In terms of conduct, the Mickey Mouse in these early films is unlike the one the world would come to know and love. In *Steamboat Willie* he chews tobacco, commits violence against any number of farmyard animals to make his impromptu music, and apparently drowns a parrot at the end. *The Gallopin' Gaucho* features a Mickey who drinks, smokes, and treats roughly Minnie, who wears pasties over her breasts as a dance hall girl. He commits more violence against animals in *Plane Crazy* and is guilty of sexual harassment against Minnie, who escapes his unwanted advances by bailing out of his airplane. She uses her bloomers as a parachute and arrives on the ground with no pants at the end. All of these capers are laced with crude humor about cow's udders, dropped pants, and chamber pots.

The truth is that this early Mickey had no distinct personality of his own but borrowed it from notable figures of the time. In *Plane Crazy*, he imitates the national hero Charles Lindbergh, who had made the first non-stop transatlantic flight in 1927 and who appears in the film in caricature as Mickey tousles his hair to look like him. As a Latin lover in *The Gallopin' Goucho*, Mickey is emulating Douglas Fairbanks, Rudolph Valentino, and other romantic leading men of the screen, and *Steamboat Willie*, of course, banks off of Buster Keaton's comedy *Steamboat Bill Jr.* released the year before. As parents noticed that children also greatly enjoyed the antics of the mouse, by 1931 they were complaining to Disney about the bad example he was setting.

Walt Disney examines a film with Mickey Mouse perched on his arm, 1935. Courtesy of the Library of Congress.

Under Disney's influence, therefore, Mickey began to develop a carefully delineated personality that would leave behind the early rambunctious Mickey, although he would continue this way for a number of years under the imaginative hand of Floyd Gottfredson in his adventurous comic strip and comic book stories. As Disney would describe the revised mouse, "Mickey's a nice fellow who never does anybody any harm, who gets into scrapes through no fault of his own but always manages to come up grinning" (Thomas 108). Years later he would add,

> All we ever intended for him or expected of him was that he should continue to make people everywhere chuckle with him and at him. We didn't burden him with any social symbolism, we made him no mouthpiece for frustrations or harsh satire. Mickey was simply a little personality assigned to the purposes of laughter. (Disney 68)

What is to account for the staying power and the continuing popularity of Mickey Mouse as an icon? There are no easy or quick answers to that question. Writing in one of his columns for *Natural History* magazine in 1979, the popular science writer Stephen Jay Gould applied the psychological theories of Konrad Lorenz to Mickey and came up with this explanation:

> In one of his most famous articles, Konrad Lorenz argues that humans use the characteristic differences in form between babies and adults as important behavioral cues. He believes that features of juvenility trigger "innate releasing mechanisms" for affection and nurturing in adult humans. When we see a living creature with babyish features, we feel an automatic surge of disarming tenderness. The adaptive value of this response can scarcely be questioned, for we must nurture our babies. Lorenz, by the way, lists among his releasers the very features of babyhood that Disney affixed progressively to Mickey: "a relatively large head, predominance of the brain capsule, large and low-lying eyes, bulging cheek region, short and thick extremities, a springy elastic consistency, and clumsy movements." (100–101)

Mickey, then, may appeal to innate instincts in all human beings, if Lorenz is right, although Gould would go on to suggest that these strong feelings of affection may be learned from our immediate experience and environment rather than being inherited from ancestral primates.

Another cultural explanation, for Americans anyway, is the heroic folk tradition of the little man, the lost soul, or what Charlie Chaplin called the Little Fellow. Americans have always had a degree of sympathy for the underdog, the person handicapped by injustice or discrimination, but the little man proves inadequate because he is overwhelmed by the anxieties and insecurities of the technological society created in the wake of the Industrial Revolution. This tradition would include such figures as James Thurber's Walter Mitty, George Herriman's Krazy Kat, Chic Young's Dagwood Bumstead, the screen personae of Buster Keaton and Woody Allen, and of course Mickey Mouse.

In fact, Disney borrowed it directly from the artist who may have been its originator in American culture, Charlie Chaplin. Developed over the years and through numerous films, Chaplin's Tramp is a timid but brave soul overcome by the difficulties of life, yet resilient and cheerful in the face of the struggle for survival, and often wresting victory out of the jaws of defeat. He is a romantic who brings style to his meager existence through passion, imagination, and indestructible hope. Disney admitted the inspiration and influence in 1948 when he said, "I think we are rather indebted to Charlie Chaplin for the idea [of Mickey Mouse]. We wanted something appealing, and we thought of a tiny bit of a mouse that would have something of the wistfulness of Chaplin—a little fellow trying to do the best he could" (Disney 68).

There is also something powerfully attractive about the very design of Mickey, the way he is drawn, even though he has slowly but surely changed over the years in small ways. The scrappy little barefoot mouse of *Plane Crazy* in 1928 became in the 1930s better dressed with gloves and yellow bulbous shoes, although he has always worn short pants. By the 1940s his solid oblong pupils had given way to more clearly defined eyes, and his snout was elongated somewhat. He later began to wear a greater variety of clothes in accordance with the roles he played in the films, as in *Mickey's Christmas Carol* (1983) or *The Prince and the Pauper* (1990), although by the time of his last appearance in a short cartoon in 1995, *Runaway Brain*, he has returned to his familiar clothing as he

Mickey Mouse greets visitors to Disney World during its opening year, 1971. Courtesy of Photofest.

fights a rampaging monster to save Minnie one more time.

He looks easy to draw, and he has undoubtedly inspired many a child to want to become a cartoonist. It isn't that easy, however, as any Disney how-to-draw or instructional book makes clear. It is a matter of concentric circles handled in just the right way, and no matter the angle at which he holds his head, the ears must remain two black circles. As John Updike has noted,

> These ears properly belong not to three-dimensional space but to an ideal realm of notation, or symbolization, of cartoon resilience and indestructibility.... A surreal optical consistency is part of the cartoon world, halfway between our world and the plane of pure signs of alphabets and trademarks.... To take a bite out of our imaginations, an icon must be simple. The ears, the wiggly tail, the red shorts, give us a Mickey.... Like totem poles, like African masks, Mickey stands at that intersection of abstraction and representation where magic connects. (8, 12–13)

Because of Mickey, Updike first tried his hand at cartooning before turning with greater success to fiction.

Children's book author and illustrator Maurice Sendak likewise was inspired by Mickey as a child to enter a creative field where the magic of imagery is the main mode of communication. As he would explain it,

> Though I wasn't aware of it at the time, I now know that a good deal of my pleasure in Mickey had to do with his bizarre proportions: the great rounded head extended still further by those black saucer ears, the black trunk fitting snugly into ballooning red shorts, the tiny legs stuffed into delicious doughy yellow shoes. The giant white gloves, yellow buttons, pie-cut eyes, and bewitching grin were delectable finishing touches.... A gratifying shape, fashioned primarily to facilitate the needs of the animator, he exuded a sense of physical satisfaction and pleasure—a piece of art that powerfully affected and stimulated the imagination. (108)

To this day, Sendak surrounds himself with reproductions of Mickey to feed his imagination.

As a result of his continuing appeal, Mickey has found himself at the center of cultural and political controversy. In 1970 a group of young underground cartoonists, led by Dan O'Neill, gathered in San Francisco, called themselves the Air Pirates after a group of villains who opposed Mickey in the comic strips of the 1930s, and set about liberating Mickey from the strictures of corporate ownership. They felt that Mickey had passed into popular folklore and could be claimed by members of their generation as public property. Thus they began to publish a series of comic books beginning with two issues of *Air Pirates Funnies* in the summer of 1971, as well as three issues of *Dan O'Neill's Comics and Stories* (a parodic but close approximation in appearance to *Walt Disney's Comics and Stories*), in which the Disney characters engaged in unusual conduct, with sex being one of the less startling activities. Needless to say, the Disney corporation sued for copyright violation and trademark infringement in a case that went on for ten years, finally to be settled with the cartoonists promising never to draw Disney characters again.

Then in April of 1989 Eternity Comics began to publish a series of reprints of the 1930 comic strips of Mickey under the title *The Uncensored Mouse*. According to copyright law in effect at the time, the strips had fallen into the public domain in 1986. Only two issues appeared before Disney stepped in to claim trademark infringement, although the front covers of the publications were totally black and featured no image of Mickey. Publication ceased as Disney and other corporations lobbied Congress for a change in copyright law. In 1998, Congress passed the Sonny Bono Copyright Extension Act, which extended copyright to the life of the author plus seventy years. The legislation has been called by the press the "Mickey Mouse law."

Although largely absent from the screen since the 1940s, but ever present as a costumed figure at Disneyland and Walt Disney World since the theme parks opened, and a continuing logo and spokesperson for all Disney enterprises, Mickey holds a central position in the popular imagination. Walt Disney himself once ruminated, "Sometimes I've tried to figure out why Mickey appealed to the whole world. Everybody's tried to figure it out. So far as I know, nobody has" (Updike 12). John Updike may have put his finger on a central matter, however, when he wrote, "The America that is not symbolized by that Imperial Yankee Uncle Sam is symbolized by Mickey Mouse. He is America as it feels to itself—plucky, put-on, inventive, resilient, good-natured, game" (10).

## WORKS CITED AND RECOMMENDED

Bain, David, and Bruce Harris, eds. *Mickey Mouse: Fifty Happy Years*. New York: Harmony Books, 1977.
Disney, Walt. *Famous Quotes*. Lake Buena Vista, FL: Walt Disney Co., 1994.
Gould, Stephen Jay. *The Panda's Thumb: More Reflections in Natural History*. New York: W. W. Norton, 1980.
Grant, John. *Encyclopedia of Walt Disney's Animated Characters*. 2nd ed. New York: Hyperion, 1993.
Heide, Robert, John Gilman, Monique Patterson, and Patrick White. *Mickey Mouse: The Evolution, the Legend, the Phenomenon*. New York: Disney Editions, 2001.
Holliss, Richard, and Brian Sibley. *Walt Disney's Mickey Mouse: His Life and Times*. New York: Harper & Row, 1986.
Jackson, Kathy Merlock. *Walt Disney: A Bio-Bibliography*. Westport, CT: Greenwood, 1992.
Lambert, Pierre. *Mickey Mouse*. New York: Hyperion, 1998.
Levin, Bob. *The Pirates and the Mouse: Disney's War Against Counterculture*. Seattle, WA: Fantagraphics Books, 2003.
Schroeder, Russell. *Walt Disney's Mickey Mouse: My Life in Pictures*. New York: Disney P, 1997.

Sendak, Maurice. *Caldecott & Co.: Notes on Books and Pictures*. New York: Farrar, Straus, and Giroux, 1988.

Thomas, Bob. *Walt Disney: An American Original*. New York: Hyperion, 1994.

Updike, John. "Introduction." *The Art of Mickey Mouse*. Ed. Craig Yoe and Janet Morra-Yoe. New York: Hyperion, 1991. 7–13.

Watts, Steven. *The Magic Kingdom: Walt Disney and the American Way of Life*. New York: Houghton Mifflin, 1997.

# Miss Manners

## *Dennis Hall*

"Miss Manners" is a figure familiar to all but the most isolated or disengaged of Americans. While many of us have some sense of what she looks like from the head shot that appears with Judith Martin's byline, we don't really need to see her. We are, rather, far more familiar with the distinctive voice of her syndicated columns and many consistently popular books with such titles as *Common Courtesy, Miss Manners' Guide to Domestic Tranquility, Miss Manners' Basic Training: Eating, Miss Manners Rescues Civilization, Miss Manners' Guide to the New Millennium,* and *Miss Manners' Guide to Excruciatingly Correct Behavior.* Although few of her readers have ever actually heard it, the rhetorical character of this voice is distinctive.

Whether we love her or loathe her, we have gotten to know Miss Manners, if not Judith Martin, through her patterns of speech, her singular taste for irony, and her authoritative habits of mind. She is an immediately recognizable force on the cultural landscape. Judith Martin, of course, does not own the entire etiquette franchise, but she possesses the largest chunk of it, as she assumed the crown once worn by Emily Post to serve as the unofficial official commentator on and arbiter of social behavior in contemporary American culture. Miss Manners is the American icon of etiquette.

Miss Manners, poised as she is between the personal reality of Judith Martin and an artistic creation, does not function as do such human icons as Marilyn Monroe or Muhammad Ali or as do such inventions as Mickey Mouse or Rosie the Riveter. Indeed, oscillating within this middle ground between real person and invention confers special iconic power upon Miss Manners, allowing her to survive change over time, to embrace contradictions, to trigger memory and nostalgia, to have a ritual function, to define generational differences, and to engender disagreement about the meaning of what she so forthrightly stands for. Miss Manners enjoys rich metonymic resonance; that is, she embodies a wide range of associated ideas that allows her to deliver meanings well beyond the practical business of giving directions on how the many parts of weddings or christenings or funerals are properly conducted, or on the forms of address or appropriate attire, or on behaviors at table or the theater, in the ballroom or the workplace, at home or the club.

In the last decade of the twentieth and into the first decade of the twenty-first century, civilized, not to mention decorous, behavior has come under intense scrutiny, owing in large measure to the pressures of political and cultural warfare, of the sudden and unpredictable creation of wealth, of the qualitative and quantitative extension of celebrity, of the "reality" phenomenon in the mass media, of the rise in the power of the opinion of everyman and every-woman and the decline in the social influence of elites of every stripe, among many other forces. Miss Manners stepped into the epistemological and ontological chaos surrounding "the practices and forms prescribed by social convention or by authority," as *The American Heritage Dictionary* crisply defines "etiquette." Her authoritative voice is archly shrill, certainly as compared to that of Emily Post, but even compared to those of her competitors and colleagues in the practice of etiquette discourse. Miss Manners is as much a sign of the dissolution of widely accepted conventions governing social behavior, from the White House to the house next door, as a sign of correct behavior. Miss Manners rides the crest of a wave of other etiquette columns and books and courses, whose popularity reflects a postmodern tear in the fabric of civility, a nostalgia for the loss of what are selectively remembered as the plain good manners of some unspecified time past. Miss Manners is the most conspicuous sign of the intense interest in these honest trifles that marks the fear of a betrayal of values with much deeper consequences, as American culture lurches into the new millennium.

Miss Manners. Courtesy of Shutterstock.

Etiquette, and Miss Manners as its most powerful personification, occupy a distinct place in the system of contemporary social intercourse and in the culture that system sustains, as much with ideas and associations about the relationships between self and other individuals and self and society, as with the specific behaviors they promote or inhibit. While often described as the lubrication that makes social intercourse possible and pleasurable, etiquette operates somewhere between those devices (as Thomas Hobbes would have it) that keep us from killing one another and those devices (as Eric Fromm would have it) that propel us to love one another. The practices and forms that Miss Manners stands for are significant for the information they convey about the practitioner and his or her relationships to others. When one is—how shall I say, "doing" etiquette—when one is engaged in the prescribed forms of conduct, engaged in observing the codes of propriety, one is engaged—particularly in this impolite and unrefined age—in conspicuous behavior, behavior singular and apparent to all but the somnambulant. When once the observance of the common proprieties went without saying, now their observance can scarcely pass without notice or comment. One's manners, whether they are the result of ignorance or habit or deliberation, whether they conform to or resist a prevailing paradigm or hover somewhere in between, are loaded with meaning.

The discourse on conduct, and more narrowly on etiquette, of course, has a long and venerable history, one too long to rehearse here. But from Castiglione's *The Courtier* (1528) to Miss Manners's *Guide to the Turn-of-the-New Millennium* (1989) a central concern has been what has variously been called *sprezzatura*, grace, ease, comfort. An atmosphere of ease is the goal, if not necessarily the lived experience, of all of Miss Manners's counsel. Ease is marked neither by rigid conformity, nor by loose nonconformity; rather, etiquette seeks to create a social space wherein one is bidden to be easy, but not so easy as to put others ill at ease. Miss Manners seeks to mediate between maintaining distance, on one hand, and indulging in intimacy, on the other hand.

Given their relatively short cultural history, Americans commonly accentuate etiquette as a sign of wealth and status, if not aristocracy, a matter of being both to the manor and the manner born. Americans often have a difficult time, as famously reported by nineteenth-century European travelers, precisely because they either escape contact altogether or rush to familiarity. Miss Manners promotes etiquette in terms of convenience and efficiency, concepts which mark behavior legitimated by middle-class earnestness and hard work, distinct from wealth and luxury. Miss Manners—in, to my mind, a singularly American turn—redefines ease and comfort in terms of efficiency and convenience, so as to maintain civility's delicate balance between unproductive distance and destructive intimacy.

Lest this mediating function seem like a painfully mechanical operation of the spirit of social intercourse, remember the strain that the postmodern condition imposes upon this interest and the needs that Miss Manners satisfies, including negotiating the separate spheres of men and women; understanding the increasing feminization of men and masculinization of women; managing the increasing confusion of public and private space; dealing with increasingly stark differences between parents and children; and between youth and middle-age and age, among a good many others. Miss Manners, reactionary in the strictest sense of the word, is an icon that traffics in associations of authority, definition, description and prescription, order and direction in the teeth of postmodern indeterminacy. As Julia Reed, reviewing the latest edition of *Miss Manner's Guide to Excruciatingly Correct Behavior*, puts it, "Though I myself am a transgressor, I find such passionate certitude not only refreshing—and often hilarious—but also extremely comforting. There should be more areas in life where there is so little room for doubt" (8).

Miss Manners speaks with the voice of authority, partially earned through the success of her column and books, reinforced by her every clear and unshakeable utterance, and by the ready acceptance of her command. While not immune to parody and other forms of postmodern irony, Miss Manners has not been the target that other reactionaries have been, most notably Martha Stewart (even before serving time). Moreover, Miss Manners confers authority on those who follow her practices and forms, even when they are not aware of it, as well as to those who cite her rule. Indeed, the resonance of Miss Manners's authority is sufficiently great that it inverts the axiom that they who assert must prove, shifting the burden of proof from the maker of the rule to the challenger of a rule. Her use of the question-and-answer format in the books as well as the column subvenes this confiscation of authority.

Miss Manners defines etiquette in the new millennium far more effectively than do her fellow columnists in magazines and free weekly tabloid papers, and than do the encyclopedic books on etiquette which continue to occupy bookstore shelves. While one might expect this proliferation of etiquette columns and books to undercut Miss Manners's hegemony, the confusion of alternatives ends up advancing her authority, by revealing that Miss Manners is, finally, the ever fixed mark in this sea of discursive instability. Her arch and often ironic authoritarianism, while it can be off-putting, is finally very comforting. Her voice speaks to the fears of contemporary culture; it is with manners as with politics, people flock to voices that speak without the slightest reservation or doubt.

Miss Manners prevails in this environment principally because of her focus and comprehensiveness. Although most of these alternative columnists employ the question-and-answer format Miss Manners exploits so effectively, they very often are limited by the narrowness of their focus: that is, their orientation to a niche market of readers in a certain generation or gender or subcultural group or socioeconomic class. In addition to their variability of focus and voice, they commonly bleed into the advice-psycho-personal idiom ranging from the successors to Ann Landers to Dr. Phil. Moreover, their use of the question-and-answer format does not exhibit the quality of Miss Manners's dialogue, which a careful combination of selection and editing and writing is able to create. Judith Martin is a major talent in this kind of writing. Most of the alternatives to Miss Manners create texts encyclopedic in character. While it may be possible for readers to construct a narrative of propitious practices and forms from them, the dialogues Miss Manners creates in her columns and books amount, like those of Plato, to a systematic philosophy of etiquette. Miss Manners's conversations elucidate principle through practice. The concrete examples that emerge from the dialogue between "Miss Manners" and the "Gentle Reader" teach by example rather than precept; after the fashion of the eighteenth- and nineteenth-century novel, they provide a representation of the real thing.

Related to this function of definition is Miss Manners's capacity to establish the existence of etiquette, her office as etiquette's creating word in what often seems the barbarism of the new millennium. Miss Manners operates as if "manners" and its venues have all but died, as if they need to be born again. One of her primary functions is to establish, to demonstrate by examples and concrete particularity, that there really are people, places, and activities characterized by ease, comfort, efficiency, and convenience, that somewhere "out there" are households and parties and restaurants and dances and older people and young people living the life that Miss Manners's account of etiquette not only describes, but promises. The pleasures of the texts Miss Manners creates are many, but in large measure reside in their definition of places and associations that go a very long way toward establishing one's identity, one's reality. She makes important social rituals possible.

Miss Manners resonates with us because she is a signally fixed bit of social discourse, succeeding in an era of discursive looseness. Miss Manners is unabashedly modern rather than postmodern. She provides an escape from the fragmented and the contingent, pointing to a relatively unified self and fixed relationships. Miss Manners, like so very many popular icons, materially signs the attempt to escape the schizophrenia of the condition of postmodernity.

## WORKS CITED AND RECOMMENDED

*The American Hertitage Dictionary*. 2nd College ed. Boston: Houghton Mifflin, 1982.

Attfield, Judy. *Wild Things: The Material Culture of Everyday Life*. New York: Berg, 2000.

Birenbaum, Arnold, and Edward Sagarin, eds. *People in Places: The Sociology of the Familiar*. New York: Praeger, 1973.

Caldwell, Mark. *A Short History of Rudeness: Manners, Morals, and Misbehavior in Modern America*. New York: Picador, 1999.

Cawelti, John. "The Concept of Formula in the Study of Popular Literature." *Journal of Popular Culture* 3.3 (Winter 1969): 381–90.

Hemphill, C. Dallett. *Bowing to Necessities: A History of Manners in America, 1620–1860*. New York: Oxford UP, 1999.

Kasson, John F. *Rudeness and Civility: Manners in Nineteenth-Century Urban America*. New York: Noonday P, 1999.

Martin, Judith. *Star-Spangled Manners: In Which Miss Manners Defends American Etiquette (For a Change)*. New York: W. W. Norton, 2003.

Reed, Julia. Rev. of *Miss Manners' Guide to Excruciatingly Correct Behavior* by Judith Martin. *New York Times Book Review* 12 June 2005: 8–9.

Visser, Margaret. *The Rituals of Dinner: The Origins, Evolution, Eccentricities, and Meaning of Table Manners*. New York: Grove Weidenfeld, 1991.

Wouters, Cas. *Sex and Manners: Female Emancipation in the West, 1890–2000*. Thousand Oaks, CA: Sage, 2004.

# Marilyn Monroe

## Ann C. Hall

Marilyn Monroe. She is omnipresent. Cultural wallpaper. Films. Photographs. Books. Cell phones. The internet. Postcards. Magazines. Cups. Souvenirs. T-shirts. Tattoos. The Ultimate Product. Forty-two years after her death, she still "sells," even in scholarly circles. A recent book by Sarah Churchwell, ostensibly about the "many lives of Marilyn Monroe," is less about Monroe and more about the numerous biographies on Monroe. As all academics know, such a tertiary work insures Monroe's status as cultural icon in both pop and scholarly circles.

Like other cultural artifacts and icons, the iconic Monroe encourages study and reflection which generates opposing viewpoints and conflicting opinions about her work, her life, and her fame. She was an actress and a comedienne, yet her obsessive need for perfection prohibited her from enjoying her screen success. She made "sex seem like eating an ice cream cone" (Mailer 306), yet she never found a satisfying romantic relationship. She represented the American rags-to-riches dream, yet she was an American rebel and the archetypal lost child. Above all, she was and continues to be beautiful, a testament to nature and her own instincts, as well as a monument to Hollywood invention, glamour, and artifice. For many, the Monroe dialectic is best represented in the shift from her birth name, Norma Jean, the natural, "real girl," to her screen name, Marilyn Monroe, the artificial Hollywood-created woman. Given the work of postmodernists, the conception of the "real" is complicated, and it is perhaps more fruitful to see the interplay of her screen personae, her off-screen publicity, and her biography in order to understand the persistent appeal of her image over the generations. As Roland Barthes explained in *The Pleasure of the Text*, textual pleasure comes not from finding the truth but from its pursuit; it is not the nude that delights, but the veils.

Norma Jeane Mortenson was born in Los Angeles, California, on June 1, 1926, to Gladys Baker, who suffered from mental illness throughout her life. With no father on the scene and Baker in and out of asylums, Monroe's childhood was at best chaotic and at worst abusive and terribly lonely. Her own account in *My Story* depicts a frightened and desperate little girl who creates "daydreams" in order to survive the uncertainty and instability of her young life. As she recalls, "Aunt Grace," a friend of her mother's who took care of Marilyn for a time, "was the first person who ever patted me on the head or touched my cheek" (15). According to Donald Spoto, Grace also instilled the desire for a film career in the young Norma Jean by taking her to the movies, particularly Jean Harlow's films of 1933 and 1934, proclaiming, "There's no reason you can't grow up to be just like her, Norma Jean, with the right hair color and a better nose" (38). And that, as they say, is history.

When Monroe, however, was sixteen and Grace could no longer care for her as a result of financial and personal limitations, Grace encouraged a relationship with a 21 year-old neighbor, Jim Dougherty. In a few months, the plan worked, and Marilyn married, thereby sparing her the abuse, isolation, and feelings of abandonment which characterized her previous stays in foster homes. Most biographers depict the marriage as pleasant, but Monroe's own description belies domestic bliss. She recalls going outside after dinner to play with neighborhood kids while Jim and his family talked after dinner. And she claims, "the first effect marriage had on me was to increase my lack of interest in sex" (28). When Jim joined the Merchant Marines in 1944, Monroe went to work at a parachute factory and was "discovered." She began modeling and taking acting lessons, pursuits that eventually led to the end of her marriage in 1946. That year also brought her name change to Marilyn Monroe.

Monroe began her career fervently, saying "it was like being in jail and looking at a door that said 'This Way Out'" (Monroe 39). Biographers agree—she relentlessly pursued perfection in her film and modeling careers. She was the ultimate starlet, one of the many young women who came and continue to come to Hollywood seeking fame and fortune. Today, Monroe continues to embody the term, as a quick Google search illustrates. Starlet costumes and wigs are defined by Monroe's wardrobe and makeup, most notably through costumes from *How to Marry a Millionaire* (1953) and *The Seven Year Itch* (1955).

Like all things, however, the starlet's life had a darker side, one which Monroe and her biographers present differently. Monroe says, "Hollywood's a place where they'll pay you a thousand dollars for a kiss, and fifty cents for your soul. I know, because I turned down the first offer often enough and held out for the fifty cents" (47). But biographer Barbara Leaming writes that by late 1947, Monroe "had joined the countless other starlets, models, and assorted young women on the Hollywood party circuit. . . . In exchange for dinner and the chance to meet some of Hollywood's most important players, the women were expected to make themselves available to" the men. Leaming also reports that Monroe moved into a cottage on the estate of one of the most influential men of the time in order "to be nearby when he wanted her at night" (15).

Whatever the case, she landed some small roles in 1947, and finally a more substantial but still small role in John Huston's *The Asphalt Jungle* (1950). Her performance in *Niagara* (1953) was the role that finally launched her career. Ironically, it is unlike her subsequent work. In it, she plays a *femme fatale*, a young woman married to a depressive and abusive man, George Loomis, played by Joseph Cotten. She and her lover plan to kill Loomis, but he thwarts the plan by killing the lover in a great *film noir* plot twist. Interestingly, the film takes great pains to avoid blaming only the woman. Monroe' character, of course, is clearly guilty of adultery and plotting her husband's death; however, not only is Loomis no picnic to live with, but also both characters have allowed passion to overtake them as powerfully as Niagara Falls. The other married couple, brilliantly played by Max Showalter and Jean Peters, in contrast, exemplify a wholesome, companionate love, a true love that reaps a daring rescue on the rapids of the Niagara river and a happily-ever-after-ending as its reward.

Monroe's next role, with Rosalind Russell in *How to Marry a Millionaire* (1953), is a comic masterpiece more akin to her later works. Both women are out to find husbands, one for love and one for money, but while Monroe's character is the more mercenary of the two, the film repeatedly illustrates her practicality, not her greed. We all need to live, after all. It is Russell who delivers one of the great lines of the film when the two are trying to get the better of a detective hired to spy on Monroe by her millionaire's father: "If we can't empty his pockets between the two of us, we're not worthy of the name woman." In the end, both women earn dividends—marriage to the men of their choice.

Monroe's classic, *The Seven Year Itch* (1955), presents her as an innocent beauty: "the celebrated skirt-blowing scene is, of course, the finest instance of Monroe's character's ability to suggest simultaneously both childlike pleasure and sexual delight" (Rollyson 78). Richard Sherman, exquisitely played by Tom Ewell reprising his stage role for the screen, possesses an overactive libido and imagination, and the film's success lies in the fact that "the girl" is unaware of Sherman's feelings. As the doe-eyed, unnamed, and beautiful neighbor, she serves as a perfect screen upon which Sherman and the audience can project fantasies. But as the set underscores, this sexual fantasy is a "stairway leading nowhere." Unlike the play version, the film keeps the relationship chaste. As a matter of fact, through Monroe's deft performance which simultaneously rebuffs Sherman's advances while bolstering his virility by admiring his fidelity to his wife and family, the film establishes a new definition of a "manly" man, one who remains true rather than one who counts his conquests while the family is away for the long, hot summer.

Monroe's role as Cherie in *Bus Stop* (1956), once again based on a stage play, takes her screen sexuality further than other films. She is clearly more experienced at sex than her cowboy partner, but she is also an honest, but gullible beauty, who will neither trick an innocent, uncultured cowboy into marriage nor will she be "roped into" a marriage by this handsome but crass man who promises her a better life. It is only in the end when she confesses her sexual experience and he promises to become more mannered and less selfish that she feels free to marry.

*Some Like It Hot* (1956) offers another version of Monroe's sexual innocence, and it is one of her finest performances. Disguised as a female band member, Joe, played by Tony Curtis, wins the trust of Monroe, aptly named Sugar Cane, the band's most delectable singer and ukulele player. After learning that Cane is interested in only millionaires with glasses, Joe dons the appropriate attire and a poor Cary Grant impersonation and claims that he is unmoved by women and their kisses. In one of the film's funniest scenes, Cane attempts to cure Joe through a series of passionate kisses. Here Monroe practices an early version of Marvin Gaye's "Sexual Healing." She has it to give, and gladly she gives to help a fellow human being, who happens to be rich and meets all the criteria she has established for a marriageable mate. The film underscores the fact that sex is fun, healing, and enjoyable; and as the other romantic relationship between Daphne, played by Jack Lemmon, and Osgood, played by Joe E. Brown, demonstrates, it is also liberally defined. Daphne explains, "You don't understand, Osgood! Aaah...I'm a man!" To which Osgood replies, "Well, nobody's perfect!" All motor off into the sunset together.

Through these and other films, even the more serious *The Misfits*, Monroe projects an innocent sexuality that could go wrong under adverse circumstances, but instead, for her and her characters, it does not. The sexuality portrayed in her film career remains life-giving, fun, enjoyable, and definitely entertaining. According to Barbara Leaming, Monroe "promises us that sex can be innocent, without danger. That, indeed, may not be the truth, but it continues to be what we wish. And that is why Marilyn remains, even now, the symbol of our secret desires" (431).

Monroe's life and modeling career, of course, were nothing like these films, but the tell-all biographies with lurid details of her "real" life and her "real" troubles perpetuate her iconic status as effectively as the films. According to Groucho Marx, Monroe was "Mae West, Theda Bara, and Bo Peep all rolled into one" (Spoto 148). This characterization adds the glamorous, the artificial, and naughty side of sexuality to Mailer's "ice-cream" characterization. Marilyn's sexuality was particularly calculated and provocative off-screen. As Barbara Leaming notes, Monroe was "brilliant with the press": everything she said "appeared to be utterly innocent and uncalculated" when it in fact was not (41). When promoting *The Prince and the Showgirl* (1956), for example, she sabotaged her own dress strap, timing its break during the press conference on the film (Spoto 379).

Early in her career, she took publicity into her own hands. Her nude calendar, for example, threatened her success, and film executives advised that she deny the photo. She would not: "Oh, the calendar's hanging in garages all over town.... Besides, I'm not ashamed of it. I've done nothing wrong. I was told I should deny I'd posed...but I'd rather be honest about it" (Leaming

41). Later, she attended an awards ceremony in 1953 in a dress that she had to be literally sewn into. She wore no "brassiere, slip, or underwear beneath the costume," prompting the following comment from columnist Florabel Muir: "With one little twist of her derriere, Marilyn Monroe stole the show" (Spoto 237). Later, a publicity session for *The Seven Year Itch* secured Monroe's naughty image:

> Several hundred professional and amateur photographers had gathered, and by midnight they were joined by almost two thousand bystanders eager for as much of Marilyn as they could glimpse.... What ensued was promptly dubbed by columnist Irving Hoffman 'the shot seen around the world.' Marilyn stood over the grating, special effects chief Paul Wurtzel controlled a huge fan below the street, and Marilyn's white dress flew up, revealing (as planned) white panties but no underskirt or half slip. (Spoto 283)

The famous photo of Marilyn Monroe standing over a grate. Courtesy of the Library of Congress.

Perhaps her most memorable moment as a "bad girl" was when she sang "Happy Birthday" to President John F. Kennedy. Once again sewn into a skin-tight garment with "nothing, absolutely nothing, underneath" and covered in sequins, she sang, using JFK's words, "in a sweet and wholesome way" for the president and 15,000 others in Madison Square Garden (Spoto 512–20). Her marriage to Arthur Miller and her decision to leave Hollywood and study with the Actor's Studio, as well as her numerous affairs with foreigners and American "bad boys," fueled the rebellious image of Monroe. She might be vanilla ice cream on screen, but off, she was red hot.

Despite her naughty side, she did not wield the same threat as other sex symbols like Mae West and Madonna, women who one can imagine would not only be capable of but might even enjoy castrating a man. Admittedly, Tony Curtis claimed that kissing Monroe during the filming of *Some Like It Hot* was like "kissing Hitler" (Spoto 400). But though director Billy Wilder tells equally unsavory stories, he ultimately says of his experience with Monroe:

> We were working with a time bomb, we were twenty days behind schedule and God knows how much over budget, and she was taking a lot of pills. But we were

> working with Monroe, and she was platinum—not just the hair, and not just her box-office appeal. What you saw on screen was priceless. (Spoto 405)

In addition to her performances and work, Monroe's dark side, her addictions, failed marriages, and obsessions fuel an image of a lost child, not a raging, rapier wielding woman. Thanks to the self-help phenomena of the 1980s and 1990s, Monroe's biographies ostensibly presented her life as a case study from the popular adult-children literature of the day: Janet Woititz's *Adult Children of Alcoholics* or Robin Norwood's *Women Who Love Too Much*. Her lapses, her despair, and her mistakes were not entirely her fault; they were the result of her upbringing. Even rescuers, her husbands and lovers, were abusive. When, for example, Monroe posed for the infamous photo shoot for *The Seven Year Itch,* she reported for work the next day with bruises, according to Spoto, as a result of a fight with then-husband Joe DiMaggio. Two weeks later, she filed for a divorce (285). Monroe then becomes a precursor for the adult children to follow. She is their symbol—the overachiever who is dying inside and using the alcohol and popular drugs of the 1960s and 1970s to ease the pain.

While watching one of Monroe's final films, *The Misfits* (1961), it is tempting to entertain the Monroe-as-victim interpretation. She is still very beautiful, but her character and her performance seem otherworldly, and given the fact that the screenplay was written by her ex-husband Arthur Miller and directed by the gambling addict, John Huston, it is amazing that she survived the film at all. She and her character appear to be fighting a losing battle in a violent world. She hopes to find and encourage love among men who know only death, murder, and destruction. In the end, several of the cowboys begin to understand love, compassion, and tenderness; but there is so little hope in the rest of the world, that this solution seems temporary at best. In Clark Gable's words in the film, "why did they have to go and change everything?"

For Sarah Churchwell, interpreting Monroe as the existential prison house for the pure, natural, Norma Jean is too simplistic (14). Yet as Gloria Steinem points out, this dichotomy furthered her popularity among her audiences across the generations, for not only was there a Norma Jean there to find, there was a Norma Jean there to be rescued:

> Men who had never known her wondered if their love and protection might have saved her. Women who had never known her wondered if their empathy and friendship might have done the same. For both women and men, the ghost of Marilyn came to embody a particularly powerful form of hope: the rescue fantasy. Not only did we imagine a happier ending for the parable of Marilyn Monroe's life, but we also fantasized ourselves as the saviors who could have brought it about. (15)

In the end, Monroe continues to appeal. There is "something" about her that draws us to speculate, simplistically or not. Her films give us the opportunity to fantasize about not only her but also our own lives. Her life invites us to examine ourselves and our understanding of glamour, ambition, and fame. And, finally, her death forces us to face our own mortality, the underside but equally essential component of life and beauty.

## WORKS CITED AND RECOMMENDED

Churchwell, Sarah. *The Many Lives of Marilyn Monroe*. New York: Metropolitan Books, 2004.
Leaming, Barbara. *Marilyn Monroe*. New York: Three Rivers P, 1998.
Mailer, Norman. "Marilyn." *Movies*. Ed. Gilbert Adair. New York: Penguin, 1999. 305–18.
Monroe, Marilyn. *My Story*. 1974. New York: Cooper Square P, 2000.
Rollyson, Carl. *Marilyn Monroe: A Life of the Actress*. New York: Da Capo P, 1993.
Spoto, Donald. *Marilyn Monroe: The Biography*. New York: Cooper Square P, 1993.
Steinem, Gloria. *Marilyn*. Photographs by George Barris. New York: Henry Holt, 1986.

# Mount Rushmore

## Susan Grove Hall with Dennis Hall

Called "The Shrine of Democracy," the sculpture of four president's heads in a granite peak among the Black Hills of South Dakota is an icon made of icons. This one curious sight now draws over three million people a year, more than the over two million acres of Yellowstone National Park. Moreover, the photographic image of Mount Rushmore has increasingly represented the nation and patriotic values to the public since the terrorist attacks of September 11, 2001, displayed on items from post office posters to drugstore disposable lighters. President George W. Bush drew upon the "shrine" appeal in announcing his Homeland Security plan on August 15, 2002, from the viewing terrace at Mount Rushmore, furnishing the media, and history, visual record of his face alongside Washington's, Jefferson's, Theodore Roosevelt's, and Lincoln's, as he addressed the audience and cameras. Because the granite visages portend leadership in the nation's birth, expansion, preservation, and development of world power in its first 150 years, and President Bush was addressing the crisis of a new century and historic era, he foregrounded himself upon the icons of the past with some daring, but adroitly, in a setting more appropriate to Americans' sense of security in a "homeland" than the country's other symbolic places in Washington, D.C., or New York City, so recently attacked, could provide. The "Shrine of Democracy" set in stone of the West seems a monument of permanence, removed from the changing politics and scandals in the White House or Capitol, serenely remote from the Statue of Liberty with its French origins and welcome to displaced foreigners.

The National Park Service (NPS), in its Visitor's Guide, brochures, and ranger programs, emphasizes its interpretation of the mountain sculpture with visual and aural repetitions of the four presidents' accomplishments on every hand, in digest histories and quotations that omit mention of political strife, social turmoil, or any enmity. The presidents are enshrined as patriarchs, the leaders who formed the nation's character and its progress; no conflict between the veneration of four men and the participatory struggle of a democracy is admitted. An impression of historical unity seems the goal.

The recently erected entryway and Avenue of Flags, through which visitors approach the site, structure their viewing in a procession toward a unity of gazing upward at the carved eyes overseeing them. The granite entry gate frames the colonnades ahead and the iconic mountaintop beyond in a visual temple leading to the "shrine." Through the pillars with flags of the states, the vision of the distant sculpture has sudden emergences and obliterations, enhancing one's approach as the progress of a pilgrimage, and reframing perspectives for camera shots. The architecture, as John Taliaferro observes, brings a "cathedralesque preamble to the altar of Mount Rushmore" where you "can savor the moment as a member of a group, or you can shut out the madding crowd and commune with the presidents, just you and the four of them" (397–98).

One of the NPS's three purposes is to provide opportunity for "contemplative" experiencing of the sculpture and its surroundings (National Park Service 2). Contemplation of this icon immediately tells us that the civil religion in which it is venerated has no connection to the Pilgrim founders, who strenuously adhered to the biblical commandment forbidding any graven images.

On the other hand, the heads on this altar do not, as does Catholic saint statuary, invite or foster prayer or imitative devotion. Aloft and aloof, colossal, bodiless, the countenances represent unique marvels of individual accomplishment, far above the rubble of stone waste and rabble of tiny people beneath their set jaws. The visitor, however, communes with the icon through the technological reverence of making photographs in the many vistas, and with friends and family framed before the polished, gleaming visages. If, as we suspect, icons serve an endeavor to reconcile competing desires for quasi-religious awe and for technological control and manipulation, here in the photographical pilgrimages Mount Rushmore performs admirably. The reality of historical time is suppressed, sheered off like the dark granite of nature, to model the four heads that countenance our national preeminence, at which we can gaze in blank, unquestioning marvel among the throng who affirm our journey to marvel, or assert an individual perspective, manipulation, and acquisition of the icon on our Kodak film.

To view mammoth human features that were blasted and chiseled from a mountain involves simple curiosity, a unifying mindless wonder at the sight, photography with a camera or postcards, and the car or tour bus essential for the trip. Such are the lures of any odd tourist attraction, fleeting sensations sponsored by commerce, in which we savor freedom granted more by automobiles than by democracy. Sculpture in the Black Hills was first proposed as a means of drawing tourists to South Dakota, in 1923 by a state historian; but the chosen sculptor, Gutzon Borglum, envisioned a national monument of massive scope and significance surpassing a tourist curiosity, one inspiring awe and excluding commercial exploitations. Borglum's stated aim for gigantic art to commemorate American "'civilization'" carved "'as close to heaven'" as possible, and his perseverance and industry to create it, indeed, engage the viewer of Mount Rushmore far more than the sight of the sculpture or ideas of liberty and democracy it allegedly conveys. After brief gazing and photographing, visitors' attention turns to the whys and wherewithals of Borglum's art, to his idiosyncratic quest and his technology. The NPS acknowledges this main current of interest in devoting two-thirds of the text in its brochure and answers to all the "Frequently Asked Questions" in its Visitor's Guide, to Borglum's rationale and the process of crafting the sculpture. It serves and abets this interest in its film and exhibits highlighting Borglum and the industry that scaled, blasted, and chiseled the mountain, in the new Lincoln Borglum Museum, his Sculptor's Studio, and through ranger talks on the Presidential Trail leading to the base of the granite rubble. In one of the Museum's popular, hands-on exhibits, you select a film image of the mountain, push the dynamite plunger, and watch the granite explode.

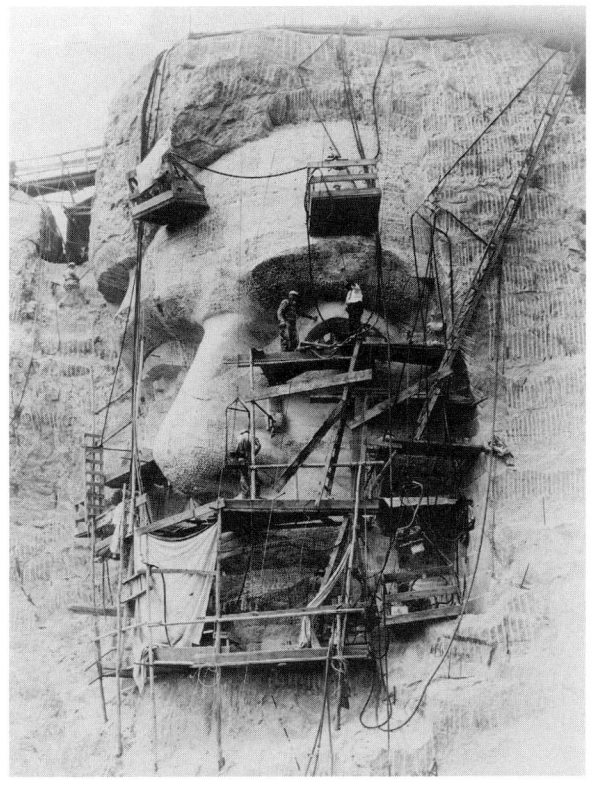

Close-up of workmen carving the head of Abraham Lincoln on the granite face of Mount Rushmore, 1937. Courtesy of the Library of Congress.

The persevering sculptor with his technology and industry becomes our marvel of individual accomplishment more than the presidents' values or democratic liberties. Borglum's aim for a monument that will outlast our time makes physical values that are abstract, that must be culturally continuous to be meaningful, must be experienced in the actions and community of life to be emotionally or morally felt. In the reification of an idea, the idea is lost, as the thing becomes much more interesting and, therefore, important. At Mount Rushmore, Jefferson's upward gaze of apparent dreaming aspiration holds little wonder after we learn the material fact of the fault in the granite which, in Borglum's original casting, would have shafted Jefferson's nose, and of Borglum's shifting the face upward to avoid the crack. Thoughts of our novel, noble government memorialized for future millennia dissipate before exhibits of Borglum's method for sealing fractures, its limitations, and the current technology and endeavors applied to retain the faces. The reification celebrated at Mount Rushmore, however, tellingly suits American passion for material culture.

Borglum, as quoted in the orientation film, wanted to make something that would last for 10,000 years, that would then represent our "civilization" even if it had passed away. The icon of endurance in stone also embodies the opposite awareness, that our civil being is constantly in change and may well be transitory. The confidence in our character and progress apparently asserted by the colossal sculpture carries with it the fear of our undoing and disappearance, which is implicit in the need for a granite monument to our historically short reign on the continent.

In our icons, so we speculate, we attempt to reconcile conflicted impulses; a look exceeding a tourist's passing gaze exposes the competing, contradictory aspects. As to disparate significations, Mount Rushmore is a tremendous icon of conflicted iconic appeals, Borglum's ambiguous need for a headstone marker for our civilization among them. Meant as bold affirmation of patriotism without ambiguity or irony, the sculpture's true, pure experiencing arrives, as touted by the NPS, in its Evening Lighting Ceremony uniting the summertime crowd in the amphitheater to stare with the spotlights and sing the national anthem. This ritual bears no small resemblance to the opening of all our ball games, and John Taliaferro's account of its assemblage of southern ladies, Boy Scouts, and black-leathered bikers into a chorus with hands upon hearts conveys the same temporary harmonization of diverse lives we sense in ceremonies for our sports (21). Another description of the floodlighting as "a heavenly view of the presidents" quickly turns to the lessons of the "full meaning" of the "Shrine" in the NPS explanations of its construction technology (Presnall 99). Any meditation on heaven's possible view of the colossal white heads on Mount Rushmore quickly encounters their problematic assertions of pride and conquest. Imagine just so far as the heavenly perspective of Theodore Roosevelt, the closest president to us in time above us, whom we unanimously revere for his conservation of nature in establishing Yellowstone National Park, gazing down on the blasted mountain.

From its proposal, the sculpture in the Black Hills drew the protest from conservationists that it would be a desecration of nature, and promoters' countering arguments that it would represent man's ordained role to improve and finish God's creation (Taliaferro 59–60). The natural spire shapes of the granite Needles towering in the Hills are suggestive of soaring cathedrals'; and their slender, erect, and curving forms evoke uniquely human attributes, yet in unearthly, mysterious transcendences. They inspire wonder, along with humbling, troubling awareness that nature's saints don't look like us, rather more like the superior aliens from outer space we fear. So the desire to anthropomorphize the Needles by carving them into Indian chieftains and western explorers—the original plan—stems from deeper longings than a tourist curiosity meets; and the presidential sculpture imposes the national visages to replace nature's discomfitting, superior aspects with faces we trust, as on our money.

The impulse to see our self-image in stone, with noble and benign providential countenance for our ways, has long been evident in reverence for New

# MOUNT RUSHMORE

Hampshire's Old Man of the Mountain. Daniel Webster acclaimed it God's own sign that "in New England He makes men" (Saine, epigraph). In Nathaniel Hawthorne's parable "The Great Stone Face," meditation on this visage gives a humble farmer wisdom, benevolence, and prophecy surpassing the hollow attainments of the renowned entrepreneur, military general, politician, and poet. The White Mountains' Old Man, however, collapsed in a storm on May 2, 2003. New England's former claim to represent the nation as heirs of the Pilgrims, moreover, has shrunk along with the physical Plymouth Rock, whose iconic rise, changing interpretations, and wane to a focus of disillusionment are superbly explored and explained in John Seelye's *Memory's Nation*. Mount Rushmore, by contrast with the Old Man, stands as an icon not of nature and humility, but of national prowess and pride. In its dark shadows lurk our fear, in our cultural insecurity within the world and our fractured, diverse communities, and our guilt.

The Black Hills were the center of the vast Plains homeland of the Lakota Sioux, and for them "a holy place, a place for vision quests" encountering the Great Spirit. Through the encroachments of settlers, wagon trains, and railroad, the hills remained land promised them when the 1868 Treaty established the Great Sioux Reservation. In 1874, however, Brevet Major General George A. Custer led his 7th Cavalry into the Hills to discover gold; and the gold rush that followed, and popular support for it, forced the Sioux from the hills. Before and after, the treatment of "the Sioux people will always be among the sorriest chapters in this nation's history," as Edward Lazarus concludes his judicious study *Black Hills White Justice* (433). Lazarus' father Arthur Lazarus, Jr., arguing for compensation of the Sioux before the U.S. Supreme Court in 1980, summarized the case:

> The United States took the bulk of the Sioux land under the 1868 Treaty and...paid them $40 million less than the land was worth. As a result of that they started [reservation life] impoverished; that was the fault of the United States. And the United States kept them from their hunting grounds, so they became dependent on the United States for food. Then, the United States first encouraged the miners to come in and then withdrew the troops. Then, the United States rounded up the Sioux and put them on the reservation and took their guns and horses so they couldn't hunt....The Sioux are among the most depressed people in the entire United States and they are so depressed, not in the least part, because the United States in 1877 took their most valuable asset, the Black Hills, and hasn't paid for it yet. (Lazarus 391)

Arthur Lazarus, Jr., won this case, and a compensation of $106 million for the Sioux; in 1987 a U.S. Court of Claims awarded them $40 million for land relinquished in the 1868 Treaty. The Sioux people, however, despite their continuing severe poverty, have rejected monetary compensation, because it represents for many an immoral sale of their sacred land and a betrayal of their essential, identifying cultural values (Lazarus 401, 424, 433).

In 1931, the Lakota Chief Luther Standing Bear, author of *My People the Sioux,* suggested to Borglum that he should sculpt the warrior Crazy Horse beside Washington and Lincoln, and Borglum agreed that a Sioux chief should be memorialized in the Black Hills. After both had died, Chief Henry Standing Bear took the cause of the Indian hero to another sculptor, Korczak Ziolkowski, who began work on a mountain ten miles southwest of Mount Rushmore in 1948, with a model of Crazy Horse on his steed, and a plan far out-scaling the presidential heads (Taliaferro 321–22, 328–29). The dynamite carving still proceeds, continued since Ziolkowski's death in 1982 by his family and a nonprofit foundation. After over 8 million tons of granite have been blasted, the visage alone, 87 feet high (Washington's is 60 feet) has emerged. The popularity of the Crazy Horse Memorial with tourists has evidence in its financing sheerly by their contributions and souvenir buying (Romero). Whether it is an appropriate memorial, however, is a debatable question among the Lakota for many reasons, among them, its enshrinement of an individual man (Larner 362–63). As a companion piece to Mount Rushmore, an icon of mastery, conquest, and progress, moreover, the statue of the warrior who bravely resisted white civilization but died in a military guardhouse, unarmed, from a soldier's bayoneting, is tragically ironic (Taliaferro 38). But its sheer size will attract tourist marvel more than its form or meaning.

Work closes on Mount Rushmore, 1944. Courtesy of the Library of Congress.

# MOUNT RUSHMORE

The bigness of Mount Rushmore obviously dominates its iconic appeal; the material, technological accomplishment evokes, and mostly consumes, our awe. Consider Steve Gottlieb's summation of "the noble sculpture" among his "Symbols of Freedom" in his photographic study *American Icons*: "One must view Mount Rushmore from so far away that even those twenty-foot noses don't seem particularly big. Dare I suggest that if you want a real sense of nose size you would do better to see the closing sequence of Alfred Hitchcock's movie *North by Northwest?*" (170). Yes, for "nose size," but not for a "real sense" of the sculpture's. Hitchcock first composed the terrifying scene of Cary Grant's and Eva Marie Saint's peril atop Mount Rushmore in his notebook sketch of the "TINY FIGURES" there with a suggested scale that enlarges the sculpture, in my estimate, by about 25 percent. The presidential faces for the filming were constructed on an MGM soundstage (Auiler 355, 340). Hitchcock's camera angles and focus magnify the noses while dwarfing Grant and Saint.

The compelling illusion to which Gottlieb testifies has significant relation to Hitchcock's genius in capturing more of our attractions to the icon than sheer awe at its size. One is the desire to get near to it, physically grasp it, and measure ourselves by it, as the film lets us pretend to do. This urge brings thousands of people a year to try to climb on the mountain, necessitates extensive ranger surveillance to keep them away from the sculpture, and motivates the new Presidential Trail which allows visitors a much closer access to the presidents; as John Taliaferro remarks, "You can look right up their noses, as Alfred Hitchock had wanted" (399). This desire draws tourists into expensive helicopter rides that approach the heads on their level, and noisily anger rangers delivering their homages to the Shrine.

A second urge Hitchcock fulfilled was the need for a popular story for the icon. The story of its sculptor's quest is tied to his generation's Teddy Roosevelt optimistic expansionism, and now bears suspicion as megalomania, or worse, as Jesse Larner relates Borglum's prior work on a Confederate monument on Stone Mountain, Georgia, to his association with the Ku Klux Klan (187–231). Hitchcock's story casts an innocent man into a heroic struggle for survival in a Cold War spy chase. That the insidious enemy nation is not identified, and its agents are powerful, attractive, and ubiquitous, plays to American fears that have abruptly heated since 9/11, of unsuspected deceptions of our innocence, and usurpations of our freedoms that can destroy them—or us. For all its outdated trappings, Hitchcock's film carries the ominous implication of Borglum's intent to create a headstone to memorialize our "civilization" long after it has disappeared. Mount Rushmore is "portentous" in the meanings of pompous and amazing, and also in portending a national anxiety which usually remains unspoken. Greil Marcus has voiced this cultural dread in contemplating something so far from the gigantic sculpture as Bob Dylan's 1967 "basement tapes":

> Just as every schooled American carries a sense of the country's beginning as event, so too does every such American harbor a sense of national ending, less

as a historical event than a fading away, a forgetting, a common loss of memory experienced all at once in a single heart: a great public event locked up in the silence of the solitary. (69)

The nation that revered Plymouth Rock as a "sacred icon" (Seelye 31) has been forgotten. But Mount Rushmore centers the conflicted aspiration, pride, power, possessiveness, guilt, and fear within American identity; and it continues to generate controversy, as well as celebration. If it is "The Shrine of Democracy," however, it enacts this role by gathering flocks of tourists, from many lands, who bring their cameras and trade them for shots, share their marvel or jokes or criticisms with strangers, and freely demonstrate their particular allegiances on their tee shirts, uniforms, or other attire, like the person on stilts costumed as a giant Gandhi who was parading on the Avenue of Flags during our July 2004 visit, bearing the sign, "We must be the change we wish to see in the world."

## WORKS CITED AND RECOMMENDED

Auiler, Dan. *Hitchcock's Notebooks: An Authorized and Illustrated Look Inside the Creative Mind of Alfred Hitchcock*. New York: Spike, 1999.

Gottlieb, Steve. *American Icons*. Lanham, MD: Roberts Rinehart Publishers, 2001.

Hawthorne, Nathaniel. "The Great Stone Face." *The Snow-Image and Uncollected Tales*. Ed. J. Donald Crowley et al. Columbus: Ohio State UP, 1974. 26–48.

Larner, Jesse. *Mount Rushmore: An Icon Reconsidered*. New York: Thunder's Mouth P/Nation Books, 2002.

Lazarus, Edward. *Black Hills White Justice: The Sioux Nation versus the United States, 1775 to the Present*. Lincoln: U of Nebraska P, 1999.

Marcus, Greil. *Invisible Republic: Bob Dylan's Basement Tapes*. New York: Henry Holt, 1997.

National Park Service. *Fiscal Year 2001 Annual Performance Plan for Mount Rushmore National Memorial*. 13 Sept. 2004 <http://data2.itc.nps.gov/parks/moru/ppdocuments/m-app-~1.doc>.

"President Talks Homeland/Economic Security at Mt. Rushmore." <http://www.whitehouse.gov/news/releases/2002/08/20020815.html>.

Presnall, Judith Janda. *Mount Rushmore*. San Diego: Lucent Books, 2000.

Romero, Librado. "Crazy Horse Writ Large and Dream to Match." *New York Times* 25 Aug. 2004, national ed.: B1.

Saine, P. J., ed. *The Great Stone Face, by Nathaniel Hawthorne*. Lebanon, NH: Blue Plate P, 2004.

Seelye, John. *Memory's Nation: The Place of Plymouth Rock*. Chapel Hill: U of North Carolina P, 1998.

Standing Bear, Luther. *My People the Sioux*. Ed. E. A. Brininstool. Lincoln: U of Nebraska P, 1975.

Taliaferro, John. *Great White Fathers: The Story of the Obsessive Quest to Create Mount Rushmore*. New York: PublicAffairs, 2002.

# Muppets

## Robert Barshay

In view of their formative role, we could well say, "Muppets are us." Jim Henson's Muppets have been the most powerful piece of children's popular culture in the second half of the twentieth century, veritable icons of Americana. They are outgrowths of the first nationally popular children's shows on television, the *Howdy Doody Show*; *Kukla, Fran and Ollie*; *The Pinky Lee Show*; *Lunch with Soupy Sales*; *Captain Kangaroo*; *Mr. Rogers' Neighborhood*; and *The Shari Lewis Show*. *The Howdy Doody Show* first aired December 27, 1947, and the others began in the 1950s. Ostensively, these shows became popular because the medium of television was relatively new, and because they were the first network programs aimed exclusively at children. The changes in children's shows since the 1950s have been quite dramatic. The seltzer shooting episodes of Clarabell the Clown, the anarchic pie throwing antics of Soupy Sales, and the vaudevillian frenzies of Pinky Lee were replaced with educational themes of math, spelling, vocabulary, and Spanish lessons in *Sesame Street*. Such a transformation in the broadcasting content of children's shows deserves some explanation.

First, children's television shows can be divided roughly into two categories: those that relied on a real human being as the source of all the content, be that moral instruction or humor, usually the vaudevillian kind, or both; and those that relied principally on a puppet(s) or a marionette(s), or both, along with a human being, to convey their entertainment and/or instructional value. The movement away from the prominence of a human element in these shows to a lesser role ultimately led to the marginalization or even total absence of visible humans. This shift eventually enabled the puppets and marionettes to control the action of the story, learning, entertainment value, and, as we will see, the subversive element that we enjoy in *Sesame Street* and the Muppets' television series and movies.

Second, the main attraction in the earliest children's shows, when dominated, usually always, by humans, was mischievous behavior performed by adults, behavior forbidden to children by their parents and teachers. But precisely because activities such as pie throwing or seltzer squirting were prohibited, children could imaginatively indulge in this behavior not allowed at home or school, and gain the approval of a grown-up, even if the grown-up was the naughty, hyperkinetic one on television who threw the pies or squirted the seltzer. Such pleasure to a repressed child of the 1950s must have been delicious because it was parentally forbidden, yet approved of at the same time by the grown-up world presented on television.

*The Pinky Lee Show* was a one-man frenetic show. Pinky sang, danced, joked, and spoke with a lisp for a full half-hour each weekday. Wearing a checkered beanie, an oversized checkered sport jacket, and a checkered bow tie, Pinky was clearly a strange descendant from his early days in vaudeville. Dismissed as a "five-foot-four lisper" by a columnist, Pinky, whose real name was Pinkus Leff, became so successful with children that his show, which debuted on January 4, 1954, became a big hit for NBC daytime, and a solid lead-in to its long-running *Howdy Doody Show*. Though beloved by children, not many adults shared their sentiment. Milton Berle once commented at a gathering of famous comedians that "if a bomb hit this joint, Pinky Lee would be a hit"; and *New York Times* reviewer Jack Gould labeled him "crude, tasteless and... a conspiracy against parents" ("TV Acres").

On September 20, 1955, during one of his hysterical routines telecast from NBC's Burbank studio, Pinky Lee collapsed from an apparent heart attack, which was later explained as a severe sinus attack ("TV Acres"). It has been said that while he was writhing on the ground, those who were producing the show as well as the kids watching it at home, thought that he was doing one of his crazy *shticks*. Under doctor's orders, the host was forced to take a year off to recuperate. Though he recovered, his reputation didn't, and he lost his show and his celebrity status, partly a result of his crude vaudevillian style.

Joan Cusack with the Muppets during *It's a Very Merry Muppet Christmas Movie*, NBC, 2002. Courtesy of Photofest.

But kids had loved his anti-establishment antics as much as adults disdained them, and their devotion made his show a hit.

The frenetic pace of the *Pinky Lee Show* brought complaints from a number of parents who felt the show got their kids unnecessarily wound up, causing discipline problems after the show was over. In fact, in August 1955, NBC agreed to tone down the gratuitous crudeness of *The Pinky Lee Show* and *The Howdy Doody Show,* "limiting the destruction of property, bad grammar, seltzer water squirting, throwing things, name-calling, and other antisocial behavior that was parentally forbidden" ("The Pinky Lee Show"). Of course, it was precisely that antisocial activity that explains the source of the success of these shows in the '50s, a time of conformity for adults and constricted behavioral standards for children.

The ultimate bad boy of children's shows was without question Soupy Sales, whose behavior reminded one of the clowns and buffoons who performed between acts at the old time burlesque shows. His program, *Lunch with Soupy Sales,* made famous for children the pie-in-the-face routine. And the slapstick *shtick* did indeed become routine. One internet source counted at least 19,000 pie-throws, mostly at Soupy, and at the height of his popularity such stars as Frank Sinatra and Sammy Davis, Jr., begged to be on the receiving end of one of his pies ("Welcome to Soupy Sales Biography!"). Soupy's urgent verbosity and mischievous grin were calculated to appeal to his audience.

*Lunch with Soupy Sales* may have been the first children's show to introduce non-human characters (with the exception of Flub-A-Dub, a hybrid creature on *The Howdy Doody Show*), and characters they were: White Fang, Black Tooth, Pookie, and Hippi. White Fang and Black Tooth were just a white dog paw and black dog paw, not much more than terrycloth sock puppets that barely reached into camera range, though Pookie and Hippi were actual puppets. White Fang, the most popular sock on television then, never spoke English; he intoned in a gruff voice that was intelligible only to Soupy. The show's popularity was based on the secret desire of its young audience to throw pies in the puss of American adulthood respectability and mores. As frosting on the "pie," such behavior was condemned with the usual moralizing, disapproval, and punishments of parents, but was loved by children and enthusiastically endorsed by the adults who programmed this show, and Soupy, the adolescently adult impresario.

*The Howdy Doody Show, Kukla Fran and Ollie, Captain Kangaroo, Mr. Rogers' Neighborhood*, and *The Shari Lewis Show* all used marionettes and/or puppets with human beings, who were dominant in the shows. *The Howdy Doody Show* was by far the most popular and long standing children's show until the appearance of *Sesame Street*. It began in January 1947 and continued through June 1956, five days a week, then from 1956 to 1960 every Saturday, all on NBC. The show bridged the transition from black-and-white to color television. All told, according to one Web site, there were 2,543 episodes ("Classic TV Shows"). What my friends and I enjoyed the most was the subversive role of Clarabell, first played by Bob Keeshan, who would subsequently become the respectable Captain Kangaroo in his own show. Like Harpo Marx of the infamous Marx Brothers movies, Clarabell uttered no words or sounds, communicated only by squeezing a small horn, and disrupted the other "straight" players by causing mischief, squirting seltzer, and generally disregarding all the rules, conventions, and customs of adult interaction—seemingly just for the pleasure of being perverse.

What made Clarabell attractive as a character was that he got away with this perversity. Although he was lightly reprimanded by "Buffalo" Bob Smith on these occasions, he was never punished or "grounded." Moreover, the reprimands came to naught, as he would indulge in the same subversive play time and time again, frequently several times in the same episode. The squirting of seltzer water in *The Howdy Doody Show* was equivalent to the tossing of pies in *Lunch with Soupy Sales.*

The other character we all loved was the Phineas T. Bluster, a sneaky curmudgeon who was deliberately disagreeable and sometimes outright dishonest. A marionette who blustered, sputtered, and schemed, Mr. Bluster was the dark sheep of the cast who secretly elicited children's affections by undermining the activities of the adults in the show. In the end his schemes and misanthropic plans never materialized, but we loved his efforts at disrupting the bland and predictable behavior of Buffalo Bob and the other "straight" characters, as we might a cranky uncle who always spouted insulting or embarrassing comments at family affairs, to the chagrin of the other adults.

As we can see, there has been a gradual shift away from human beings to non-humans, mainly puppets and marionettes, as the dominant focus of children's shows. Pinky Lee, Soupy Sales, and others of that ilk were slammed by critics and parents alike for being vulgar, unseemly, wild, undisciplined, and, yes, naughty. In a word, they subverted adult respectability. However, puppets, marionettes, and, more recently, Muppets can act subversively in ways unacceptable for adult actors in children's shows. When a Muppet sticks his tongue out at cleanliness and acts perversely, or stuffs his mouth at every opportunity (and eats with his mouth open as crumbs fly all over), not only do children laugh, but parents think such behavior cute. For Muppets are cuddly, furry, and adorable, unlike their vaudevillian forbears.

The adult view of the Muppets was shaped by *Sesame Street*, the first popular show in which the Muppets dominated a children's show. It first appeared on television on November 10, 1969. Parents loved *Sesame Street* not only because it would not harm their children, as it was patently without violence, frightening happenings, or dark undertones of any sort, but also because the program would teach them numbers, letters, words, and good family values. Thus mothers plopped their children in front of the television in the morning because it kept them quiet—a cheap and easily accessible babysitter—and because it was a source of seemingly wholesome entertainment and vital education. Moreover, many parents of the 1970s were aware that *Sesame Street* originated from the Children's Television Workshop and was subsequently picked up and telecast by the Public Broadcasting Service, which had the imprimatur of a near-divine entity, or so it seemed to enlightened moms of the time. Watching *Sesame Street* was the equivalent of playing with educational toys, but cheaper.

So *Sesame Street* was popular with children as well as their parents. I believe that children enjoyed the show for some of the same reasons that children in the 1950s enjoyed their comedies. First, some of the prominent Muppets were subversive of respectable adult norms and standards of behavior. Cookie Monster is, after all, the incarnation of one of the seven deadly sins—gluttony. Not only does he gorge himself in virtually every episode in which he appears, he gorges himself on cookies, a dessert which children may enjoy only if they eat first their vegetables and other boring foods. So here we have a creature who stuffs himself with a beloved delicacy, one which children may be deprived of if they don't comply with adult eating rules, such as eating their spinach or liver. His maniacal focus on stuffing himself on cookies simulates obsessive/compulsive behavior, such that concerns for others and their interests do not register at all on his sensitivity barometer. He is what children wish they could be at home.

Some years ago, *Sesame Street* created a satirical segment called "Monsterpiece Theatre," in which one "Alistair Cookie" is portrayed by Cookie Monster. Naturally, he sported a silk ascot and a velvet jacket, and sat on a wing chair surrounded by leather-bound books. At the end of the sketch, he mumbles, "Me love culture," through a mouthful of chocolate chip cookies (Hymowitz). Though it is doubtful that many children who enjoyed that show were actually familiar with "Masterpiece Theatre," most were able to understand on some level that the trappings of high culture were being mocked by the "monsterfication" of low culture. The intellectual pretensions to which adults often aspire were being leveled by what children most admire: unmitigated appetite run amuck, without censorship or punishment, all conveyed in bad grammar.

One of the most famous Muppets is the Oscar the Grouch, whose appeal is that he not only can be grouchy—a forbidden middle-class trait—but that he is always grouchy, particularly to the adult humans on the show. Many American adults impose upon their children a militant niceness as *de rigueur* behavior. This standard of behavior may be experienced by the children as unnatural, though they would not be able to express that in words or thought. For most children, to be grouchy when other children are nasty to them, or when they don't feel good, or when they sense they have been insulted, is natural, though more often than not they will be instructed to suppress grouchiness under any circumstances. So they identify with Oscar the Grouch who gets away with grouchiness all the time, despite the admonitions of the surrogate parents on the show. For children who are constantly reminded to clean up their room or pick up their clothes off the floor, seeing Oscar the Grouch live in a trash can out in an urban street only evokes admiration for the ultimate rejection of adult hygiene and rectitude.

In the previous television shows, prominent vaudeville behavior contributed enormously to their appeal. Though we don't have the pie-in-your-face and seltzer water in-your-pants kind of burlesque in *Sesame Street*, we have the "watered down" version of Abbott and Costello in Muppets with Ernie and Burt. Burt is the pointy headed one who is the butt of Ernie's verbal assaults, or sometimes playful ignorance. More to the point, Burt, as the straight man of the team, and Ernie, as the jokester, engage in the repartee of vaudeville duos. And the sketches, like the traditional vaudeville acts of the George Burns and Gracie Allen prototype, mock the values and expectations of the straight man, which represent respectable society. It's the ignorance of the Ernies in the world that wreaks havoc upon the settled order of things. Humor, even the benign kind practiced by Ernie, subverts culture that takes itself too seriously.

I have heard grumblings from some parents objecting to Burt and Ernie's sharing the same bedroom. Notwithstanding potential challenges from the fundamentalist right or the adherents of gay and lesbian critical theory, no "queer" conspiracy or latent homoerotic content complicates their relationship. After all, preschool and elementary school children share the same bedroom with friends of the same sex, chatting past their bedtime, in sleepovers, and would use that model to relate to the Ernie and Burt relationship. Homophobia is part and parcel of the adult world, but unknown to the more honest world of children's friendship. We see the same vaudevillian dynamics at work in the characters of Statler and Waldorf, two curmudgeons who appeared weekly in *The Muppet Show* (1976–1980) and *Muppets Tonight!* (1996–1997). These old codgers sat together in the mezzanine boxes, humorously insulting the other acts that appeared on the television show in the guise of a variety show. The fast repartee, the straight man and jokester roles, and the perverse joy of being not nice were all trademarks of their routines that children loved. The zingers were aimed not just at the performances of the Muppet entertainers, but, more important, at polite society in which all effort is to be commended, no matter the merit, a value that adults attempted to inculcate in their children.

In one conversation between these senior citizens—who look somewhat similar to the infamous Mr. Bluster—one says to the other that he likes the last act. The other asks why, evoking the response, "because it *is* the last act." Children appreciate the truth over nice falsehoods, particularly when expressed with humor and in the mouths of funny looking adults. Old people and children have in common an indifference to socially acceptable behavior that attempts to call something it is not: the former because they don't care, and the latter because they don't understand the concept.

To become an icon of American popular culture, the Muppets have to resonate with adults even more than with children, as they are the ones who employ *Sesame Street* as a dependable babysitter and invaluable classroom. Kay S. Hymowitz indicates that it has been more successful than any other children's show not only in this country, but also all over the world. Moreover, "In the United States, *Sesame Street*'s popularity is staggering; 77 percent of American preschool children from all areas, ethnic groups, and income levels watch the show once a week or more. In many locales they can take their pick of three or more broadcasts a day" (1). In addition to its popularity over a quarter of a century, it has won fifty-eight Emmys, two Peabody Awards, and four Parents' Choice Awards, and also become the subject of retrospectives at the Smithsonian Institution and the Museum of Modern Art (2). Possibly it is even more popular with parents than with children, for very different, perhaps opposite reasons. The most important reason that *Sesame Street* resonates with adults is that for them the show has been culturally constructive, particularly so when it first came on the air in the late 1960s and 1970s, a time when cultural values were in turmoil and conflict.

*Sesame Street* celebrates diversity in its cast of humans, who are white, African American, Hispanic, and Asian. As Hymowitz points out, "the rainbow cast is inclusive, embracing a deaf woman using sign language and a child in a wheelchair" (3). More important, the cast of Muppets, the focus of the interest for children, is equally diverse. The main Muppet is Kermit, who is a green frog, and proud of his identity and color. The brilliance of the show is that such diversity is not ideologically exhorted, but rather is demonstrated naturally and unselfconsciously in an urban environment. Moreover, though the show does not gloss over the disagreements and conflicts that occur among friends and acquaintances, the Muppets treat each other with basic respect, dignity, and fairness. Implicit in all the relationships is belief that though each of the Muppets has different strengths, talents, and flaws, and identities, none is ridiculed or scorned for those differences. In short, tolerance is demonstrated in their relationships, a more powerful lesson than preaching about its importance.

So the popularity of the Muppets, as reflected in *Sesame Street* and in other media, continues to powerfully engage both adults and children, who often have different views on what is amusing, important, and interesting. A pie-in-the-face or a squirt of seltzer down the pants is not the only way of mocking adult prissiness, sanctimony, or pretentiousness. The Muppets's behavior maintains the anti-adult messages from the earliest television show of the 1950s by poking fun in less physical ways at the values of respectability, niceness under all circumstances, cleanliness, order, and conformity. At the same time, the Muppets, as seen in the early television episodes, the movies, and most enduringly in *Sesame Street*, appeal to adults, because by their behavior, by their personalities, by virtue of whom they represent, and by their relationships with humans and, most important, with each other, they reflect the values of diversity, tolerance, and the dignity of all creatures. And, of course, the children learn their alphabet and numbers, and are exposed to Spanish, while their mothers can go about their business around the house knowing that their children are in good, albeit furry, hands.

## WORKS CITED AND RECOMMENDED

"Classic TV Shows—Howdy Doody with Buffalo Bob Smith and Clarabell." 30 July 2004 <http://www.fiftiesweb.com/tv/howdy-doody.htm>.

Finch, Christopher. *Of Muppets & Men: The Making of the Muppet Show*. New York: Alfred A. Knopf, 1981.

Hymowitz, Kay S. "On 'Sesame Street,' It's All Show." *City Journal* Autumn 1995. 9 Aug. 2004 <http://www.city-journal.org/html>.

Italia, Bob. *Behind the Creation of...the Muppets*. Ed. Rosemary Wallner. Edina, MN: Abdo & Daughters, 1991.

"The Pinky Lee Show." 28 July 2004 <http://www.tvparty.com/lost pinky.html>.

Sherman, Bill. *Muppography*. 20 June 1997. 16 July 2004 <http://vr.ncsa.uiuc.edu/BS/Muppets/muppography.html>.

"TV Acres: Children's Show Hosts—Pinky Lee." 28 July 2004 <http://www.tvacres.com/child_pinkylee.htm>.

"Welcome to Soupy Sales Biography!" 28 July 2004 <http://www.amdest.com/stars/ssales/html>.

# NASCAR's Bristol Motor Speedway

## Barbara S. Hugenberg and Lawrence W. Hugenberg

> Bristol is phenomenal, much like Green Bay (Wis.), where everybody stands behind their Packers. It's like a Magic Kingdom, in both Virginia and Tennessee.
> — Olin Burton Smith, who purchased Bristol Motor Speedway in 1996 (UMI Publications 117)

You drive to Bristol, Tennessee, from miles away (because every hotel room within twenty-five miles is rented by NASCAR fans), you park your car two miles away from the track on the side of the road (because all the parking lots are full or you refuse to pay $40 to park in someone's front yard), you walk up the hill to the raceway, you hear the rumble of a couple of cars racing around the track as teams practice and tune their cars to anticipated track conditions, and you enter the track and notice 160,000 seats in a large bowl surrounding this half-mile oval track (originally exactly a half-mile track, it was reshaped in 1969 and became a .533-mile track, according to *Bristol Motor Speedway History*). The recreational vehicles arrive during the week preceding the race and NASCAR fans run their American and Confederate flags up homemade flagpoles. Other fans set up their "shrines" for their favorite drivers with tents, coolers, chairs, flags, banners, and other equipment in the team colors. On race day, the hillside by the track is covered with hundreds of recreational vehicles, shining in the sunlight, and appearing to be stacked on top of each other in a sea of green grass (or brown mud if it rains).

The area around the track fills up hours before the race, as fans shop in the makeshift NASCAR memorabilia yard sale where vendors set up tents in residents' front yards or along the town sidewalks. Other fans arrive early to catch a glimpse of their favorite driver arriving at the track by helicopter or leaving their mobile home, parked right next to the track, to begin their race preparations. The stands start filling up long before the start of the race or even the beginning of pre-race ceremonies: the parachuting of military personnel into the center of the track, the introduction of the drivers as they circle the track waving to the stands, the invocation by a local religious figure, the presentation of the United States flag by a military honor guard, the singing of the national anthem by a well-known entertainer, and the fly-over by military aircraft. Finally, you hear the four most famous words in racing shouted by a corporate executive of the company sponsoring the race, "Gentlemen, start your engines!"

As the forty-three racecars rumble to life with their 800-horsepower engines, the stands fill with exhaust fumes. The cars roll off pit road and down the track behind the pace car and the noise of the cars is deafening (so you put in your earplugs). The noise level at Bristol Motor Speedway is constant and loud because it is a short track encircled by the 160,000-seat stands. As a result of this constant, loud noise, Bristol Motor Speedway is known as "Thunder Valley." At other NASCAR tracks the noise levels are less constant because tracks are larger or stands are smaller and cars become more and more separated as the race progresses. After several laps, the pace car drops off the track, pulls into pit road, and the race starter, perched above the track at the start-finish line, drops the green flag. The forty-three cars race past the start-finish line straining to get to top speed. Two and three cars wide they enter the first turn, which is banked so high that track workers have to climb on their hands and knees to the top of the track to clear debris or soak up an oil spill.

Then it happens: drivers are banging into each others' bumpers or rubbing other cars as they carom around this small track, and finally one of the cars is spinning out of control and hits the wall—bits and pieces of the car explode all over the track. Sometimes, as a car is spinning other cars are captured by the initial wreck and are sent into the wall at the top of the track or into another car in front of them that has slowed down. The yellow caution flag is thrown to slow down the race field behind the pace car, which gives the crew time to sweep up bits and pieces of racecar left in the wake of the wreck. After the track is cleared and deemed safe, the entire cycle begins again with the pace car exiting the field, the sprint towards the start-finish line and the inevitable wreck. The fans cheer the constant action and the wrecks—unless it is their favorite driver spewing oil or losing fenders. This same sequence happens over and over throughout the 500 laps—green flag racing, caution flag, green flag racing, caution flag, and so on.

In UMI Publications' *Bristol Motor Speedway: 40 Years of Thunder*, the racing at Bristol Motor Speedway is described as "old-fashioned beating and banging that reminds fans what the sport used to be. In fact, the most famous remark about the place came from a Winston Cup driver, who said when asked how it feels to race at Bristol, 'It's like flying a F-16 in a high school gym'" (141). Matt McLaughlin, a long-time reporter for Speed Channel, wrote the following regarding the popularity of Bristol Motor Speedway for NASCAR fans:

# NASCAR'S BRISTOL MOTOR SPEEDWAY

Aerial view of the Bristol Motor Speedway. AP/Wide World Photos.

> Yes, in the grand scheme of things racing pales to religion, but when it comes to what has formed this crazy cult of stock car fans, Bristol is indeed the closest thing we have to a tent revival. It's part revival, part rock and roll show, part demolition derby, part brass knuckled rumble, part Bruce and the E Street Band Detroit Medley encore, part Christmas morning for six year olds, and 100% pure racing. I've said it before and I'll say it again Brothers and Sisters, don't take me to the river preacher take me to the banks of Bristol. (Ben Trout, Senior Manager of Communications, Bristol Motor Speedway, letter, June 1, 2004)

If attending a NASCAR race at Bristol Motor Speedway is your first, you become hooked on NASCAR and a life-long fan of this track, if not all of NASCAR. One fan wrote in the October 21, 2004 issue of *Scene Magazine*,

> This year, I was invited to join my girlfriend on an all-expenses-paid one-week cruise to Bermuda to celebrate both her and her son graduating from college and her daughter graduating from the eighth grade. Guess what weekend they planned to leave? The weekend of the Bristol night race.... After much soul searching and the comment from my racing buddy at work that, "Bermuda would be there forever, but Bristol only happens once," I decided to decline the invitation to go to Bermuda and go to Bristol. Now most "normal" folks would think I was nuts, but us rabid NASCAR fans are different. ("From Our Readers," *Scene* 28: 83)

When non-fans think of NASCAR racing, they may think of rednecks, fast cars, all left turns, NASCAR dads, and wrecks. Moderate NASCAR fans move beyond these simple perceptions to think of several famous tracks where they attended races or watched them on television: Daytona, Indianapolis Speedway (home of the Brickyard 400), Charlotte, or Atlanta. Or they might think of famous drivers; such as Richard Petty, Bobby Allison, Dale Earnhart, Jeff Gordon, or Benny Parsons. Other moderate NASCAR fans might recall the track where they witnessed their first NASCAR race (Darlington, Rockingham, Martinsville, Bristol, or Talladega). However, when many longtime, devoted fans think of NASCAR many of their immediate thoughts go to their experiences and/or the reputation of Bristol Motor Speedway. For these fans, Bristol Motor Speedway is an icon, "independent of time and place" (Martin 207). This image is frequently the result of witnessing their first NASCAR race at Bristol and becoming hooked on NASCAR racing at that point. Or it might be the result of attending a spring race or the August night race at Bristol Motor Speedway, and listening to the roar of the forty-three cars, seeing the other 160,000 plus fans rooting for their favorite driver, and seeing banging, rubbing competition among forty-three drivers for hundreds of laps. The contest does not have the regulating device of other tracks, the restrictor-plate which limits the vehicles' speed at times of concerns with safety. A fan extolled the virtues of NASCAR racing at Bristol in writing,

> So put me on the Bristol side of this debate. It is a spectator's track, not a TV track. If you want to see a bunch of cars go really fast, go to a restrictor-plate race. If you want to see a stock car race, then go to Bristol. ("From Our Readers," *Scene* 27: 84)

This latter statement about racing is our experience with NASCAR as well. In August 2003, the *Bristol Herald Courier* reported,

> A majority of more than 96,000 fans reaffirmed that the Sharpie 500 is the hottest ticket in Winston Cup Racing. NASCAR online polled site visitors asking them, "If they could attend just one Winston Cup race, which would it be?" The Sharpie 500 collected 50,043 votes (52 percent) placing the August night race classic at the top of the list. ("Fans Say...")

Bristol Motor Speedway is a focal point for NASCAR fans during the spring, but the hardest ticket for NASCAR fans to secure is for the August night race each year:

> Both NASCAR Winston Cup Series races—one in the spring and one in August—are sold out well in advance. Having precious tickets and suggesting a Bristol race to anyone who enjoys racing is like inviting a preacher to a screening of what awaits in the hereafter. (UMI Publications 7)

Tickets on eBay sell for hundreds of dollars over their face value. Tickets for these races are also sold through ticket brokers at highly inflated prices. Fans lucky enough to be selected to purchase tickets via the lottery sponsored by the Speedway do not give them up. In fact, there are fans who sell their tickets for the spring race, receiving sufficient profits to purchase their season tickets for both races.

The town of Bristol is divided down the center of State Street by the state border between Tennessee and Virginia. Bristol, Tennessee, is a small town with a population of approximately 25,000 people. The first NASCAR race at Bristol International Speedway, as it was called originally, took place in July 1961. Forty-two cars started the Volunteer 500 and only 19 cars finished the race. The second race occurred in October the same year, the Southeastern 500. The first night race at Bristol Motor Speedway took place in August 1978. The original stands held only 18,000 fans. The increased seating capacity and interest in these races predicted and paralleled the growth of NASCAR. According to *Bristol Motor Speedway History,* by April 1997 there were 118,000 seats with 22 new skyboxes (making Bristol Motor Speedway the largest sports arena in Tennessee); by August 1998 there were 131,000 seats and 100 skyboxes at the track; by the March 2002 race, seating capacity was raised to 147,000; and by the August 2002 night race, seating capacity reached 160,000. In this growth, "Bristol Motor Speedway was truly a 'build-it-and-they-will-come' sort of thing. To many it must have seemed every bit as bizarre as hacking out a baseball diamond for ghosts in the middle of an Iowa cornfield" (UMI Publications 9).

There is nothing so impressive in sports as approaching the track from the city and walking up the hill to the track. To NASCAR fans, this speedway is the "Shining City on the Hill." It is completely surrounded by the stands in the shape of a perfect oval. Fans carry in their coolers full of beer or plastic bottles of Jack Daniels or some other clear liquid, probably brewed locally, in plastic milk jugs. They carry their chair backs, coolers, and food up the stands, row after row to their seats at the top of the stands, in rows there counted by double and triple letters. Fans of all ages perform this ritual—most of them twice a year for the spring and August races. Sitting in the stands is a microcosm of white America with fans coming from all over the country to this NASCAR Mecca. There are young and old fans, children, men and women, fans from every walk of life, tall and short. Few people of color, however, attend NASCAR races at the Bristol Motor Speedway.

Fans scream for their favorite drivers and, because of the nature of the track, are certain their voices are heard above the thundering engines. The four corners of the track are pitched at approximately the same angle (36 degrees) as the stands rising from the edge of the track. Because of this unique configuration at Bristol, fans in the first row to the top row of the stands, can see directly into the car and see their favorite drivers' faces or helmet as they pass. This "intimate" relationship with the drivers during the race is unique to Bristol. This contributes to the fans' perceptions of this track—this place—this hallowed ground of communion with the heroic daredevil drivers.

But these perceptions are only part of the fans' idyllic infatuation with Bristol Motor Speedway. Another part of this fascination is the racing that occurs once the green flag is dropped. NASCAR fans familiar with the phrase, "If-it-ain't-rubbin', it-ain't-racin,'' see the most track-related contact between the drivers of any NASCAR track. This is, in the eyes of many fans, stock-car racing at its finest and racing the way it ought to be. On every lap, cars are rubbin' against each other in all four turns. Sometimes this contact causes a car to spin up the track and crash into the wall. As the race progresses, more and more cars lose more and more pieces, to the point where at the end of the race, their cars are circling the track with no front fenders or hood or no back fenders and a crumpled trunk. Also, as the race progresses, some drivers lose their patience with other drivers so the contact between them becomes more and more intentional, and the race for track position becomes more and more intense, and, because two cars cannot occupy the same space at the same time, there is more and more rubbin' and more and more wrecks. Bob Pockrass, a staff writer for *Scene Magazine*, observes, "Such is life at Bristol where tight racing results in drivers bumping each other to get someone out of their way, followed by retaliation."

One of many memorable events at Bristol occurred during the 2002 spring Busch Series race when Kevin Harvick was wrecked by Greg Biffle and attacked him in pit row after the race. At the same race, Jack Sprague was standing on the pit wall at the end of the race waiting for Jimmy Spencer who wrecked him on the last lap. When these events occurred, fans rose to their feet as one and cheered. Another memorable event occurred when Jeff Gordon "bumped" Rusty Wallace, who had not won a race in a very long time at that point, near the end of the race, causing Wallace to temporarily lose control of his car so Gordon could pass him for first place to win the August 2002 night race. In the 2004 Spring race, Tony Stewart and Scott Wimmer were each penalized a lap by NASCAR during the race for bumping into each other a couple of times—first when Stewart hit Wimmer in the back when he slowed down to avoid a crash and later when Wimmer, in retaliation, ran into Stewart as they were racing side by side.

Broadcasters add to the idyllic persona of Bristol Motor Speedway during their pre-race, race, and post-race comments. They tell the fans that this track tests each driver's patience because they are always in close quarters with other drivers for 500 laps. Broadcasters tell viewers prior to the race that some drivers will become so frustrated at times during the race, because they are being held up by slower cars or they have been bumped or rubbed for the past two hours, that they will initiate contact with other drivers causing them to spin out or temporarily lose control of their cars. Commentators predict increasing contact between drivers to heighten fans' anticipation and, hopefully, fulfillment of the NASCAR fan's mantra, "If-it-ain't-rubbin', it-ain't-racin.'' They tell the fans that car owners and crew chiefs do not like these

# NASCAR'S BRISTOL MOTOR SPEEDWAY

Bristol races because of the amount of sheet metal on their expensive cars that is bent, scratched, dented, mangled, and/or demolished during one race at Bristol; not to mention two races at Bristol. The fact that drivers will race hard side by side, rub against cars in the turns, bump slower cars out of the way in the short straight-aways draws fan to Bristol for the races—they believe the racing at Bristol is a throw-back to historic, traditional NASCAR racing from decades ago.

If the track at Bristol were similar to other tracks on the NASCAR Nextel Racing Circuit, fans would not express the demand for tickets the owners of Bristol Motor Speedway currently enjoy. Fans are drawn to this half-mile track because of the racing, the intimacy, and the reputation of the track. The most famous track in NASCAR with the most popular race in the Nextel Series will continue to attract new fans to the sport and reinvigorate the affections of more long-time fans to NASCAR.

## WORKS CITED AND RECOMMENDED

*Bristol Motor Speedway History*. 3 Aug. 2004. 20 Nov. 2004 <http://www.bristolmotorspeedway.com/track_info/speedway_history/>.

"Fans Say Sharpie 500 Is Number One Again." *Bristol Herald Carrier* 11 Aug. 2003. 22 Oct. 2004 <http://www.gospeedway.com/bristolnumber1/news4.html>.

"From Our Readers." *Scene Magazine* 27 (1 Apr. 2004): 84.

"From Our Readers." *Scene Magazine* 28 (21 Oct. 2004): 83.

Martin, Linette. *Sacred Doorways: A Beginner's Guide to Icons*. Brewster, MA: Paraclete P, 2002.

Pockrass, Bob. "Boiling Point." *Scene Magazine* 27 (1 Apr. 2004): 36.

Trout, Ben. Letter to the authors. 1 June 2004.

UMI Publications. *Bristol Motor Speedway: 40 Years of Thunder*. Charlotte: UMI Publications, 2004.

# Niagara Falls

## Patrick McGreevy

Nearly all Americans can conjure an image of Niagara Falls. It confronts them in books, magazines, newspapers, on cans of Niagara Spray Starch and boxes of Nabisco Shredded Wheat. They have seen footage on television, and in movies like *Superman II*, *Canadian Bacon*, and countless others. They know it is a place of natural power and beauty, long associated with romance and honeymoons. They have heard tales of stunts, accidents, and rescues. Many know that its casinos attract millions of gamblers. Many also know that its power now serves to generate a great deal of electricity, and some remember that cheap electricity was directly related to the Love Canal disaster. A few know that it is also a place of religious shrines, and of suicide.

Reports of a great waterfall on the St. Lawrence reached Europe before the founding of Britain's first permanent colony in Virginia. By the end of the seventeenth century, Niagara Falls had become an emblem of North America itself—the wild heart of a continent most Europeans considered the polar opposite of their own long-civilized countries. As such, Niagara represented the wildest of nature. While this has remained the most persistent symbolism of the falls, the meanings Americans have associated with nature have been bewilderingly varied.

Although well known for over 150 years, it was only with the opening of the Erie Canal in 1825 that Niagara became accessible for ordinary travelers. This access coincided with the rise in the United States of a new commercial and industrial middle class with the leisure and the resources to travel for pleasure. Niagara Falls emerged as the chief goal of the North American "Grand Tour" that always included the Hudson River and the Erie Canal. A great many Europeans joined American travelers on this pilgrimage to the falls. Niagara quickly became a fashionable resort, the haunt of literary, artistic, and educated travelers (McKinsey; Sears; Adamson).

Although earlier European visitors lacked a vocabulary to express what they felt at Niagara, the new middle-class tourists were well schooled in the aesthetics of the natural sublime that helped them to value and express the complex mixture of terror and joy that scenes like the falls seemed to inspire.

The overwhelming and apparently limitless in nature is attractive, they believed, because it awakens a recognition of the viewer's own inner dimensions of spiritual depth, imagination, or reason. Anthony Trollope, for example, suggested this prescription for a sublime experience at Niagara:

> To realize Niagara, you must sit there until you see nothing else than that which you have come to see.... At length you will be at one with the tumbling river before you.... You will fall as the bright waters fall, rushing down into your new world without hesitation and with no dismay; and you will rise again as the spray rises, bright, beautiful, and pure. Then you will flow away in your course to the uncompassed, distant, and eternal ocean. (140–41)

Because of the different ways women and men were socialized during this period, women were much less likely to measure themselves the equal of a colossal waterfall, and therefore to use the language of the sublime. In an earlier visit, Trollope's mother, Frances, could not bring herself to express any sense of mastery over the scene. Although she was quite familiar with the conventions of the sublime, she concluded: "It is not for me to attempt a description of Niagara; I feel I have no powers for it" (303). Unlike the men who accompanied her, she was unable to enter the "appalling cavern" behind the Horseshoe Falls. "I lost my breath entirely," she wrote, "and the pain in my chest was so severe, that not all my curiosity could enable me to endure it" (308).

Niagara's antebellum visitors were also deeply affected by romanticism—and its particular American expression, transcendentalism, which emphasized the correspondences between American nature and the sacred, often viewed reflexively as an individual spiritual meaning. Caroline Gilman, an 1836 visitor who had been deeply influenced by Emersonian transcendentalism, described Niagara by moonlight. "One feels thoroughly *alone*," she wrote, "while overhanging that thundering mass of waters, with the silent moon treading her tranquil way. I thought of *soul*, and this almighty Fall seemed but a drop compared to the cataract of mind" ([emphasis in original] 116).

Because many saw nature itself as sacred, they often spoke of a visit to Niagara as a pilgrimage. At first glance, this may seem to be at odds with Niagara's infamous circus atmosphere. Museums of morbid curiosities and freaks, as well as public attractions—like sending animals over the falls in a boat—were present at Niagara from about 1830; daredevil stunts began in the 1830s. P. T. Barnum once tried to purchase Goat Island, which sits between the two waterfalls, as a permanent site for his big top. Today, dozens of museums and circus acts—and most recently two gambling casinos—have enhanced this tawdry aspect of Niagara's landscape. Yet Niagara's circus atmosphere corresponds to the exotic fairs and markets that always surrounded medieval Christian pilgrimage sites; as anthropologist Victor Turner suggests, both the sacred and the profane belong together, apart from the ordinary world of day-to-day life.

Niagara Falls, 1886. Courtesy of the Library of Congress.

Many visitors had imagined Niagara so romantically that they could not help but be disappointed by the natural reality. To the first generation of distinctively American writers and painters, however, romanticism was intertwined with nationalism. As Elizabeth McKinsey has convincingly argued, for the antebellum northern middle class, Niagara Falls became an icon of the American Sublime. The United States may not have a deep history or a long-settled landscape, but with spokesmen like James Fenimore Cooper and Thomas Cole, the nation could boast of its forests, the Natural Bridge, and Niagara Falls. In the relentless power of Niagara, many Americans could see a metaphor for their own nation's burgeoning energy.

From the opening of the Erie Canal until the end of the century, Niagara's visitors produced a torrent of words and images. Writers like Margaret Fuller, William Dean Howells, and Mark Twain, and painters like Thomas Cole and Frederic Church, along with countless others, contributed their interpretations of Niagara Falls. In a more popular vein, word of mouth, guidebooks, advertisements, songs, and stories explored similar themes in a complex blending of folklore and popular culture. In more recent times, advertisements, Broadway melodies, and Hollywood movies have served the same purpose.

One of the most persistent and recognizable of Niagara's associations is with romance, sexual passion, and honeymooning. Couples celebrating their wedding journeys began to arrive in the 1830s. Certainly no other North American place is more associated with this practice. In the Hollywood and Broadway productions of the 1930s and 1940s, when sex could only be openly explored within marriage, Niagara Falls was shorthand for the sexual culmination of courtship. Henry Hathaway's 1953 film *Niagara*, staring Marilyn Monroe and Joseph Cotten, exploited these connotations. The theme had already been well established by nineteenth-century poetry, novels, and travelers' accounts. Sexual urges, like other passions, were often characterized as something wild and natural within that required channeling. The wildness of Niagara was contained within its gorge just as the wildness of passion should be contained within the institution of marriage. In the early twenty-first century, sexual enhancement drugs are still generally advertised as aids to marriage—as opposed to facilitators of rape. Is the name "Viagra" a coincidence?

A common response to Niagara Falls throughout the nineteenth century was an urge to confront and symbolically conquer it; some expressed this urge in words, others preferred to walk on tightropes or ride barrels over the cataract. While stunts had appeared in the 1830s, the first successful trip over the falls in a barrel was accomplished in 1901 by Annie Edson Taylor, a middle-aged Michigan school teacher who never profited from her accomplishment.

The first touristic competitors to Niagara Falls were the Erie Canal locks at Lockport, about twenty miles to the east. Here was a technological marvel that demonstrated new human capabilities; to some, it seemed obvious that it was the canal that had made Niagara a sensation. Indeed, the locks ascend the same escarpment over which Niagara glides. Nathaniel Hawthorne, who visited the falls in 1834, was initially very disappointed by the falls but later complained that many Americans were more impressed by the locks at Lockport. The first great technological marvel at Niagara itself was Jacob Reobling's Railway Suspension Bridge that began to carry trains and carriages over the gorge just below the falls in 1855. Although not as well remembered as Reobling's Brooklyn Bridge, it became a tourist attraction in its own right and made its creator famous.

Perhaps the most obvious way of taming Niagara was to harness its power for industry, a notion that appeared as early as the late eighteenth century. Indeed the founders of the first village at Niagara Falls named it after the greatest manufacturing city in the world, Manchester. The first large-scale power development was a hydraulic canal that cut diagonally across the Village of Niagara Falls, New York, creating a concentrated manufacturing district that thrived from 1875 to 1900 at the top of the gorge a few hundred feet downstream from the falls. An international movement to free the immediate vicinity of the falls from industry and private exploitation of tourists led to the creation the Niagara Reservation (1885) in New York—designed by Frederick Law Olmsted—and Queen Victoria Park (1887) on the Ontario side. For the first time in American history, a wild landscape had been preserved by government action.

By the 1890s, momentum began to gather for a much larger power development at Niagara Falls. Niagara was becoming an icon of the future. Many ideas were proposed. King Camp Gillette, who would later become famous and wealthy for inventing the razor blade, suggested that efficiency and logic would eventually lead to a single great city where the all of North America's manufacturing could be concentrated. He believed there was enough power at Niagara to supply such a city. The flamboyant entrepreneur William T. Love wanted to create a utopian "Model City" by diverting water from the upper Niagara River through a power canal; one mile of the canal was completed when financial problems halted the project. The scheme that eventually reached fruition created enormous excitement. Thomas Evershed suggested digging a deep tunnel under Niagara Falls, New York, into which would pour water from the upper river, turning turbines and generating electricity. The Niagara Falls Power Company consulted with recognized experts such as Lord Kelvin, Thomas Edison, and George Westinghouse to help design this unprecedented project. In a decision that would set the basis for much of our twentieth-century world, Nikola Tesla's unpopular idea of alternating current was chosen against the advice of Kelvin and Edison, but this decision turned out to be the key to transmitting electricity. In 1896, the company successfully initiated the first long-distance transmission of electricity to power the streetlights of Buffalo, a phenomenon that was fully exploited and demonstrated at Buffalo's Pan-American Exposition in 1901 (Adams).

Beginning at the turn of the century, a nascent electrochemical industry concentrated at Niagara Falls to take advantage of the inexpensive power. The Hooker Chemical Company used the abandoned canal from William T. Love's failed utopian project as a toxic waste dump. Ironically, the canal finally achieved the notice Love had hoped for when harmful chemicals began to ooze to the surface in the 1970s after the City of Niagara Falls had tragically allowed a school and a residential neighborhood to be built there. The Love Canal disaster gave impetus to the burgeoning environmental movement of the 1970s; it fostered an awakening of concern about toxic chemical pollution that, in turn, led to state and federal legislation.

Niagara Falls has a longstanding connection to the rhetoric of disaster. For anyone who wished to emphasize the impending catastrophe of some political action or policy, it is hard to imagine a more effective, and immediately understood, image than of a ship heading into the Niagara Rapids. In his 1867 book *Shooting Niagara: And After?* Thomas Carlyle used just such an analogy to criticize the entire direction taken by the industrial world. The most recent example is a widely quoted warning from former Central Command chief General Anthony Zinni. Appearing on the CBS program *60 Minutes* on May 23, 2004, Zinni criticized President Bush's rhetoric of "staying the course" in Iraq: "To think we are going to stay the course; the course is headed over Niagara Falls."

Analogies of disaster have their roots in the history of actual deaths at the falls. Many have perished accidentally. Others have died attempting stunts. A great many more have committed suicide. There is no place in North America where more people—as many as fifty-three in a single year—have taken their own lives. Nineteenth-century poets often compared the Niagara River to the course of life; the falls itself represented the abrupt end of life. Perhaps the world's largest collection of horror museums is clustered here, successfully exploiting the awareness of human mortality the falls has so often awakened in visitors (McGreevy 41–70).

Although humans have redirected the power of Niagara itself to their own purposes, the cruel fact remains that, as individuals, we are not the equal of nature: we are all eventually swallowed by it. But horror is not the only reaction to mortality. For some, the connotations are of eternal peace. We see this not only in written responses to Niagara Falls, but also in the establishment of several shrines and a monastery. In 1861 the Catholic Church officially declared Niagara Falls a pilgrim shrine to Our Lady of Peace (McGreevy 34). Indeed a number of peace conferences have been held at Niagara. Partly in celebration of the world's longest undefended border, the Peace Bridge—which spans the river upstream from the falls—was dedicated in 1927. Leonard Henkle, another utopian entrepreneur, proposed the construction in 1895 of a colossal "International Hall" where representatives of all the nations could meet to settle their differences peacefully and work to eliminate war and poverty. Finally, at the end of World War II, Niagara Falls nearly became the site of the United Nations Headquarters; only the Rockefeller family's gift of land persuaded the committee to choose Manhattan (McGreevy 65–68).

Despite the commercialization and environmental problems, Niagara Falls attracts more visitors than ever, an annual horde of over 10 million. It is no longer an elite resort; in fact, with its gambling casinos and kitschy attractions, it probably reminds many visitors of Las Vegas. Although its public image has changed through time, there seems little chance that Niagara Falls will lose its purchase on the imaginations of Americans.

## WORKS CITED AND RECOMMENDED

Adams, Edward Dean. *Niagara Power: History of the Niagara Falls Power Company*. 2 vols. Niagara Falls, NY: n.p., 1927.

Adamson, Jeremy Elwell. *Niagara: Two Centuries of Changing Attitudes, 1697–1901*. Washington, DC: The Corcoran Gallery of Art, 1985.

Dow, Charles Mason. *Anthology and Bibliography of Niagara Falls*. 2 vols. Albany: State of New York, 1921.

Gilman, Caroline. *The Poetry of Travelling in the United States*. New York: S. Colman, 1838.

McGreevy, Patrick. *Imagining Niagara: The Meaning and Making of Niagara Falls*. Amherst: U of Massachusetts P, 1994.

McKinsey, Elizabeth. *Niagara Falls: Icon of the American Sublime*. Cambridge: Cambridge UP, 1985.

Sears, John F. *Sacred Places: American Tourist Attractions in the Nineteenth Century*. New York: Oxford UP, 1989.

Trollope, Anthony. *North America*. London: Chapman & Hall, 1862.

Trollope, Mrs. Frances. *Domestic Manners of the Americans*. London: Whittaker, Treacher, 1832.

Turner, Victor. "The Center Out There: Pilgrim's Goal." *History of Religions* 12 (1973): 191–230.

# Jack Nicholson

## Thomas A. Van

As of early 2005, Jack Nicholson has appeared in seventy-eight films, in many of them for only a few minutes, but the range of his dramatic interpretations is phenomenal. He has played well an enlisted sailor and a Marine colonel; a private detective, a mafia hoodlum, and a comic book villain; an obsessive-compulsive, a psychotic, and a psychologist; cowboys, the homeless, Prince Charmings, and satyrs, the Devil himself, even a publishing executive who turns into a wolf. An icon in a temple (or a supermarket) enjoys *iconostasis*, or what some have called "motionless magnificence." But performing artists, particularly movie actors and their directors, search relentlessly for new roles in new plots, as they hope that name recognition will sell tickets. For the viewer, the transaction at the box-office offers a comfortable paradox: always the exciting promise of something absolutely new, but done by established and familiar personae. From these moving targets, popular opinion and memory sort and construct icons, one of them Nicholson.

Nicholson's earliest movie work was in the B-movie thrillers of Roger Corman, starting with his role as a troubled adolescent in *Cry Baby Killer* in 1958, followed by *Little Shop of Horrors* in 1960, where he plays a masochist in a dentist's office. His early films were not box office successes, with the exception of two westerns which became cult hits in France; but *Head*, which he wrote and produced in 1968 about a television executive who experiments with LSD, got the attention of Dennis Hopper and Peter Fonda, who were casting for a movie about motorcycling hippies. The rest is cinematic history. The films Nicholson was involved in during the ten years before *Easy Rider* enjoy cult status, sometimes as pure camp, but often as myth: the unpromising youth of a hero before his ascent to fame. But if the interest in Nicholson's earliest films is based on what was yet to come, a great deal of critical opinion about Nicholson's most recent movies is based on what he did earlier. Reviewers and fans talk about "classic" Nicholson films and use them as a standard for comparisons. Five films usually top any list of his best. That they all came out between 1970 and 1975 is remarkable: *Five Easy Pieces* (1970), *Carnal Knowledge* (1971), *The Last Detail* (1974), *Chinatown*

(1974), and *One Flew Over the Cuckoo's Nest* (1975). Any discussion of Jack Nicholson as an American icon begins with them.

Nicholson's work in the early 1970s stunned Hollywood, which recognized immediately what it had been needing. Marlon Brando and James Dean had introduced new idioms for presenting what was supposed to be the authentic masculine self in postwar America. Gone was the stoic decency and reliable patriotism of Cooper and Bogart. The new offerings were disenchanted brooding, artful inarticulateness, sexual turmoil at the fork, and fits of what was supposed to be totally instinctive behavior. There would be no going back. By 1970 a country which had begun to doubt its leaders and its policies was distraught and angry. Nicholson's characters, stark and powerful in themselves, vented that anger. From the screen they issued a stream of verbal abuse and sarcasm more memorable than the story lines. Brando and Dean, who tended to rely on suggestive understatement, seem almost subdued by comparison. If they implied introspection, Nicholson unapologetically, almost lyrically, proclaimed narcissism.

Nicholson's portrayal of an alcoholic Southern ACLU lawyer in *Easy Rider* (1969) brought him national attention, but the plot (bikers versus rednecks) stayed with the obvious. The American icons in that movie are the Harley-Davidsons. The much subtler *Five Easy Pieces*, which came out the following year, offers the first fully developed Nicholson persona, in one of his finest performances. Nicholson plays Robert Eroica Dupea, a sensitive and volatile young man who has rejected his upbringing among a family of classical musicians for a drifting life as a laborer. As the film opens, he has a job he hates in a Texas oil field and a troubled relationship with Rayette, a waitress who deals with her emotional distress by playing or singing Tammy Wynette songs. He is psychologically abusive to her and routinely unfaithful. When Dupea finds out that his father is dying, she accompanies him to a family reunion which merges a past and present he despises. He complicates things further by having a brief but intense affair with his brother's fiancée, before she ends it. After a drunken bender, Dupea leaves his home again, heading back to Texas with Rayette. But suddenly he abandons the apparently pregnant Rayette, at a gas station along the highway, and hitches a ride in a semi bound for the far North.

It is choice melodrama, well acted, which juxtaposes two very different areas of America, Texas and coastal Oregon; but the real flashpoints for Dupea are culture and class. The consensus required to produce cultural behavior also imposes predictability and conformity, which enrage him. The identity of one community is too often predicated on the absence of the traits which give identity to another: there is no Chopin among oil rigs and no Tammy Wynette in a music conservatory. To Dupea, cultural markers and boundaries offer invitations for attack. He has never been able to stomach Rayette's taste in music or her country ways, but he excoriates a salon of Oregonian aesthetes when they sneer at her for saying she misses her television programs. He tells them they are a "bunch of pompous celibates." With his brother's beautiful fiancée, cultural boundaries can be crossed sexually, giving him an opportunity to bring something wild and instinctive to a place ruled mainly by the discipline of musical performance. But he does not cross any boundary intending to stay. Dupea moves Katherine to tears when he plays Chopin perfectly, then stuns her when he insists he has absolutely no feeling for it. In refusing to join her emotional response to the beauty of Chopin, he is refusing to come back home to the caste of aesthetes. Yet earlier, in a traffic jam on a Texas highway, he could leave his car and mount the back of an open pickup to vamp happily on an old upright, as the truck pulled out in another direction. Dupea's willed fate is to need to be somewhere else.

Dupea's frustration with society and consequent retreat into nature is only time-honored Romanticism. The Nicholson iconography in *Five Easy Pieces* owes most to the affair between Nicholson and the camera eye, which dutifully attends a superb cast, but which favors only him. One way to realize this favoritism is to watch the movie with the sound off. Physically, he is wiry and compact, but coiled. His movements, like his words, can be sudden, but completed with a poise which is almost balletic. The men he brawls with in this movie are taller, heavier, and stronger, so naturally he gets the worst of it. They have the heavy walk and lumbering posture of stage bullies. Nicholson's stride recalls the soft lope of a coyote. The adversaries are usually dull-eyed, with slack, beefy faces. Nicholson's sculpted face, somewhat off-scale with the rest of him, is the expressive center of most scenes. It is a face ruled by a knife-like glance, with dark acrobatic brows and a ruthless smile almost too big for its container, which can range from an invitation to Saturnalian wildness to a contempt words cannot contain.

Jack Nicholson in Stanley Kubrick's *The Shining*, 1980. Courtesy of Photofest.

The Nicholson hero may get the worst of a storyline, but he never loses in the exchange of aggressive remarks. He delivers the final (and quotable) piece of insolence, which usually ends the scene. To a mass audience, he is the center of attention they cannot be, giving the toothy snarl they would like to send back at whatever controls and ignores them. Regardless of the plot, his audience knows that it is being treated as an insider, as someone who is able to appreciate hip responses and crafted verbal aggression. Dupea is selfish, unfaithful, even self-destructive, but he is never false or lame, which can't be said of anyone else around him. The other characters, whether decent or hateful, have no idea that they lack his authenticity, but the audience knows.

There are conventions behind these edgy exchanges. Taunts and raillery have long been staples of dramatic comedy. Most television sitcoms are, at base, vaguely plotted insult contests, with timely infusions from a laugh track. The abusive lines in a Nicholson script are offered at calculated intervals as *noir* confections for his admirers. The laughter they cause is sadistic, and it comes in many shades. When Dupea verbally devastates someone socially more powerful than he is, there is usually an approving roar. The laughter following his sudden venom to a waitress about the details of a chicken sandwich or to an easily intimidated girl friend is more tentative, but with a Nicholson hero, routine insensitivity is usually accepted as a point of style.

The powerful and complicated dynamics between Nicholson the master actor, the directed and edited cinematic eye, and audience expectations were just beginning. *Carnal Knowledge,* written and directed by Mike Nichols, vivisects male sexual behavior, with Nicholson and Art Garfunkel playing the selfish sinners. Shrewdly observant and sententious, it has become a classic in gender studies. Nevertheless, interpreting Nicholson's presence and performance here is wildly problematic, because even in a morality play it takes more than homiletics to contain, much less banish, a fascinating devil. In cinema, so much the more so. The movie astutely argues that sex is a game mainly for the benefit of male consumers and that the playing field is the female body. As young men, Nicholson's Jonathan and Garfunkel's Sandy are undergraduate roommates at a private college, sexually involved with the same woman, unbeknownst to Sandy. They meet several times later in life to compare sexual experiences, until Sandy seems appalled by Jonathan's predatory history. Not only does Jonathan not deny his selfishness: he proclaims it. At one point he screams at a voluptuous and abused mistress, "I'm already taken. I'm taken by me." It's more a war cry than the confession of a lost soul. Jonathan's selfish quest for ecstasy, while it dehumanizes an entire gender, is also Faustian, and militantly unrepentant.

*Five Easy Pieces* and *Carnal Knowledge* introduced the range of the Nicholson persona. To this day, *The Last Detail*, *Chinatown*, and *One Flew Over the Cuckoo's Nest* create the standard for evaluating Nicholson performances. The Robert Towne scripts for the first two are some of the best screenwriting in the history of cinema. Most Nicholson films in the following thirty years or so attempted to duplicate the dark and uncompromising intensity of these three films. Too often, the result was mere echo and repetition, or worse, parody. All three films offer an unsweetened picture of the American underclass. In *The Last Detail* Nicholson's character Billy "Bad Ass" Buddusky and his sidekick Mule are career sailors who have to escort another sailor, Meadows, from Norfolk to Portsmouth, where he will do eight years in the brig for attempting to steal forty dollars from the contribution box of the admiral's wife's pet charity. Bad Ass's minor scheme to rob the Navy on their per-diem expenses changes when he and Mule realize that the vague creature in handcuffs and navy blues is little more than on overweight petty thief with a sweet tooth: Meadows is passive, uncomplaining, and a loner. Bad Ass and Mule are not particularly concerned about the severity of Meadow's sentence, which is only unfairness in an unfair world; but Bad Ass perceives Meadows's personality as an insult to the human condition. He wants to get their infantile prisoner some of the experiences he does not know he has missed, before he disappears into Portsmouth.

For three days, Meadows's guards are his comrades. He carouses with them, joins in when they brawl with Marines, smokes dope, and goes to a brothel, all probably for the first time. Bad Ass wants Meadows to recognize pleasure in all its variety and to reach out and take. As the hours race on, Meadows comes to life. He finally wants something, which is the one thing he can't have: freedom to live the life he has just now been introduced to. When he tries to escape, Badass beats him savagely, before delivering him to Portsmouth. Too late, Meadows has found something to cry about.

Meadows is pathetic, but sympathy for him does not drive this story. The movie is a tribute to the unadvertised vitality of American life at the margins. It is life on an enlisted man's salary, of cheap diners, bus stations, sleazy bars, whorehouses, and fist fights; but it contains essential values of individualism and personal loyalty. Bad Ass and Mule are ornery sailors, but they befriend Meadows from a patriotism deeper than the uniform and the code which goes with it. They had no control over whatever produced his sad case, but they acted out an enlightened alternative to it.

*Chinatown* involves a much more explicit encounter between a hero, a rotten entrepreneurial system, and the victims he is powerless to protect from it. In the film, Chinatown and the rest of Los Angeles are beholden to a few powerful individuals with a ruthless will to acquire. The rule for the police, or for that matter anyone who wants to survive, is to not ask questions and to "do as little as possible." Nicholson plays Jake Gittes, a private detective who insists on seeing what others have been taught to ignore. His sarcasm and cold, skeptical gaze unsettle every conscience, guilty or innocent. In the end, when ruthless corruption again has its way, Jake's glare alone asserts a sense of justice that prevails against crass self-interest and ironic indifference. In addition to his not-for-sale detective character, the sophisticated appetites and style of this hero add to the film's refinement of the hard-boiled detective into Nicholson's image.

In the background of *The Last Detail* and *Chinatown* lurks a question: why help people abused by a system which will win anyway, when helping them will probably only add to their misery? Such suspicion invites one not to act but to become part of the passivity which fuels that system. Bad Ass and Gittes ignore the invitation, and so does Nicholson's Randall Patrick McMurphy in *One Flew Over the Cuckoo's Nest*. There the system to be hopelessly resisted is a public insane asylum, a house full of Meadowses, with a head nurse monitoring all of them to keep them passive. The inmates queue for their tranquillizers every morning to the strains of Mantovani. Later on, Head Nurse Ratchett will preside over humiliating group therapy sessions. Enter McMurphy, who has decided to act insane in order to be put in the asylum temporarily and avoid prison farm work. Too late, he finds out that his release depends not on time served but on the whim of those in charge of the asylum.

McMurphy plays the trickster every sleepwalking community dreads and needs. The men's pointless predictability ignites him. He tries to teach them about the excitement of uncertainties, like watching a World Series game, or discovering that they might be able to outplay the asylum staff in a pick-up basketball game. But taking the whole ward deep sea fishing in a stolen boat is his greatest trick, because it puts the asylum in the double bind of wanting to discipline McMurphy and having to admit that he has made a fine contribution to patient morale. Finally, McMurphy organizes a drunken party at which the patients trash the ward and McMurphy's girlfriend gives the youngest inmate, Billy Bippey, his first sexual experience. When Nurse Ratchett sees the carnage next morning, Billy guiltily commits suicide, at which McMurphy assaults Ratchett and earns a lobotomy. Life in the asylum then goes on as usual, with one exception: the huge Native American who has witnessed all this mercifully smothers what is left of McMurphy, breaks out, and heads north. He leaves behind a geyser foaming from a water fountain he overturned on the way out—an erotic tribute to a dead trickster, who led rites of mid-winter paganism in the house of the dead, but also modeled a type of ancient sacrifice and redemption.

Dubbusky, Gittes, and McMurphy see the contexts in which they have to function as farcical, but they themselves are not farcical. If a Nicholson character is being laughed at, he cannot be the existential resister or heroic loser. In *As Good as It Gets* (1997) Nicholson plays an obsessive-compulsive writer of romances who insults Jews, gays, women, blacks, Latinos, and every other polite person in his painful way. He is a poster boy for political incorrectness who becomes sensitive and caring, but not before delivering his quota of shocking remarks. After that, Nicholson played a recently retired police detective in *The Pledge* (2001) and a recently retired insurance executive in *About Schmidt*, neither of whom know what to do with themselves; then he went on to a bit of high (and posh) comedy about seniors in love in *Something's Gotta Give* (2003), which begins with Nicholson's character having an infarction as he is about to bed a much younger woman. Viagra and Lipitor jokes abound, until the right lovers are reunited in Paris on a bridge over the Seine.

The Nicholson persona and person blend and separate regularly. Reports of his angry fits and endless amours are a publicist's dream. When Nicholson loses his temper at a basketball game or attacks somebody's windshield with a golf club in the midst of a traffic snarl, he somehow seems more real both on and off screen. Reports of Nicholson's sexual endowment and stamina have provided benchmarks for male fantasies, as well as "in-jokes" for whenever a Nicholson character fails sexually. Stealth publicity made the same use of Warren Beatty's sexual reputation. When Beatty played the impotent Clyde Barrow in *Bonnie and Clyde* (1967) or a hairdresser in *Shampoo* (1975) pretending to be gay so that he could cuckold a rival, there was a harvest of knowing guffaws. These same fans maintain a watch on Nicholson's advancing age, receding hairline, and expanding girth, all of which the actor has been using lately to court an aging population at the box office.

In the reign of his combined performance and personality in the popular imagination, Nicholson has updated the role of Frank Sinatra. "Old Blue Eyes" projected a unique romantic image through changing decades, throughout publicity of his drunken brawls at the Waldorf, his physical and verbal confrontations with the press, his womanizing, and his outrages as leader of the "Rat Pack." His rhythmic stylings of ballads, from the big band era on, still set the standard, like Nicholson's early crafting of screen characters. Furthermore, Sinatra brought a swinging hedonism from the bandstand to radio and records for the working class which had been through the Depression and World War II and impatiently awaited pleasure; Nicholson has continued and elaborated the restive desire, uninhibited behavior, and anger in fantasies of successive audiences bent on having more of everything. Whereas Sinatra's poignant ballads, however, became the idiom for male loneliness and romantic melancholy, and his suicide attempts after his breakup with Ava Gardner publicized his vulnerability, Nicholson's screen persona has never veered from machismo, never disclosed reflection on his affections or sorrow.

It pleases Nicholson fans to assume that his love life on screen and his personal relationships are extensions of one another, but the fans are more interested in the statistics than in the psychology of his amours. They are much more curious about the biographical sources of the disenchantment and cynicism he specializes in. A much circulated story is supposed to explain Jack's interior and with it some of the roles he has played. The story is true. What it has to do with Nicholson personally or with his art is another matter. When he was thirty-seven, Nicholson found out from a researcher for *Time* magazine that the people he thought were his parents were really his grandparents, and that the woman he thought was his elder sister was really his mother, who had born him out of wedlock when she was sixteen. All of them were deceased when Nicholson learned this, and he had already done some of his finest work; but many of his followers will swear that this explains all about Jack: the continual anger, the attitude toward women, and so on. A grain of salt would help here. The singer Bobby Darin's mother turned out to be his grandmother, and his sister his mother, through a teenage pregnancy. Fans used this story, rather than Darin's doomed rheumatic heart, to account for his insecurities—it at least offered a respite from blaming Sandra Dee.

Nicholson's iconic contribution to American culture has much to do with the paradox in Alexis de Tocqueville's observation that Americans are uncomfortable being in a minority on any issue. They at once wish to hold a minority (individualist or rebellious) position, and to see it as the dominant stance that is affirmed by others and will prevail. Nicholson has acted out pungent invitations to resist and ridicule unthinking cooperation and assimilation. That can be done with a mocking grin, a coarse uncensored phrase, or just authentic individual behavior which is fair and commonsensical. On some days, anyone ought to be able to stand up like Nicholson's Joker in *Batman* and say "What this town needs is an enema," and expect a second to the motion. Perhaps David Mamet would oblige.

## WORKS RECOMMENDED

Bingham, Dennis. *Acting Male: Masculinities in the Films of James Stewart, Jack Nicholson, and Clint Eastwood*. New Brunswick, NJ: Rutgers UP, 1994.

Brode, Douglas. *The Films of Jack Nicholson*. New York: Carol Publishing Group, 1990.

Crane, Robert David, and Christopher Fryer. *Jack Nicholson, Face to Face*. Philadelphia: Lippincott, 1975.

Douglas, Edward. *Jack the Great Seducer: The Life and Many Loves of Jack Nicholson*. New York: HarperCollins, 2005.

McGilligan, Patrick. *Jack's Life: A Biography of Jack Nicholson*. New York: Norton, 1994.

Thompson, Peter A. *Jack Nicholson: The Life and Times of an Actor on the Edge*. Secaucus, NJ: Carol Publishing Group, 1997.

# Olmsted Park

*Thomas J. Mickey*

To walk in a public park is the right of every American. The idea of a "public park" has a history in this country that originates with one man, Frederick Law Olmsted. In the nineteenth century Olmsted undertook the design and construction of Central Park in New York. That was his first of many such endeavors in landscape design. Though he went on to design private estates like Biltmore and college campuses like Stanford, it is his legacy of the public park that all Americans revere.

Nature has always been an area of contention. Just to figure out a definition of nature that everybody agrees on is an impossible task. When we approach the question of controlling nature, we are in an even thornier place. Today to exert control over the land, including trees, stone, and water, means to open the door to environmental questions from many quarters.

In the nineteenth century of Olmsted's America, nature represented the last frontier for human solace. People, according to Olmsted, were living the new industrialized life in big cities. Factory work, severe working conditions, and scant employee benefits squeezed the worker at the same time as the culture witnessed the rise of the robber barons in its midst. Olmsted envisioned a park with scenic vistas that included trees, an extensive lawn, and pathways to give the city dweller an escape and an opportunity to relax and renew in the outdoors. Such a vision of the park inspired Olmsted his whole life. Olmsted proposed a view of nature that he felt would really help modern society.

This country was not quite 100 years old when Olmsted began his work on Central Park. It was just beginning to realize its potential, especially through the growth of urban populations in major cities along the East Coast. As people from other nations immigrated to America, they frequently settled in cities where others like themselves had already come to build a new home. Life in urban environments created congested living conditions. Tenement houses were routine in large cities like New York, Philadelphia, and Boston.

Olmsted was raised in a religious family who gave him an altruistic vision that characterized his life's work. He always felt that people were entitled to certain rights, no matter what their color or origin of birth. It never occurred to him to

# OLMSTED PARK

think that there was any other way to treat people. He carried that spirit with him throughout his life. Early on, he thought slavery was dehumanizing and should be abolished. His position originated from a deeply felt humanism that motivated all he did. He considered the natural beauty found in extensive lawns and trees to be something that would comfort, inspire, and benefit all people.

The idea of using nature in a way to show that all people can live together propelled his desire to create a public park. All people can enter the park and mingle with one another. Olmsted did not value the tradition of hierarchical social classes of people. The public park, as he envisioned it, would be a real expression of democracy. Here all people were welcome. People of all classes would mingle with one another. In that process they would learn about their differences and commonality, and create a stronger country.

In regard to the view of nature as under human control, an idea popular at many times in history, Olmsted wanted to control nature for the best of reasons: to create a more democratic way of life. This goal also guided his recommendations for national landmarks like Yellowstone and Niagara Falls. He wanted these natural treasures open for all to enjoy and not set off as concessions to make money for a few.

The area that Central Park covers was originally a swamp with mounds of soil and lots of rock. Olmsted along with his associate Calvauz Vaux designed

Saturday afternoon in Central Park, ca. 1900. Courtesy of the Library of Congress.

a plan to fill that space with rolling hills, pathways, trees, and water. It would be a refuge from the turmoil and confusion of the city.

Today when you walk in Central Park, you are struck by the daring and courage it took for Olmsted to position his vision for that space. The street that runs parallel to the park on the west is called Central Park West. As you walk north from the Park Plaza, the glorious old New York hotel, and into the park, you feel like you are in another world. At one point you follow a gravel stone path far below street level. Through the trees you can see apartment buildings rising above you on Central Park West; but here you are in a spot of natural beauty, a true refuge for the weary city dweller.

Public parks followed in other cities around the country, including Boston, a project Olmsted also undertook. The Boston public park system designed by Olmsted has the glorious name of the Emerald Necklace. His approach there was to link several green areas together. Bodies of water like the Charles River and Jamaica Pond have pathways that line them just like the water walkways along the water in Central Park. The Emerald Necklace stretched for seven miles.

His work in Milwaukee is illustrated in his design for Lake Park, along the shores of Lake Michigan, marked by the characteristic rolling lawn with an occasional tree. Today in Wisconsin the county parks number 600. And so he designed other parks around the country as well. As Olmsted designed one park, he brought his experience of the earlier parks to the current project.

Olmsted opened up America to appreciate nature in the city. To him, that contact with nature was something people needed in order to be fully human. Through giving people the public green space of a park, Olmsted felt he contributed in a way that his own privileged life dictated he must act.

As a result of his foresight and benevolent spirit, the country has thousands of parks today. For example, the Boston Parks and Recreation Department now oversees 2,200 acres of parkland including 215 parks and playgrounds, 65 squares, urban woodlands and street trees, 3 active cemeteries, 16 historic burying grounds, and 2 golf courses. The department also programs a wide range of community events and live entertainment in the parks under its jurisdiction.

Within the city limits of Seattle, the first public park was Denny Park, a gift to the city by David T. Denny in 1884. In 1887 the Board of Park Commission was established to oversee development of the Seattle park system. Seattle Parks Commissioners hired the Olmsted Brothers landscape architecture firm in 1903 to design a comprehensive system of parks and boulevards for the city. The Olmsted Plan for Seattle's parks spurred the early development of the Seattle park system and has been the basis of its modern day park system.

Olmsted worked on many parks around the country. Later in his life his sons took over the landscape business and continued a public park focus. From 1857 to 1950 the firm designed over 5,000 projects, one-third of which were residential.

The basic idea of the park was something Olmsted addressed in his middle years. His earlier life involved a series of different jobs both on the East Coast and in California. He often depended on the money that his father loaned him. It was only when at mid-life he entered the new field of landscape design that he found himself in a profession and became self-sufficient.

That journey took many years.

Olmsted's ideas about nature originated with his family. His father loved to contemplate nature at the Connecticut homestead of the Olmsted family. Domesticity and civilization became common themes in Olmsted's prolific writings. He saw home life as the place to establish personal meaning, and involvement in the community as a way to secure social meaning. Both were extremely important to him.

Also, on a visit to England Olmsted fell in love with the rural English landscape. He especially admired and referred to the English public park called Birkenhead.

A more important early influence on Olmsted, however, came from the American horticulturalist and landscape designer Andrew Jackson Downing, from Newburgh, New York. Downing edited and wrote *The Horticulturalist*, a magazine that proposed the picturesque view of nature. The home landscape, according to Downing, was composed of trees, shrubs, and pathways. The lawn around the home was to be an extensive grassy area with little emphasis on ornamental flowers.

Olmsted wrote letters to Downing and considered him his mentor. It was Downing who proposed the idea of a public park in New York, which later became Central Park. Because Downing died in 1852 at the early age of 37 in a tragic boating accident, he was unable to see his vision of Central Park become a reality. Five years later Olmsted picked up the gauntlet when he was 35. Olmsted actively sought the Central Park supervisor job. Downing had brought an engineer and draftsman from England, Calvert Vaux, whose friendship with Downing lasted seven years. It was through Downing that Olmsted met Vaux, who would become his collaborator on Central Park and several other landscape projects.

A public relations genius before public relations was seen as a profession, Olmsted often sought to publicize his vision and his work. Throughout his life he pursued recognition and status for his accomplishments. Fitted with a strong ego, Olmsted often ran up against opposition to his ideas, and that stress cost him, especially in his physical health. He often worked to exhaustion. He was frequently frustrated with bureaucracies of government and business, but nevertheless kept pursuing his vision. He measured a park's success in terms of its ability to give the citizen who enters it an appreciation of nature. In his writings, he proposed reasons for establishing national and state parks.

From early in his life, Olmsted urged the importance of protecting natural beauty, whether mountains, forest, or scenic areas like those of California. He thought California, where he lived from 1863 to 1865, one of the most beautiful places in the country. It is in California that he began to show the mind of a landscape architect, an artist whose media are the natural resources of landform, plants, stone, and water.

In California he designed the Oakland Cemetery and thus began his work as a landscape architect, in 1865. He designed Berkeley like Central Park, with pathways to take advantage of the view. He avoided a gridiron pattern in his designs for outdoor space, because they seemed so unnatural compared to what he saw as nature.

Some consider Prospect Park in Brooklyn, built after Central Park, his masterpiece of park design. It exhibited Olmsted's essential elements for a public park: meadows, woodland, and lake. Here too there was never any decorative planting, only what he called the natural look.

However, the Biltmore Estate in North Carolina, built by George W. Vanderbilt, remains the best-preserved work of Olmsted. One of Olmsted's decisions was to plant rhododendrons along the entrance road to the estate. A perfect choice by a real plantsman!

Olmsted also played a major role in setting the landscape theme for the Columbian Exposition, the world's fair in Chicago, from 1890 until it opened in 1893. There a park, which was part of the Exposition and boarded the lake, was Olmsted's design.

In 1881 he moved from New York to Brookline, Massachusetts, where he would continue his work as landscape architect and set up his own firm with his sons. In Brookline he found the "communicativeness" he sought all his life. That term Olmsted used to describe social contributions and obligations, but also the pleasures of the ideal citizen.

His ideas took form in writing and editing for a magazine, *Garden and Forest* (1888–1897), which he founded along with Charles Sprague Sargent, director of the Arnold Arboretum in Boston, and Olmsted's friend, horti-

Bird's-eye view of Central Park, 2004. Courtesy of Corbis.

cultural editor and writer William Augustus Stiles. It was an early American journal devoted to horticulture, botany, landscape design and preservation, national and urban park development, scientific forestry, and the conservation of forest resources.

Family problems like the death of his son and his daughter's disability weighed on his shoulders. His own health finally gave out and he had to be hospitalized. He died at the McLean Hospital in Belmont, Massachusetts, in 1903.

Though his personal and family life presented him with many problems, Olmsted continued to work as a landscape architect as long as he could. He, in fact, is credited with starting the profession of landscape architecture. While some of his designs have not been preserved, his lasting legacy is his vision of the public park, which can be found in every American city and state, and in many sizes and shapes.

Today the country needs that public space defined by trees and lawn and pathways more than ever. In many cities around the country, real estate values have escalated. Though their land value is high, the continued construction of new public parks and the ongoing funding to maintain existing parks say how much they mean to a democratic society.

In a society so obsessed with instant messaging, the need to enjoy nature is not easily met. We think we have to be doing something "constructive" all the time. Yet isn't the act of contemplating nature a sublime action in itself? The need to enjoy the outdoor green space of the public park is more important than ever.

Although society and culture have changed, the public park today is a refuge just as it was in the nineteenth century. Thanks to Frederic Law Olmsted, the public park stands open for all to enjoy.

## WORKS RECOMMENDED

Beveridge, Charles E., and Paul Rocheleau. *Frederick Law Olmsted: Designing the American Landscape*. Ed. David Larkin. New York: Rizzoli, 1995.

Fein, Albert. *Frederick Law Olmsted and the American Environmental Tradition*. New York: G. Braziller, 1972.

Hall, Lee. *Olmsted's America: An "Unpractical" Man and His Vision of Civilization*. Boston: Little, Brown, 1995.

Olmsted, Frederick Law, Jr., and Theodora Kimball, eds. *Forty Years of Landscape Architecture: Central Park [by] Frederick Law Olmsted, Sr.* 1928. Cambridge, MA: MIT P, 1928, 1973.

Parker, Christopher Glynn. "A Celebration of the Life and Work of Frederick Law Olmsted, Founder of American Landscape Architecture." 3 Jan. 2006 <http://www.fredericklawolmsted.com/>.

Roper, Laura Wood. *FLO: A Biography of Frederick Law Olmsted*. Baltimore, MD: Johns Hopkins UP, 1973.

Sutton, S. B., ed. *Civilizing American Cities: A Selection of Frederick Law Olmsted's Writings on City Landscapes*. Cambridge, MA: MIT P, 1971.

# One-Room Schoolhouse

## Ray B. Browne

America has always been a nation which prided itself on the education of its citizens, and it has tried to provide facilities for all who sought to better educate themselves. To do so the citizens have had to integrate the cultures of the countries from which they emigrated into the great "melting pot" of American culture, and become a part of the "Citie on a Hill," as the Puritans called it. They could fulfill a new way of life, the "American Dream," as later generations characterized it, and live "the American Way of Life," which always included the goals of social equality and political democracy. From the beginning of the American experience, education has been looked upon as an indispensable and the one-room schoolhouse has been its icon. In 2006 some 400 one-room schoolhouses remain, most in Montana and Nebraska, each with one to seven pupils.

By the middle of the nineteenth century, most Americans, with the conspicuous exception of slaves and Indians for many generations, were at least minimally literate. They developed their literacy by reading materials largely imported from and imitative of British culture, principally the King James Bible and various catechisms. By the middle of the twentieth century, three-quarters of Americans had a high school or higher education.

The American Revolution introduced a general debate about the purpose and most effective methods of teaching, the remnants of which survive into the twenty-first century. In the new and opening frontier there was, of course, the book of nature, which many people felt was the ideal for a new nation. On a more formal basis, some schools, looking to the past, favored the teaching of republican principles. Thomas Jefferson, on the one hand, advocated a layered system, consisting of elementary schools, followed by academies and then universities, so as to develop a politically responsible population of elite leaders. Toward this goal he founded the University of Virginia in 1819, which opened for classes in 1825. Benjamin Franklin, on the other hand, favored a more democratic curriculum that instructed in English and taught practical subjects such as drawing, calculation, and the immediate past rather than classical or ancient history. He and many others advocated establishing a "common school," what became known as the American "public school."

The approach that evolved in the nineteenth and early twentieth centuries from these conflicting views, known as the Quaker system, was based on ideas advocated by Joseph Lancaster, a Quaker, and Andrew Bell, a Church of England clergyman. Their goal was an inexpensive form of mass education, teaching literacy and religious precepts. The system assumed a single teacher who could control several hundred children, using "monitors" who in turn trained younger children to drill still younger children. The curriculum consisted of reading, writing, and arithmetic for boys and needlework for girls. The curricula were modified on the receding frontier as needed.

Depending on the number of students, the location of the school, the qualifications of the teacher, and the attitude of students' parents, the school could be an unqualified success, or, often, a limited failure. The plan for these schools was promising, but the execution generally exposed its weaknesses. There was, first of all, the difficulty in finding a central location for a student body that was often dispersed over wide, commonly rural, areas. Then there was the trouble of finding a teacher who was educationally and emotionally qualified.

The one-room schoolhouse, often called a "blab school," was a mixture of all levels of instruction being conducted at the same time. Generally, various levels of instructional needs were grouped together; the higher level instructed the next level below it, and that level then taught the level below it. The "schoolmarm," for the teacher was generally a woman, reserved herself for teaching the highest level, but made herself available to all levels as various needs arose. Sometimes the teacher knew enough to cover all subjects at all levels; sometimes she was just a figurehead. But she was always overworked. In remote areas she arrived at the school early to prepare the school for the coming day; in the winter, she gathered firewood and built a fire, often in a cast iron stove, to make the coming day bearable.

In a classroom filled with children of varying ages, sometimes discipline got out of hand. Often in rural areas students were overgrown farm boys who had no desire to be in school and took out their dislike of being cooped up all day by bullying the younger and smaller students. Sometimes they took their anger out on the teacher and threatened her with physical violence. There are records of students physically attacking their teachers. Sometimes efforts to maintain strict rules of discipline led to absurd consequences, as a cartoon from *Harper's Weekly* of May 21, 1875, illustrates: a Negro lady, who returned to school to learn to read and write, is forced to stay in and study during recess because she had not learned her lessons for the day. She was 71 years old.

Through the years and across the country, millions of children of all ages attended such schools and succeeded after leaving them. The most famous, of course, was Abraham Lincoln, who occasionally attended classes in log schoolhouses for less than a year altogether, but learned, as he said, "to read, write and cipher to the Rule of Three."

A one-room schoolhouse near Marlinton, West Virginia, 1921. Courtesy of the Library of Congress.

Reading and learning are central themes in Hamlin Garland's popular memoir, *A Son of the Middle Border* (1917), which details, particularly in the eleventh chapter, "School Life," experience of the one-room schoolhouse. After the Civil War, Garland's family was drawn westward into Iowa, Wisconsin, and the Dakotas by a father who, like many Americans of the day, was looking for El Dorado, seeking their fortunes in the ground or on the farm. For them, the sun rose in the west. Though the youngsters in the family had to work continually, they attended school when they could. The schoolhouse stood for education and for the community's capacity to weather the storms that racked the prairie. Garland recounts how once a snowstorm

> leaped upon us at the close of a warm and beautiful day in February [which] lasted for two days and three nights, making life on the open prairie impossible even to the strongest man. The thermometer fell to thirty degrees below zero and the snow-laden air moving at a rate of eighty miles an hour pressed upon the walls of our house with giant power. (110)

After the storm passed,

> we met our schoolmates that day, like survivors of a shipwreck, and for many days we listened to gruesome, tales of stages frozen deep in snow with all their

# ONE-ROOM SCHOOLHOUSE

passengers sitting in their seats, and of herders with their silent flocks around them, lying stark as granite among the hazel bushes in which they had sought shelter. (111)

Yet for all the safety it provided, the temperature in the schoolhouse never seemed to be comfortable. As Garland describes it,

> It was always too hot or too cold in our schoolhouse and on certain days when a savage wind beat and clamored at the loose windows, the girls, humped and shivering, sat upon their feet to keep them warm, and the younger children with shawls over their shoulders sought permission to gather close about the stove. (115)

At Garland's school, and most others, the texts were McGuffey's Readers, which introduced the students to all kinds of literature—to Whittier, Bryant and Longfellow, and to Cooper's novels *Deerslayer* and *The Pilot*. But the main bread on which the students feasted was, of course, Shakespeare, whose literature "became a part of [their] thinking," Garland says, and helped the students "measure the large figures of [their] literature" (113).

Because many Americans themselves attended such schools (or have relatives who did or know someone who attended or taught in them), there has grown up a mystique about their power to "teach the basics," and, more significantly, to shape character. *Harper's Weekly* (February 13, 1875) pictures an idealized version of the one-room school as a teaching and learning

Interior of a one-room schoolhouse in Crossville, Tennessee, ca. 1934. Courtesy of the Library of Congress.

community with teacher and children gathered round the stove, tempered with touches of reality in the representations of the cold and the decaying room. Some of the merit attributed to the one-room school is certainly deserved; some is perhaps exaggerated. I myself attended such a small one-room schoolhouse in Ohio County, in Western Kentucky, in 1930 and found it less than fulfilling. It depended too much on discipline and order. In general, the feeling that the hickory stick is the magic instrument of teaching prevailed, as it has done throughout most of educational history. Uninformed psychology has insisted that violence, or at least firm pressure, has been effective in forcing society, or portions of it, into compliance. But the question takes on different dimensions when applied to education. In the school, the hickory stick perhaps has been as much the devil's stick of negative results as the magic wand of positive accomplishment.

In twenty-first-century American society, the concentration of school children into larger and larger groups and schools and the development and dissemination of distance learning technology has all but eliminated the reality of the one-room school. Perhaps the closest modern equivalent is the small kindergarten, though the differences are obvious. Yet we continue to hold the one-room school in high regard, as an icon of the large part education has played in America's past and plays in its future. Bowling Green State University has such a school building on its campus, built in 1875 in Huron County, Ohio, and moved and reassembled brick-by-brick after nearly 100 years of use. Twenty-minute tours are conducted of the building inside and out to demonstrate what teaching and learning was like in the nineteenth century. It is one of many one-room school shrines across America.

Perhaps the most romanticized version of one-room school nostalgia is the popular song "School Days (When We Were a Couple of Kids)," with words by Will D. Cobb, music by Gus Edwards, first published in 1908. On publication the song sold over a million copies, and it is still occasionally heard. The words take us back to the dear old golden rule days, to "readin' and 'ritin' and 'rithmetic," all taught to the tune of a hickory stick. In the song, love greased the troubles encountered in the one-room school. With us today, distance in time and advancement in educational facilities enhance and polish the icon of education which once glowed in the weak rays of the oil lamp that guided young people on the path of our educational system.

American icons are often static and represent the unchanging, but the one-room schoolhouse has grown from its original purpose. It represents American educational development, as well as the personal advancement of individual Americans. As opportunities for those achievements have opened up, so has the icon of the one-room schoolhouse developed. The single room has grown into a complex of buildings, the single teacher into a group of trained specialists, the administration into a hierarchy of overseers. Although their training and purposes are well placed, sometimes the results are not ideal. Maybe that is why we look back to what we think were the good old days when all educational needs could be met and problems solved through a system we idealize by turning the antiquated one-room schoolhouse into a formal, sufficient educational icon.

## WORKS CITED AND RECOMMENDED

Fuller, Wayne E. *One-Room Schools of the Middle West.* Lawrence: UP of Kansas, 1994.

Garland, Hamlin. *A Son of the Middle Border.* 1917. New York: Macmillan, 1935.

Leight, Robert L., with Alice Duffey Rinehart. *Country School Memories: An Oral History of One-Room Schooling.* Westport, CT: Greenwood, 1999.

Manning, Diane. *Hill Country Teacher: Oral Histories from the One-Room School and Beyond.* Boston: Twayne, 1990.

One-Room School House Center. 28 Dec. 2005 <http://www2.johnstown.k12.oh.us/cornell/states.html>.

Pringle, Laurence P., with illustrations by Barbara Garrison. *One Room School.* Honesdale, PA: Boyds Mills P, 1998.

Williams, Cratis D. *I Became a Teacher: A Memoir of One-Room School Life in Eastern Kentucky.* Ed. James M. Gifford. Ashland, KY: Jesse Stuart Foundation, 1995.

# Oscar

## Robert Holtzclaw

He's an inanimate object that stands just over one foot tall and weighs less than ten pounds, yet each year rich and successful men and women spend millions of dollars to woo him, careers rise and fall based on where he goes, and hundreds of millions of people around the world watch to see the decisions he makes. Like the biggest stars in Hollywood, he needs only one name. He is Oscar.

Considering the glitz, tension, and high-stakes business dealings with which he is now associated, Oscar had quite modest beginnings, arising almost as an afterthought in the planning stages of the Academy of Motion Picture Arts and Sciences (AMPAS). From these humble origins, however, the statuette and all it represents have grown into a highly coveted sign of peer approval and career success. The prestige of an Oscar victory is part of the allure, but a more concrete motivation is also at work: winning the award, particularly in the major categories, can add millions of dollars to a film's box-office gross and subsequent DVD and video revenue and also increase the salary for future projects of the winners. Speaking in a 2004 Arts and Entertainment (A&E) television "biography" of Oscar, critic and film scholar Neal Gabler summed up the golden man's reputation this way: "Oscar is a celebrity—more famous than just about any star in Hollywood."

Such fame and success for the Academy's yearly prizes could never have been predicted when the idea was first developed. The Academy of Motion Picture Arts and Sciences itself began in 1927, and its initial primary goals were to mediate labor disputes in the film industry, promote advancements in movie technology, and help rehabilitate the somewhat unsavory public perception of Hollywood and the film business. The idea of an award from the Academy was a minor component of AMPAS's overall mission; according to Robert Osborne, writing in *70 Years of the Oscar*, the "presentation of awards [was] definitely a secondary matter" (15).

Two years after AMPAS's creation, on May 16, 1929, the first Academy Awards presentation was held at the Blossom Room of the Hollywood Roosevelt Hotel. The event was a far cry from the lavish, lengthy ceremony it has become in the subsequent seventy-five years. The night featured dinner, and conversation, but the actual award presentation ceremony took approximately five minutes (including the first Best Picture award to *Wings*). Recipients were announced in advance, with their names printed in the programs, and there were no production numbers and no long speeches—just a quick acknowledgment of the winners as part of the evening's festivities.

The Oscar statuette has reached iconic status in the years since that tentative first night; it is instantly recognizable, even in silhouette, throughout the United States and much of the world. The award's design has changed very little since it was created in 1928 by MGM art director Cedric Gibbons and sculptor George Stanley. Oscar stands 13½ inches tall and weighs 8½ pounds, and he is made of the alloy britannia metal with 24-karat-gold plating. The actual figure is a knight holding a crusader's sword, standing upon a reel of film with five spokes which represent the five original branches of the Motion Picture Academy—actors, directors, producers, technicians, and writers.

Precisely how the Academy Award got the nickname "Oscar" is not certain: there are competing theories, however, which only add to the statue's storied history. The most prevalent account, and the one officially endorsed by the Academy itself, asserts that Academy librarian Margaret Herrick once commented that the statue resembled her uncle, Oscar Pierce. According to this version, other Academy workers began using the term and it spread informally throughout the industry.

Although Herrick herself confirms this story and it is the official Academy version, two other theories also have some support. Both involve celebrities, and are perhaps more quirky and enticing to believe in terms of the creation of the Oscar legend. The first of these involves playwright Oscar Wilde. When asked if he had ever won the Newdigate, a poetry award, he is said to have offhandedly replied "While many people have won the Newdigate, it is seldom that anyone gets an Oscar." Hearing of Wilde's clever remark at a dinner party years later, playwright Charles MacArthur reportedly said to his wife, actress Helen Hayes, "I see you've won an Oscar" (referring to her 1932 Academy Award for *The Sin of Madelon Claudet*), and the term spread from there ("How Did Oscar Get His Name?"). If this is the case, Wilde essentially (and accidentally) named the award for himself before it was even created.

The other competing theory attributes the nickname to actress Bette Davis, who is said to have remarked that from the rear, the statue resembled her then-husband, Harmon Oscar Nelson. This risque comment was supposedly passed around at various dinner parties and industry gatherings until "Oscar" became the preferred term for the statuette.

Whatever its origin, "Oscar" crossed over into public use in 1934, when Walt Disney referred to the award by that name during his acceptance speech and a newspaper columnist used the term in print. The Academy itself resisted adopting the nickname for several years. AMPAS tried, unsuccessfully, to

A giant Oscar statue at the entrance of the red carpet in Los Angeles. Courtesy of Shutterstock.

garner support for calling their award "the golden trophy" or "the statue of merit," and the entertainment paper *Weekly Variety* attempted to popularize "the iron man." But "Oscar" won out, and the organization officially began using the nickname in 1939. Perhaps AMPAS's initial reluctance to embrace the term can be attributed to the organization's desire to bestow a more "dignified" name on its prestigious award, not a nickname based on a librarian's uncle, a controversial playwright, or the rear end of Bette Davis's husband.

Oscar's significance built slowly during its first decade, functioning primarily as an important industry award that received some national attention but faded quickly until the next year. The transformation of Academy Awards night into an entertainment event began in earnest at the 1940 awards. This year, for the first time, attendees were informed that cameras would be present and the ceremony would be captured on film, with highlights to be shown at theaters before their main features. Knowing that the general public would see the ceremony led to some changes in the format and atmosphere; the stars dressed more formally and extravagantly, presentation and acceptance of awards became more structured, and the entire event began to take the shape of a briefer version of the ceremony as it is seen today. Entertainer Bob Hope also made his first appearance as host of the awards in this year, a role he would fill many times in the future. Celebrities' clothing choices have now become one of the most prominent elements of the entire evening, as there is pre-show speculation about which designers will be chosen by various stars, commentary during the red-carpet arrivals, and post-show media analysis of the winners and losers in the fashion competition.

Another element of the Oscar mystique also came into play after the 1940 ceremony. The Academy had stopped its practice of announcing the winners in advance several years earlier, but news outlets were still informed of the victors in advance (so they could print them up for the next morning's paper) and had agreed not to leak the results prematurely. In 1940, however, the *Los Angeles Times* published the results early, and the now-famous secrecy and "sealed envelopes" were introduced the following year. This little scandal itself led to more publicity for the Oscars, increasing the public's interest and, consequently, the award's value within the industry.

The next big year in the development of Oscar's iconic status came in 1954, when NBC broadcast the ceremony to a national television audience for the first time. This inaugural telecast set a television ratings record, and by 1958 viewership had reached 100 million people. Now, of course, the program is a television ratings event with few equals in the broadcast industry. Each Oscar telecast draws almost 1 billion viewers worldwide, employs approximately 35 cameras and 500 workers, and goes into preproduction five months before its air date—a dramatic change from the brief, almost casual nature of the first few years of Academy presentations. Television and the movie industry both benefit from the event, and the two rivals for consumers' entertainment time and money happily join forces each year.

Some recognition of the basic value of an Oscar win came very early in the Award's history, however, and along with this recognition came one of Oscar's lingering controversies: the idea of "campaigning" for the award. AMPAS executive director Bruce Davis has said the primary rule is to "run a dignified campaign—don't beg" ("Oscar"). However, some strategies and expenditures continue to draw attention and criticism. Steve Daly, in his 2004 article "Noms That Were Bombs," reports that "Oscar-season advertising, say Hollywood observers, has gotten completely out of hand in recent years. Even the Academy has been moved to decry 'monetary outlays and questionable tactics that have far outstripped anything in the past'" (88). Voters (the approximately 5,800 academy members) are often unhappy with overly aggressive advertising, and campaigning studios must balance this potential problem with the perceived need to draw attention to the work. With varying degrees of tact and subtlety, studios often launch elaborate, expensive campaigns for their movies and stars. In his *Parade* article "How Much Is Oscar Worth?" Sandy Kenyon states that "for the studios, an Oscar can add up to tens of millions of dollars in additional revenue. That's why, combined, they spend an estimated $50 million...to win them" (16).

The first Oscar campaign controversy came in just the second year of the award's existence. In 1930, actress Mary Pickford invited the five judges to her Pickfair estate for an elaborate dinner, and then a few weeks later she won the Best Actress Oscar. After this incident, the rules for selecting the winner were changed. Perhaps the most criticized Oscar campaign during the award's first fifty years was actor Chill Wills's unsuccessful attempt, in 1961, to secure a Supporting Actor victory for his work in *The Alamo*. The entire *Alamo* campaign is considered one of the more excessive in Oscar history, but it did result in seven nominations, including Best Picture (with only one win, for sound). The ad placed by Mr. Wills's publicist, however, is considered among the most extreme. Turned down by *Daily Variety* but accepted by *The Hollywood Reporter*, the ad pleaded: "We of the *Alamo* cast are praying—harder than the real Texans prayed for their lives at the Alamo—for Chill Wills to win the Oscar." Wills lost to Peter Ustinov, and later the Academy's Board of Governors issued a rare public denouncement, terming *The Alamo*'s attempts an "excessive and vulgar solicitation of votes" (Daly 89). This and other controversies have helped keep ad campaigns somewhat under control, but controversies continue to erupt, with Miramax Studio's hard-driving (and sometimes successful) campaigns a target of criticism in recent years. Some observers, however, find nothing wrong with overt attempts to influence voters: Peter Bart, a journalist for *Variety*, has said "Why pretend it's the Nobel Prize? It's not. It's okay to advertise and campaign" ("Oscar").

The annual telecast itself is often criticized for its overall length, lousy production numbers, and long-winded speeches, but the controversies and surprises of the program are part of the reason viewers keep coming back year after year. Among the many incidents that have outlived their fleeting moments on screen and entered the public consciousness as Oscar legend are the following three:

1. In 1974, as David Niven was speaking to the audience, 33-year-old Robert Opal streaked across the stage flashing a peace sign and wearing nothing but a smile. Niven turned around to see why people were laughing and gasping, and upon seeing Mr. Opal he remarked that the poor chap had made the unfortunate decision to gain attention by "showing his shortcomings" to the world (Osborne 224). The shock of the streak, and the wit of Niven's quick retort, had people talking for some time.

2. Sally Field, perhaps to her regret, made an unscripted remark upon winning her second Oscar (in 1985) that has since come to be closely associated with her and used in various other movies and television shows, often as parody. Field's reaction to her victory was probably one that many award winners have felt, but she made the mistake of saying it aloud and acknowledging her pleasure too directly: "I can't deny the fact that you like me, right now, you like me."

3. While Oscar telecasts through the years have a sad (or perversely entertaining) history of awful musical numbers, one of the most maligned is from the much-ridiculed 1989 telecast, produced by Allan Carr. The opening number featured a performance of "Proud Mary" by the singing and dancing duo of Rob Lowe and a woman in a Snow White costume; horrendous in every measurable way, it is imprinted on the minds of many viewers and was even singled out in *Vanity Fair* magazine as "the worst moment in the history of television" ("Oscar").

Beyond these more amusing highlights, however, Oscar has also cemented its iconic status through a number of much-discussed controversies. George C. Scott announced that he had "contempt" for the Academy and would refuse to accept an Oscar if he won (which he then did, in 1971 for *Patton*), and Marlon Brando sent Sacheen Littlefeather (actually an actress named Maria Cruz) to refuse his 1972 Oscar because of "the treatment of American Indians... by the film industry" (Barr, Brown, and Schwartz). Some winners who did accept their Oscars also stirred up controversy and attention. Vanessa Redgrave, accepting a Best Supporting Actress award in 1978 for *Julia*, used the occasion to comment on the Middle East conflict by denouncing the "zionist hoodlums" she saw as interfering with efforts to reach an appropriate resolution. That phrase in particular, and her remarks in general, led to strong reaction from the assembled audience and debate within the media and general public. Later in that broadcast, writer Paddy Chayevsky denounced Redgrave when it was his turn at the podium: "I am sick and tired of people exploiting the occasion of the Academy Awards. Her winning is not a pivotal moment in history and does not require a proclamation. A 'thank you' would have sufficed" ("Oscar").

More recently, controversy has continued through such events as the Academy's decision to award a special career-spanning Oscar to director Elia Kazan, revered by some for his craft and artistry while disliked by others for his actions during the Hollywood Blacklist era. His appearance onstage at the Oscars was met by a mixture of cheers, boos, and even stoic silence from those who elected not to join in the standing ovation. And documentary filmmaker Michael Moore elicited strong reaction when he accepted his Oscar in 2003 for *Bowling for Columbine*, making reference to the election of a "fictitious president" who is now waging a "fictitious war" in his criticism of President Bush and the war in Iraq. Moore's comments, too, were received with a loud mixture of cheers and boos, both for their content and the perceived appropriateness (or lack thereof) of using the Academy Awards as a venue for such speeches.

All these facets of Oscar combine to secure his place as a cultural icon in America and throughout the world—his history, the great movies and performances he commemorates (and has overlooked), the spectacle of the Oscar ceremony, the controversies, the millions spent in his pursuit. Winners value the recognition from their peers (and the subsequent salary increases they often receive), while movie fans enjoy the chance to see the human side of their favorite stars as they win or lose on awards night, and to experience vicariously some of the glamour and the tension. Contests to predict the winners spring up both officially (in newspapers and magazines) and through many office pools, and debates inevitably erupt over the wisdom or folly of Oscar's choices. Everyone's a movie critic, and this extends quite naturally into the role of Oscar critic too.

Perhaps two final quotes from the *A&E Biography* of Oscar can help to encapsulate the nature of his enduring appeal and his significance to both the public and the industry. Actor and director Ron Howard notes the pervasive influence of Oscar and the way it seeps into our consciousness at a very young age: "It's been ingrained in our psyches.... Even a third-grade oral report [might begin or end with] 'I'd like to thank the academy.'"

And the master himself, Federico Fellini, is succinct and incisive in his comment on the Academy Award's importance in the massive, expensive, creative world of the movie business: "In the mythology of the cinema, Oscar is the supreme prize."

## WORKS CITED AND RECOMMENDED

Barr, Karyn, Scott Brown, and Missy Schwartz. "Oscar's Memorable Moments." *Allstarz.org* 21 Feb. 2001. 4 Apr. 2004 <http://www.allstarz.org/oscars/moments.htm>.

Daly, Steve. "Noms That Were Bombs." *Entertainment Weekly* 6 Feb. 2004: 87–90.

"How Did Oscar Get His Name?" *Timesjlt.com* 19 Mar. 2002. 23 Mar. 2004 <http://www.timesjlt.com/mar19/mainframeoscarname.htm>.

Kenyon, Sandy. "How Much Is Oscar Worth?" *Parade* 29 Feb. 2004: 16.

Osborne, Robert. *70 Years of the Oscar*. New York: Abbeville, 1999.

"Oscar." *A&E Biography*. Braverman Productions. A&E Television Networks. 22 Feb. 2004.

# Patchwork Quilt

## Judith Hatchett

I'm probably among the last generations of Americans whose mothers, aunts, or grandmothers spread homemade quilts under shade trees on hot summer afternoons and said, "I'll make you a pallet," meaning that children should stay on or near the quilt, thus out of the house, and make themselves content with a cigar box full of crayons and many coloring books. That my grandmother had in the distant past actually made these quilts we took for granted, if we thought about it at all, as part of her ancient lifestyle that included gardening, canning, and chopping the heads off her own chickens. To us baby boomers, these were things old people had done because they didn't know any better.

As I think about those quilts today, though, I am haunted by questions I didn't know to ask and can now never answer. Why did my grandmother make the quilts—was it habit, perceived necessity, or pleasure? Did she take pride in them? If so, why didn't she mind throwing them on the ground or seeing them hauled off in the backs of cars for afternoons of picnics or sunbathing? Why didn't anyone save them? I realize that I don't remember how any of her quilts looked, but I do remember keenly the smell of them—grass and cotton and sunlight.

As I began to research and reflect on quilts and quilt-making, I realized that the unanswered questions surrounding my own family's quilter permeate the history of quilt-making, a history in which fragments are pieced together to form a design that conjures powerful but different reactions. I began to understand that in the history of quilts and our perceptions of them lie many tensions—between beauty and usefulness, appreciation for and denigration of women's labor, individual and communal efforts, and most especially, between stories told and stories silenced. I also became intrigued by the way quilts appear in American literature and the ways their symbolic presentations reflected their actual history. Eventually I chose to examine the ways two contemporary Kentucky writers employ the quilt as symbol and to juxtapose their treatment of the quilt against the actual history of quilts.

The texts I chose to examine were by Bobbie Ann Mason and Silas House, but choices abounded. A Web site called *Quilts, Quilters, Quilting, and Patchwork in Adult Fiction* lists over 150 literary works that center on quilts. Visitors are invited to submit their own annotated entries, so the list is constantly growing. That the patchwork quilt seems a near-perfect embodiment of all things American makes this extensive literary treatment understandable. The quilt's combination of art and utility evokes collective memories of our pioneer pasts, wherein thrift and ingenuity turned castoff scraps into creative coverlets that warmed both bodies and souls of families struggling to make their lives and fortunes in a New World.

As my personal, historical, and literary reflections revealed, the quilt is so inextricably entwined with American history that it looms a far more complex icon than our national myths might acknowledge. Writers who seize upon the quilt and foreground it as a symbol within their narratives may or may not encompass the contradictions and ambivalence reflected in the real history of quilt-making.

In his first novel *Clay's Quilt*, Silas House presents quilts as unambiguously positive objects, at once comforting and beautiful. The chief quilter in the story is Clay's Uncle Paul, although several members of Clay's family—even his rebellious mother Anneth, who was murdered when Clay was four—have helped to quilt at one time or another. Readers encounter no conflict between quilt as art and quilt as bedcover, such as that in Alice Walker's short story "Everyday Use," wherein the two views of quilts represent mutually exclusive lifestyles. Clay and his family appreciate the beauty and warmth of quilts in equal measure. While House's symbolism is obvious, and deliberately so, it is also effective in underscoring the novel's theme that, no matter the difficulty, Clay must take up the fragments of his life and form his own orderly pattern.

In this novel, then, quilts and quilt-making are instructive. Paul tells Clay about the crazy quilt: "'They don't go by no real design. It's all up to the quilter'" (37). Clay also learns from Paul that his mother would choose only bright colors for quilts because she refused to see, as Paul explains, that "'a quilt needs some browns and grays to even it all out'" (38). When he handles the scraps from Paul's basket, Clay knows he can feel "geography and history beneath his fingertips" (37). Clay instantly associates the quilt scraps with the scraps of information he has gleaned about his mother's life and wishes that he "might stitch them together, and have a whole that he could pull up to his neck and feel warm beneath.... If he did, he would take two corners in his hands, snap the whole out onto the good air, and let it sail down smooth and easy to settle on the ground. It would be a story made up of scraps, but that was all he had" (40). At the novel's end, Clay feels wholeness for the first time when he receives a Flying Bird quilt that Paul had made from scraps of Anneth's clothing. *Clay's Quilt*, then, views quilt-making as a trope for seizing the elements of one's life—even if they are leftover, cast off, or clashing—and shaping them into something strong, lovely, and useful.

This use of quilt as symbol also reflects core American values such as hard work, building something from nothing, importance of family, and individual responsibility for coping with whatever life brings. Such connections resemble those of Eliza Calvert Hall's *Aunt Jane of Kentucky*, published in 1907, wherein Aunt Jane tells stories and offers advice while working on quilts. Aunt Jane also associates piecing quilts with making sense of life: "'how much piecin' a quilt's like livin' a life? . . . The Lord sends us the pieces, but we cut them out and put 'em together pretty much to suit ourselves'" (74).

Joan Mulholland argues in the *Journal of American Culture* that quilts are and always have been a form of discourse, a language shared among a quilter, the quilter's teacher—usually her mother—and the quilter's community (1–3). Thus Clay, his Uncle Paul, and Aunt Jane "read" the quilts as both instruction and emblem of how to approach life. In Bobbie Ann Mason's "Love Life," Opal Freeman reads her family quilts quite differently. A retired algebra teacher who spends her evenings drinking peppermint schnapps and watching MTV, Opal is bemused by her niece Jenny's interest in the quilts Opal keeps wrapped in plastic and stored in a closet. "'Do you know what those quilts mean to me?' she asks Jenny. 'A bunch of old women ruining their eyes.'" Opal then declares that she will take up aerobic dancing (10). Opal at first refuses to show Jenny the quilt she is most curious about—the family burial quilt, which Opal refers to as "'that old rag'" (3), which she later complains is "'too ugly to put on a bed and too morbid to work on'"

Four women working on a patchwork quilt, ca. 1910. Courtesy of the Library of Congress.

(15). Jenny declares the quilt to be beautiful but Opal says, "'It's as ugly as homemade sin'" (14). Opal gives the quilt to Jenny, who says she will learn to quilt and complete the blocks for family members who have died since Opal inherited the quilt and stopped the tradition of adding a block upon each death. Although it remains doubtful that the unsettled Jenny, single like her aunt, will actually learn to quilt, Opal feels no regret upon relinquishing the family heirloom and reflects again on "'All those miserable, cranky women, straining their eyes, stitching on those dark scraps of material'" (15). While watching MTV from her recliner, Opal covers herself with a comforter, presumably mass-produced and therefore in no way oppressive. Opal therefore reads her family quilts as stifling and depressing, and as instructing her to lead a life she clearly rejects.

House and Mason, like the other 150 or so writers included on the *Quilts in Fiction* Web site, recognize the iconic power of the quilts in the American consciousness and build their narratives around them, but the two writers project their significance in contrasting ways. The history of quilts and quiltmaking explains how this can be: the affirming and oppressing stories read in the quilts are actually one narrative. Quilts do have two sides, a duality that extends through their origins, their makers, and their use.

The most obvious duality is that between a quilt's beauty and its usefulness. The American patchwork quilt, as it evolved from European needlework traditions, was born of necessity. Protectionist Navigation Acts of the 1660s prevented colonists from producing wool and cotton, and even after the acts were repealed cloth was prohibitively expensive. Even the scrap pieces required for quilts were scarce because settlers had few changes of clothes. Colonial women pieced scraps together, added padding and a back cover, and then quilted the three layers to form a coverlet both strong and warm (Mulholland 1–2). Yet here also begins a major mystery for our reading of quilts. A colonial woman could assemble a "tack" quilt—the basic three layers, warm and strong, yet hastily and artlessly put together—in a single day (Walkley). So why did these women add hours and hours of stitching to their already daunting workloads in order to work their scraps into decorative patterns and shapes? And why, generations later, did frontier women, equally burdened, do the same?

Students of quilt history argue that from the outset American women began to "speak" through their quilts—perhaps their only form of self-expression—and quite deliberately to distinguish quilt-making from other chores. Both Ann Mulholland and Christina Walkley contend that many pioneer women also saw quilting as a sign of gaining control in lives made chaotic by harsh conditions. Walkley quotes an early Texas settler:

> Sometimes you don't have no control over the way things go. Hail ruins the crops, or fire burns you out. And then you're just given so much work in a life and you have to do the best you can with what you've got. That's what piecin'

is.... Your fate. But the way to put them together is your business. You can put them in any order you like. Piecing is orderly. (2)

On the other hand, social pressure eventually became a strong force in women's quilt-making. Young girls were expected to sew quilt blocks by the age of five and were given "stints"—certain specified amounts of stitching—to do each day. By the nineteenth century young women were expected to produce a quilt set of at least twelve quilts that spoke to their communities about not just their needlework skills but also their worth as potential wives. This portfolio told the community that "the girl not only knew her job in life but she was able and willing to perform it" (Mulholland 2–3). Naturally young women who resented the forced labor and assumption of inevitable destiny read quilts as restrictive guides into lives they did not choose but were often forced to accept.

A further duality in quilt production is that between piecing and quilting, both of which may be done by one or many. Here again are a bright and dark side. Certainly the quilting bee offered isolated farm women a social release as well as collaborative production of useful home goods. Other collaborations were forced, as when slave-owning women might choose to piece all or part of a quilt's cover and then order their slaves to do the quilting. This collaboration extended the artistry of quilts, however, because the slaves incorporated their own design and self-expression (Mulholland 4). Another problematic type of collaboration occurred when entrepreneurial women paid other women to produce quilts that they then sold for profit. As will be discussed later, this means of production blurred the connection between owner and creator in ways that often exploited the creator.

Other dualities within quilting further underscore its complexity as a national icon as well as literary symbol. Its history involves a give-and-take, for example, between creativity and technology. One might assume that using machines would threaten a pre-industrial art like quilt-making; but the advent of the sewing machine in the nineteenth century actually increased the creativity of quilters because it reduced the hours of hand-stitching and enabled more reflection on and experiment with design. The artistic aspect of the quilt was further enhanced as the industrial revolution enabled women to purchase inexpensive cloth for the sole purpose of quilt-making. By the Victorian era, wealthier women produced quilts—or had them produced—solely for display. Significantly, though, during hard economic times, such as the Civil War or the Depression, women would return to piecing and quilting by hand and forming quilts from leftover materials.

Other advances did adversely affect the creativity of quilt-making. During the Colonial Revival of the 1930s, quilts became popular and sought after, and quilt patterns were published in magazines or could be ordered by mail. While this popularity increased the quilting population, it homogenized quilt design, with many regional quilt names being changed or blended, and distinct community designs forsaken for popular national ones (Waldvogel 12–29). Beginning late in the nineteenth century, another contrast appeared. Whereas earlier generations of women had been expected to be modest about their quilting skills, women could now enter quilts in county fairs and even win prizes. *Hearts and Hands: The Influence of Women and Quilts on American Society* documents how, during the nineteenth century, quilts enabled women to enter an increasingly public discourse as they "used their quilts to register their responses to, and also their participation in, the major social, economic and political developments of their times" (Hedges 11). A further contrast emerged, then, between the modest homemaker bent quietly over her quilting and the abolitionist or suffragette designing and displaying a quilt with a public and political message.

The chapter in quilt history that best encapsulates the dualities and ironies of quilting is that of the Sears and Roebuck quilt competition within the 1933 Chicago World's Fair. A public relations coup for Sears, the contest attracted 25,000 entries. The quilt revival of the 1930s only partially explains the excitement created by the contest: the prize money explains the rest. Merikay Waldvogel and Barbara Brackman's *Patchwork Souvenirs of the 1933 World's Fair* contains their carefully researched account of the contest, interviews with participants, and photographs of surviving quilts and quilt pieces. This account also explains how Sears designed the contest: prizes were awarded locally, regionally, and nationally, with local winners receiving $5 or $10 and regional winners receiving as much as $200. The grand prize was $1,000 plus a $200 bonus if the winning quilt incorporated the Fair's theme of A Century of Progress. Today the prize would be the equivalent of about $20,000 (35). Inez Ward, of Horse Cave, Kentucky, recalls that when she received news of her $200 prize, she ran to the fields to tell her husband and father-in-law: " 'They were so excited. They brought the team to the house and decided that was enough work for the day' " (Waldvogel 45).

An astonishing six of the thirty finalists were from Kentucky. Waldvogel and Brackman acknowledge that "Geography may have played some part as Kentucky's location allowed its quiltmakers to send quilts to mail-order houses in Memphis, Atlanta, or Chicago," thus tripling the chances for a prize. But they also argue that even increased odds were not so important as the "legendary" quality of Kentucky quilts during the 1930s (Waldvogel and Brackman 56). An ironic likelihood is that Kentucky was able to fare so well in the Century of Progress competition because the state, and particularly its women, had actually experienced so little progress. For Kentuckians the Colonial Revival was hardly that, but instead a sudden attention to the ways they had been and were still living. These quilters were quilting for the most part as they always had, some with the additional stress of contracting their work for very modest pay. With little education, isolated homes, and few job opportunities, Kentucky women turned to sewing as the only way to support themselves or their families. At least the contest offered the possibility of more customers. One of the Kentucky winners, Susie Jackson Combs, intentionally used the contest as free advertising for her quilts and received over 200 orders as a result (Waldvogel and Brackman 57).

Although extremely popular, the Sears contest sparked much controversy. Despite Sears's offering a bonus for quilts illustrating the fair's theme, only two final prizes were awarded to themed quilts. The competition rules did not distinguish, moreover, between originally designed quilts and those made from kits. The judges Sears selected preferred traditional quilts, just as they valued stitching over design and creativity. Thus they awarded the grand prize to the Unknown Star, submitted by Margaret Rogers Caden of Lexington, Kentucky, because they were impressed by the intricacy of the padded quilting, even though the design and color were both considered ordinary by skilled quilters (Waldvogel and Brackman 46). We can make our own judgments only through photographs and replicas, though, because the prize-winning quilt disappeared after being presented to Eleanor Roosevelt.

The darkest problem with the contest was not exposed at the time, even though it fueled Lexington gossip for decades: the problem that Margaret Caden did not make her prize-winning quilt, even though she signed the required Sears document stating that the work was entirely her own. "The Quilt of the Century" had been pieced and quilted by four Kentucky women who knew about neither contest nor prize. Margaret Caden, who contracted out all the quilts sold through her Lexington shop, long continued to profit from the quilt by selling its pattern and renaming it the Bluegrass Star. When the quilters eventually found out about the prize, they realized that they were in no position to protest. As the daughter of one quilter explained: "'It was Depression times; my father was an invalid, and they had to have their jobs. That was the reason my mother kept her mouth shut'" (Waldvogel and Brackman 55). Defenders of Margaret Caden have suggested that she had no intention of deliberate deception but was defining quilting as the collaborative process she knew it to be. Her choice of Chicago for her regional submission gives her away, however. Speculation is that she avoided the other submission sites available to Kentuckians because they were in the Southeast where the judges would know, as one anonymous interviewee put it, that "'Margaret Caden did not know which end of a needle to thread'" (Waldvogel and Brackman 59).

This questionable conclusion to the Century of Progress quilt competition further extends the ways quilts "speak" to their makers, communities, and viewers, and emphasizes the dualities intrinsic to this American art. Thus when Silas House presents quilts as positive, instructive, and equally useful and beautiful, he is telling one true story of quilts. Bobbie Ann Mason's story is also true. Just as Opal views the work on quilts as drudgery, she may also be discomfited by their historical connection with marriage and submission to community standards. The traditions associated with the burial quilt force Opal to read her life not as a happy professional woman who has chosen to be single, but as an "Old Maid" who must complete the quilt and as a child whose parents wanted a boy to carry on the family name. When she sees

A woman working on her quilt in San Francisco. Courtesy of Getty Images/PhotoDisc.

women quilting together not as a festive quilting bee, but a group of "miserable, cranky women straining their eyes," she recalls ways the collaborative nature of quilting has been exploited, and the bitterness such exploitation could cause. Importantly, the reader can neither see nor read the quilt—Opal calls it ugly, but Jenny says it is "gorgeous" and "beautiful."

Likewise, readers who associate quilt-making with oppression will salute Opal as a pioneer exploring new ways for single women to live. Others may view her break from the past and its traditions as self-destructive. Both *Clay's Quilt* and "Love Life" end with quilts being passed to young adults who welcome them as connections to their unknown pasts. In a larger sense, quilts do that for all Americans. As we read an art form that has evolved from horizontal to vertical—from pioneer beds to museum walls—we can see how inextricably quilts are bound with American history and our attitudes toward it. Like that history, their stories are both comforting and complicated by conflict—and many have never been told.

Those untold stories return me to my grandmother. When I asked my mother why Granny Wade produced so many quilts, she answered, "I think she didn't want our home to look cheap." She also recalled my grandmother and the neighborhood women gathering to can their produce, to exchange slips of plants, and to quilt. These women were all born farm women, but exiles driven to town by hard times, who during the Depression used nineteenth-century skills they were too poor to abandon to sustain neighbors affluent enough to have lost something.

I have lost forever the opportunity to read my grandmother's quilts, and I can have no certainty about what they meant to her, except to know that she would never in her entire life have used the word "discourse" in connection with them. Some historians might contend that she must have devalued her quilts if she let them be thrown under sweaty grandchildren, sunbathers, and picnic meals. I like to think that for my grandmother and hundreds of women before her, quilts were a form of beautiful largesse, perhaps the only form they had to offer to those they loved, their only opportunity to practice the careless generosity of the better off. I hope it is true that they created beauty and comfort and threw both into the world of everyday use, offering a single final blessing from their abundance: "Enjoy these quilts and wear them out. There's plenty more where they came from."

## WORKS CITED AND RECOMMENDED

Hall, Eliza Calvert. "Aunt Jane's Album." *Aunt Jane of Kentucky*. 1907. Lexington: UP of Kentucky, 1995. 55–82.

Hedges, Elaine. *Hearts and Hands: The Influence of Women and Quilts on American Society*. San Francisco: Quilt Digest P, 1987.

House, Silas. *Clay's Quilt*. New York: Ballantine, 2002.

Mason, Bobbie Ann. "Love Life." *Love Life: Stories by Bobbie Ann Mason*. New York: Harper and Row, 1989. 1–18.

Mulholland, Joan. "Patchwork: The Evolution of a Woman's Genre." *Journal of American Culture* 19.4 (Winter 1996): 57. *Academic Search Premier*. EBSCO. Midway College Library. 10 Mar. 2005 <http://web28.epnet.com/>.

*Quilts, Quilters, Quilting, and Patchwork in Adult Fiction*. Ed. Betty Reynolds. 29 Apr. 2005 <http://infohost.nmt.edu/~breynold/quiltfiction.html>.

Waldvogel, Merikay. *Soft Covers for Hard Times: Quiltmaking and the Great Depression*. Nashville: Rutledge Hill P, 1990.

Waldvogel, Merikay, and Barbara Brackman. *Patchwork Souvenirs of the 1933 World's Fair*. Nashville: Rutledge Hill P, 1993.

Walker, Alice. "Everyday Use." *In Love and Trouble: Stories of Black Women*. New York: Harvest-Harcourt, 1973. 47–59.

Walkley, Christina. "Quilting the Rocky Road." *History Today* 44.11 (Nov. 1994): 30. *Academic Search Premier*. EBSCO. Midway College Library. 26 Jan. 2005 <http://web28.epnet.com/>.

# Walter Payton

## Clyde V. Williams

They walked past, slowly and quietly, almost reverentially. Each of the 36 of them reached out and touched the outstretched bronze hand. Then they assembled beneath the south goal post, where a painted paper curtain urged the Columbia Wildcats to a Homecoming victory over rival Poplarville High. (Columbia, Mississippi, October 18, 2004)

Created by Columbian Ben Watts, paid for by Columbia citizens, and dedicated in July 2003, the bronze statue stands just north and slightly east of the stadium's scoreboard, at the top of which appears "Walton Payton Field." Marcus Wood, CHS's new football coach in 2003, initiated the idea of his players' touching Payton's bronze hand before each home game that autumn as "an additional tribute to Walter and what he meant to the school and community." Each Columbia Wildcat has his photo taken beside the statue, and before each road game, players visit the statue. "The kids especially like the words on the plaque below the statue," Wood said.

Thirty-four years earlier, on the sweltering night of September 4, 1970, Columbia High defeated nearby Prentiss High 14–6 before a capacity crowd. In his play-by-play radio broadcast, sportscaster Frank Glenn excitedly chronicled CHS's two touchdowns—Walter Payton's runs of 70 and 88 yards. That September 1970 game marked Columbia High's first football game as an integrated team and school, and the first time that thousands of African Americans and white adults participated in a significant public event in the south Mississippi city of 6,000. As Payton's high school coach and close family friend Charles Boston later recalled: "To me, that did it for integration [issues]. I don't think they looked at Walter as a black boy, but as a [Columbia] Wildcat" (John).

Walter Payton thus became the central figure in one of Columbia, Mississippi's most important events in its 185-year history. He played a fundamental role in a major cultural change.

Leading his football team to an 8–2 record, however, reflected but one aspect of his first and only year at Columbia High. He continued his interest in music as a drummer in the CHS band, and performed respectably on the baseball field; and he won the state broad jump championship in May 1971, several days before he graduated at age 16.

Payton's reputation as a star athlete dramatically increased during the 1971–1974 seasons at Jackson State University, a small historically black institution in Mississippi whose sport team competed at the National Collegiate Athletic Association's (NCAA) Division I-A level. He started and played 37 games at J-State, where in 1973 his 160 points led the nation in scoring and led the Tigers to a South Western Athletic Conference (SWAC) title, the latter having more importance to Payton than his scoring record.

Since the 1960s, individual statistics in American intercollegiate football have become as significant as team records. As professional football emerged as America's team sport of choice in the last third of the twentieth century, pro teams and scouts scrutinized individual statistics carefully. In Payton's J-State career, they found durability and effectiveness (he carried the ball 584 times for 3,563 yards and scored 66 touchdowns) and versatility (he passed for 474 yards, kicked five field goals, and added 53 points-after-touchdown), in all, contributing a school record of 464 points. In one game he scored a conference record 46 points. In December 1974, he ranked fourth in ballots for the Heisman Trophy, awarded to America's best college football player. That year's Heisman winner, Archie Griffin, played halfback at Ohio State, which competed in the NCAA's prestigious Division I Big Ten Conference.

Payton's coach, Robert Hill, who held J-State's single-season rushing record of 1,623 yards—one of the few school offensive records that Payton did not break—called him "college football's best running back." Many observers in 1974 and later attributed Payton's loss of the Heisman to his playing in the relative obscurity of the Division I-A SWAC. A Jackson city commissioner stated that had Payton played for a team in Division I's Southeastern or Big Eight conference, he would have been "a serious candidate [winner] for the Heisman" (James). The Heisman vote and award occurred several weeks before Payton graduated, after 3½ years, from Jackson State, at age 20.

Both Payton's statistics and his character attracted close attention from National Football League scouts. During spring 1975, the Chicago Bears, with the NFL's fourth overall draft selection, chose Payton in the first round.

Departing Mississippi in July 1975 for the Bears' training camp in Platteville, Wisconsin, and ultimately to their game venue, Chicago's Soldier Field, he followed hundreds of thousands of the state's African Americans who migrated to Chicago, often via Jackson, Memphis, and St. Louis, during the first three-quarters of the twentieth century—a migration which reversed during the final decades of the century.

> As the Columbia Wildcats prepared for their October 2004 Homecoming game against Poplarville, video editors at the Fox Sports Network in New York and Atlanta neared completion of their work on *Beyond the Glory!*

*Walter Payton* for nationwide broadcast on October 31. It was filmed in Columbia and elsewhere. In a Chicago suburb, visitors to the Lake County Discovery Museum viewed displays in an exhibition honoring Walter Payton. Across the land, knowledgeable football coaches from children's community leagues to middle school and high school conferences invoked Payton's name when they encouraged their players to teamwork and hard work.

During the decade before Payton arrived in Chicago, the Bears' losing record did not diminish the team's solid base of fan support, especially among blue-collar citizens. During his first nine years as a Bear, Payton's team had seven losing seasons and made NFL playoffs only in 1977 and 1979, losing in opening rounds both years. Before the end of his fifth season, Payton had broken the team record for yards gained rushing. In Chicago, sportswriters characterized him as the one bright hope for the team's future and praised his dependability (he missed playing only one game during his entire career), his commitment to the team, and his enthusiasm for the game. Despite his team's record and its limited talent, especially in areas that would have enhanced Payton's personal offensive statistics, Payton's comments to the press did not criticize teammates; instead, he often thanked fans for their support.

Payton's numbers began to add up; during his fifth year, he had broken twenty Bear offensive records and three NFL records.

By early in his eleventh season (1984), he surpassed former Cleveland runner Jim Brown's 19-year NFL rushing yardage record of 12,312 yards. As 1984 began, Payton trailed former Pittsburgh star Franco Harris in the chase to overtake Brown; but on October 7, Payton broke Brown's record. As Payton and Harris approached the record, Brown indicated his hope that Payton would emerge as winner because, Brown said in wire-service stories, Payton never ran out of bounds to avoid punishing open-field tackles, while Harris tried to escape being hit by skipping out of bounds. What Brown did not know was that crashing into opponents, actually seeking contact, had been an underlying principle of Walter Payton's offensive play from his high school years.

During the 1984 regular season and playoff games, Payton ran for 1,684 yards and set a team record with 45 pass receptions. Before the Bears–Washington Redskins game for the division championship, Payton told Knight-Ridder's Bob Verdi that the Bears' team and franchise needed to defeat Washington, and, perhaps thinking of the perpetual failure of the Chicago baseball Cubs to win a championship, he added, "the city of Chicago needs it" (Verdi). The Bears won that game, but lost the conference championship to San Francisco the next week.

Setting the rushing record, together with the team's success, resulted in Walter Payton's gaining substantially greater attention outside the Chicago area, and made him one of the NFL's most recognized players nationally. Two other events—the Bears' Super Bowl championship in January 1986, and Payton's retirement in 1987—solidified his place in the league's history and in American popular culture.

The Bears' 15–1 regular 1985 season record, two playoff victories, and smashing New England 46–10 in the Super Bowl drew massive attention to the team, to Payton, to flamboyant quarterback Jim McMahon, and to rookie offensive lineman William "Refrigerator" Perry. A rock-rap piece, "Super Bowl Shuffle," had played around the clock days before the big game in New Orleans. *Time* magazine featured Payton and Perry on the cover of its January 27, 1986, edition, and Tom Callahan's cover story concentrated on Payton, whom he called the game's "Regal running back," adding: "How Payton has endured these eleven seasons, physically and spiritually, still so near to the top of his game, is more than a wonder" (46–47).

Chicago Bears star Walter Payton poses with the Gordon's Gin Black Athlete of the Year Award in New York, 1985. AP/Wide World Photos.

Perhaps the most dramatic moment of Payton's career came at its end, on January 10, 1988, in a 21–17 loss to Washington. On the Bears' final play, needing eight yards for a first down to give the team a chance for a tying field goal, McMahon passed to Payton, who gained seven yards. Game over. But the chilled crowd repeatedly yelled his name, then quieted, then left Soldier Field, with Payton still sitting on the Bears' bench. Mitch Albom's analysis noted:

> For a while it seemed as if he might never leave. His head was bowed, his body limp. After 13 years and 199 games, and more yards than any football player has ever gained, there were tears running down a grown man's cheeks. Walter Payton did not want to go home. (D1)

At his departure, he carried dozens of team and league records; the most important included career rushing yards (16,726), career rushing attempts (3,838), seasons with 1,000 or more yards (10), yards gained rushing in a single game (275). He left at the top of his profession, at age 33.

> As a receiver coming out of the backfield, or throwing the ball, or carrying out a fake, or chasing down the opponent on an interception or fumble, he did everything. Guys in that arena, a superstar like he was, they don't have to do that. But he did it because he was setting the best example he could for his teammates. (Mike Ditka, qtd. in Payton, with Yaeger 103)

Payton's final NFL coach, Mike Ditka, a gruff guy not commonly given to commending his own—or opposition—players, repeatedly and enthusiastically praised Payton, calling him "The best blocker by far that they've [other NFL coaches] ever seen at running back" (Payton, with Yaeger 103).

Statements about him from his relatives, friends, fellow athletes, coaches, and writers consistently reiterated several key elements of Walter Payton's character: determination and preparation, privacy and quiet, and generosity.

Coach Boston observed that, as a high school junior learning the game, in practice Payton simply would run over rather than around teammates attempting to tackle him. Boston taught the youngster the stiff-arm to elude tacklers; Watts's bronze statue of Payton, whose hand current players touch before games, depicts that element of his game.

Coaches and teammates gave him one of several nicknames, "The Big-Eyed Boy," which Coach Boston explained: "Before games, Walter's eyes seemed to get bigger and bigger. When you looked at him with his helmet on, all you seemed to see was his eyes, almost like fiery coals." Years later an opponent noticed this intense concentration and determination. After losing to the Bears 23–19 in the 1984 divisional playoff game, the Washington Redskins stellar defensive end Dexter Manley said of Payton: "He's like Superman...you look in his helmet at those eyes and say, 'Where is this guy coming from? Where do you find people like this?'" (Boeck D6). High school teammate Forest Dantin, soon after Payton's death in 1999, said, "Walter was always very intense and wanted to win" (Boothe A16). At that time, family friend and East Marion (Mississippi) High School coach Les Peters said, "he always had a burning desire to succeed, and he did" (Boothe A16).

Gannett News Service writer Greg Boeck called him "The complete football player, the NFL's most treasured asset" (D6). The Knight-Ridder chain's Mitch Albom saw him as "A running back who so dazzled the sport that he defied logic" (D1).

These repeated plaudits by NFL players and writers reflect the fact that numbers alone, no matter how impressive, do not fully characterize an athlete. For instance, after the Bears defeated Washington to earn their conference championship appearance in 1985, Redskins defensive back Curtis Jordan said, "Whatever Payton gets, and he's gotten it all because he may be the best ever, he deserves it" (Boeck). A Payton block knocked Jordan out of that game with a cracked shoulder.

Coach Boston also recalled that during Payton's childhood, Walter would gallop around neighborhood yards carrying smaller children on his back. His brother Eddie recalled their father instilling a strong work ethic in his children; one that included heavy manual labor in the yard and family garden. Walter commonly ran alone on the sandy banks of the nearby Pearl River, and later, his physical conditioning regimen became legendary in the NFL. His physical training occurred year-round, every year, until he retired. In 1986, Dallas Cowboy coach Tom Landry called Payton, "Tremendously strong, stronger than any other player ever at his size [5'10", 205 lbs.]" (Isle 6). Moreover, he mastered his offensive play assignments and his opponents' defensive tendencies. "He was always prepared, physically and mentally, for any opponent, at any level," Coach Boston said.

Once a Chicago reporter asked him to enumerate his favorite things. Payton responded, "Hunting and privacy." Peters noted, "He was a private person," and Dantin added, "He never raised his voice or fussed at the other [players]" (Boothe A16). Fans and observers saw an additional manifestation of his avoiding the spotlight even during games. When he made an especially dazzling play, he would hand the ball to the referee and trot back to the team huddle. After scoring, he typically handed the ball to a Bears lineman before heading back to the sidelines. Coach Boston, a quiet man himself, had emphasized to Payton and his other youthful charges, "Remember when you score, you didn't get there by yourself." Throughout his football career, Walter Payton placed teammates and his team before his personal goals; at all levels, he acknowledged and expressed gratitude for their efforts.

> Sweetness—the grace, ease, and speed of a great running back's movements? Sweetness—kindness and generosity of spirit?

Stories of how Walter Payton's nickname became "Sweetness" circulated around Jackson and Chicago from the mid-seventies. Perhaps it derived from the adjective "sweet," that word which then and now shows youth approval of a person, event, or action; certainly it could describe Walter Payton's activities on the gridiron.

But it could as well describe the gentleness and generosity of the Jackson State football star who as a student worked with physically and intellectually disabled children. It could describe the man who understood the importance of children receiving toys at Christmas and established a foundation which provided toys and volunteers to distribute them to hundreds of thousands of Chicago-area children. And the man whose rise from rural south Mississippi to wealth and fame in the great metropolis led him to create a college scholarship program at his alma mater, a program which seems about to expand nationally.

It could describe the tenacity of a man who, loving privacy, upon retiring from football became an active, persuasive spokesperson for many charitable organizations and who participated in many events to support those organizations. It could describe Walter Payton's successful efforts during his final year of life in 1999 to encourage Americans to become organ donors, to save or prolong the life of fellow citizens; it could describe what NFL Commissioner Paul Tagliabue called "The grace and dignity he displayed in final months" and how his teammates and friends recalled his facing death during those months which concluded on November 1, 1999. He was 45.

For the Columbia High Wildcats and Coach Wood, their October 18, 2004, 44–12 Homecoming win was comfortable and convincing. All 36 team members played. As the team trotted off Walter Payton Field, a younger Wildcat who had gotten to play most of the final quarter looked over to the statue, winked, waved, and gave a "thumbs-up" sign. The words on the plaque beneath the statue of Walter Payton say, "None of us are as strong as all of us."

## WORKS CITED AND RECOMMENDED

Parts of the entry incorporate the author's discussions with Coach Charles Boston, Marcus Wood, and public school officials in Columbia, Mississippi; with Coach Eddie Payton at Jackson State University; and descriptions from the author's extended visits to Columbia in October and December 2004.

Albom, Mitch. "How 'Sweet' He Was: Final Chapter on Storied Career." *Jackson* (MS) *Daily News* 11 Jan. 1988: D1+.
*Beyond the Glory! Walter Payton.* Fox Sports Network. 31 Oct. 2004.
Boeck, Greg. "Payton Gets January Shot at Long Last." *Clarion-Ledger* 1 Jan. 1985: D6.
Boothe, Kristan. "Columbia Mourns Loss of Its Hometown Hero." *Columbian-Progress* 4 Nov. 1999: A16.
Callahan, Tom. "'Sweetness' and Might." *Time* 24 Jan. 1986: 46–49.
Isle, Stan. "Rosen: 24-Man Roster, Very Interesting." *The Sporting News* 27 Jan. 1986: 6.
James, Billy. "Payton Still Hoping for Heisman." *Meridian Star* 8 Nov. 1974: 12.
John, Butch. "Columbia: Is This Payton Place?" *Clarion-Ledger* 19 Jan. 1986: A1+.
Payton, Walter, with Don Yaeger. *Never Die Easy: The Autobiography of Walter Payton.* New York: Villard, 2000.
Verdi, Bob. "Beating Redskins Will Quench 'Sweetness' Craving for Payton." *Clarion-Ledger* 30 Dec. 1984: D10.

# Polyester

## *Patricia A. Cunningham*

Microfibers and performance textiles are key players in contemporary fashion. Yet hip consumers don't recognize them as polyester. And if they did, they might be too young to recall that by the late 1970s, wearing polyester, or any synthetic fabric, was decidedly uncool. However, that was not always the case. When it was first introduced, polyester was a highly touted new synthetic fiber that was first made into woven fabrics for men's suits in the early 1950s. Polyester was a "miracle fiber" known for its wrinkle-free qualities, toughness, and resiliency. But its negative qualities—low moisture absorption, oily soiling, static, and pilling problems—soon put it in a bad light. Its real downfall came when the price dropped and it became the fiber of choice for double-knit fabrics used for inexpensive menswear. The knits were often produced in pastel "fashion colors" for men's leisure suits. The fashion for leisure suits fizzled quickly, and they became a much despised and parodied clothing item that quickly sent polyester down the road to infamy as an icon of bad taste, and even of all that was wrong with American society.

Since the late 1970s, many dollars have been spent by the textile industry to remove the stigma. Thanks to the introduction of micro-denier fibers and performance fabrics, such as Coolmax, they have almost succeeded; but it has not been without the help of textile technology and changing American lifestyles. Although polyester became an icon of ugliness, the miracle fiber of the twentieth century has been transformed into a high-tech necessity for the twenty-first century. The story begins and ends in the laboratory.

Much of the credit for the discovery of polyester, as well as nylon, belongs to a young American scientist, Wallace Carothers, who worked at DuPont from 1928 until his untimely death in 1937. Carothers discovered polyester while working on a project to understand the nature of polymers. Carothers sought to convince fellow scientists that polymers were long chain molecules held together by ordinary chemical bonds. His research on polyester, carefully patented by DuPont and widely published, led to the later development of polyester into a spinnable fiber. This development was accomplished by two Englishmen, Rex Whinfield and his assistant James Dickson, working at

Calico Printers Association. In 1941 they received a patent on a process for producing a spinnable polyester fiber from ethylene glycol and terephthalic acid. However, World War II interrupted further development until 1944, when ICI (Imperial Chemical Industries) began serious development of polyester, which they named Terylene. Through the Co-operation Agreement on Patents and Processes with ICI, DuPont acquired polyester fiber patents for the United States in 1946. They first named their fiber Fibre V, but renamed it Dacron in 1951 (Brunnschweiler and Hearle 30–39).

Initially, DuPont was anxious to produce a yarn that would replace wool for men's suitings. Certainly polyester had the requisite resiliency that prevented a fabric from wrinkling easily. However, in the process of developing the fiber, DuPont encountered numerous processing problems, product limitations, and performance deficiencies. Nonetheless, the first commercial entry was a man's tropical weight suit manufactured by Witty Brothers that was advertised in the *New York Times* in June 1950. Schoeneman of Baltimore offered a cord suit in 1952; Hart, Schaffner, & Marx presented a blend of wool and polyester in 1953, the same year that Cone Mills announced oxford cloth shirts in a 65 percent cotton/35 percent polyester blend. Clearly trade interest in the fiber was high. However, the initial interest of consumers was low. They needed to be educated about the wash and wear qualities of new synthetic fibers (Brunnschweiler and Hearle 44–47).

Throughout the 1950s gains were made in all aspects of the business. American consumers, in particular, became keen on "better living through chemistry," and technology that gave rise to a new contemporary style. Disneyland's *Tomorrowland* even featured a futurist house (c.1986) built entirely of plastic by Monsanto. An early sponsor of Disneyland, Monsanto later featured a giant oil lamp with mannequins wearing "Polyester." Yet there were challenges to the euphoria for plastics.

At the same time, opposition to technology and technocrats emerged, dramatized, for instance, as widespread fear generated by the invention of indestructible clothes, in the film *The Man in the White Suit* (1951). After all, what would happen if clothes never wore out? Fiber wars also developed. The natural fiber interests (wool and cotton) struck out at synthetics. Cotton manufacturers used advertising campaigns to promote ease of care and comfort qualities of resin-treated 100 percent cotton. They believed that their wash and wear fabrics were superior to anything made of blends of polyester and cotton. The campaigns were effective; Dacron prices for filament yarns fell by 20 percent (DeMeo 358–59). Competition from Kodel, an Eastman Chemical polyester (of slightly different chemical makeup), exacerbated the problem for DuPont. But then, DuPont counterattacked with a program to improve the qualities of polyester through modifications, such as high luster and pill resistance, and the introduction of new fiberfill products (Brunnschweiler and Hearle 47).

Nonetheless, the competition did not cease; in fact, it increased. In the early 1960s, the original polyester patents expired. Many companies throughout the world joined in the polyester merry-go-round. DuPont now had more than cotton and Kodel to contend with. They had worldwide competition that was fierce. Diversification that opened up markets to polyester, and expansion beyond staple and filament yarns into non-clothing industrial end use, continued unabated (Brunnschweiler and Hearle 40–47). In the 1960s, polyester was an icon, but not of bad taste. It served as a beacon for a new high-tech world that would move Americans beyond merely being modern. But this association did not last. In many respects polyester became its own worst enemy, fueled by the success in knitwear. The knitwear industry began using textured polyester (crimped) filament yarn (such as Taslan, developed in 1953 by DuPont) for double-knit fabrics for women's and later men's clothing. The success of this combination brought about a boom for polyester. It provided a catalyst for innovation and technological change that resulted in an unprecedented exciting era for the textile industry. Knits were everywhere. The inevitable bust came with overproduction of knitting machinery and fabric. Demand waned when fashion took a different course.

Of course, it is the man's leisure suit, often constructed of double-knit polyester jersey, that is credited with the downfall of polyester. However, at first, leisure suits were quite acceptable, as was polyester as a fabric for suits. Things began to change when the widely read fashion and textile industry magazine *American Fabrics and Fashions* suggested using textured polyester knits for men's suits. In an article titled "The Knitted Suit for Men, What Are We Waiting For?" their keenest argument rested on the property of resiliency provided by both the knit and the polyester. It was the perfect travel suit; it could be rolled up for a week without wrinkling (n.p.). Using double knits for men's suits was another means to expand the market. Men's traditional suits were in fact made of polyester wovens and wool-polyester blends. However, menswear moved toward more fashionable styles at this time. The menswear designers Pierre Cardin and Hardy Amies offered a variety of new looks for men, the Mao jacket being just one. They used polyester. In the thick of this Peacock Revolution in menswear, more casual styles, such as the shirt suit, or leisure suit, emerged as a viable alternative to the traditional business suit. It was more formal than jeans.

The leisure suit was a major trend in 1974, but by the end of the decade it had become passé. John Travolta's polyester-clad disco dancing character in the 1978 film *Saturday Night Fever* provides a quick glimpse of the polyester suit's association with tackiness, showiness, and the working class. Or think of Elvis in his Las Vegas period wearing rhinestone-studded jumpsuits. But the demise in part was owing to price. Polyester that had once been made into fabrications sought after by high-end suit designers was now available at low price points. The now low cost of the fabric made it accessible to the shoddy end of the menswear market. Proliferation was its downfall. Polyester had lost its luster as the fiber of the future. Its heyday was over. The leisure suit became the icon of bad taste in America, and with it polyester. As testament to the power of the leisure suit to evoke disdain in the late 1970s, it is purported that Lutece, New York City's most famous restaurant, posted a small sign, "Please! No Leisure suits!" (Stern and Stern 154).

The leisure suit does not have to take all of the blame for the fall of polyester, however. Fashion changed; anti-plastic thinking was energized by antiwar, anti-establishment sentiment in a strong youth culture. The hippie movement grew out of these sentiments. Hippie culture demanded everything natural. In general, during the seventies Americans became more aware of the environment, fueling an interest in all things natural. It is not surprising that cotton made a comeback. Consumers wanted to be environmentally correct, and so demanded natural fibers. Fashion also took a turn toward looser fitting clothing, and the stretch imparted by knits was no longer a necessity. Casual dress meant fewer men wore traditional suits. More young people were wearing jeans with L.L. Bean jackets and hiking boots. Although the dress for success movement began to counter the casual look, it too warned against polyester.

The 1980s were tough times for synthetics. The decade was one of opulence. Natural fibers prevailed; silk especially had a great revival. Furs, silk brocade, linen, cotton, and cashmere were the preferred prestige materials. Women had entered the workplace in droves and needed smart, professional looking clothes. Knits were viewed as too casual; John Malloy's dress-for-success ideology supported tailored suits for both men and women. Even the push for "casual Fridays" did not support the wearing of leisure suits. Casual dress meant khaki pants and cotton knit polo shirts for men. Nonetheless, technological developments continued in the polyester industry. Polyester continued to be produced and improved, finding new markets and growth in diversity of uses. Japanese designers took fashion by storm in the 1980s, and their tradition includes a keen interest in textiles. Issey Miyake introduced his 100 percent polyester "Pleats Please" collection in the late 1980s. The line remains popular with consumers, and has become a signature style for Miyake. Miyake and other Japanese designers continue to collaborate with textile firms, and have no qualms about using polyester and other synthetics (Handley 132–35).

Yet, for all of the expansion of the fiber, the jokes persisted. It seemed that no matter how much the industry sought to recover the image of polyester, the leisure suit and thus polyester remained a source for humor. Polyester and leisure suits together became emblematic of "the loser," as in the video game *Leisure Suit Larry* and in John Waters's film *Polyester* (1981). Even worse, in the Spenser series of detective novels by Robert B. Parker, polyester is drawn on as a symbol of consumer values. The idea that the leisure suit wearer has no taste allows Parker to use polyester as a symbol "of not knowing any better." Ill-fitting polyester clothing is deemed inappropriate. At one point in a novel, Spenser quips, "you can't look tough in Ban-Lon." (In this case, one must ignore that Ban-Lon is a trade name for another synthetic fiber, nylon. That would be bad taste too.) The basis for the reader's understanding the meaning comes from what Jackson Lears calls "acquisitive consumption."

Inept tasteless consumption is associated with inappropriate social behavior; whereas people who act appropriately, it is assumed, consume appropriately—that is, with good taste. The purchase of a leisure suit seems clearly inappropriate behavior, and is understood as such by the public and thus the reader (Goodwin 739–45). As noted in the *Enclyclopedia of Bad Taste,* leisure suits became an "emblem of the churl, the bumpkin and the cheapskate" (Stern and Stern 154).

During the 1990s American culture began to look back at the 1970s; The decade produced at least one nostalgic television series, *That '70s Show.* Certainly 1970s clothing styles were revived by the fashion industry. In Des Moines, Iowa, a local radio host, Van Hardin, continued to put on a Leisure Suit Convention that he started in 1988. The convention has been an opportunity for folks to bring out their leisure suits, don their disco duds, and have fun. The convention offers dancing to 1970s music, a fashion show, and awards for the best dressed. While these piqued an interest in the seventies and leisure suits, it is, perhaps, two discoveries that really aided the comeback of polyester. First, recycling of post-consumer plastics by Wellman Inc. set the stage for a polyester revival (Brunnschweiler and Hearle 105–7). Such items as soda bottles made from a rigid form of polyester were recycled into new fleece fabric, the most well-known one being Polartec. The fleece was then manufactured into cold weather clothing that became popular almost immediately, and remains so. Second, microdenier fibers (less than 1 denier) made a strong entry into the marketplace. They are the "dual knights" that rescued polyester from a certain death (at least in the clothing business). Given that polyester could not shake its bad image for many years, it is not surprising that the word polyester is underplayed in both of these new textiles.

Yet, one of the unique aspects of the new polyester is that few people realize they are, in fact, wearing polyester. In the 1990s, especially, the fiber industry still felt the sting of the leisure suit. In order to counter this association, they chose to refer to polyester as "microfiber." (Microfiber can also be made of nylon and rayon, so it is not always polyester.) More important, perhaps, was that microfibers were expensive compared to higher denier fibers, and thus needed a new name to make that distinction clear: the lower the denier the finer the yarn. As observed by both Elaine Underwood and Susannah Handley, the industry coined unusual names for the microfibers (Tactel, Micromattique, Micronesse, and Microspun), and promoted them widely. (It seems that they were following the tactic used for Ultrasuede, made popular by the American designer Halston; no one knew that Ultrasuede was polyester!) The fiber industry promoted the new microfibers with designers as well. Many consumers, when asked, could not distinguish between the feel of the microfibers and silk; the uniqueness of fabrication made with microfibers have made them popular not only with high-end fashion designers, but also with artists who create one of a kind "art to wear" (Underwood 16; Handley 145–68).

Since their introduction, the microfibers have had great success in high performance active wear because fabrics made from them, such as Coolmax, are comfortable to wear, tough, and attractive. They breathe, they don't trap moisture, they don't pill; in fact, some of them behave like our skin. The sportswear industry has been quick to pick up on these factors and predicts great growth in the market for high-tech fabrics for urban and country living, as well as for serious amateur and professional athletes, and those who engage in active sports such as bicycling, hiking, running, and skiing (*Coolmax*). There is no question that the 1990s were the "body boom" decade that has continued into the twenty-first century. Going to the gym has become an important feature of the American lifestyle. The online publication *Textiles Intelligence,* devoted to business and market analysis for the world's fiber, textile, and apparel industries, sees the performance apparel market as one of the fastest growing sectors of the international textiles and clothing industry. A summary of a report on product developments ("Product Overview") reveals that they looked at consumer lifestyles and made a forecast that active sports will continue to grow; thus they could predict that high performance textiles will also see growth. Polyester fibers are part of the picture; just look at the garment label ("Product Overview" 1–2).

Although unknown to many Americans, polyester has been touching almost every aspect of our lives, and will continue to be part of them; it is the mass-market polymer. Textiles are incorporated into about one-third of industrial and engineered products. Polyester yarns, fabrics, and non-wovens are used in many of them. They include tents, awnings, sewing thread, rope, hoses, webbing, car seats, home furnishings, flexible storage tanks, automobile tires, and outer skin for boats. Monofilaments are used in screens, stencils, printed circuits, and industrial and surgical filters. Rigid polyester plastics show up in furniture, irons, and tools. Finally, thermoplastic elastomers appear in athletic shoes, ski boots, telephone cords, gear wheels, hair brushes, and even flex joints for windsurf masts (Brunnschweiler and Hearle 276–86). The list of uses is inexhaustible. It is worth recalling, perhaps, that the space suit for the first lunar landing in 1969 was made of DuPont products—nylon, Dacron, Lycra, Neoprene, Mylar, and Teflon. In the end, the story of how polyester became a signal for bad taste is but a blip in the larger picture of polyester and the rise of technology in America. Polyester has surpassed the level of perceptible icon; it has become the ubiquitous fiber of our lives.

## WORKS CITED AND RECOMMENDED

Brunnschweiler, David, and John Hearle, eds. *Tomorrow's Ideas & Profits: Polyester: 50 Years of Achievement.* Manchester, U.K.: Textile Institute, 1993.

*Coolmax.* 8 July 2005 <http://coolmax.invista.com/faqs.html>.

DeMeo, Stephen. "Dacron Polyester: The Fall from Grace of a Miracle Fabric." *Science as Culture* 5 (1996): 352–70.

Goodwin, Cathy. "Good Guys Don't Wear Polyester: Consumption Ideology in a Detective Series." *Advances in Consumer Research* 19 (1992): 739–45.

Handley, Susannah. *Nylon: The Story of a Fashion Revolution*. Baltimore, MD: Johns Hopkins UP, 1999.

"The Knitted Suit for Men, What Are We Waiting For." *American Fabrics and Fashions* 1 (1967): n.p.

"Product Overview." *Textiles Intelligence* 12 (2005): 1–2. 8 July 2005 <www.textilesintelligence.com>.

Stern, Jane, and Michael Stern. *The Encyclopedia of Bad Taste*. New York: HarperCollins, 1990.

*Textiles Intelligence* 12 (2005): 1–2. 8 July 2005 <www.textilesintelligence.com>.

Underwood, Elaine. "Can a Reborn Polyester Dethrone King Cotton?" *Adweek's Marketing Week* 15 Apr. 1991: 16.

# Poster Child

## *Mary Johnson*

"Poster child." "Poster boy." "Poster girl." An individual—usually a youth, but not always—whose name or image is invoked to stand in for an issue, the "poster child" is an icon unique to contemporary society. It can occur only in a society with a mass media—or means of mass dissemination—for without mass dissemination, it would lose its iconic power.

A search of Google brings up thousands of instances of the term, few of them actually having to do with the image of a child on a poster: Thomas Edison is called the ADD (Attention Deficit Disorder) Poster Child. Slovenia is the "Poster Child for the New Europe." To liberals, Halliburton is the "Poster Child of the War Profiteers"; to conservatives, Rosie O'Donnell is the "Poster Child for Homosexual Adoptions."

Matthew Shepard, the young Wyoming college student brutally murdered in 1998 for being gay, became the poster boy for hate crimes legislation. Columbine High School student Cassie Bernall, murdered in the April 1999 massacre, became the poster child of the Christian Youth movement when the story spread that she had been shot for saying that she believed in God. Five-year-old Elian Gonzalez, rescued by the U.S. Coast Guard in November 1999 in waters off Miami, was for a time the poster child of Cuban-American discord.

In all these cases, an individual (in the case of Halliburton, a corporate "individual"), standing in for an issue, provides a single face, and thus a focus, for a larger and usually unwieldy abstract notion. In one sense, the individual might be said to be serving as an icon, albeit sometimes temporary, for an issue.

But it is actually the poster child itself, as a modern conceit, that is the icon.

The poster child originated, of course, on a real poster. A creation of those who sought public support to cure one disease or another, the poster child began calling out to our nation during the first half of the twentieth century, her smiling face and appliance-laden body—wheelchair, braces, crutches—working hard to instill pity and just enough guilt to get the money flowing. Although Donald Anderson was, the Smithsonian Institution tells us, the first

March of Dimes poster child, poster children have most often been little girls. Six-year-old Mary Grimley served as polio's poster child, dining with President Roosevelt at the Warm Springs rehabilitation center and posing in her wheelchair for publicity shots.

The idea behind these twentieth-century posters—to use the image of a supposedly suffering child to tug at the heartstrings—sprang from a sentiment that found its flowering in the Victorian age. Tiny Tim is as good a poster child as we are likely to find, and although Charles Dickens didn't put the child with his crutches on an actual poster, Tim Cratchit served the exact same purpose as did Anderson and Grimley: he was there to remind us of our obligation to the less fortunate. He set the tone for all disease poster children that would follow: that of the "happy cripple" who, because he is meek and enduring, calls forth the best in those of us who do not so suffer—at least this is the lesson as the Victorians would have us take it.

Indeed, during the 1840s in our own nation, thousands of little books of moral instruction for children published by Christian tract societies followed the path laid down by Tiny Tim. The titles themselves are instructive: *The Deformed Boy*, *The Happy Mute*, *The Little Hunchback*, *Poor Matt*, *The Clouded Intellect*, *The Patient Cripple*, *Crazy Mary*, *Blind Nelly*, *The Lame Boy*, *The Deaf Boy's Triumph*. The child in each of these stories is, like Tiny Tim, a kind of "pre-poster child"— and like him, each carried to readers an overtly religious message: to accept one's lot in life, no matter its difficulty; to be grateful if one's lot is not as hard as others, and in all cases to provide Christian charity to the less fortunate.

In a world without television, movies or the Internet, these unflinchingly illustrated little booklets, under the guise of moral instruction, also taught both adults and children, both non-disabled and disabled, how to understand disability: to understand that it was the role of the disabled child to be cheerful and enduring, and that disability was sent by a God to instill moral character or to serve as a means whereby Christians could exercise charity and thus save their souls.

Tiny Tim, seen here in the 1938 version of Charles Dickens's *A Christmas Carol*, set the tone for all disease poster children that would follow. Courtesy of Photofest.

Thus the original message of the poster-child icon became fixed, paving the way for the work that would be done by the children that first graced the posters and then populated the telethons of the 1950s and 1960s: the brave and smiling little girls with their braces and cerebral palsy, the cheerfully hopeful Jerry's Kids of the Muscular Dystrophy Labor Day Telethon, which persists to this day.

Today, disease foundations still use the poster child for fundraising. An Arthritis Foundation poster shows a pretty little girl with a big bow in her hair: "This little old lady has arthritis," reads the poster. A poster for a Shriner's hospital shows a little girl—at first standing with crutches, then dropping them and running off to play: "Giving kids back their childhood," reads the poster.

Children raise more money than adults, white kids bring in more money than black kids, and girls are better than boys at tugging the heartstrings, fundraising executives of the nation's Easter Seals chapters were told at a national session that included how-to's for making their poster child campaigns a monetary success. The public sympathizes with images of "the most weak," they were counseled. Such thinking isn't by any means confined to executives of disease charities. United Way agencies, which offer all manner of human services to those in need, will more often than not use a disabled child as their poster image. Children with visible disabilities—using crutches, walkers, or wheelchairs—are thus frequently found on United Way posters.

Poster children can be expected to do more than merely lend their physical image to a group's fundraising poster. They appear at charity events. If the group sponsors a telethon, they are an integral part of that as well, performing on stage with celebrities. Yet their performances, unlike those of the celebrities, are not expected to necessarily showcase a talent: they are there for a different purpose. Just as the celebrity's job is not only to entertain, but to play the role of the beneficent helper, someone for the viewer to identify with, the poster child's job is to play the opposing role, that of the suffering victim whose fate can be ameliorated only by the beneficent helper.

Other than the fact that their role is that of a victim, poster children function, ironically, much as do beauty pageant winners. Like the Miss Ham and Yam beauty queen, the Sickle Cell Disease Association of America's National Poster Child, according to its Web site, serves as "Goodwill Ambassador" by:

- "Making public appearances on behalf of the Association;
- Acting as an emissary to various public officials including the President of the United States;
- Being a positive example and role model to others with sickle cell disease;
- Educat[ing] the public and assist[ing] in securing public and private sector support" (12 July 2005 <http://www.sicklecelldisease.org/info/poster.phtm/>).

This list of "duties," paired with the role the child assumes on the poster and in the telethon, gives us an insight into the dual nature of the iconic image of the poster child. For the poster child serves as both hero and victim, an image that both attracts and repels us, an image from which, its creators hope, we will be unable to turn away.

Today the term "poster child" has come to mean any individual who "puts a face on a problem." Thus we have Matthew Shepard, Cassie Bernall, Elian Gonzalez, and Terri Schiavo, each of whose names can be expected to elicit strong feelings—stronger feelings, certainly, than we would have for the issue alone, had we not come to associate it with its "poster child." For that is the power of the icon: the emotional power that can be called forth from us by focusing on an individual human being transcends (or so it appears) the power generated by a mere disembodied idea. As a symbol for hate crime, Matthew Shepard has served admirably: a Matthew Shepard rally on Capitol Hill soon after his death brought out celebrities including Ellen DeGeneres and Barbra Streisand. Melissa Etheridge wrote the song "Scarecrow," dedicating it to Shepard. Elton John presented a concert in Laramie and played "Don't Let the Sun Go Down on Me" in Shepard's memory. Peter, Paul, and Mary performed at a concert in Shepard's memory. The play "The Laramie Project" has been performed by community theaters across the nation. In 2002, NBC broadcast a made-for-television movie, *The Matthew Shepard Story*, starring Stockard Channing and Sam Waterston.

The poster child has succeeded far beyond its original purveyors' dreams, moving from image to icon in the course of little more than a century. So reliable is this emotional calling forth that it cannot in fact really be contained or managed, as much as we might wish to do so: the "poster child" for any one issue will just as easily represent its opposite, for, as it embodies an issue, it does so completely: issues that polarize us will not be less, but more, polarized by invoking the icon. Thus Terri Schiavo becomes our poster child both for the right to life and the right to die. Elian Gonzalez is invoked as both the poster child of "the revolution" and the poster child of anti-Castro sentiment.

Once embedded in the public mind, the successful poster-child image takes on a life of its own and is set adrift from its moorings. Misty Bernall's book *She Said Yes: The Unlikely Martyrdom of Cassie Bernall* (1999) landed on the Publishers Weekly bestseller list with 350,000 copies in print, and the Bernalls appeared on *Today*, *20/20*, and *Larry King Live*, despite reports that the story the book told simply never happened. The now-discredited tale—other Columbine youths have confirmed that Bernall's "witnessing" never occurred—has nonetheless continued to inspire what supporters claim is a massive surge in Christian youth group rolls.

The original poster-child icon—and its extension far beyond disability— could never have been brought about without the mass media. Journalists have been taught that to humanize what would otherwise be dull statistics;

they need to put "a face on the problem." Thus no far-reaching story can be told without focusing on an individual who is supposed to embody the issue.

Depending on how well the reporter does the job—and depending on how cleverly the individual is chosen—the "poster child" does indeed draw our attention to an issue. Whether we focus on the issue as a result of focusing on the individual, though, is a more iffy proposition. Is it not often true that the more the image is focused on, the more the larger implications of the story cease to exist? Then the very reason for the poster child in the first place—to draw attention to a larger problem—is subverted. How many times did we look at Matthew Shepard's boyish smile before the horror he suffered began to recede, replaced by only his image? Terri Schiavo's face and smile told us one thing: that she was aware, trapped and unable to communicate, but conscious all the while, smiling at her mother. Medical experts insisted on a different understanding: that her brain was shrunken, atrophied; that she had no conscious awareness. Thus is the poster child also able to obfuscate rather than enlighten.

In order to focus on the poster child icon and understand its power, we cannot forget that although the term "poster child" has come to mean any individual who puts a "face on the problem," the original manifestation of the poster child icon was intentionally that of a child, and was always an image about disability.

The original poster-child image was intended to call forth pity and sympathy from a superior perspective. The relationship is intentionally unequal; it is by the looker giving to the cause of the poster child that the looker gains. That effect has remained unchanged from the original crippled children stories of the nineteenth century, which were designed to instill in the Protestant populace the habit of Christian charity toward the less fortunate. "Less fortunate" is part of the original content of this icon.

Just as the poster-child cannot be separated from the media campaign that makes use of her, the icon of the poster child can only call forth feelings that are invested in the larger issue which the poster child represents. Thus, in its original manifestation, the poster child icon goes hand in hand with the image of, and our common feelings about, disability, which have been shaped by the fundraising charities that created and so effectively made use of the poster child. The feelings are a mix of pity, fear, and hope—feelings which we have yet as a nation to untangle. They rely for their power on stereotypes about disability that people today who have disabilities, particularly those who have grown up with their disabilities, are still fighting to free themselves from in order to live normal lives.

That is why in recent years this manifestation of the poster child has come under fire from disability rights activists, many of whom were actually poster children themselves.

"When I was in first grade, my teacher passed out a flyer to encourage everyone to get their polio vaccinations," Cyndi Jones told the curator at the Smithsonian Institution. "She said, 'Cynthia's photo is on this flyer.' As the flyers were passed out, to my horror, I saw that the March of Dimes had used one of my poster-child photos and above my photo pasted, 'NOT THIS.' I can still feel the sense of hurt and betrayal. I was cute, intelligent, even sparkled. How could they say that about me? That day I became an activist" (15 July 2005 <http://americanhistory.si.edu/polio/howpolio/disability.htm>).

A close look at many of the Mary Grimley poster-child photos reveals something a bit different than the "cheerful invalid" that Grimley was supposed to be projecting: mouth closed in a frown, eyes defiant and proud, this forthright stare suggests to us a child less than impressed with the label of "poor crippled girl." In 2000, Mary Grimley—now Mary Grimley Mason—produced her autobiography, *Life Prints*, for the Feminist Press. In it she recounts growing up as the embodiment of the poster-child icon and her decades of living within—and struggling against—its strictures.

## WORKS CITED AND RECOMMENDED

Albrecht, Gary L., ed. *Encyclopedia of Disability*. Thousand Oaks, CA: Sage, 2006.

Barnes, Colin, Mike Oliver, and Len Barton. *Disability Studies Today*. Malden, MA: Blackwell Publishers, 2002.

Bernall, Misty. *She Said Yes: The Unlikely Martyrdom of Cassie Bernall*. Nashville: Word Publishing, 1999.

Goggin, Gerald, and Christopher Newell. *Digital Disability: The Social Construction of Disability in New Media*. Lanham, MD: Rowman and Littlefield, 2003.

Mason, Mary Grimley. *Life Prints: A Memoir of Healing and Discovery*. New York: Feminist P at City U of New York, 2000.

National Public Radio. "Beyond Affliction: Inventing the Poster Child." 3 Jan. 2006 <http://www.npr.org/programs/disability/ba_shows.dir/pos_chld.dir/pos_chld.html>.

Rogers, Linda J., and Beth Blue Swadener, eds. *Semiotics and Dis/ability: Interrogating Categories of Difference*. Albany: State U of New York P, 2001.

Smith, Bonnie, and Beth Hutchison, eds. *Gendering Disability*. New Brunswick, NJ: Rutgers UP, 2004.

Termain, Shelley, ed. *Foucault and the Government of Disability*. Ann Arbor: U of Michigan P, 2005.

# Elvis Presley

## *George Plasketes*

Long live the King—and Elvis Presley has. Like no other king. Like no other person, place, or thing. There is no image or icon in American popular culture with more paramount, profound, and pervasive resonance than Elvis. Look or listen no further than the mere mention of "Elvis" or an utterance of "The King." The rare first-name-basis only carries considerable cultural credibility and an inexhaustible iconic catalog of references, subreferences, and cross-references. Elvis reigns as the icon of icons, the all-inclusive metaphor, an omnipresent lodestar of American culture.

Elvis's biography has been a rich source of images and iconography. The story is a synthesis of the familiar heroic journey, an allegory and cautionary tale, and "rags to riches" mythic narrative, replete with revisions that run from rags to riches to reinvention to ruin to resurrection and "Once upon a time" meanings and magnitude. From his birth and humble beginnings in Mississippi to his hip shaking, sneering establishment rattling, rock-and-roll arrival in the 1950s, to Memphis and movies, to Las Vegas's entertainment excess, to an early demise that was both disappointing and doubted, followed by an enduring, eventful afterlife, Elvis has evolved into an epic encore of Second Coming proportions.

Purists insist that music is the most distinct and comprehensive body of evidence Elvis endowed, and thus the foundation and thread of what I call his "*icon*tinuity." In contrast, when Sir Elton John had difficulty raising funds for a Princess Diana memorial two years after her death, observers argued that the waning interest and her leveling legacy were primarily a result of the absence of any significant body of work. There is no great speech, no defining moment, no crowning contribution beyond Diana's charity work and the inherent recognition accompanying her aristocracy. Royal observers suggest that lack ultimately separates her, or any contender, from the supreme icon hierarchy of Elvis, martyr JFK, archetypal rebel James Dean, and sex symbol Marilyn Monroe, a Fab Four that have remained relevant decades beyond their deaths.

# ELVIS PRESLEY

Elvis endowed America's cultural heritage with more than music. His signature songs, the unique black and white fusion of rockabilly, blues, and gospel, are far from the sole defining dimension of his vast mythology. An abundance of familiar reference points enhance Elvis's composition and cultural chronology into a collage that resembles a "Connect the King's dots" contest. As the transcendent iconic figure, Elvis embodies other elements which sustain his sex, drugs, rock-and-roll identity, as well as sense of the sacred. The iconic inventory includes artifacts and objects (Cadillacs, souvenirs, and memorabilia); facial features (sideburns, lip snarl); gestures (hip shake and martial arts moves that defined his latter-day career and training manuals for impersonators); places (Tupelo, Memphis, Graceland, Hollywood, Las Vegas); clothing, costume, and style (rhinestone jumpsuits, belt buckles, gold lamé, black leather, scarves, sunglasses); fatty foods (deep fried peanut butter and banana sandwiches); and sayings ("Thank you, thank-you-very-much," "Elvis has left the building"). His story also contains defining moments such as concerts and comebacks, including his alleged death which spawned a grass roots social/psychological/religious movement of true believers and a cult of fanaticism manifest in the Elvis is Alive phenomenon; groundbreaking appearances (*The Ed Sullivan Show*), turning points (drafted into the Army), career shifts (movies), bizarre political encounters (approaching Richard Nixon about becoming a Federal Drug and Narcotics agent). There are heroes and villains (his mother Gladys, father Vernon, twin stillborn brother Jesse Garon, wife Priscilla, daughter Lisa Marie, Colonel Parker, Dr. Nick) and personas (rebel, sneering androgynous punk, Hollywood hunk and hero, bloated, addicted Vegas act, religious figure, zombie). And there is legacy; his daughter Lisa Marie, whose ex-husbands include Michael Jackson and Nicholas Cage, is two records into her own music career.

These iconic conventions constitute an elusive, expanding, enigmatic, exploding, enduring Presley presence that permeates postmodern culture and subculture. It is both pulse and plague; prism and puzzle. A kingdom of consumer oddities, commodities, and endless Elvistas defines the Elvis "icontinuum." Through mass meditation and mass media attention, occupation and preoccupation, images of

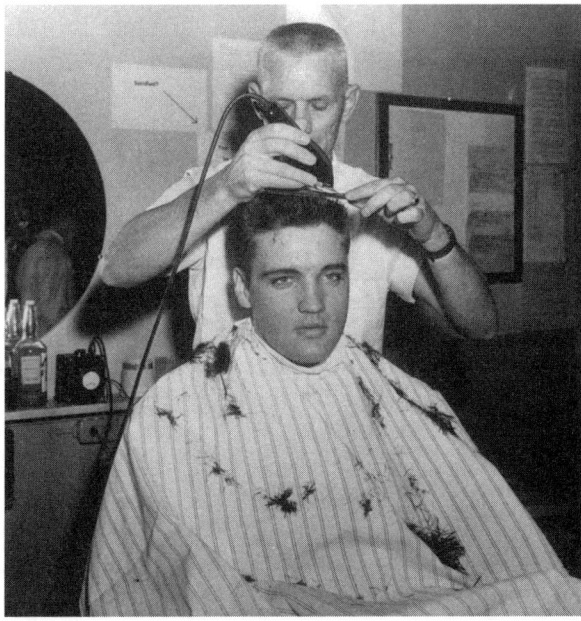

Elvis Presley receiving his first Army haircut at Fort Chaffee, Arkansas, March 25, 1958. AP/Wide World Photos.

Elvis—from black velvet and blue suede, to pink and pastel, to vinyl, solid gold, rhinestone, or 100 percent cotton—consume and captivate our consciousness and imagination like no other. Elvis's likeness—whether jailhouse or jumpsuit, junk or junkie, punk or parody, Cadillac or coffin—has been pressed, placed, preserved, and packaged in plastic and on postage stamps; credit cards, checks, and currency; art and artifact; greeting cards and cologne ("For All the King's Men"). Businesses, boulevards, and babies bear and borrow his name, a revered and registered trademark. There are waves of UFO-like sightings, "Elvisitations," ritualistic pilgrimages to Graceland, death and anniversary commemorations in January and August, and his living likeness in legions of impersonators. His omnipresence hauntingly hovers, from a King-connected constellation "rock star" in the heavens to highway horizons on billboards to the depths of Ruby Falls, 1,100 feet inside Lookout Mountain in Chattanooga, Tennessee, where "Elvis '75" is magic markered onto the side panel of a utility light.

An excessive enterprise, empire, and entity, Elvis appears on memorabilia and merchandise, in roadside relics and Graceland's gift shops; at fast-food chains, in front yard flea markets and backyard shrines; on World Wide Web sites in cyberspace and sporting events; at parties and parades; or as part of promotions, protests, and pranks, even as Presidential personas. In 1992, Elvis was a kindred spirit "running mate" for then-Arkansas governor Bill Clinton in his successful campaign to win the White House as king of the country.

The mass media and popular arts have been prolific purveyors of the pervasive and perpetual Elvis-lution. A Presley prism, they reflect and disseminate Elvis icons in messages, meanings, metaphors, and motifs with multiple points of view defined by generation, genre and gender, race, religion and region, social class and occupation. For example, the literary landscape is no longer limited to tell-tale biographies, blurred between factual fiction and fictional fact, but now includes Elvis cookbooks, encyclopedias, photo collections, travel guides, poems, children's books, novels, and short stories in science fiction, fantasy, romance, and mystery genres, and even subliterary modes such as comic books.

Beyond the bookshelves, Elvis representations routinely appear in tabloids, talk shows, advertisements, situation comedies, dramas, songs, radio formats, films, videos, musicals, paintings, portraits, performances, plays, parodies, and puns and fat jokes ("Love Meat Tender," "Return to Slender"), sculptures, shrines, needlepoint, quilts, cartoons, comic strips, graffiti, ballet, books, newspapers, magazines, politics, and sporting events.

In the process, the story is retold, revised, and reinterpreted; the images transformed and transported, juxtaposed with everything and everyone. Elvis is not only the King, but has been widely recast, reconsidered, and reconstructed as the Queen, the Fisher King, King of Kings, and King Kong. A clown, clone, cartoon character, Cajun and Kennedy; athlete and addict; drug and drag; Dean and Dylan; Air Jordan and Jordanaires. He is Seinfeld,

Springsteen, and the Statue of Liberty; landmark, legend, lyric, and Lazarus; vampire, Venus, Valentino, and Virgin Mary; Pelvis, Melvis, Hellvis, and Hitler; high priest, pauper, prince, prescription pill popper, parody, politician, and president; pioneer and New England Patriot (logo); primadonna, Madonna, Mona Lisa, and Marilyn; mascot, messiah, and murderer; demon, deity, and Disney; ghost, god, glutton, and gimmick; saint, sinner, savior, succubus, and siren; Bigfoot, Buddha, Beavis, and Butthead; beauty, beast, and burden; Pez, pet, prophet, and profit.

One of the forces driving Elvis's icontinuity lies in dichotomies reflected in his two distinct careers and personas, unique until Madonna redefined reinvention repeatedly during the past quarter century. The endless Presley points and puzzle pieces contain contradictions and contrasts crisscrossing American popular culture. Overweight and overwrought, exhumed, exploited, and exhausted, Elvis's image accommodates dualities ranging from royalty and rip-off, grunge and gospel, Graceland and Disgraceland, the glamourous and grotesque, aesthetic and athletic, fact and fiction, the hysterical and historical, the iconic and ironic, the exalted and exiled. He epitomizes the feminine and masculine, good and evil, heaven and hell, young and old, faith and doubt, rich and poor, comic and tragic, black and white, life and death, mirror and mirage, whisper and shout, primitive and profound, mainstream and fringe, sacred and sexual, unique and universal, convention and invention. He is vision and voice; kitsch, catechism, and contagion; time and space; prophecy, parody, paradox, and paranormal; fetish and fashion; corpse and corporation; rhetoric, rumor, ritual, and religion; occupation and preoccupation; genre, generation, and gender; the cosmic, concrete, coincidence, complex, and contradictory; demographic and the democratic.

The pinnacle of the Presley polarity and presence was best illustrated in the 1992 Presley-dential stamp election when voters decided which Elvis they wanted to be King, choosing between the "young 1950s" and "late model Vegas" Presley poses. The winner would be represented on a 29-cent postage stamp. The stampaign was a precursor to recent election controversies, as the die-hard "Elvis Is Alive" faction declared the election invalid, pointing to United States Postal Service regulations which stipulate that people must be dead ten years before their image can be considered for a stamp. The accumulation of these art and infotainment expressions, or "ricochets" as characterized by William Fox in his novel *Dixiana Moon* (1981), might best be captured in one of the final frames of John Crawford's eight-panel cartoon, "Baboon Dooley Rock Critic Consults the Deity!" (1988). A divine voice from the heavens reveals the "the Great Secret of Existence" to Baboon, that "the universe is one big Elvis Presley."

Such religious allusions and pious parallels are prevalent dimensions of Elvis's myth and iconography that converge with consumerism and cult of personality. Elvis has always been viewed as a Messiah figure, his story a passion play of "Greatest Story Ever Told" proportions that includes a doctrine, disciples, deification from faithful followers, and spiritual suggestions of resurrection, redemption, prophecy, conversion, and a second coming. "And unless you understand that Elvis Presley was more than anything a spiritual leader of our generation, there's really no way to assess his importance, much less than the meaning of his music he created," writes music critic–biographer Dave Marsh in Elvis's obituary (1992).

Fragments of both traditional and non-traditional religions and cult conventions are widely represented in Presley-terian devotion, a range that includes Catholic, Southern Baptist, Scientology, Numerology, and mysticism. Beyond the cognitive dissonant fanaticism of the "Elvis Is Alive" movement, one of the most obvious manifestations can be identified in the millions of faithful followers and curious consumers who are part of a congregation that makes an annual Presley pilgrimage through the gates of Graceland, where, suggests the Paul Simon lyric, "we all shall be received." Ritualistic commemorations of Elvis's January birthday and August death are marked by candlelight vigils, cross-shaped floral arrangements, and weeping worshipers. Souvenirs are anointed saintly relics. Rooms, houses, and gardens are transformed into shrines and altars decorated with Elvis icons. Impersonators are high priests disseminating a musical gospel. One of the most haunting heavenly images is located in the Memphis mansion's Meditation Gardens, where a giant marble statute of Jesus, arms outstretched, stands in front of a cross. "Presley" is inscribed on the base beneath; the juxtaposition wickedly surreal. Whether catechism, coincidence, or comic, such King and King of Kings comparisons continue to mark the Elvis icontinuum.

The scope and depth of Elvisiana, its sightings, citings, and sightseeing, have generated another level of iconic inquiry beyond artistic and entertainment expressions, Graceland gatherings, and annual impersonator conventions. More formal assemblies dedicated to the study of this cultural phenomenon have emerged on college campuses and at regional, national, and international conferences, where groups gather to contemplate the King. Elvis has gradually become a serious subject of scholarly studies. Among institutions offering courses on the King are the Smithsonian and the University of Iowa, where "Elvis as Anthology" is part of the English and African-American World Studies curriculum. In April 1994, EducArts, a nonprofit organization dedicated to interdisciplinary education, sponsored a symposium, "Icons of Popular Culture I: Elvis and Marilyn," at the Georgetown University campus. In August 1995, the University of Mississippi, host of yearly seminars on native son William Faulkner, held an International Conference, "In Search of Elvis." Though traditionalists resisted, citing the lack of academic merit, the conference convened. "We see this as broadening the areas of Southern culture," says conference co-director William Ferris. "What we're doing is raising an academic recognition of not only Elvis but popular culture in general...because of the power that these things have in our lives" (Hardy).

The Elvis Icontinuum is vast, varied, and unavoidable. The Mojo Nixon and Skid Roper novelty song "Elvis Is Everywhere" (1986), though a more playful observation than stunning revelation, remains relevant. In *Dead Elvis: Chronicle of a Cultural Obsession* (1991), cultural critic Greil Marcus, author of some of the most perceptive works on Elvis, places Elvis's "permanent ubiquity" and "infinite circularity" in a Big Bang context, writing of the "universe he [Elvis] detonated still expanding, the pieces still flying, taking shape, changing shape again and again"; a boundless, fluid form that cannot be contained (viii).

Boundless and binding. The symbols, signposts, sightings, and citations solicit some response, be it a smile, smirk, suspicion, scorn, or celebration. Whether fanciful fascination, accidental attraction, casual confrontation, or critical inquiry, Elvis has proved irresistible. Presley participation and pursuits are pluralistic, no longer the exclusive domain of obsessive El-fans. Iconic attraction and involvement are inevitable, an El-virus we are all capable of contracting. Marcus foresaw the fixation nearly thirty years ago, referring to it as a "helpless commitment" because "a self made man is rather boring one thing, a self made king is another" (Marcus, *Mystery Train* 143).

On a daily basis, we continue to filter through the flood of fallout and fragments, the pieces of the Presley puzzle scattered across Elvisiana, contemplating the King and his Kingdom, the lessons learned and lost in his life and legacy. We are endlessly entangled in dead-or-alive discussions and dialogue, debating his demise. We measure the messages, metaphors, and meanings delineated by generation, gender, and genre, race, region, and religion, occupation, social class, style, or era, comparing and contrasting points along the Elvis Icontinuum, hoping to uncover connections, closure, and clues not only to Elvis, but to our own individual and collective identities.

This curious convergence of consumerism and all-encompassing iconicity is a condition described by Isabel Bonney, a character in Jack Womack's futuristic novel *Elvissey* (1993): "I knew no escape from the King... while E's presence was daily extruded into our lives, it unavoidabled [sic] that we be baptized in his flood" (62). Collectively we have been baptized, a congregation of post-Presley iconographers—expressionists and impressionists, artists, writers, and musicians, painters, performers, politicians, poets, and prophets; critics and scholars, accidental tourists and innocent bystanders—endlessly exploring and experiencing Elvis's life, death, and afterlife through the complex conundrum and overflowing, overlapping collection of chaos represented in his iconicity. In words and images, sights and sounds, allegories and metaphors, litany and language, parallels and parables, quotes, comments and comparisons. History and mystery mingle, the messages simultaneously muddled and magnified, dissipating further into myth. There is no end to the Elvis-story, its ricochets, resonance, and multilayered meanings. Nick Tosches was right when he wrote in *Country* (1977), "I think Elvis Presley will never be solved" (47). Elvis Presley persists as the paragon of icontinuity, his chronology an infinite Icontinuum. It's good to be King.

## WORKS CITED AND RECOMMENDED

Crawford, John. "Baboon Dooley Rock Critic Consults the Deity." Cartoon. *Spin* June 1988: 32.

Fox, William Price. *Dixiana Moon*. New York: Viking, 1981.

Hardy, Lawrence. "Lifeline: All Shook Up." *USA Today* 7 Aug. 1995: D1.

Marcus, Greil. *Dead Elvis: A Chronicle of a Cultural Obsession*. New York: Doubleday, 1991.

———. *Mystery Train: Images of America in Rock 'n' Roll Music*. 2nd ed. New York: Dutton, 1982.

Marsh, Dave. *Elvis*. 2nd ed. New York: Thunder's Mouth's P, 1992.

Tosches, Nick. *Country: Living Legends and Dying Metaphors in America's Biggest Music*. New York: Stein and Day, 1977.

Womack, Jack. *Elvissey*. New York: Tom Doherty Associates, 1993.